STEADY GAINS
AND STALLED PROGRESS

STEADY GAINS
AND STALLED PROGRESS

*INEQUALITY AND THE BLACK-WHITE
TEST SCORE GAP*

KATHERINE MAGNUSON AND JANE WALDFOGEL

EDITORS

Russell Sage Foundation • New York

The Russell Sage Foundation

The Russell Sage Foundation, one of the oldest of America's general purpose foundations, was established in 1907 by Mrs. Margaret Olivia Sage for "the improvement of social and living conditions in the United States." The Foundation seeks to fulfill this mandate by fostering the development and dissemination of knowledge about the country's political, social, and economic problems. While the Foundation endeavors to assure the accuracy and objectivity of each book it publishes, the conclusions and interpretations in Russell Sage Foundation publications are those of the authors and not of the Foundation, its Trustees, or its staff. Publication by Russell Sage, therefore, does not imply Foundation endorsement.

Library of Congress Cataloging-in-Publication Data

Steady gains and stalled progress : inequality and the black-white test score gap / edited by Katherine Magnuson and Jane Waldfogel.
   p. cm.
  Includes bibliographical references and index.
  ISBN 978-0-87154-567-1
  1. Educational tests and measurements—Social aspects—United States. 2. Educational equalization—United States. I. Magnuson, Katherine A. II. Waldfogel, Jane.
  LB3051.S83 2008
  371.26′013—dc22

2008020353

Text design by Suzanne Nichols.

RUSSELL SAGE FOUNDATION
112 East 64th Street, New York, New York 10065
10 9 8 7 6 5 4 3 2 1

Contents

About the Authors   vii

Introduction   1
Katherine Magnuson and Jane Waldfogel

PART I   A LONG-TERM VIEW   31

Chapter 1   Inequality and Black-White
                Achievement Trends in the NAEP   33
                Katherine Magnuson, Dan T. Rosenbaum,
                and Jane Waldfogel

Chapter 2   Changes in Families, Schools,
                and the Test Score Gap   66
                Mark Berends and Roberto V. Peñaloza

Chapter 3   Income Inequality and Racial Gaps
                in Test Scores   110
                Mary E. Campbell, Robert Haveman,
                Tina Wildhagen, and Barbara L. Wolfe

PART II   EXPLAINING GAPS AT SCHOOL
                 ENTRY AND DURING SCHOOL   137

Chapter 4   Can Gaps in the Quality of Early
                 Environments and Noncognitive
                 Skills Help Explain Persisting
                 Black-White Achievement Gaps?   139
                 David Grissmer and Elizabeth Eiseman

Chapter 5   Segregation and the Test Score Gap   181
                 Jacob L. Vigdor and Jens Ludwig

Chapter 6   The Role of Inequality in
                 Teacher Quality   212
                 Sean P. Corcoran and William N. Evans

Chapter 7   Culture and Stalled Progress in
                 Narrowing the Black-White
                 Test Score Gap   250
                 Meredith Phillips

PART III   CONCLUSIONS AND POLICY
                 IMPLICATIONS   287

Chapter 8   School Policies and the Test Score Gap   289
                 Helen F. Ladd

Chapter 9   What We've Learned About Stalled
                 Progress in Closing the Black-White
                 Achievement Gap   320
                 Ronald F. Ferguson

                 Index   345

About the Authors

Katherine Magnuson is assistant professor of social work and a faculty affiliate at the Institute for Research on Poverty at the University of Wisconsin at Madison.

Jane Waldfogel is professor of social work and public affairs at Columbia University.

Mark Berends is professor of sociology at the University of Notre Dame and director of the National Center on School Choice.

Mary E. Campbell is assistant professor of sociology at the University of Iowa.

Sean P. Corcoran is assistant professor of educational economics at the Steinhardt School of Culture, Education, and Human Development at New York University.

Elizabeth Eiseman is a graduate student at the Darden School of Business at the University of Virginia.

William N. Evans is Keough-Hesburgh Professor of Economics at the University of Notre Dame and a research associate at NBER.

Ronald F. Ferguson is a lecturer in public policy at the Kennedy School of Government and the Harvard Graduate School of Education and the faculty director of the Achievement Gap Initiative at Harvard University. He is also senior research associate at Harvard's Wiener Center for Social Policy.

David Grissmer is a principal scientist at the Center for Advanced Study of Teaching and Learning at the University of Virgina.

Robert Haveman is professor emeritus of public affairs and economics and faculty affiliate at the Institute for Research on Poverty at the University of Wisconsin at Madison.

Helen F. Ladd is the Edgar T. Thompson Professor of Public Policy Studies and professor of economics at the Sanford Institute of Public Policy at Duke University.

Jens Ludwig is professor of social service administration, law, and public policy at the University of Chicago and a faculty research fellow at NBER.

Roberto V. Peñaloza is a statistician at the National Center on School Choice at Vanderbilt University.

Meredith Phillips is associate professor of public policy and sociology at the University of California at Los Angeles.

Dan T. Rosenbaum is assistant professor of economics at the University of North Carolina at Greensboro.

Jacob L. Vigdor is associate professor of public policy studies and economics at Duke University and a faculty research fellow at NBER.

Tina Wildhagen is assistant professor of sociology at Smith College.

Barbara L. Wolfe is director of the LaFollette School of Public Affairs, professor of public affairs, economics, and population health sciences, and a faculty affiliate at the Institute for Research on Poverty at the University of Wisconsin at Madison.

Introduction

KATHERINE MAGNUSON AND JANE WALDFOGEL

black vs. white

A hundred and forty-five years after the Emancipation Proclamation and fifty-five years after *Brown v. Board of Education,* segregation is no longer the law of the land, and in principle black and white children have the benefit of equal opportunities. Yet, across many dimensions, black Americans do not start life on equal footing with their white neighbors. Racial and economic inequalities shape children's experiences from very early on and as a result, on average, black and white children face very different life chances. For example, the average black child spends nearly six years in poverty, in contrast to less than one year for the average white child (Magnuson and Votruba-Drzal 2008). The long list of other related disadvantages that black children are disproportionately likely to experience is equally concerning: lower-quality schools, less access to health care, and more dangerous neighborhoods.

What do such disparities in life chances mean for black children? Among the gaps that remain between black and white children, many would agree that the most consequential is the disparity in their school outcomes. On average, black children come to school scoring lower than white children on measures of school readiness, do not do as well on tests of reading and math achievement in elementary and middle school, and are less likely to graduate from high school and go on to college. Collectively referred to as achievement gaps, these differences operate much like the proverbial half-full (or half-empty) glass of water. Some observers point out how much blacks have gained relative to whites since the days when black and white children attended separate schools. Others lament that though meaningful progress has been made, the remaining gap is substantial and a powerful explanation for the poorer standing of black Americans.

What explains these achievement gaps? It should come as no surprise that the issue has defied simple explanation. The causes and meaning of racial differences in IQ and other measures of cognitive ability have long been controversial.

A century ago, it was thought that differences in intelligence and cognitive ability, whether across individuals or across population groups, were

1

mainly explained by biological, and primarily genetic, processes. Today it is generally understood that, although intelligence and cognitive ability are heritable at the individual level, differences in these attributes across population groups are primarily explained by differences in environmental conditions.

Several stylized facts offer important support for this conclusion. First, social scientists point out that racial groups are socially constructed, not biologically determined. In the United States, race is a cultural invention with membership based on phenotypic characteristics. It is therefore unlikely that genetic factors explain differences between racial groups (Smedley and Smedley 2005). Second, research has found that individual differences in cognitive performance in advantaged environments appear to be driven in large part by genetic processes, whereas individual differences in disadvantaged environments appear to be more closely linked to environmental influences (Turkheimer et al. 2003). Because black children are disproportionately likely to be economically disadvantaged, this suggests that environmental factors are a potentially important determinant of their achievement. Finally, although the genetic view would have predicted relatively stable scores and differences across population groups over time, the data indicate that cognitive and IQ scores have been steadily increasing over the past 100 years and that differences across population groups have narrowed. Taken together, this evidence is persuasive that the fundamental causes of between group differences in IQ and related measures of cognitive ability lie in differing experiences and unequal opportunities, rather than differences in genes (Flynn 2007).

Given the preponderance of evidence suggesting that environmental conditions explain differences in black and white students' achievement, it is all the more urgent to understand and address the proximal and specific causes of black-white achievement gaps. Without such knowledge, little can be done to shift the odds in favor of black children's success. Test scores serve a gatekeeping function for consequential life course transitions, in particular, high school graduation and college entry. College completion, in turn, is increasingly necessary if young people are to go on to jobs that pay more than poverty-level wages (Danziger 2007; Kirsch et al. 2007). In today's knowledge economy, the premium placed on cognitive skills is greater than at any time in the past, and is likely to only rise in future. At the same time, the penalty to having low levels of skills is higher than ever, and will also only be higher in future as low-skills jobs are increasingly outsourced or filled by technology. Addressing low skills is a matter not just of equity but also of efficiency: the greatest economic resource of the nation and the fuel for economic growth is a highly skilled workforce.

A decade ago, Christopher Jencks and Meredith Phillips (1998) concluded that the single greatest remaining challenge to racial equality was the persistence of the black-white test score gap. The same statement could certainly be made today. Although some argue that test scores are just one factor contributing to life chances, it is now widely recognized that disparities in test scores and school achievement are a major determinant of unequal outcomes across important domains (Barton 2003; Belfield and Levin 2007). The United States has made great strides in closing gaps between blacks and whites, but will never achieve racial equality without equality of school achievement. Explaining achievement gaps is not just an academic exercise; it is an economic and social imperative. The payoff to more schooling, and the penalty to poor educational attainment, is too great to allow us to close racial gaps in other outcomes without first addressing this fundamental problem.

When we began work on this book five years ago, the data indicated that the progress in gap-closing that had so captured attention in the 1970s and early 1980s had come to a halt in the late 1980s and 1990s. Some have argued that progress was permanently stalled and that no further gains in closing black-white gaps would be seen. Yet, by the time we were halfway through the book, evidence was emerging that the black-white test scores gaps are closing again. As a result, we are optimistic about the prospects for further improvements and all the more motivated to ask what factors account for the remaining gaps and what policies might address them.

History is helpful here. Over the past thirty to forty years, our country has seen first a period of remarkable progress in narrowing black-white achievement gaps, then another in which these gaps notably failed to converge, and then yet another in which progress in closing the gaps resumed. Just as the rings inside tree trunks or the layers within glaciers provide clues as to the conditions under which they were made, these historical patterns of alternating gains and stalled progress in closing test score gaps can tell us something about the conditions that are related to gap closing and those that are related to stagnation in gaps.

The chapters in this book look closely at these historical patterns and use the variation in gaps and conditions over time to deduce which economic and social factors have been important in gap closing and which are implicated in periods of stalled progress. The goal is to better understand the sources of remaining racial gaps in achievement and also to assist policy makers to make better choices about policies they might implement to close black-white achievement gaps in future.

This is an opportune time to be asking these questions. The most recent national data (shown later in this introduction) indicate that black-white achievement gaps are now lower than they have been at any time since such tests were first administered in this country. At the same time, the federal No Child Left Behind Act, which passed with bipartisan support, requires states and localities to report the average student achievement within schools separately by race as well as by other important student characteristics. These reporting requirements have transformed racial achievement gaps into a real, tangible, and local issue in many school districts. For this, and many other reasons, states and localities are undertaking unprecedented school reforms in hopes of improving student performance on standardized tests as well as reducing achievement gaps. There has also been an explosion of interest at both the state and federal level in preschool programs to help ensure that children are ready for school and to help redress gaps in school readiness. Given this window of opportunity, it is the right time to ensure that we understand the sources of remaining gaps and do all that we can to eliminate them. Only then will we have fulfilled the promise of a society of equal opportunity, one in which children are not handicapped or advantaged by virtue of their birth into a particular racial group.

Steady Gains and Stalled Progress

This volume reports the results of a conference that was convened at the Russell Sage Foundation in November 2006. The conference considered a host of factors that might explain recent trends in the black-white test score gap. We focused in particular on the role that increasing economic and social inequality may have played. There are many ways in which changes in economic and social dimensions of inequality might affect trends in black and white children's achievement, and the conference authors tackled the major ones. In particular, they examined the role of income inequality and related family-level factors, influences prior to school entry, school-related factors such as segregation and teacher quality, and other factors including how children spend their time outside of school. The hypotheses the authors examined are not mutually exclusive. Rather, each represents a possible piece of a puzzle that when taken together may help explain the pattern of steady gains and stalled progress and may also help identify policies to promote further gains.

To set the stage for the chapters that follow, we provide some background on the black-white test score gap and then summarize recent trends in the gap as well as recent trends in economic inequality and related social inequalities that may have affected it. We then provide an overview and summary of the volume.

The Black-White Test Score Gap

The black-white test score gap has been a stubbornly persistent feature of the American landscape. However, the magnitude of the gap and the patterns of achievement underlying the gap have not been constant over time. What accounts for the pattern of steady gains and stalled progress in closing the gap? In particular, how does the stalled progress in the 1980s and 1990s relate to the rise in economic and social inequality, which began shortly before progress began to stall? The short answer is that research to date has not provided an answer to these questions. In their landmark volume on the black-white test score gap, Jencks and Phillips (1998) examined the steady gains that occurred in the 1960s and 1970s and identified the most important factors accounting for converging test scores, chief among them being changes in families, civil rights and antipoverty initiatives, and school reforms. However, in the decade after the publication of that volume, it became apparent the steady gains analyzed in the Jencks and Phillips volume had stopped. Analysts have yet to satisfactorily explain this phenomenon, which we refer to as stalled progress. Derek Neal, who conducted the most comprehensive analysis to date, concluded that "it is not clear why the process of black-white skill convergence appeared to stop in 1990" (2006, 570). Nor has research established why progress in closing the black-white gap may have resumed again after 2000. Are we now entering another period of steady gains? If so, why?

Trends in the Black-White Test Score Gap

The single best source on trends in the black-white test score gap is the National Assessment of Educational Progress Long-Term Trend data (NAEP-LTT). The NAEP-LTT has been administered to nationally representative samples of nine-, thirteen-, and seventeen-year-olds (fourth graders, eighth graders, and twelfth graders, respectively) at regular intervals since the early 1970s, with the most recent administration (as of this writing) in 2004 (Perie, Moran, and Lutkus 2005). The NAEP-LTT provides reliable data on trends in achievement over time, because the tests have remained substantially the same at each assessment.

NAEP-LTT data are available at regular intervals for both reading and math, although the tests for these two subjects were administered in different years before the 1990s. The reading long-term trend data begin in 1971 and run through 2004; the math long-term trend data that we were able to obtain begin somewhat later, in 1978, but again run through 2004.[1] We use these data to document trends in black-white test score gaps in reading and math for nine-, thirteen-, and seventeen-year-olds.[2] Following the convention employed in previous research, we use data reported by the test administrator to code children as black or white and focus on trends for these two subgroups.[3]

Trends in Reading

Figure I.1 displays the long-term trends in reading scores. For all three age groups, narrowing in the early period is attributable to relatively steep gains in achievement for black children compared with their white peers. However, it is notable that achievement levels off earlier among the

Figure I.1   NAEP-LTT Reading Scores–Nine-, Thirteen-, and Seventeen-Year-Olds

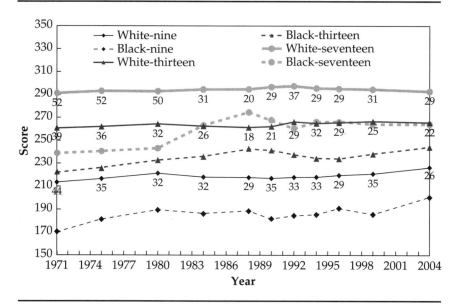

Source: Authors' compilation.
Notes: Numbers presented in the chart reflect the gap in levels of achievement between black and white children of a particular age.

younger children, by about 1980, and remains fairly flat for nearly twenty years before rising again between 1999 and 2004. Trends in the gaps follow this pattern, converging before 1980, with the gap for nine-year-olds dropping from 44 points in 1971 to 32 points in 1980, and then stagnating between 1980 and 1999, with the gap ranging from 29 to 35 points. In 2004, the gap for nine-year-olds fell to 26 points as a result of the improvements made by black children.[4]

In contrast, the black-white reading test score gap for thirteen-year-olds and seventeen-year-olds narrowed until 1988, with seventeen-year-olds making especially large gains in the early 1980s, after which black children's achievement declined, causing the black-white gap to widen. By 1994, the achievement gap among thirteen-year-olds was 32 points, just as large as it had been in 1980. In 2004, the thirteen-year-olds exhibited the same increase in performance as the nine-year-olds, but such gains were not apparent among the seventeen-year-olds.

Figure I.2 presents the reading test score trends disaggregated by both race and gender. Among nine-year-olds, girls consistently outscore boys, but the trends for girls and boys are quite similar. Among thirteen-year-olds, trends for black boys and girls are similar up to 1988, but then there is some suggestion that boys may have displayed an earlier and sharper fall

Figure I.2   NAEP-LTT Reading Scores–Nine- and Thirteen-Year-Olds

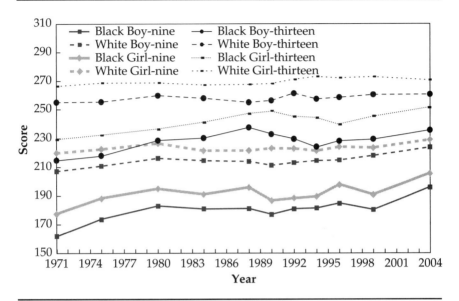

Source: Authors' compilation.

in scores than girls, although both groups recover in the 1990s. These patterns suggest that boys may have been more affected by whatever caused the downturn in reading scores for black thirteen-year-olds than girls. Although we do not present these data for seventeen-year-olds, trends were quite similar to those presented in figure I.2 for thirteen-year-olds. For high school seniors, there were gender differences in the levels of reading achievement, and perhaps a slightly earlier and sharper fall among boys after 1988 than girls.

Given our focus on inequality, it is of interest to know whether these trends are being driven by changes at the top or the bottom of the test score distribution. We therefore also examined trends by percentiles of the score distribution as well as by parental education. In results not shown, but available on request, we found that considerable and stagnating black-white gaps during the late 1980s and 1990s were apparent at both the top and bottom of the distributions with just slight variations in the achievement patterns.

Trends in Math

As was the case for reading, black and white math test scores converged until the 1980s for nine-, thirteen-, and seventeen-year-olds. Figure I.3 plots the long-term trend in math scores. Due to improvements in the relative

Figure I.3   NAEP-LTT Math Scores–Nine-, Thirteen-, and Seventeen-Year-Olds

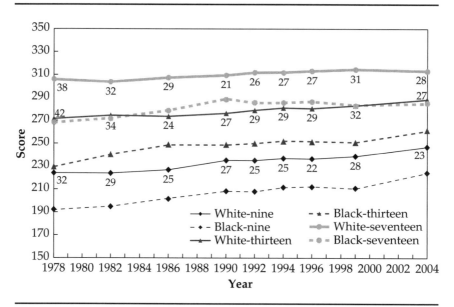

Source: Authors' compilation.
Notes: Numbers presented in the chart reflect the gap in levels of achievement between black and white children of a particular age.

achievement of black students, between 1978 and 1986, the black-white gap in math scores declined from 32 to 25 points for nine-year-olds and from 42 to 24 points for thirteen-year-olds. However, this remarkable convergence was not maintained. Among nine-year-olds, black children's scores increased at nearly the same rate as white children's scores in the 1990s, so that by 2004, the black-white gap was 23 points, nearly the same as it had been in 1986. Among thirteen-year-olds, black children's achievement scores remained largely flat (until the upturn in 2004), while white children's scores continued to rise, albeit slowly. Among seventeen-year-olds, improvements in math achievement persisted through 1990, with test scores gaps converging from 38 points to 21 points. These gains, however, were not long-lasting. Black seventeen-year-olds' achievement dropped, and by 2004 the corresponding black-white test score gap was only one point smaller than it had been in 1986.

Figure I.4 plots the same trends by both race and gender and indicates that the trends by age and race do not vary by gender. Nor are there notable gender test score gaps in either race group. These results stand in contrast to those for reading, where (as shown in figure I.2) girls have an advantage over boys and where black thirteen-year-old boys possibly suffered an ear-

Figure I.4   NAEP-LTT Math Scores–Thirteen- and Nine-Year-Olds

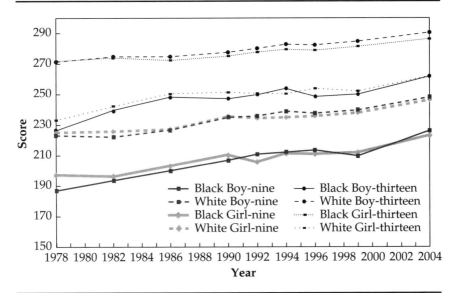

Source: Authors' compilation.

lier and sharper downturn than their female counterparts. Examining gender differences for seventeen-year-olds (not presented in the figures but available on request), we find that white girls had lower levels of math achievement than white boys, but no gender differences among black students. Among high school students as among younger children, trends in test score gaps did not differ by gender. Again, in results not shown but available on request, we also examined trends by test score percentile and parental education. For the most part, these data suggest that patterns of test score gap gains were similarly stalled during the late 1980s and 1990s at the bottom and the top of the test score distribution.

Synthetic Cohorts

It is also useful to trace the relative standing of particular cohorts of children over time. Although the NAEP does not follow individual children or cohorts, the fact that cross-sections of children four years apart in age are tested at roughly four-year intervals means that the data can be used to construct synthetic cohorts. Considering the data in this way makes apparent that much of the eighth-grade gap was already present by fourth grade. Indeed, previous research suggests that a sizable black-white achievement gap is present when children enter school (Fryer and Levitt 2004; Jencks and Phillips 1998).

Figure I.5   Synthetic Cohorts for Reading Achievement NAEP-LTT

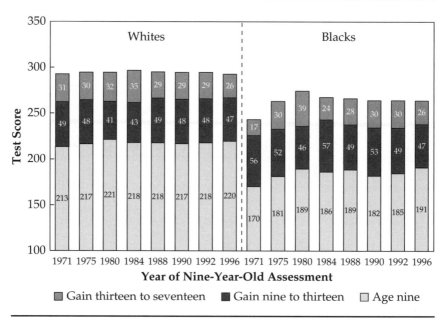

Source: Authors' compilation.

Ronald Ferguson has analyzed the NAEP cohort data and points out how distinctive the reading test score patterns are for children born in 1975 who were nine years old in 1984 (see figures I.5 and I.6; see also Ferguson 2007, chapter 2). In 1988, at age thirteen, this cohort had the smallest black-white reading gap of any prior cohort at age thirteen, and yet four years later, at age seventeen, that gap had more than doubled, suggesting that some shock may have occurred to affect the reading progress of black teenagers during this period. The later cohorts of black children did slightly better, but still faced larger black-white gaps at age seventeen than previous cohorts had.

Summary

Taken together, the evidence presented in figures I.1 to I.6 points to several important stylized facts. Over the past three decades, the black-white gap has displayed a period of steady gains, a period of stalled progress, and most recently what looks to be another period of improvement. Yet, differences in the patterns of achievement test scores underlying these trends are important. First, the trends in reading and math achievement levels differed, in particular during the period of stalled progress. During this time, reading scores for white and black children remained largely flat or

Figure I.6   Synthetic Cohorts for Math Achievement NAEP-LTTT

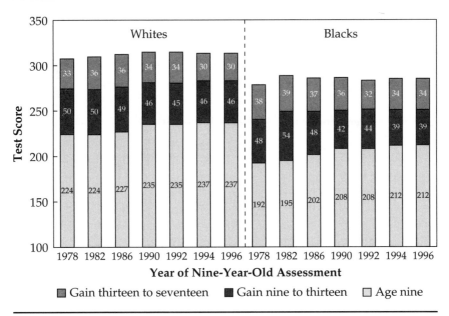

Source: Authors comp ilation.

declined, whereas math scores increased, but gains for black and white students were similar. Second, there are some important differences by age. The convergence of reading test scores appears to have ceased earlier among the nine-year-olds than thirteen-year-olds, possibly suggesting a cohort effect, yet declines in reading were particularly pronounced for cohorts of children who were teenagers in the late 1980s and 1990s, possibly suggesting a period effect. Stalled progress in math test scores occurred at roughly the same time for all age groups, which is more indicative of a period effect. Third, gender differences, both in levels and trends, appear to be important in understanding overall patterns in reading, but less important for math. Given these patterns, it seems likely that the explanations for convergence and stagnation are not one and the same, and may even differ by subject, gender, cohort, and age.

Trends in Economic Inequality and Related Social Inequality

In this section, we briefly review the current state of knowledge on economic and social inequality and consider how changes in both types of inequality might affect trends in the black-white test score gap. As noted earlier, the economic circumstances in which black and white children are

raised differ considerably. Understanding the role of inequality is important because, as we shall see, the recent growth in economic inequality has
disproportionately affected black Americans, who were more likely than
white Americans to be at lower levels of the earnings, income, and wealth
distribution to start with. Thus, to the extent that growing economic
inequality has social consequences, these are likely to be more apparent
on average for black Americans than for white Americans.

Social Consequences of Economic Inequality

One reason to consider the association between economic inequality and
children's test scores is the potential for social consequences of economic
inequality (Neckerman 2004). Social consequences are of particular concern because they may affect the current generation of children as well as
future generations. Because income and wealth are implicated in many
aspects of family life, there are numerous ways that economic inequality
could lead to inequality in social outcomes among families and children.
Children in families at the bottom of the income and wealth distributions
may have access to fewer resources in and out of the home, may receive
poorer child care or health care, or may attend poorer-quality schools and
have less effective teachers (see, for example, Haveman et al. 2004; Meyers
et al. 2004; Phillips and Chin 2004). In addition, increased financial hard-
ship may diminish their parents' capacity to provide warm and supportive parenting (McLoyd 1998).

Long-run effects of increased economic inequality are also potentially
important. If increased economic inequality leads to increased disparities
in college attendance, current economic inequality may result in economic
and social inequality in the future (Ellwood and Kane 2000; Kane 2004;
Dickert-Conlin and Rubenstein 2007). A further concern is the long-run
impact of economic inequality on family formation, which might arise if
low incomes deter men from marriage and lead to more children being
raised in single-parent families (Ellwood and Jencks 2004; Martin 2004).

The effects of economic inequality on social dimensions of inequality
discussed so far are examples of what William Evans, Michael Hout, and
Susan Mayer termed mechanical consequences (2004). These effects are
called mechanical because they reflect the fact that, to the extent an economic factor affects an individual's well-being and life chances, any increase
in economic inequality, holding all else constant, will lead to an increase in
inequality along these social dimensions.[5]

Evans and his coauthors (2004) also pointed to the role that can be
played by externalities, which involve the influence of factors external to
individuals on their outcomes. One type of externality has to do with relative deprivation. Relative deprivation theory suggests that individuals
assess their well being by comparing themselves to others, especially those

who are better off than themselves. Thus, an increase in economic inequality could adversely affect individuals at the bottom of the distribution by increasing the magnitude of the differences between themselves and the better-off comparison group, leading to poorer self assessments and possibly other adverse outcomes.

A second type of externality that Evans and his coauthors discussed is a possible link between economic inequality and state spending decisions. Here, however, it is not clear what effect growing economic inequality might have. One scenario would suggest that as economic inequality increases, states might undertake policies and programs that lead to an increase in financial redistribution from wealthier to poor individuals, either because the median voter has lost economic ground and thus favors more redistribution or because the rich favor reducing inequality. However, it is also possible that as the rich gain financial resources, they exert more power over the political process and that redistributive spending, which they do not see as in their interests, falls.

A third type of externality highlighted by Evans and his coauthors (2004) has to do with economic segregation. If the neighborhoods in which families live become more economically segregated because of increasing economic inequality, such segregation could have adverse consequences for children in low-income families. This may be especially important for understanding trends in achievement gaps given the close connections between neighborhood composition and school composition.

Trends in Economic Inequality

Given the possible social consequences of economic inequality, the unprecedented growth in economic inequality over the past three decades in the United States is especially worrisome. We begin with a discussion of trends in earnings, which for most Americans are the primary source of income and wealth. Two striking trends characterize the period from 1979 to 2004. The first is a decline in the earnings of the bottom 10 percent of the earnings distribution relative to the median (that is, the 50th percentile). The second is an increase in the earnings of the top 10 percent of the distribution relative to the median, with a particularly steep increase for the top 1 percent (see, for example, Piketty and Saez 2003). Thus, the growth in earnings inequality has been driven by changes at both the bottom and the top of the distribution, though the growth in inequality at the top of the distribution has been larger.

Many theories have been advanced to explain this unprecedented growth in the inequality of earnings, and most experts agree that several factors have contributed (Katz and Murphy 1992; Levy and Murnane 1992; Juhn, Murphy, and Pierce 1993; Levy 1998; Katz and Autor 1999; Autor, Katz, and Kearney 2006, 2008; Levy and Temin 2007). Skill-biased technological change, which refers to the increased demand in the labor market for highly educated workers, has been important. As demand for highly skilled workers has grown, the wages employers are willing to pay to attract and retain such workers have also risen. Changes in executives' compensation have also been a factor for those at the top of the earnings distribution. At the other end of the distribution, changes in international trade, and in particular the auto and steel industry, have resulted in fewer well-paid blue collar jobs for workers without a college education. The decline of unions and the failure of the minimum wage to keep pace with inflation have further eroded the earnings of low-wage workers. In addition, increases in immigration of low-skilled workers have increased the supply of low-wage workers and may have exerted downward pressure on wages for less-educated native workers (Borjas, Freeman, and Katz 1997). Of course, earnings and employment continue to be affected by cyclical changes in the economy. The late 1990s economic boom, in particular, provided some boost to workers at the bottom of the distribution, whose earnings rose in real terms for the first time in several decades (Mishel, Bernstein, and Allegretto 2007). Following the economic expansion, however, low-skilled workers still had lower earnings relative to the median than they had in 1979.

Because earnings are the major component of family incomes, these trends in earnings inequality are reflected in trends in family income inequality. However, because family incomes are also affected by other factors, in particular, family structure and patterns of family members' employment, family income inequality trends may differ somewhat from earnings inequality trends. Figure I.7 (from Congressional Budget Office 2007) shows trends in the incomes of families with children at different points of the family income distribution. If incomes were equally distributed, families in each fifth or quintile of the distribution would have one-fifth of total family income. However, this is not the case. In 1979, those in the top fifth already held 34 percent of all family income, and, the distribution had become even more unequal by 2004, as the top quintile's share of total family income rose to 47 percent. The gains were even more dramatic for the top 1 percent (not shown in the figure), whose share rose from 5.7 percent to 15.3 percent. Over the same period, the share held by all other quintiles fell. In particular, the share of those in the bottom fifth fell from 6.3 percent in 1979 to 5.1 percent in 2004; this decline would have been even worse had it not been for income gains for this quintile in the late 1990s as more single mothers went to work (Congressional Budget Office 2007). Levels of family wealth inequality are even higher than income inequality, because wealth is much more concentrated at the very top of the distribution (Kennickell 2000), though it is not clear whether inequality in family wealth has been growing as rapidly as inequality in family income (Scholz and Levine 2004).

Figure I.7   Distribution of Family Income

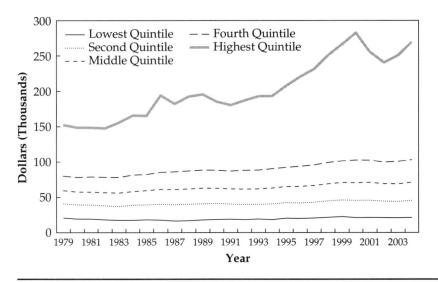

Source: Congressional Budget Office (2007).

What do these trends in overall economic inequality imply for black-white economic inequality? If black and white Americans had the same distribution of earnings, income, and wealth, then the increased dispersion of the past several decades would not have affected black-white inequality. However, because black and white economic circumstances were already very unequal, with black Americans more likely than white Americans to have low earnings, income, and wealth, and less likely to have high earnings, income, and wealth, the recent growth in economic inequality would be expected to exacerbate existing disparities (Altonji and Blank 1999). Of course, at the same time other factors may have operated to reduce black-white inequalities. Levels of education among black Americans have risen sharply, as has the quality of the schools they attend (Krueger, Rothstein, and Turner 2006). In addition, civil rights, antidiscrimination, and affirmative action initiatives have probably reduced discrimination in the labor market (Holzer and Neumark 2006). These factors, in the absence of increased economic inequality, would have reduced black-white gaps in earnings, income, and wealth (Altonji and Blank 1999).

Trend data for black-white earnings inequality reflect the influence of these competing trends. In the 1970s, black-white earnings gaps narrowed because of the inequality-reducing factors delineated (increased levels and quality of education and reduced discrimination), but from the late 1970s onward, the black-white earnings gaps stopped closing (Altonji and Blank

Figure I.8   Median Family Income and Child Poverty Rate by Race

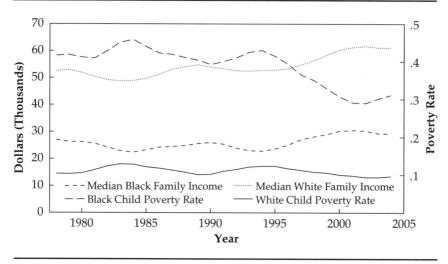

Source: Authors' compilation.

1999; Krueger, Rothstein, and Turner 2006). Similar trends are evident when we examine black-white income gaps among families with children in the March Current Population Survey (see figure I.8). In this case, however, the gaps are probably also affected by other co-occurring trends, in particular, the greater decline in marriage among black families than among white. One of the strongest protective factors for family income over this period, as low-skilled workers lost ground in the labor market, was the presence of a second earner. Black families, though, are much less likely than white families to have two parents present, and this gap has widened over the past thirty or forty years (figure I.9). Finally, as noted, overall inequality in wealth is far greater than inequality in earnings or income. The same is true for black-white inequality in wealth (Shapiro and Oliver 2006; Scholz and Levine 2004).

Inequality and Trends in the Black-White Test Score Gap

The chapters in this volume examine a number of ways in which increased economic inequality, and related social dimensions of inequality, may have contributed to recent trends in the black-white test score gap and, in particular, to the stalled progress that began in the mid- to late 1980s. Because economic and social dimensions of inequality are interrelated, and because many factors affect student achievement, we would not expect any single

Figure I.9   Rates of Two-Parent Families by Race

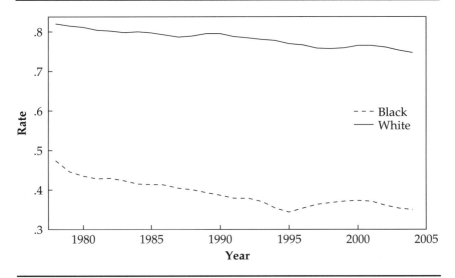

Source: Authors' compilation.

aspect of inequality to play a predominant role. Rather, it is likely that many aspects of increased economic and social inequality may have acted together to stall the progress that black children had been making relative to their white peers up to the 1980s. Moreover, given that trends in reading and math gaps have not been constant over time but rather have been characterized by periods of steady gains as well as stalled progress, with some variation by age, cohort, and gender groups, we would not expect one set of factors to explain all the trends over time. As Ronald Ferguson emphasizes in chapter 9, the black-white test score gap has not been a unitary phenomenon over the past forty years, and its causes are likely to be multiple and complex.

A Long-Term View

The first three chapters take a long-term view. In chapter 1, Katherine Magnuson, Dan Rosenbaum, and Jane Waldfogel analyze the links between inequality and black-white achievement trends for nine-year-olds using NAEP-LTT data from the 1970s to 2004. The NAEP-LTT series is the single best source of data on trends in black and white test scores, but contains only limited data on family-level factors. The authors therefore augment the NAEP data by merging in information about the average characteristics of black and white families with children from the March

Current Population Survey (CPS). They find that controlling for the child's characteristics (that is gender, parent's level of education, and whether the household receives a newspaper, as reported in the NAEP) and the average characteristics of families of the same race group in that child's state (that is, average maternal age and education and share of families with single parents, from the March CPS) does help explain a portion of the black-white test score gap. Moreover, they also find some evidence suggesting that when income inequality in a state becomes higher, children's test score performance is lower. However, income inequality appears to be negatively related to the performance of all children and thus does not seem to be directly implicated in the stalled progress in closing the test score gap. Rather, the state and family characteristic that seems to be most related is parents' education. Improvements in black parents' education was a key factor identified in the Jencks and Phillips (1998) volume as underlying the gains in closing black-white test score gaps in the 1960s and 1970s. The analysis in chapter 1 suggests that the slower progress in closing parental education gaps in the 1990s may be a factor in explaining the stalled progress in closing the black-white test score gaps in those years.

Mark Berends and Roberto Peñaloza, in chapter 2, also take a long view, analyzing how changes in families and schools have affected the black-white test score gap for seventeen-year-olds during the thirty-two years from 1972 to 2004, taking advantage of detailed data from four cohorts of high school seniors. Consistent with earlier work (Berends et al. 2005), they find that family factors, such as the increasing education level of black parents and smaller family sizes in black families, played an important role in helping to close the black-white test score gaps in the 1970s and early 1980s. They analyze whether changes in family factors such as these continued to benefit black children after the 1980s, or whether other changes in family factors may have disadvantaged black children relative to white children. They find that for the most part, changes in family factors continued to benefit black students, but that these were offset by increasing disparities in the characteristics of schools that black and white students attend, such as the percentage minority and socioeconomic characteristics of fellow students. This result stands in contrast to the earlier period, when school improvements pursuant to the civil rights movement contributed to gains in closing black-white gaps.

Focusing on the role that family income plays, in chapter 3, Mary Campbell, Robert Haveman, Tina Wildhagen, and Barbara Wolfe use data from the National Survey of Adolescent Health to analyze the extent to which income predicts test scores for young adults age eighteen to twenty-eight and then, based on those estimates, how recent changes in income inequality are likely to have affected trends in the gaps in student test scores. They find that changes in the distribution of income per se are likely to have played only a small role in explaining trends in black-white test score gaps, because income matters most to test scores at the bottom of the income distribution, whereas the increase in income inequality has been greatest at the top. However, they also find that blacks attend schools with higher levels of income inequality and that, though attending a more unequal school decreases black students' test scores, it slightly raises those of white students. These results point to income inequality within schools as a mechanism by which increasing income inequality could have contributed to stalled progress in closing black-white test score gaps.

Explaining Gaps at School Entry and During School

Previous work on black-white test score gaps has found that substantial gaps are already present when children enter school, and that black-white gaps tend to widen during the school years (Phillips, Crouse, and Ralph 1998; see also Fryer and Levitt 2004, 2005; Murnane et al. 2005; Clotfelter, Ladd, and Vigdor 2006). These findings suggest the importance of examining the causal mechanisms that might underlie black-white gaps at school entry as well as during the school years. The next four chapters take up this challenge.

In chapter 4, David Grissmer and Elizabeth Eiseman use nationally representative data from the Early Childhood Longitudinal Study—Kindergarten Cohort to examine black-white gaps at school entry. Expanding on previous research that has focused mainly on academic skills, they examine noncognitive skills, including fine and gross motor skills and child behavior, in addition to reading and math skills. They find that substantial black-white gaps in both cognitive and noncognitive skills are present at school entry, suggesting the need to better understand the development of both those domains in early childhood. Their work also points to the potential role that early childhood programs might play in closing black-white gaps. In particular, there is strong evidence that early education programs delivered in preschool settings can improve children's school readiness, with particularly large effects for high-quality programs serving disadvantaged children. However, the extent to which preschool programs will be able to further reduce test score gaps will depend on black children gaining an advantage over white children in enrollment rates or benefits from enrollment, or both (Magnuson and Waldfogel 2005).

Chapters 5 and 6 focus on the role of school-related factors in explaining black-white test score gaps. As noted, the fact that achievement gaps widen after school entry points to the importance of understanding what role schools might play and how that role may have changed over time. During the 1970s and early 1980s, school reforms and changes associated with the civil rights movement were credited with reducing black-white gaps in reading and math (Ferguson 2007; Ferguson with Mehta 2004).

With inequality increasing along many dimensions in the 1980s and 1990s, did inequality in school factors contribute to the stalled progress in closing the test score gaps during that period? Chapters 5 and 6 tackle this question.

In chapter 5, Jacob Vigdor and Jens Ludwig consider the role of changes in neighborhood and school segregation, which previous research has identified as important factors contributing to black-white achievement gaps (Clotfelter, Ladd, and Vigdor 2003; Clotfelter 2004; Card and Rothstein 2006). During the 1970s and 1980s, there were substantial reductions in both neighborhood and school segregation, and these reductions contributed to the narrowing of the black-white test score gap. However, in the 1990s, although neighborhood segregation continued to decline, progress in integrating schools slowed, and in some districts worsened. As a result, Vigdor and Ludwig conclude that if schools had desegregated as quickly as neighborhoods had, the black-white test score gap today would be smaller. Their analysis also suggests that if schools had continued desegregating as rapidly in the 1990s as they had in earlier decades, progress in closing the black-white test score gap might have continued rather than stalled. Vigdor and Ludwig's analysis implies that reducing segregation in schools, or addressing the reasons that segregated schools widen achievement gaps, could further reduce the black-white test score gap in future.

In chapter 6, Sean Corcoran and William Evans consider the role of another important school factor, teacher quality. Disparities in the quality of teachers to which black and white children are exposed have been identified as a key contributor to the black-white achievement gap (Ferguson 1998, 2007; Ferguson with Mehta 2004; Hanushek and Rivkin 2006; Phillips and Chin 2004). Did this aspect of inequality worsen when progress in closing black-white gaps in reading and math stalled? The analysis in this chapter suggests that the answer depends on which grades one considers. At the elementary level, the gaps in teacher qualifications, characteristics, and attitudes between teachers of the average black student and the average white student did widen during the 1990s; however, at the secondary level, they mostly narrowed or held constant. Thus, growing inequality in teacher quality may be impeding progress at the elementary level, but is not likely to be a factor explaining the stalled progress of children at the secondary level.

That black-white test score gaps widen during the school years does not necessarily mean that school factors alone are acting to widen those gaps. Factors such as how children and youth spend their time after school and during the summers and how much support their parents provide for learning may also affect children's achievement. Given the growth in economic and related social inequality in recent years, these out-of-school factors may have affected test score trends (Ferguson 1998, 2007; Ferguson with Mehta 2004). Meredith Phillips considers this question in chapter 7.

She concludes that trends in factors such as the time students spend reading for pleasure, doing homework, or watching television, as well as the amount of reading materials in the home and parental monitoring of homework and television watching, are not strongly correlated with trends in black-white test score gaps for thirteen-year-olds or seventeen-year-olds. However, she finds some links between lower rates of computer ownership and lower math scores for black students, as well as an association between an increase in disciplinary problems and a decrease in test scores for black seventeen-year-olds. There is thus some evidence that out-of-school factors may have played a role in the recent period of stalled progress, at least for some groups.

Conclusions and Policy Implications

The final two chapters reflect on the evidence about recent trends in the black-white test score gap and the factors that might explain them. Each then offers thoughts about the prospects for future gap closing and what policies might facilitate this.

In chapter 8, Helen Ladd provides a critical overview of the role that school reform policies might play in promoting gains in closing the black-white test score gap. She reviews five types of school policies that have been proposed or justified because of their potential to reduce racial test score gaps. She concludes that few education policies are likely to play a major role in reducing the black-white achievement gap, but argues that well designed policies are still a critical component of any gap-reduction strategy. Ladd identifies two school-based strategies that hold particular promise—reducing class sizes in the early grades and evening out the quality of teachers across schools serving different racial groups.

In chapter 9, Ronald Ferguson revisits the evidence on the trends in test score gaps, in particular highlighting cohort trends. He argues that changes in popular as well as school culture (for example, trends in students cutting classes and in grade inflation) may be important explanations for gap trends. He then identifies policies that might address these aspects of popular culture and school culture and thus contribute to further progress in closing test score gaps in future. Ferguson also emphasizes that the causes of black-white achievement gaps are multiple and complex and that a multifaceted approach will be needed if further progress is to be made.

What Have We Learned?

The persistent gap in test scores between black and white children remains one of the greatest challenges of our time. The chapters in this volume help us better understand the reasons why the United States has experienced both steady gains and stalled progress in its efforts to close the black-white test score gap and provide some direction about steps the country might take to make further progress in future.

Two key conclusions stand out. First, growing economic and related social inequality has probably impeded progress in closing black-white test score gaps. Second, however, to the extent that rising inequality has played a role, its effects have been complex, working through factors at both the family and school level. Growing disparities in family income do not appear to have had large direct effects on test scores. Rather, growing disparities in income and related social dimensions have threatened progress in closing black-white achievement gaps through their effects on families and schools, which in turn influence test scores.

At the family level, the convergence in parental education of black and white children has been important in closing test score gaps. However, as others have noted (see, for example, Long, Kelly, and Gamoran 2005), the convergence in mean levels of parental education was mainly due to improvements at the lower end of the educational distribution (high school completion), and considerable gaps in postsecondary education remain. Findings presented in chapters 1 and 2 suggest that overall improvements in parental education were operating to close the gaps between 1974 and 2004. Nevertheless, in 2004, sizable gaps—in parental education, particularly postsecondary education, and test scores—remained. Thus there is considerable scope for further improvement here.

At the school level, the evidence in this volume points to several factors related to economic and social inequality that worsened for black students relative to white students and that look to have played a role in stalling progress in closing the black-white test score gap. In particular, chapters 4 and 5 point to the slowdown in school desegregation, and chapters 6 and 7 highlight the lower quality of teachers black students have relative to the quality of those white students have.

As Vigdor and Ludwig discuss in chapter 5, analysts differ as to how segregation should be measured, and over time trends in segregation can look quite disparate depending on what measure is used. The other factor affecting estimates is how much influence segregation is estimated to have in any given model. Vigdor and Ludwig use a dissimilarity index, which shows little or no increase in segregation in recent years, combined with estimates of segregation effects from rigorous models that attempt to identify causal effects by holding constant school effects. As a result, their estimate of the role that segregation has played in stalled progress is quite small. In contrast, Berends and Peñaloza in chapter 2 use the percentage of minority students to measure segregation. Segregation on this measure increased markedly between 1982 and 2004 and is estimated to be strongly associated with test scores for high school seniors in their regression models that do control for school effects. Accordingly, their estimates suggest that segregation increased over the past two decades and that the increase contributed to a widening of the black white gap for this age group. The two chapters concur that the progress in desegregation of the 1960s and 1970s either came to a halt or was reversed in the 1980s and 1990s, and that this is a factor in the stalled progress of those decades.

Inequality in teacher quality is another factor that disadvantages black students and is likely to have played a role in the stalled progress. In chapter 6, Corcoran and Evans provide new evidence on black-white student gaps in teacher quality using data from the Schools and Staffing Survey. They conclude that black-white gaps in meaningful aspects of teacher quality have widened over the past few decades, though mainly for elementary school rather than secondary school children. In chapter 7, Ladd argues that disparities in teacher quality are at least in part attributable to segregation, noting that efforts to desegregate schools would reduce disparities in teacher quality by placing more black and white students in the same schools (though they still might have different teachers within those schools). The two chapters concur that teacher quality is a key input in students' educational achievement and that reducing disparities in teacher quality across black and white students would likely reduce black-white test score gaps.

Of course, there may be other factors—not examined here—that help explain recent trends in the black-white test score gap and in particular why progress in closing the gap stalled in the 1980s and 1990s. The chapters in this volume have examined the facets of social inequality that seem most likely to matter and for which we had adequate data. But there are some potentially important omissions. We did not consider differences in child health and how those might affect progress in closing the gap. Other researchers have found that though disparities in child health exist, they are not a large factor in explaining gaps in test scores at school entry (Currie 2005) or in later school years (Jackson 2007). Nevertheless, improvements in child health probably did play a role in the progress of the 1960s and 1970s (see, for example, Almond and Chay 2006), and the role of child health merits further attention in future work.

We also do not consider trends in parental incarceration, which have had such disproportionate effects on black families (Bushway, Stoll, and Weiman 2007; Wildeman forthcoming). Although we think it is likely that the impact of incarceration works at least partially through factors examined in this book, such as income and family structure, it too merits further examination.

Finally, we have not considered psychological factors, such as the attitudes with which black and white children approach tests and the meaning that school work and tests has for them (see, for example, Aronson 2002; Cohen et al. 2006; Fuligni 2007). Because of data limitations, such psychological factors are not included in our analyses of social inequality, but are nonetheless important to understanding the achievement gap, and thus should continue to be studied.

Looking Ahead

The trends in the black-white test score gap over the past thirty to forty years provide ample evidence that such gaps are amenable to change, as both William Dickens and James Flynn (2006) and Ronald Ferguson (chapter 9, this volume) argue. Where do we stand now and what can we look forward to in the future? The most recent long-term trend data, from the 2004 NAEP-LTT, suggest that we may be entering another period of convergence, though sizable gaps remain. We would not want to make too much of the 2004 data until we can see whether the progress persists through the next administration of the NAEP-LTT in 2008 (scheduled to be released in 2009). Nevertheless, the 2004 results are encouraging and point to the possibility that we may be entering another period of steady gains.

We can only speculate as to how much more progress could be made in closing the racial test score gap if economic and social inequality were declining instead of increasing. In the meantime, the studies in this volume clearly point the way to some policies that would make a difference. First, there is a role for expanding black children's enrollment in high-quality preschool programs that help children enter school with higher reading and math skills. Second, there is a role for policies to improve the quality of education that black children receive once they are at school—through reducing class sizes, improving teacher quality, reducing school segregation, and increasing accountability. Third, there is a role for parents and community members to play in addressing how youth spend their time outside of school and their behavior in school. Fourth, given evidence that low incomes constrain black youth from attending college, there is a role for expansions in college financial aid programs such as Pell Grants. Together, such policies, if successful, would not only improve educational outcomes and reduce disparities in the current generation of children but also improve outcomes and reduce gaps in the next generation by increasing the share of black parents with higher education, in particular, a college degree.

Notes

1. We are grateful to the Russell Sage Foundation for their generous funding of the work reported in this volume. We obtained a copy of the beta version of the NAEP-LTT data from the U.S. Department of Education, National Center for Education Statistics under a restricted data license agreement. The mathematics testing began in 1973 but we were not able to obtain the data from before 1978. We are grateful to NCES for making these data available to us and to

Yougeon Lee for assistance with the data. Additional funding for NAEP analyses was provided by the William T. Grant Foundation.

2. Information on the overall black-white gap has also been reported by NCES in several reports (see, most recently, Perie, Moran, and Lutkus 2005). One concern about data on the seventeen-year-olds is that only twelfth grade students are tested, and thus trends in test scores may be affected by trends in dropout rates.

3. It is also possible to code children using race as reported by the child him or herself. Results using this variable are very similar to those shown here. Hispanic children are not included here but are included in the analyses in chapter 3.

4. Researchers often measure black-white test score gaps as a proportion of a standard deviation. The standard deviations for these tests change slightly over time, but are typically around 40 points for reading and 36 points for math. Dividing the difference in test scores by the standard deviation yields an effect size for the gaps, which ranges from about 1 to about 0.75.

5. Another way that economic inequality can affect social dimensions of inequality or long-run economic inequality is via what Evans and his co-authors call relational effects. Relational effects refer to the impact of income (or other economic factors) becoming stronger or weaker over time (thus, they refer to changes in coefficients). In the extreme, income differences could be less consequential in affecting an outcome in a period when income inequality was rising, if over the same period the effect of income on that outcome had fallen. For instance, as public kindergarten has become the norm, the effect of family income on children's kindergarten enrollment has diminished, such that now kindergarten enrollment is more or less universal (Meyers et al. 2004). On the other hand, growing income dispersion could be more consequential than previously thought, if the effect of income on an outcome has grown over the same period. This may be the case with regard to health, as income now appears to have a stronger effect on health than it once did (Eibner and Evans 2004).

References

Almond, Douglas, and Kenneth Chay. 2006. "The Long-Run and Intergenerational Impact of Poor Infant Health: Evidence from Cohorts Born During the Civil Rights Era." Unpublished paper. Columbia University and University of California, Berkeley.

Altonji, Joseph, and Rebecca Blank. 1999. "Race and Gender in the Labor Market." In *Handbook of Labor Economics*, vol. 3, edited by Orley Ashenfelter and David Card. Amsterdam: Elsevier Science.

Aronson, Joshua. 2002. *Improving Academic Achievement: Impact of Psychological Factors on Education.* San Diego, Calif.: Academic Press.

Autor, David, Lawrence Katz, and Melissa Kearney. 2006. "The Polarization of the U.S. Labor Market." *American Economic Review Papers and Proceedings* 96(2): 189–94.

———. 2008. "Trends in U.S. Wage Inequality: Revising the Revisionists." *Review of Economics and Statistics* 90(2): 300–323.

Barton, Paul E. 2003. *Parsing the Achievement Gap: Baselines for Tracking Progress.* Princeton, N.J.: Educational Testing Service.

Belfield, Clive R., and Henry M. Levin. 2007. *The Price We Pay: Economic and Social Consequences of Inadequate Education*. Washington, D.C.: Brookings Institution Press.

Berends, Mark, Samuel R. Lucas, Thomas Sullivan, and R. J. Briggs. 2005. *Examining Gaps in Mathematics Achievement Among Racial-Ethnic Groups, 1972–1992*. Santa Monica, Calif.: RAND Corporation.

Borjas, George, Richard Freeman, and Lawrence Katz. 1997. "How Much Do Immigration and Trade Affect Labor Market Outcomes?" *Brookings Papers on Economic Activity* 1997(1): 1–90.

Bushway, Shawn, Michael A. Stoll, and David F. Weiman. 2007. "The Regime of Mass Incarceration: A Labor Market Perspective." In *Barriers to Reentry: The Labor Market for Released Prisoners in Post-Industrial America*, edited by Shawn Bushway, Michael A. Stoll, and David F. Weiman. New York: Russell Sage Foundation.

Card, David, and Jesse Rothstein. 2006. "Racial Segregation and the Black-White Test Score Gap." NBER Working Paper 12078. Cambridge, Mass.: National Bureau of Economic Research.

Clotfelter, Charles T. 2004. *After Brown: The Rise and Retreat of School Desegregation*. Princeton, N.J.: Princeton University Press.

Clotfelter, Charles T., Helen F. Ladd, and Jacob L. Vigdor. 2003. "Segregation and Resegregation in North Carolina's Public School Classrooms." *North Carolina Law Review* 81(4): 1463–511.

———. 2006. "The Academic Achievement Gap in Grades 3 to 8." NBER Working Paper 12207. Cambridge, Mass.: National Bureau of Economic Research.

Cohen, Geoffrey L., Julio Garcia, Nancy Apfel, and Allison Master. 2006. "Reducing the Racial Achievement Gap: A Social-Psychological Intervention." *Science* 313(5791): 1307–10.

Congressional Budget Office. 2007. "Changes in the Economic Resources of Low-Income Households with Children." Washington: Congressional Budget Office.

Currie, Janet. 2005. "Health Disparities and Gaps in School Readiness." *Future of Children* 15(1): 117–38.

Danziger, Sheldon. 2007. "Fighting Poverty Revisited: What Did Researchers Know 40 Years Ago? What Do We Know Today?" *Focus* 25(1): 3–11.

Dickens, William T., and James R. Flynn. 2006. "Black Americans Reduce the Racial IQ Gap: Evidence from Standardization Samples." *Psychological Science* 17(10): 913–24.

Dickert-Conlin, Stacy, and Ross Rubenstein, editors. 2007. *Economic Inequality and Higher Education: Access, Persistence, and Success*. New York: Russell Sage Foundation.

Eibner, Christine E., and William N. Evans. 2004. "The Income-Health Relationship and the Role of Relative Deprivation." In *Social Inequality*, edited by Kathryn M. Neckerman. New York: Russell Sage Foundation.

Ellwood, David T., and Christopher Jencks. 2004. "The Uneven Spread of Single-Parent Families: What Do We Know? Where Do We Look for Answers?" In *Social Inequality*, edited by Kathryn M. Neckerman. New York: Russell Sage Foundation.

Ellwood, David T., and Thomas J. Kane. 2000. "Who Is Getting a College Education: Family Background and the Growing Gap in Enrollment." In *Securing the Future: Investing in Children from Birth to Adulthood*, edited by Sheldon Danziger and Jane Waldfogel. New York: Russell Sage Foundation.

Evans, William N., Michael Hout, and Susan E. Mayer. 2004. "Assessing the Effect of Economic Inequality." In *Social Inequality*, edited by Kathryn M. Neckerman. New York: Russell Sage Foundation.

Ferguson, Ronald R. 1998. "Teacher Perceptions and Expectations and the Black-White Test Score Gap." In *The Black-White Test Score Gap*, edited by Christopher Jencks and Meredith Phillips. Washington, D.C.: Brookings Institution Press.

———. 2007. *Toward Excellence with Equity: An Emerging Vision for Closing the Achievement Gap*. Cambridge, Mass.: Harvard Education Press.

Ferguson, Ronald R., with Jal Mehta. 2004. "An Unfinished Journey: The Legacy of Brown and the Narrowing of the Achievement Gap." *Phi Delta Kappan* 85(4): 656–69.

Flynn, James. 2007. *What Is Intelligence? Beyond the Flynn Effect*. Cambridge: Cambridge University Press.

Fryer, Roland G., and Steven D. Levitt. 2004. "Understanding the Black-White Test Score Gap in the First Two Years of School." *Review of Economics and Statistics* 86(2): 447–64.

———. 2005. "The Black-White Test Score Gap Through Third Grade." NBER Working Paper 11049. Cambridge, Mass.: National Bureau of Economic Research.

Fuligni, Andrew, editor. 2007. *Contesting Stereotypes and Creating Identities: Social Categories, Social Identities, and Educational Participation*. New York: Russell Sage Foundation.

Hanushek, Eric A., and Steven G. Rivkin. 2006. "School Quality and the Black-White Achievement Gap." NBER Working Paper 12651. Cambridge, Mass.: National Bureau of Economic Research.

Haveman, Robert, Gary Sandefur, Barbara Wolfe, and Andrea Voyer. 2004. "Trends in Children's Attainments and Their Determinants as Family Income Inequality Has Increased." In *Social Inequality*, edited by Kathryn M. Neckerman. New York: Russell Sage Foundation.

Holzer, Harry, and David Neumark. 2006. "Affirmative Action: What Do We Know?" *Journal of Policy Analysis and Management* 25(2): 463–90.

Jackson, Margot I. 2007. "Understanding Links between Children's Health and Education." Working paper. Los Angeles, Calif.: University of California at Los Angeles.

Jencks, Christopher, and Meredith Phillips. 1998. "Introduction." In *The Black-White Test Score Gap*, edited by Christopher Jencks and Meredith Phillips. Washington, D.C.: Brookings Institution Press.

Juhn, Chinhui, Kevin M. Murphy, and Brooks Pierce. 1993. "Wage Inequality and the Rise in Returns to Skill." *Journal of Political Economy* 101(3): 410–42.

Kane, Thomas J. 2004. "College-Going and Inequality." In *Social Inequality*, edited by Katherine M. Neckerman. New York: Russell Sage Foundation.

Katz, Lawrence F., and David H. Autor. 1999. "Changes in the Wage Structure and Earnings Inequality." In *Handbook of Labor Economics*, vol. 3, edited by Orley Ashenfelter and David Card. Amsterdam: North-Holland.

Katz, Lawrence F., and Kevin M. Murphy. 1992. "Changes in Relative Wages, 1963–1987: Supply and Demand Factors." *Quarterly Journal of Economics* 107(2): 35–78.

Kennickell, Arthur B. 2000. "An Examination of Changes in the Distribution of Wealth from 1989 to 1998: Evidence from the Survey of Consumer Finances." Prepared for the Conference on Saving, Intergenerational Transfers, and the Distribution of Wealth, Jerome Levy Economics Institute, Bard College, Annandale-on-Hudson, N.Y., June 7–9, 2000. Accessed at http://www. federalreserve.gov/pubs.

Kirsch, Irwin, Henry Braun, Kentaro Yamamoto, and Andrew Sum. 2007. *America's Perfect Storm: Three Forces Changing Our Nation's Future.* Princeton, N.J.: Educational Testing Service.

Krueger, Alan B., Jesse Rothstein, and Sarah Turner. 2006. "Race, Income, and College in 25 Years: Evaluating Justice O'Connor's Conjecture." *American Law and Economics Review* 8(2): 282–311.

Levy, Frank. 1998. *The New Dollars and Dreams: American Incomes and Economic Change.* New York: Russell Sage Foundation.

Levy, Frank, and Richard J. Murnane. 1992. "U.S. Earnings Levels and Earnings Inequality: A Review of Recent Trends and Proposed Explanations." *Journal of Economic Literature* 30(3): 1333–81.

Levy, Frank, and Peter Temin. 2007. "Inequality and Institutions in 20th Century America." NBER Working Paper 13106. Cambridge, Mass.: National Bureau of Economic Research.

Long, Daniel, Sean Kelly, and Adam Gamoran. 2005. "Whither the Virtuous Cycle? Past and Future Trends in Black-White Inequality in Educational Attainment." Unpublished manuscript. University of Wisconsin, Madison.

Magnuson, Katherine A., and Elizabeth Votruba-Drzal. 2008. "The Enduring Influences of Childhood Poverty." Unpublished manuscript. University of Wisconsin, Madison.

⇢ Magnuson, Katherine A., and Jane Waldfogel. 2005. "Early Childhood Care and Education, and Ethnic and Racial Test Score Gaps at School Entry." *The Future of Children* 15(1): 169–96.

Martin, Steven P. 2004. "Women's Education and Family Timing: Outcomes and Trends Associated with Age at Marriage and First Birth." In *Social Inequality,* edited by Kathryn M. Neckerman. New York: Russell Sage Foundation.

⇢ McLoyd, Vonnie C. 1998. "Socioeconomic Disadvantage and Child Development." *American Psychologist* 53(2): 185–204.

Meyers, Marcia K., Dan Rosenbaum, Christopher Ruhm, and Jane Waldfogel. 2004. "Inequality in Early Childhood Education and Care: What Do We Know?" In *Social Inequality,* edited by Kathryn M. Neckerman. New York: Russell Sage Foundation.

Mishel, Lawrence, Jared Bernstein, and Sylvia Allegretto. 2007. *The State of Working America, 2006/2007.* Washington, D.C.: Economic Policy Institute.

Murnane, Richard J., John B. Willett, Kristen L. Bub, and Kathleen McCartney. 2005. "Understanding Trends in Racial/Ethnic Achievement Gaps during Elementary School." In *Brookings-Wharton Papers on Urban Affairs 2005,* edited by Gary Burtless and Janet Rothenburg Pack. Washington, D.C.: Brookings Institution Press.

Neal, Derek A. 2006. "Why Has Black-White Skill Convergence Stopped?" In *Handbook of the Economics of Education,* edited by Eric Hanushek and Finis Welch. Amsterdam: North-Holland.

Neckerman, Kathryn M., editor. 2004. *Social Inequality*. New York: Russell Sage Foundation.

Perie, Marianne, Rebecca Moran, and Anthony D. Lutkus. 2005. *NAEP 2004 Trends in Academic Progress: Three Decades of Student Performance in Reading and Mathematics*. Washington: U.S. Government Printing Office.

Phillips, Meredith, and Tiffani Chin. 2004. "School Inequality: What Do We Know?" In *Social Inequality*, edited by Kathryn M. Neckerman. New York: Russell Sage Foundation.

Phillips, Meredith, James Crouse, and John Ralph. 1998. "Does the Black-White Test Score Gap Widen After Children Enter School?" In *The Black-White Test Score Gap*, edited by Christopher Jencks and Meredith Phillips. Washington, D.C.: Brookings Institution Press.

Piketty, Thomas, and Emmanuel Saez. 2003. "Income Inequality in the United States: 1913–1998." *Quarterly Journal of Economics* 118(1): 1–39.

Scholz, John Karl, and Kara Levine. 2004. "U.S. Black-White Wealth Inequality." In *Social Inequality*, edited by Kathryn M. Neckerman. New York: Russell Sage Foundation.

Shapiro, Thomas, and Melvin Oliver. 2006. *Black Wealth, White Wealth: A New Perspective on Racial Inequality*. New York: Routledge.

Smedley, Audrey, and Brian D. Smedley. 2005. "Race as Biology Is Fiction, Racism As A Social Problem Is Real: Anthropological and Historical Perspectives on the Social Construction of Race." *American Psychologist* 60(1): 16–26.

Turkheimer, Eric, Andreanna Haley, Mary Waldron, Brian D'Onofrio, and Irving I. Gottesman. 2003. "Socioeconomic Status Modifies Heritability of IQ in Young Children." *Psychological Science* 14(6): 623–28.

Wildeman, Christopher. Forthcoming. "Parental Imprisonment, the Prison Boom, and the Concentration of Childhood Disadvantage." *Demography*.

PART I

A LONG-TERM VIEW

Chapter 1

Inequality and Black-White Achievement Trends in the NAEP

KATHERINE MAGNUSON, DAN T. ROSENBAUM, AND JANE WALDFOGEL

How do recent changes in economic inequality and related social dimensions of inequality relate to trends in black-white test score gaps? In this chapter, we provide new evidence on the question, analyzing the links between inequality and black-white achievement trends for nine-year-olds using the National Assessment of Educational Progress Long-Term Trend data (NAEP-LTT) from 1975 to 2004. The NAEP-LTT series is the best single source of data on trends in black and white test scores, but contains only limited data on family-level factors. We therefore augment it by merging in information about the average characteristics of black and white families with children, by state and year, from the March Current Population Survey (CPS). These average characteristics cannot tell us about an individual child's family but can tell us about the average family contexts that children of each race group experienced in a particular state and year. We also merge information about state-level annual income inequality among all families with children from the March CPS. This measure will not capture an individual child's position in the income distribution but will provide information about overall income inequality in that state and year.

To briefly preview the results, we find that controlling for the child's characteristics, as reported in the NAEP, and the average characteristics of families from the same race group in that child's state, from the March CPS, does help explain a portion of the black-white test score gaps in math and reading, with parental education appearing particularly important. We also find that when income inequality in a state is higher, children's math and reading test scores are lower. However, income inequality seems to adversely affect a broad range of children, suggesting that increases in inequality have suppressed performance overall but may not have widened black-white achievement gaps.

Background

As noted in the introduction to this volume, different socioeconomic standing among white and black children has been a common explanation for test score gaps (Magnuson and Duncan 2006). Parents' education, in particular, has been singled out as an important determinant of children's achievement and a possible source of convergence (Haveman and Wolfe 1995). Although the educational attainment of both white and black parents has been increasing, the black gains have been relatively larger, suggesting that they might explain the comparatively larger test score gains among black students relative to their white counterparts. Michael Cook and William Evans (2000), for example, found that the convergence of parental education between white and black students accounted for 25 percent of the convergence in thirteen-year-olds' NAEP-LTT black-white test score gaps between 1970 and 1988. Likewise, both David Grissmer, Ann Flanagan, and Stephanie Williamson (1998) and Mark Berends and Roberto Peñaloza (chapter 2, this volume) have pointed to changes in parental education as an important source of gap convergence through the early 1990s.

The role of parental education in explaining patterns of test score gaps in more recent years, however, has not been considered (see also chapter 2 this volume). National trends in maternal education suggest that the greatest convergence probably occurred before the early 1990s. The gap in years of education between white and black mothers in the March CPS narrowed a full year, from 1.7 years (11.3 versus 9.4 years) in 1967 to just 0.7 years (13.4 versus 12.7 years) in 1994. Since 1994, however, the gap has remained constant or increased as both white mothers' and black mothers' education has increased at similar rates, to 13.9 and 13.0 years, respectively, in 2005.[1]

It is important to note that tracking national trends in parental education is complicated by measurement challenges. An important source of error in the March CPS and other studies is the practice of asking about years of education completed but not about degrees attained. In particular, respondents who did not complete high school but obtained a General Educational Development (GED) certificate may report that they have completed twelve years of schooling, the same level reported by respondents with a high school degree, even though studies have shown that a GED is not equivalent to a high school degree (Heckman and LaFontaine 2006). Given that the proportion of GED recipients has risen over time, CPS trends overstate growth in true educational attainment. Although confounding GEDs with high school completion likely leads to an overestimate of the increase in mothers' educational attainment over time, doing so affects similar proportions of white and black mothers and is likely to have a very small impact on the measurement of educational gaps between the two groups.[2]

Parental education levels may have been improving and even converging, but other dimensions of socioeconomic standing, particularly incomes, have not. Recent studies of economic inequality and related social dimensions of inequality provide ample evidence that inequality has grown rapidly in the United States over the past thirty years (Neckerman 2004). Little research, however, has examined the implications of rising inequality for the black-white test score gap.

As discussed in the introduction, there are several theories about why economic inequality might affect test scores and the black-white test score gap.[3] First, changes in the income distribution may affect test scores directly by changing the financial resources available to families. Research suggests that family income is a strong predictor of children's achievement (Duncan and Brooks-Gunn 1997). The effects, however, appear to be nonlinear, with increments in family income at the lower end of the distribution mattering much more than those at the higher end. In addition, it appears that poverty is more detrimental to the achievement of young children than of older children (Duncan and Brooks-Gunn 1997; see also chapter 3 in this volume). The growth in economic inequality, to the extent that it is fueled in part by declining incomes at the lower end of the income distribution (as it was in the 1980s), may lead to a decline in achievement among disadvantaged young children, including blacks, relative to more advantaged children, including whites (for whom achievement either does not change or increases slightly).

Alternatively, rather than the absolute level of resources that parents have to invest in their children, it may be that a family's relative income is most important to the children's achievement (Mayer 2001). Children's perception of the economic standing of their family relative to other families may exert an influence on their learning and achievement (Evans, Hout, and Mayer 2004). In this case, as income inequality increases, students whose families have few resources may feel both more deprived and more discouraged about their ability to succeed in school. If this leads to their putting less effort into their schoolwork (Evans, Hout, and Mayer 2004; Mayer 2001), then their achievement may decline. If so, increasing inequality would lead to lower test scores for children at the lower end of the income distribution, and could lead to widening gaps in test scores between more and less advantaged groups. However, because young children may not engage in these types of social comparative processes as much as older children, this process may be muted.

It is also possible that increasing income inequality may shift the perceived payoffs to academic success and thus increase the incentives for all students to work harder in school (Mayer 2001). Specifically, if increasing economic inequality is in part due to wage increases among highly educated workers, then as the reward to higher levels of education (and the penalties to lower levels of education) increase, students may be more motivated. If this were the case, we might expect to see rising levels of overall educational achievement alongside rising income inequality. However, it may also be that there is an optimal level of inequality in this regard, and that if inequality is too high, low-achieving students may be discouraged and may decrease their effort (Freeman and Gelber 2006). Again, this theory may be most applicable to older students, as younger students may be less aware of the perceived payoffs of educational attainment.

Rising income inequality could also have indirect effects on test scores and black-white test score gaps. One mechanism for such indirect effects has to do with economic segregation. If rising income inequality is accompanied by increased economic segregation, then some school districts will likely get richer as others become poorer. These disparities in resources in turn might lead to disparities in teacher quality and other aspects of school quality, and therefore the achievement of disadvantaged children may decline compared with the achievement of their more advantaged counterparts.[4]

Despite studies that have considered the effects of family income on children's achievement, there has been almost no empirical work linking trends in income inequality to trends in children's school outcomes. Susan Mayer's study of the effects of economic inequality on children's educational attainment is the most relevant (2001).[5] Using microdata on individual children from the Panel Study of Income Dynamics, in combination with state-level data on family characteristics from the census, Mayer estimated the effect of income inequality (as measured by the Gini coefficient of family income in the state when the child was fourteen) on children's subsequent educational attainment between 1970 and 1990. She found that income inequality has effects on adolescents' educational attainment that range from negative to neutral (and occasionally positive), depending on the specification. However, when she examined students separately by income group, she found that income inequality is associated with decreases in college enrollment and graduation for adolescents from lower-income families and with increases in the same outcomes for higher-income adolescents.

Mayer's 2001 study is the closest previous study to ours, but it is important to note several points of difference. First, Mayer analyzed educational attainment rather than achievement test scores, and the influence of income inequality may differ across these outcomes. For example, income inequality may affect college enrollment and graduation because of income constraints at the point of college entry among students with otherwise similar characteristics and test scores (see, for example, Ellwood and Kane 2000;

Kane 2004). If this is the case, income inequality might affect educational attainment but not necessarily test scores. Conversely, income inequality may depress test scores at the bottom of the score distribution, among students unlikely to attend college. In that case, we might see effects of income inequality on test scores that are not present when analyzing college attendance.

Second, Mayer analyzed educational outcomes for young adults as a function of inequality when they were fourteen. Our focus here is instead on test scores for nine-year-olds, which we analyze as a function of their reported family characteristics as well as those of families with children of the same race group in their state over the previous three years. If inequality influences adolescents more (or less) than it does nine-year-olds, this too could lead to divergent results. Finally, our analysis covers a more recent period than Mayer's study did.

In examining whether income inequality is associated with test scores, it is important to consider the level at which inequality should be measured. Mayer provided a rationale for using data on state-level inequality, as opposed to local- or national-level inequality (2001). She argued that though one might want to control for local characteristics, those measures are likely to be confounded by selection bias if families select the areas they live in for reasons related to educational performance. Although state-level characteristics do not capture all possible influences on educational performance, they do capture some relevant aspects of the environment in which a child grows up as well as some aspects of state policy that are likely to matter for school performance. National factors also may be very important, but it is impossible to estimate their effects in a national sample. Thus, studying the effects of state-level characteristics offers the advantage of their being less likely to be biased than local measures and being more readily estimated than national measures. For these reasons, following Mayer, we use inequality measured at the state level, among all families with children. This approach assumes that both black and white families are influenced by the overall level of income inequality rather than the level of inequality within racial groups.

Sample and Methods

We use microdata from the NAEP-LTT, which provides the only consistent time trend of black and white students' performance on tests of reading and math skills. The NAEP-LTT has been administered to fourth, eighth, and twelfth graders periodically from 1971 to 2004, and in keeping with its goal of monitoring longitudinal trends in achievement, the NAEP-LTT assessments have been kept as similar as possible over time. We begin our analysis with data from 1975 because this is the earliest year of individual data we were able to obtain.

The analyses in this chapter focus on the nine-year-olds (fourth graders). We focus on nine-year-olds because they are the youngest group for which NAEP-LTT data are available. This age group is of interest given that large black-white gaps are already present at school entry, widen in the first few years of school, and persist thereafter (Fryer and Levitt 2006). We restrict our sample to white and black students administered the reading and math tests in years in which state-level identifiers are available in the data so that we can merge in state-level variables from the CPS.[6] We also make use of some information on children's family background captured in the NAEP.[7] We examine both reading and math test scores because, as discussed in the introduction, trends in these test scores have differed somewhat over the period we examine.

We combine these data with state-level information about family characteristics of white and black children taken from the March Current Population Survey. We also merge data on overall state-level family income inequality from the CPS. As we discuss, these variables provide a measure of the context in which children in that state and year are growing up.[8]

NAEP Data

To link student and state characteristics to students' performance within states over time with minimal error, it was necessary for each state included in the analyses to have an adequate number of black and white students. We chose to include only states and years which had at least twenty-five black children with assessment data for at least two assessment years, and for which state-specific CPS data were available.[9] These restrictions result in a sample that is primarily drawn from large states (see tables 1.A1 and 1.A2 for the list of included states and sample sizes for each for the math analyses and reading analyses).

Reading and Math Skills   In each year, the NAEP includes several booklets of questions for each subject. All items are given to approximately the same number of students, but no student is given all the items. Given this design, the Educational Testing Service uses multiple imputation methods to create a set of plausible reading and math test scores for each student. Although the tests have remained substantively similar over time, with the same test items being administered in the years between 1984 and 2004, Item Response Theory (IRT) methods have been used to equate earlier tests with these later tests using shared items.

The reading tasks required students to read and answer primarily multiple-choice questions based on a variety of text materials. Questions measured students' ability to read either for specific information or for general understanding. The math skills assessment contains constructed-response and multiple-choice questions that measure knowledge of basic facts, numerical operations, measurement, and the ability to apply mathematics to daily-living skills, such as those related to time and money. Students' performance on the long-term trend assessments is summarized on a 0 to 500 scale for each subject area. The weighted mean for math achievement in our sample was 228, with a standard deviation of about 36. The weighted mean for the reading scores was about 211, with a standard deviation of about 41.

Race and Sex   The NAEP collects data on students' racial background from the assessment administrator, student self-reports, and school records. We follow the NAEP reporting convention of using the administrator's assessment of the students' race and limit our analyses to white and black nine-year-olds. Children were also asked to report their sex, and we include this measure as a covariate (1 = male, 0 = female).

Parental Education and Newspaper Receipt   After 1978, students reported on each of their parent's educational attainment using five categories: did not finish high school, graduated high school, had some education after high school, completed college, and I don't know. In 1975, only the first three categories were used. These responses were combined to reflect the highest level of education for either parent or missing information. To make the parental education variables comparable over time, we combined categories three and four in the later years. Very few students (less than 10 percent for all years) reported that their parents had only completed some education after high school (category three). With nine-year-olds reporting their parents' education, it is not surprising that this variable had considerable amounts of missing data, over 30 percent for both the reading and math sample. Means for nonmissing values are presented in table 1.1.

Children were asked whether their household regularly receives a newspaper. Their responses were used to construct a dichotomous measure of newspaper receipt (1 = yes, 0 = no; see table 1.1). Again, there was missing data for this variable, approximately 8 percent for both the math and reading samples.

CPS State-Level Data

State-level characteristics for families with children age six to eighteen years old were created from annual March CPS data. Before 1978, some states were combined into one reporting category in the CPS. In instances in which states were combined, we dropped students living in these states from the sample for 1975 and 1978 because we were unable to create state-specific characteristics. To both reduce error and capture the cumulative state environment that nine-year-old children had experienced, the CPS

Table 1.1   Means and Standard Deviations for Independent Variables, by Race

| | Black | | White | |
	Mean	Standard Deviation	Mean	Standard Deviation
Math Analyses				
NAEP variables				
Parent education: less than high school	0.11	0.32	0.09	0.28
Parent education: high school	0.30	0.46	0.26	0.44
Parent education: more than high school	0.59	0.49	0.66	0.48
Male	0.48	0.50	0.50	0.50
Receive newspaper regularly	0.73	0.44	0.77	0.42
State-level CPS variables				
Years of maternal education	11.65	1.03	12.73	0.70
Single-parent family	0.51	0.08	0.19	0.04
Two-parent family	0.39	0.07	0.77	0.04
Average maternal age	37.08	1.04	38.83	1.10
50:10 income ratio	4.60	0.92	4.36	0.74
90:10 income ratio	10.91	2.82	10.29	2.34
Child poverty rate	0.40	0.09	0.10	0.02
Reading analyses				
NAEP variables				
Parent education: less than high school	0.11	0.32	0.10	0.30
Parent education: high school	0.33	0.47	0.30	0.46
Parent education: more than high school	0.56	0.50	0.60	0.49
Male	0.48	0.50	0.50	0.50
Receive newspaper regularly	0.70	0.46	0.76	0.43
State-level CPS variables				
Years maternal education	11.62	0.86	12.50	0.72
Single-parent family	0.51	0.07	0.19	0.04
Two-parent family	0.39	0.07	0.78	0.04
Average maternal age	36.93	0.97	38.67	1.12
50:10 income ratio	4.76	0.92	4.62	0.88
90:10 income ratio	11.20	2.53	10.75	2.24
Child poverty rate	0.39	0.10	0.11	0.02

Source: Authors' compilation.
Note: Means and standard deviations are provided for nonmissing data.

variables are averaged over three years, the year in which the NAEP assessment was administered and the two previous years.[10] In addition, for most variables the means are created separately by race (exceptions are noted). Descriptive statistics for these variables are provided in table 1.1.

It is important to stress that these characteristics tell us about the cumulative state environment that nine-year-old children experienced but do not measure the characteristics of a particular child's family. Using maternal education as an example, the CPS variable we use captures the average level of education of mothers, not whether a given child had a more or less highly educated mother. Thus, if we find that this variable is positively associated with test scores, we cannot infer that having a more highly educated mother raises one's test scores (this is known as the ecological fallacy problem). It may be that having more well-educated mothers in the state raises test scores for children (even if their own mothers do not have a college education) because their peers have higher levels of achievement or because more highly educated parents support better schools or libraries or act in some other way to improve educational outcomes.

Maternal Education and Age   The average level of mothers' educational attainment was created from the CPS data. The resulting variable measures the average number of years of education mothers within a state completed.[11] As noted earlier, the CPS does not distinguish between high school completion and obtaining a GED, which will lead to an overestimate of the average years of education of both black and white mothers. In addition, a measure of mothers' average age was constructed. Descriptive statistics for these variables are presented in table 1.1.

Family Structure   Three types of family structure were identified for families with children in the CPS: two-parent, single-parent, and no-parent households. An indicator of each was constructed to capture the share of children in each state experiencing particular family types. Unfortunately, because of a change in the way in which household and family relationships, and mother-child relationships in particular, were coded in 1976, we were unable to create a consistent time trend for family structure variables before 1976; consequently, for 1975, we use a single year of family structure data (1976) rather than a three-year average.

Income Inequality and Poverty   Annual family income was used to identify the median family income for all families in the state (black and white combined), as well as the 10th and 90th percentile of income for all families in the state.[12] From these data, we created two indicators of income inequality commonly used in inequality research, the ratio of the 50th percentile to the 10th percentile income (referred to as the 50:10 ratio) and the ratio of the 90th percentile to the 10th percentile income (the 90:10 ratio). Following

Mayer (2001), we construct these income inequality measures across all families, rather than separately by race group. This assumes that families are affected by the overall level of income inequality rather than the level of inequality within a race group. To capture the differential economic position of white families and black families and, in particular, the share of families with very low incomes, the child poverty rate, measured separately for white and black children, was also constructed. This is simply the share of families with children with incomes below the federal poverty line.

Methods

To consider whether the lack of progress in closing black-white achievement gaps may be due to changing family and social characteristics, we first present basic descriptive information on racial trends in children's achievement and the possible explanatory variables. Next, we turn to regressions in which we use changes within states over time to identify the association between family and state characteristics and changes in black-white test scores. The regression model for these analyses is

$$Ach_{is} = B_1 Black_{is} + B_2 FamChar_{is} + B_3 StateChar_{is} + B_4 Year_{is}$$
$$+ B_5 Black_{is} * Year_{is} + B_6 Black_{is} * < HS_{is} + B_7 Black_{is} * HS_{is}$$
$$+ B_8 Black_{is} * > HS_{is} + B_9 StateFE_{is} \tag{1.1}$$

The achievement of child i in state s is modeled as a function of their race, specifically whether they are black, a vector of NAEP measures of family background ($FamChar_{is}$), a vector of state s characteristics ($StateChar_{is}$) taken from CPS data, and a set of year indicators ($Year_{is}$). In addition, we include two sets of interaction terms. The first set reflect the interaction of race and year ($Black_{is}^* Year_{is}$); these variables indicate the difference in black children's achievement relative to white children's achievement in a particular year.[13] The second set of interaction terms are the NAEP-reported parental education variables interacted with whether the child is black ($Black_{is}^* < HS_{is}$, $Black_{is}^* HS_{is}$, $Black_{is}^* > HS_{is}$); these variables capture any difference in the association between parental education and children's achievement across races. Eric Grodsky, Demetra Kalogrides, and Julie Siebens found that parental education was less strongly associated with achievement among black children than white children (2007). This may reflect the fact that black parents attend lower quality schools or attain lower levels of education within educational categories. Finally, to isolate the effects of changes in family and social characteristics within states, rather than across states, all analyses include state fixed effects.[14] In this way, our work differs from Mayer's 2001 research as she only included region fixed effects in her main specification.

We introduce the family and state characteristics into the regression analyses in sequential steps. First, we enter only the race and year indicators as well as the black by year interaction terms. Next, we enter the NAEP family characteristics, including the interactions between parental education measures and whether the child is black. Finally, we enter the CPS state measures. In analyses not presented, we also tested for interactions between the state characteristics and whether the child is black, but these terms were not statistically significant and so were not included in our final specification.

Of primary interest is whether the inclusion of child, family, and state characteristics reduces the coefficients associated with the black indicator, which measures the average difference between blacks and whites during the reference year. Also of key interest is whether including these variables reduces the coefficients for the black by year interactions, which indicates whether changes in the black-white gap in achievement over time are explained. It should be noted that this approach assumes that the effects of family and state characteristics remain constant over time, and studies suggest that this is likely to be the case (Cook and Evans 2000).

Because each student has five plausible test scores, generated by multiple imputation techniques, we use STATA's micombine procedure to analyze the data. One concern with these data is correcting the standard errors to take into account the complexity of the survey sampling design and the nested nature of the data. Although survey design information can be used to produce accurate standard errors at the student level, many of our key explanatory variables are measured at the state level. Consequently, we use Huber-White standard error corrections clustered at the state level.[15]

Descriptive Results: Trends

Figure 1.1 plots trends in math and reading skills for black and white nine-year-olds in our samples from the NAEP data. For both math and reading, the figure shows large black-white gaps that are largely constant through the late 1970s, 1980s, and 1990s, becoming narrower only toward the end of the period. From the late 1970s to 2004, the black-white math gap closed from 29.9 points to 16.1 points and the reading gap closed from 30.6 to 17.6 points. It is important to note that we find more convergence by 2004 in our sample than is the case in the full NAEP-LTT sample.[16] This suggests that there was less convergence in the states we do not include in our analysis sample (states with smaller samples) than in those we included.

As noted in the introduction, the underlying trends in black and white achievement differ across the two skill areas. The trend lines for math skills indicate that math skills have risen for both black and white nine-year-olds since the 1970s. In contrast, reading scores for both black and white nine-year-olds changed only minimally over the period, though the data for

Figure 1.1   Trends in Nine-Year-Olds Math and Reading Skills, NAEP Data

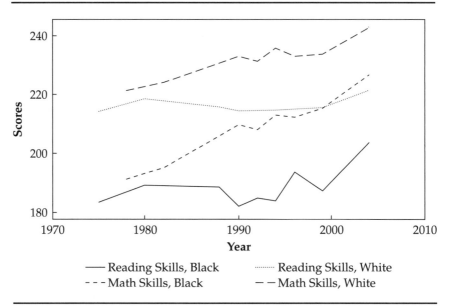

Source: Authors comp ilation.

black nine-year-olds, albeit somewhat noisy, suggest an increase in reading skills after 1999.

Figure 1.2 plots trends in maternal education and newspaper receipt as reported by the children in our math sample. Trends in the reading sample are similar. The data indicate an increase in the share of mothers with more than a high school degree from the late 1970s to the late 1980s. Indeed, from the late 1990s onward, black nine-year-olds are nearly as likely (or as likely) as white nine-year-olds to report that their mother has more than a high school education. This convergence in maternal education is considerably greater than we would expect based on national data and may reflect errors in reporting, given that the information is being reported by nine-year-olds and the items have considerable missing data.

Data on family newspaper receipt (also presented in figure 1.2) show declines in the share of both black and white families receiving a newspaper over the period. There is a small black-white gap in newspaper receipt, which initially widens during the 1990s before appearing to close in 2004.

Because the data on family characteristics in the NAEP are limited, and may be reported with error by children, we also consider data on the characteristics of black and white families with children from the March CPS. Descriptive statistics shown in table 1.1 indicate sizable race gaps on these

Figure 1.2   Trends in Maternal Education and Newspaper Reciept, NAEP Data

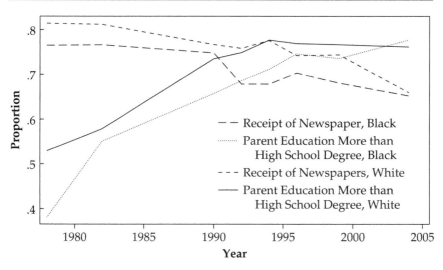

Source: Authors' compilation.

characteristics, with black children being more likely to have less educated mothers and younger mothers, to live in single-parent families, and
to live in families with incomes below the poverty line.

Figure 1.3 presents the trends over time in state aggregated levels of
maternal education. As expected, the trends for our sample closely parallel national trends, with convergence in levels of mothers' years of education through the early 1990s and then little or no additional convergence.
Further analyses of these data (not shown but available on request) indicate that the convergence in years of education during the 1980s is fueled
by relatively larger increases in black mothers' high school completion and
receipt of some postsecondary schooling compared with white mothers.
Although the share of white and black mothers with a college degree rises
over the period, this share rises more quickly for whites from the late 1980s
onward, with a particularly sharp increase in the early 2000s, which largely
explains why convergence in education levels appeared to slow considerably during the mid-1990s.

We also use the March CPS data to calculate measures of family income
inequality for all families with children by state and year.[17] Figure 1.4 plots
the trend over time in the 90:10 ratio and the 50:10 ratio. The trend lines for
both measures indicate an increase in inequality from the late 1970s to 2004.
Although there is some decline in inequality in the late 1990s attributable
primarily to increases in incomes in the bottom income decile, the trend

Figure 1.3   Trends in Black and White Maternal Education, State CPS Data

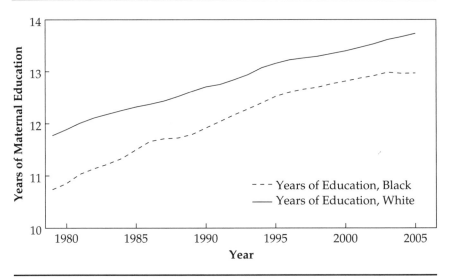

Source: Authors' compilation.

lines turn upwards again after 2000, and by the end of the period, inequality on both measures is notably greater than at the start. The 90:10 ratio rises from a level of about seven in the late 1970s to about eleven in 2004 (indicating that the family income of the top decile moves from being seven times as large as that of the income in the bottom decile to being eleven times as large).

Regression Results

The results of the math regressions are shown in table 1.2. As discussed earlier, we begin by entering only the indicators for race and year along with race by year interaction terms. The results from model 1 (in column 1) indicate that in 1978 on average black students score 30.7 points below white students on the math test. That the standard deviation on this measure is about 36 means that black students are scoring about 0.85 standard deviation lower than white students. The positive and significant year coefficients indicate a significant gain in math test scores apparent by 1990, which persisted through the decade, and another sharp gain evident in 2004. The positive and significant coefficients for the black by year variables indicate that these gains in math scores were steeper for black students than for white.

We next enter the NAEP family characteristics (model 2). As expected, the results indicate that children with more educated parents and those whose families receive a newspaper have higher math scores. However, the significant negative interaction terms indicate that the association

Figure 1.4   Trends in Income Inequality, State CPS Data

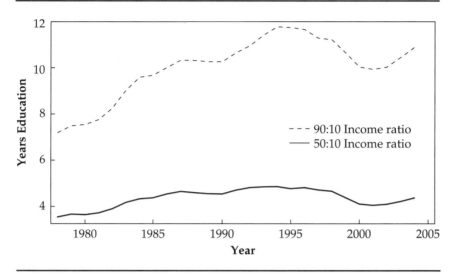

Source: Authors' compilation.

between parental education and achievement is weaker among black children than among white. Adding these measures of family background slightly reduces the black coefficient, the year coefficients, and the black-by-year coefficients suggesting that changes in family characteristics may explain some of the time trend in math scores for both black and white students.

Next, we enter the CPS measures of maternal education, family structure, and maternal age for black and white families with children (table 1.2, model 3). As discussed earlier, because these are not characteristics of the child's family, we do not interpret them as telling us what role the characteristics of a child's parents play, but rather the associations in a given state and year between test scores and the average characteristics of families of the same race. We find no significant effects for family structure but positive effects for maternal age and the average level of maternal education. Adding these state characteristics—in particular, the measures of maternal education—substantially reduces the magnitude of the black coefficient, from −30.7 in model 1 and −25.2 in model 2 to −14.7 in model 3. Including these variables does not, however, further reduce the year coefficients or the black-by-year coefficients. These results suggest that a portion of the initial black-white gap during the period can be explained by differences in the average educational attainment of black and white parents, but that the greater gains of black children relative to white during the latter part of the period are not explained by improvements in parents' educational attainment.

Table 1.2 Summary of Regressions of NAEP Math Test Scores on Family Characteristics and State Characteristics

	(1)	(2)	(3)	(4)	(5)	(6)	(7)	(8)	(9)
NAEP variables									
Black	−30.7***	−25.2***	−14.7***	−25.1***	−15.3***	−25.1***	−15.2***	−17.7***	−13.9***
	(1.97)	(1.88)	(4.50)	(1.92)	(4.53)	(1.94)	(4.57)	(3.69)	(4.66)
Parent education: high school		11.1***	11.1***	11.1***	11.0***	11.1***	11.0***	11.0***	11.1***
		(1.60)	(1.60)	(1.62)	(1.62)	(1.61)	(1.61)	(1.61)	(1.60)
High school X black		−3.51**	−3.66**	−3.43**	−3.58**	−3.45**	−3.60**	−3.34**	−3.59**
		(1.30)	(1.30)	(1.30)	(1.31)	(1.30)	(1.31)	(1.34)	(1.33)
Parent education: more than high school		23.7***	23.5***	23.6***	23.5***	23.6***	23.5***	23.6***	23.5***
		(1.45)	(1.44)	(1.47)	(1.46)	(1.47)	(1.46)	(1.45)	(1.44)
More than high school X black		−7.30***	−7.34***	−7.27***	−7.32***	−7.27***	−7.31***	−7.24***	−7.31***
		(1.34)	(1.35)	(1.33)	(1.35)	(1.34)	(1.35)	(1.36)	(1.36)
Receive newspaper		6.97***	6.98***	6.93***	6.95***	6.94***	6.96***	6.97***	6.99***
		(0.66)	(0.65)	(0.66)	(0.66)	(0.66)	(0.66)	(0.66)	(0.65)
Male		0.19	0.23	0.18	0.22	0.18	0.22	0.19	0.23
		(0.42)	(0.41)	(0.42)	(0.42)	(0.42)	(0.41)	(0.41)	(0.41)
State CPS variables									
Average maternal education			5.31***		4.85***		4.96***		4.39**
			(1.41)		(1.49)		(1.50)		(1.91)
Share of families with single parents			4.50		4.16		4.14		10.9
			(11.4)		(11.4)		(11.5)		(12.3)
Average mother age			1.40*		1.20		1.25		1.39*
			(0.68)		(0.72)		(0.72)		(0.67)
50:10 income ratio				−2.40***	−2.02**				
				(0.82)	(0.90)				

90:10 income ratio						−0.77**	−0.63*	−23.8**	−12.8
						(0.31)	(0.33)	(9.58)	(11.2)
Child poverty rate									
Year = 1982	1.54	0.44	0.31	1.15	1.15	−0.22	1.07	−0.32	0.84
	(1.32)	(1.04)	(1.04)	(1.03)	(1.03)	(1.41)	(1.07)	(1.44)	(1.06)
Year = 1990	10.4***	8.45***	8.26***	11.0***	11.0***	6.55**	10.9***	6.34**	8.63***
	(1.30)	(1.26)	(1.24)	(1.62)	(1.62)	(2.47)	(1.75)	(2.63)	(1.23)
Year = 1992	10.8***	8.82***	8.63***	11.8***	11.8***	6.40*	11.7***	6.21*	9.16***
	(2.05)	(1.97)	(1.95)	(2.27)	(2.27)	(3.06)	(2.52)	(3.34)	(2.07)
Year = 1994	14.2***	11.5***	11.3***	14.3***	14.3***	7.55**	15.0***	7.98**	11.8***
	(1.96)	(1.80)	(1.78)	(2.23)	(2.23)	(3.20)	(2.50)	(3.54)	(1.66)
Year = 1996	11.2***	9.59***	9.40***	12.4***	12.4***	4.39	12.9***	4.58	9.90***
	(2.37)	(2.29)	(2.28)	(2.71)	(2.71)	(3.95)	(2.98)	(4.23)	(2.22)
Year = 1999	12.7***	10.9***	10.7***	13.1***	13.1***	4.40	13.8***	4.74	11.0***
	(1.82)	(1.57)	(1.54)	(2.16)	(2.16)	(3.12)	(2.34)	(3.36)	(1.45)
Year = 2004	23.2***	21.8***	21.6***	23.6***	23.6***	11.8**	24.7***	12.3**	21.7***
	(2.04)	(2.11)	(2.11)	(2.16)	(2.16)	(4.18)	(2.64)	(4.57)	(2.13)
Black X year = 1982	2.45	0.24	1.26	−0.29	0.83	−0.58	0.78	−0.62	0.70
	(2.33)	(2.10)	(2.19)	(1.92)	(2.17)	(1.92)	(2.17)	(1.93)	(2.34)
Black X year = 1990	8.55**	6.31**	7.55**	0.83	7.79**	6.88**	7.93**	7.00**	7.92**
	(3.00)	(2.86)	(2.74)	(2.17)	(2.83)	(3.32)	(2.83)	(3.33)	(2.97)
Black X year = 1992	7.83***	6.05**	7.29***	7.79**	7.91***	5.88**	7.80***	5.74**	7.56***
	(2.69)	(2.39)	(2.33)	(2.83)	(2.30)	(2.27)	(2.33)	(2.29)	(2.41)
Black X year = 1994	8.03***	6.19**	7.87***	7.91***	7.69**	5.52	7.68**	5.48	7.28**
	(2.76)	(2.61)	(2.67)	(2.30)	(2.73)	(3.33)	(2.72)	(3.34)	(2.76)

(continued)

Table 1.2   Summary of Regressions of NAEP Math Test Scores on Family Characteristics and State Characteristics (*Continued*)

	(1)	(2)	(3)	(4)	(5)	(6)	(7)	(8)	(9)
Black X year = 1996	9.86***	7.40**	9.02***	7.69**	9.11***	8.24**	8.97***	8.09**	7.34**
	(2.58)	(2.79)	(2.75)	(2.73)	(2.80)	(3.40)	(2.81)	(3.40)	(2.81)
Black X year = 1999	12.2***	9.75***	11.3***	9.11***	11.1***	8.47**	11.0***	8.43**	9.96***
	(2.70)	(2.63)	(2.58)	(2.80)	(2.59)	(3.10)	(2.59)	(3.10)	(2.27)
Black X year = 2004	14.2***	11.3***	12.8***	11.1***	12.6***	11.1***	12.5***	11.1***	9.95**
	(3.30)	(3.25)	(3.20)	(2.59)	(3.12)	(3.04)	(3.13)	(3.05)	(3.53)
Constant	214***	196***	196***	205***	205***	104***	201***	97.4***	198***
	(1.50)	(1.84)	(1.84)	(3.56)	(3.56)	(29.5)	(2.86)	(28.7)	(1.78)
Observations	36,138	36,138	36,138	36,138	36,138	36,138	36,138	36,138	36,138
R-squared	0.12	0.19	0.19	0.19	0.19	0.19	0.19	0.19	0.19

Source: Authors' compilation.
Notes: Standard errors are in parentheses. A measure of the proportion of children in a state residing without parents is included in models 3, 5, 7, and 9. All models include state fixed effects. Missing data dummy variables for NAEP parental education and newspaper receipt are also included.
***p-value<.01; **p-value<.05; *p-value<.10

Next, we add controls for our measures of family income inequality. We are interested in whether inequality reduces children's test scores and whether it affects black-white differences in test scores. We first add the 50:10 ratio, both with and without measures of the state characteristics from the CPS (table 1.2, models 5 and 4, respectively). In both models, the ratio has a significant negative effect on math scores, though the estimate is smaller when a measure of state maternal education is entered. Including the ratio results in somewhat larger coefficients for the set of year variables, suggesting that over-time progress in math may have been hindered by rising income inequality. The estimate of the black coefficient or the black by year coefficients, however, is not altered by adding the ratio (comparing results in model 4 to results in model 2, and results in model 5 to results in model 3), suggesting that black and white children's test scores were similarly affected by the average level of inequality in their states and by trends in inequality.

When we add the 90:10 family income ratio (in models 6 and 7), results are similar. The 90:10 ratio has a significant negative effect on math scores. The coefficients are smaller in absolute value than the coefficients on the 50:10, but this in part reflects scaling, because the level of the 90:10 is about twice as large as the level of the 50:10. Again, including the 90:10 in analyses yields larger year estimates than models with only state-level parental education, suggesting that over-time progress in math was hindered by rising income inequality. But with the black coefficient and the black by year coefficients remaining similar after the addition of the 90:10 income ratio, it appears that black and white children's achievement may have been similarly affected by the average level of inequality in their states.

In our final specifications, we include the average poverty rate of black and white families with children. In contrast to the inequality measures (which are estimated over all families with children), the poverty measures are race-specific, although still aggregate (that is, these measures capture the average living circumstances of white or black children rather than of an individual child). When we add the average poverty rate into a regression without other controls for family characteristics from the CPS (model 8), it has a significant negative effect on math scores. Adding this control substantially reduces the black coefficient (from −25.2 in model 2 to −17.7 in model 8) but has a minimal influence on the black by year coefficients, suggesting that poverty is implicated in the overall black-white gap but that trends in black-white poverty gaps have little association with those in test score gaps. However, when we add the average poverty rate to a model that includes measures of other family characteristics from the CPS, its magnitude falls by half and it is no longer significant. This result suggests that other state measures of family characteristics (maternal education, family structure, and maternal age) are confounded with state poverty rates.

The results of the reading regressions are shown in table 1.3. As in the math analyses, we begin by entering only the indicator of race along with year controls and black-by-year interaction terms. The results from model 1 indicate that in 1975 black students scored 30.5 points below their white counterparts on reading skills. That the standard deviation on this measure is about 41 means that black students were scoring about 0.74 standard deviation lower than white students. In contrast to the results for math, the year coefficients and black-by-year coefficients are typically insignificant in the reading model, except in 2004 when there is a sharp overall upturn, as well as a significant black by year interaction. This reflects the consistency of student reading test scores over time, until their increase in 2004.

When we enter the NAEP family characteristics into the regression (model 2), we find that children with more educated parents and children whose families receive a newspaper have significantly higher reading scores, though again the significance of parental education by black inter-action terms suggests that the effects of parental education on achieve-ment are weaker among black children than among white children. These measures of family background, however, have a relatively small effect on the black coefficient, in that it is reduced by just 5 points by their intro-duction. We next add the CPS measures of the average maternal educa-tion level, family structure, and maternal age of black and white families with children. We find a positive effect of the average level of maternal education, and adding this control reduces the black coefficient by approx-imately four more points to −21.8 (in model 3). Adding these controls also further reduces the effect of several year variables and eliminates the pos-itive year effect in 2004, suggesting that improvements in family charac-teristics, particularly mothers' education, were working to boost children's reading scores during the period. These additional controls, however, do little to change the estimated effects of the black by year interaction terms, suggesting that test score gains due to maternal education were similar among white and black children. Given that children's test scores were largely unchanged during this time, the results suggest that some other unmeasured factor was working to counteract the benefit of increases in maternal education.

Next, we add measures of family income inequality. We first add the 50:10 ratio, both with and without controls for family characteristics from the CPS (models 5 and 4, respectively). In the first model, the 50:10 ratio has a significant negative effect on reading scores, but controlling for the 50:10 does not alter the black coefficient or the black by year coefficient, again sug-gesting that black and white children were similarly affected by the average level of inequality and trends in inequality in their states. In the second model which includes state-level characteristics, the coefficient for the 50:10 ratio is smaller and nonsignificant as is the measure of state-level maternal education, suggesting that these variables are confounded. Results for the 90:10 ratio (in models 6 and 7) are similar.

Table 1.3   Summary of Regressions of NAEP Reading Test Scores on Family Characteristics and State Characteristics

	(1)	(2)	(3)	(4)	(5)	(6)	(7)	(8)	(9)
NAEP variables									
Black	−30.5***	−25.5***	−21.8***	−25.1***	−21.9***	−25.1***	−22.0***	−24.3***	−22.0***
	(2.04)	(2.30)	(6.05)	(2.31)	(6.13)	(2.31)	(6.10)	(3.93)	(5.99)
Parent education: high school		14.4***	14.3***	14.3***	14.3***	14.3***	14.3***	14.4***	14.4***
		(1.60)	(1.60)	(1.61)	(1.61)	(1.62)	(1.61)	(1.60)	(1.60)
High school X black		−4.05*	−4.07*	−4.02*	−4.04*	−4.03*	−4.06*	−4.03*	−4.09*
		(2.17)	(2.14)	(2.17)	(2.14)	(2.17)	(2.14)	(2.16)	(2.14)
Parent education: more than high school		25.9***	25.9***	25.9***	25.8***	25.9***	25.8***	25.9***	25.9***
		(1.90)	(1.90)	(1.91)	(1.91)	(1.92)	(1.92)	(1.90)	(1.90)
More than high school X black		−8.26***	−8.39***	−8.26***	−8.37***	−8.26***	−8.38***	−8.26***	−8.38***
		(1.78)	(1.79)	(1.78)	(1.79)	(1.78)	(1.79)	(1.78)	(1.79)
Receive newspaper		8.26***	8.27***	8.23***	8.25***	8.22***	8.24***	8.26***	8.27***
		(0.84)	(0.84)	(0.83)	(0.83)	(0.83)	(0.83)	(0.84)	(0.84)
Male		−8.89***	−8.90***	−8.89***	−8.90***	−8.90***	−8.90***	−8.89***	−8.90***
		(0.83)	(0.83)	(0.83)	(0.82)	(0.83)	(0.83)	(0.83)	(0.83)
State CPS variables									
Average maternal Education		5.40*		4.81		4.64		6.41*	
		(2.77)		(2.77)		(2.74)		(3.24)	
Share of families with single parents		9.01		8.17		7.82		4.09	
		(17.1)		(16.9)		(17.1)		(17.0)	
Average mother age			1.09		0.87		0.96		1.02
			(0.66)		(0.59)		(0.61)		(0.69)
50:10 income ratio				−1.60**	−1.24				
				(0.74)	(0.81)				

(continued)

Table 1.3   Summary of Regressions of NAEP Reading Test Scores on Family Characteristics and State Characteristics (Continued)

	(1)	(2)	(3)	(4)	(5)	(6)	(7)	(8)	(9)
90:10 income ratio						-0.67*	-0.51		
						(0.32)	(0.34)		
Child poverty rate								-4.47	10.2
								(14.3)	(14.9)
Year = 1980	4.46*	3.22	0.95	-0.055	-1.23	0.88	-0.55	3.07	1.20
	(2.34)	(2.04)	(2.32)	(2.49)	(2.72)	(2.26)	(2.48)	(2.22)	(2.43)
Year = 1988	1.44	1.22	-3.89	-0.56	-4.67*	0.55	-3.70	1.10	-4.17
	(2.03)	(1.91)	(2.88)	(1.68)	(2.63)	(1.67)	(2.72)	(2.06)	(2.89)
Year = 1990	0.19	0.30	-5.85	-1.78	-6.77*	-0.59	-5.70	0.18	-6.30
	(3.34)	(2.71)	(3.93)	(2.43)	(3.50)	(2.46)	(3.57)	(2.93)	(4.04)
Year = 1992	-0.030	-0.55	-7.32*	-2.27	-7.91**	-1.02	-6.75*	-0.61	-8.05*
	(2.48)	(2.25)	(3.58)	(2.16)	(3.24)	(2.05)	(3.39)	(2.28)	(3.86)
Year = 1994	-0.099	-1.05	-9.40*	-2.60	-9.63*	-0.72	-8.01	-1.11	-10.2*
	(3.37)	(2.85)	(5.07)	(2.38)	(4.73)	(2.42)	(4.89)	(2.95)	(5.28)
Year = 1996	0.48	0.024	-9.86**	-1.58	-9.89**	0.19	-8.38**	-0.040	-10.8**
	(2.29)	(2.19)	(4.27)	(1.98)	(3.85)	(1.92)	(3.97)	(2.25)	(4.44)
Year = 1999	2.05	1.91	-8.97	-0.13	-9.21*	1.64	-7.70	1.78	-9.76*
	(3.54)	(2.65)	(5.33)	(2.64)	(4.99)	(2.59)	(5.08)	(2.87)	(5.44)
Year = 2004	10.4***	10.3***	-3.67	7.95***	-3.64	9.96***	-2.05	10.1***	-4.53
	(1.90)	(1.94)	(5.98)	(2.29)	(5.58)	(1.78)	(5.56)	(2.09)	(6.09)

	(1)	(2)	(3)	(4)	(5)	(6)	(7)	(8)	(9)
Black X year = 1980	-0.033	1.51	1.17	0.90	0.70	0.98	0.84	1.66	0.66
	(2.58)	(2.71)	(3.38)	(2.73)	(3.33)	(2.76)	(3.37)	(2.82)	(3.70)
Black X year = 1988	3.88	3.47	2.42	3.02	2.13	3.14	2.37	3.70	1.53
	(3.30)	(3.72)	(4.57)	(3.65)	(4.36)	(3.66)	(4.45)	(4.01)	(5.30)
Black X year = 1990	-2.09	-2.41	-2.33	-2.49	-2.49	-2.33	-2.23	-2.15	-2.92
	(4.14)	(4.16)	(5.26)	(4.18)	(5.21)	(4.18)	(5.28)	(4.77)	(5.72)
Black X year = 1992	0.85	-0.0059	-1.66	-0.20	-1.66	-0.12	-1.48	0.23	-2.36
	(3.34)	(3.36)	(4.46)	(3.34)	(4.37)	(3.32)	(4.42)	(3.65)	(4.90)
Black X year = 1994	-0.62	0.54	-1.46	0.079	-1.67	0.092	-1.47	0.61	-2.14
	(4.21)	(3.97)	(4.45)	(3.89)	(4.33)	(3.84)	(4.40)	(4.03)	(4.75)
Black X year = 1996	8.13**	6.98*	5.33	6.62*	5.15	6.59*	5.32	6.86*	5.07
	(3.61)	(3.73)	(4.92)	(3.69)	(4.79)	(3.66)	(4.84)	(3.62)	(5.00)
Black X year = 1999	2.44	2.24	0.22	1.64	-0.14	1.58	0.045	2.18	0.062
	(4.32)	(3.80)	(5.44)	(3.75)	(5.26)	(3.74)	(5.33)	(3.66)	(5.61)
Black X year = 2004	11.5***	11.1***	10.6**	10.5***	10.00**	10.5***	10.2**	10.7***	10.8**
	(3.45)	(3.26)	(3.99)	(3.34)	(3.96)	(3.37)	(3.99)	(3.18)	(3.91)
Constant	207***	191***	87.3**	201***	110**	199***	107**	192***	77.2*
	(2.15)	(2.13)	(39.8)	(4.91)	(41.4)	(4.62)	(40.0)	(3.46)	(42.5)
Observations	38,014	38,014	38,014	38,014	38,014	38,014	38,014	38,014	38,014
R-squared	0.10	0.18	0.18	0.18	0.18	0.18	0.18	0.18	0.18

Source: Authors' compilation.

Notes: Standard errors are in parentheses. A measure of the proportion of children in a state residing without parents is included in models 3, 5, 7, and 9. All models include state fixed effects. Missing data dummy variables for NAEP parental education and newspaper receipt are also included.

***p-value<.01, **p-value<.05; *p-value<.10

Finally, we estimate models controlling for the average poverty rate of black and white families with children. In contrast to the math results, we do not find a significant association between the average poverty rate and children's reading scores, even without other controls for average state CPS family characteristics (model 8).

These math and reading results indicate that income inequality is associated with lower scores on both reading and math tests and imply that the finding is equally true for black and white students. (Controlling for inequality did not affect the black coefficient or the black by year coefficients.) To test this more directly, in supplemental analyses, we re-ran our models separately for black and white students. The results (not shown but available on request) confirm that the 50:10 and the 90:10 family income ratios are negatively associated with reading and math scores for both black and white students. They suggest that, if anything, the magnitude of the association tends to be slightly larger for white students than for black students.[18]

Because we do not have data on students' family incomes, we could not divide our sample by family income and test for whether associations with income inequality are stronger for students in the bottom of the distribution. Instead, taking advantage of the student-reported data on parental education in the NAEP, we divided students into three education groups, by whether their parent had less than high school, only a high school degree, or more than high school. As noted earlier, these categories may be defined with error, given that we are relying on reports from nine-year-olds and there is a good deal of missing data on this item, but the subgroup analyses provide some indication as to whether the associations between income inequality and test scores differ by parental education group. In results not shown but available on request, the coefficients on the income inequality measures are negative and mostly stable across the parental education groups for math outcomes. For reading outcomes, point estimates were consistently negative for all education groups, though they were considerably larger for the less-educated groups, and much closer to 0 for the more highly educated. These patterns of findings provide further support for the conclusion that income inequality is negatively associated with test scores for all groups. However, we note that income inequality might have less negative effects (or even positive effects) if we could identify children in families at the top of the income distribution.[19]

Discussion and Conclusions

In our analyses, we tried to explain two trends in achievement among black and white children. During the period we consider, there was improvement in black and white students' math achievement of roughly equal proportions through 1999, followed by somewhat greater gains by black children in 2004. In contrast, for reading, there was little change in achievement for either group until 2004, when again black children made greater gains.

Our regression results suggest that individual and state-level family characteristics are important in understanding racial achievement gaps. We confirm findings from earlier studies that suggest that a substantial proportion of the black-white gap is attributable to different levels of parental education and differential returns to parental education (see also chapter 2 this volume). In math nearly half and in reading nearly a third of the initial gap in achievement in the late 1970s was explained by individual and state-level measures of family background, particularly parental education. We do not find that state-level income inequality or poverty explains initial gaps once other family characteristics are taken into account, though we do note that these income measures appear to be somewhat confounded with family characteristics such as parental education.

Turning to explanations for trends in achievement, our results provide mixed support for the hypothesis that rising inequality impeded progress in closing the black-white test score gap. When we consider characteristics such as parental education, we find some evidence that rising levels benefited children's achievement, though perhaps less so for black children than for white children. According to the CPS state-level data in 1978, the average level of maternal education was just 10.6 years for black mothers and 12.0 years for white mothers. By 2004, the averages had risen to 13.0 and 13.7, respectively. Educational gains for black parents account for about a 3.4 point convergence of the black-white math test score gap by 2004. This is roughly an effect size of .12, about 25 percent of the convergence in test scores between 1978 and 2004. Given the lower levels of returns to parents' education for black children compared with white, a very small amount of this is attributable to individual parent's education (0.5). Indeed most of this convergence (2.9 points) is attributed in our models to improvements in average characteristics of mothers of a particular race group within states.[20]

For reading, again, rising levels of parental education were beneficial for all children. We also found that maternal education played a small role in explaining the convergence of test score gaps, accounting for about 2.2 points, an effect size of about 0.05 and about 27 percent of the convergence. As before, given the lower returns to education of individual black parents, most of this convergence was attributable to the average educational attainment of mothers of a particular race group within states. We caution, however, that, as emphasized earlier, the NAEP measure of individual parents' education was reported by nine-year-olds, likely with considerable error, and thus our estimates of the effects of parental education may be biased. Another potential source of bias is that differences in maternal education may be correlated with other factors we are not measuring in our data (such as genetic endowments, occupational status, or assets).

When we consider measures of income inequality, we find that these do little to explain the black-white gaps or trends in the black-white gaps over time. Instead, we find that income inequality is negatively associated with math and reading test scores for both black and white children. Our results from analyses with the 50:10 ratio of family income imply that, if income inequality had remained at its 1978 levels, average math scores would be 1 point higher in 2004, and average reading scores would be 0.7 points higher. Thus, it appears that rising income inequality is impeding the overall performance of American school children, by roughly similar amounts in both math and reading. However, the magnitude of the effect is quite small, and such inequality is not necessarily contributing to gaps in achievement between black and white children. We note that we are not able with our data to analyze high-income versus low-income children separately. It may be that if we could do so, we would find stronger negative effects of income inequality for those at the bottom, and less negative (or even positive) effects for those at the top. This is a question that would benefit from further research.

Our results point to some interesting similarities and differences across the math and reading results. As expected, we find that family characteristics (in particular, maternal education) are strongly predictive of test scores for both sets of skills, but controlling for family characteristics from the NAEP and CPS data explains much more of the black-white gap in math than it does in reading. Adding those characteristics reduced the black-white math gap in 1978 by 52 percent (from 30.7 points to 14.7) but reduced the reading gap in 1975 by only 29 percent (from 30.5 points to 21.8).

Another point of difference between the math and reading results is the notable contrast in the underlying trends, evident both in the raw data and in the regression results. Both black and white students made gains over this period in math, with black students making somewhat larger gains at several time points, in 2004 in particular. In contrast, reading performance was pretty much flat for both black and white students, except for the upturn for both groups in 2004. These differing trends suggest that in explaining black and white student progress over this period, the factors that are pertinent to math may differ from those that are pertinent to reading.

At the same time, the data point to the possibility that some common factor acted to raise performance in both math and reading for all students in 2004. We can only speculate as to what that factor might be. One possibility is some peculiarity in the tests that year, though that seems unlikely given that we are using the long-term trend data. Another possibility is that students' improved performance in 2004 reflects the impact of certain school factors such as the increasing emphasis on accountability and testing that occurred in the late 1990s and early 2000s (see chapter 8, this volume). This too is a subject that would benefit from further research as additional years of NAEP-LTT data become available.

Several limitations to the empirical analysis presented in this chapter should be noted. First, the NAEP-LTT data provide the only long-term trend information on children's achievement, but the data on children's family background characteristics are meager. We must rely on nine-year-olds' reports of their parents' education, which we suspect is reported with error. In addition, information is not collected on family income. Better quality data on these dimensions of family's socioeconomic standing would vastly improve our ability to understand influences on black-white test score gaps. In addition, the NAEP-LTT data do not provide state identifiers for all years during the 1980s, and the omission of these time points from our analyses is unfortunate.

In this study, we have attempted to identify the effects of changes in state-level economic inequality and family characteristics on test score gaps, holding constant state and year effects. Although this approach is commonly credited with reducing possible bias, it is of course possible that our analyses suffer from omitted variable bias, and that the state-level characteristics for which we have measures are merely proxies for a range of related trends. That is, there may have been changes within states over time that are correlated both with changing family characteristics and trends in test score gaps. If this is the case, then our estimates of the effects of state-level characteristics may be biased. In addition, the NAEP data have a relatively small proportion of black children within each state, particularly in the later years of the test. Consequently, small sample sizes led us to include children who live in only relatively large states. This may have introduced measurement error and makes it difficult to generalize our findings to all children. Finally, our model assumes that the returns to family characteristics have remained the same over time.

In spite of these limitations, our results provide some new evidence as to the influence that changing economic inequality, and its social correlates, may have had on changes in student achievement and black-white test score gaps. These results suggest that the achievement of both black and white children has been hindered by rising economic inequality. This may have little bearing on the black-white test score gap, but it is certainly not good news for the United States overall. On the other hand, it does seem to be good news that the increasing educational attainment of black parents has played a role in closing test score gaps. In the long run, further increasing the education of black parents looks like a promising route to closing the black-white test score gaps.

Acknowledgments

We are grateful to the Educational Testing Service for providing the restricted use Beta Version of the NAEP-LTT files, to Youngeon Lee for assembling the NAEP files, and to Meredith Phillips for assistance in using the NAEP data. We are also grateful to Mary Campbell and Sandy Jencks for helpful comments. Funding support was provided by the Russell Sage Foundation and the William T. Grant Foundation.

Table 1.A1   Sample Distribution for NAEP Reading Analyses

State	1975 Total	1975 Black	1980 Total	1980 Black	1988 Total	1988 Black	1990 Total	1990 Black
Alabama	0	0	553	123	102	51	0	0
Arkansas	0	0	807	114	85	32	0	0
California	1,906	162	1,667	142	470	37	396	28
Florida	614	183	1,259	348	0	0	200	29
Georgia	0	0	259	49	183	82	66	30
Illinois	1,316	253	1,243	190	171	48	134	50
Kentucky	0	0	570	64	0	0	0	0
Louisiana	0	0	0	0	168	53	116	65
Maryland	0	0	1,218	332	0	0	75	27
Michigan	0	0	1,039	193	0	0	0	0
Mississippi	0	0	0	0	0	0	74	47
New Jersey	400	75	187	29	267	42	204	28
New York	1,871	348	1,428	447	354	84	215	26
North Carolina	0	0	1,038	205	144	41	0	0
Ohio	603	105	742	158	287	50	0	0
Pennsylvania	781	78	1,196	257	0	0	162	45
Texas	858	204	1,279	120	216	44	214	28
Virgina	0	0	0	0	0	0	184	28
Total	8,349	1,408	14,485	2,771	2,447	564	2,040	431

Source: Authors' compilation.

Notes

1. Estimates from authors' calculations using data from March CPS; details available on request.
2. James Heckman and Paul LaFontaine (2007) suggest that this is more of a problem for men than women and for the most recent cohorts (who may not yet be parents). Data they compiled indicate that 4 percent of white women and 4.5 percent of black women who were likely to be mothers of school-age children in 1995 had obtained GEDs. These percentages had risen to 6 percent for white women and 7.7 percent for black women in 2005.
3. In this chapter, we focus on the short-run effects of income inequality. However, it is possible that there are long-run effects of inequality that may also affect trends in test score gaps. For example, if rising economic inequality during the 1980s discouraged low-income youth from attending college or forming stable two-parent families, then as they reached the child-bearing years in the late 1990s and early 2000s, lower levels of education and higher rates of single-parenthood may be detrimental to their children's achievement. Mary Campbell and her colleagues, for instance, found that increases in economic inequality are associated with increases in the share of black youth dropping out of school (2005). Although these long-run effects are possible, because of data limitations we are unable to model these processes.

1992		1994		1996		1999		2004		
Total	Black	Total	Black	Total	Black	Total	Black	Total	Black	Total
0	0	82	35	0	0	109	51	0	0	846
0	0	0	0	0	0	167	36	0	0	1,059
0	0	520	44	303	35	422	26	641	40	6,325
309	37	0	0	245	71	0	0	317	52	2,944
111	62	142	36	135	62	286	110	282	96	1,464
222	36	336	56	132	49	133	29	0	0	3,687
0	0	83	29	0	0	0	0	0	0	699
0	0	146	31	0	0	0	0	60	27	490
0	0	0	0	100	29	0	0	0	0	1,393
216	71	0	0	0	0	214	41	0	0	1,469
0	0	0	0	0	0	164	57	56	29	294
60	24	114	40	141	35	0	0	0	0	1,373
231	61	332	45	243	25	212	36	311	71	5,197
0	0	135	32	247	70	0	0	0	0	1,564
182	29	0	0	0	0	285	57	0	0	2,099
341	32	0	0	0	0	154	36	298	49	2,932
420	85	0	0	319	27	246	58	280	43	3,832
0	0	0	0	115	45	94	29	0	0	393
2,092	437	1,890	348	1,980	448	2,486	566	2,245	407	38,014

4. There may also be links between income inequality and other types of spending that are consequential for children's achievement. As economic inequality increases, voters may support lower levels of funding for public programs, if they feel more able to opt out of public provision, or may support higher levels, if they fear political instability (Mayer 2001).

5. A second paper considers how economic segregation affects children's educational attainment (Mayer 2002). Campbell and her colleagues estimate the links between economic inequality and several measures of school attainment (2005).

6. The NAEP-LTT data do not have state identifiers in the 1986 math sample and in the 1984 and 1988 reading sample

7. We use only a relatively small set of family background variables from the NAEP, because the set of background questions that has been consistently asked of all children over time is quite limited.

8. It is important to note that the CPS prior to 1978 was not designed to be state representative. Nevertheless, the CPS is the best available source of data on family characteristics for the period we examine.

9. The choice of twenty-five as a threshold for inclusion is arbitrary, but results were not sensitive to variation around this cut-off. (An alternative approach would be to include all states regardless of sample size and to place a lower weight on estimates from small states; however, even then, including states with very few observations could introduce error.) Applying

Table 1.A2   **Sample Distribution for NAEP Math Analyses**

| | 1978 | | 1982 | | 1990 | | 1992 | |
State	Total	Black	Total	Black	Total	Black	Total	Black
Alabama	367	94	0	0	0	0	0	0
California	1,595	85	715	113	554	47	573	28
Connecticut	161	32	0	0	0	0	136	26
Florida	334	42	0	0	0	0	443	85
Georgia	0	0	543	157	120	52	187	81
Illinois	514	111	657	49	192	43	0	0
Kentucky	0	0	0	0	0	0	0	0
Louisiana	473	217	340	167	181	103	322	119
Michigan	1,032	130	567	81	334	30	310	71
Mississippi	170	107	0	0	130	78	0	0
Missouri	176	52	0	0	0	0	168	32
New Jersey	250	150	590	84	190	37	108	30
New York	1,176	201	1,238	226	355	40	335	60
North Carolina	638	272	0	0	0	0	0	0
Ohio	412	123	531	125	306	33	328	64
Pennslyvania	501	62	511	128	252	61	459	31
South Carolina	359	131	210	105	0	0	0	0
Tennessee	404	143	199	74	0	0	0	0
Texas	813	187	869	142	327	38	593	106
Virgina	271	116	0	0	207	45	0	0
Total	9,646	2,255	6,970	1,451	3,148	607	3,962	733

Source: Authors' compilation.

these restrictions as well as requiring the NAEP data to have state-level identifiers reduces our sample considerably, from 94,382 to 36,171 for reading
analyses and from 69,557 to 38,105 for math analyses. The largest reductions
are attributable to missing state identifiers for math in 1986 and for reading in
1984 and 1988.

10. The NAEP assessment for nine-year-olds occurs in the winter of the specified
year (January–March). It is important to note that these three-year averages
do not capture the characteristics of the state during the child's preschool
years. If state characteristics in early childhood matter and differ from those
during the past three years, our analyses will omit those effects.

11. The CPS uses categorical responses that combine mothers with lower levels
of education. We assign mothers a value for years of education based on the
midpoint value of each response category. We also conducted analyses using
four variables measuring the proportion of mothers within a state falling into
the following four categories: less than high school, high school graduate or

| 1994 | | 1996 | | 1999 | | 2004 | | |
Total	Black	Total	Black	Total	Black	Total	Black	Total
136	49	151	25	200	80	101	27	955
734	59	475	49	584	39	778	54	6,008
0	0	0	0	0	0	0	0	297
0	0	326	103	0	0	406	61	1,509
181	63	164	36	402	151	250	93	1,847
468	52	201	80	187	42	0	0	2,219
103	27	0	0	0	0	37	0	140
177	48	0	0	0	0	0	0	1,493
0	0	0	0	298	73	216	10	2,757
136	33	0	0	273	83	31	19	740
0	0	0	0	167	32	0	0	511
161	25	163	34	0	0	0	0	1,462
442	72	353	44	348	87	318	68	4,565
171	53	358	101	0	0	0	0	1,167
0	0	0	0	380	90	185	37	2,142
0	0	0	0	267	63	304	28	2,294
96	33	95	68	0	0	0	0	760
170	54	0	0	0	0	0	0	773
0	0	437	33	307	55	305	35	3,651
0	0	217	66	153	45	0	0	848
2,975	568	2,940	639	3,566	840	2,931	432	36,138

GED, some postsecondary education, and a college degree. The results were substantively similar to those reported in table 1.2 and table 1.3.

12. The income measure from the CPS captures money income but does not reflect taxes and noncash benefits because that information is not available until 1979.

13. We also estimated supplemental models in which we analyzed outcomes for black and white children separately. In light of the relatively small sample size for black children, we could not reject the hypothesis that the coefficients were the same in the models for black children and white children. Therefore, we present results from pooled models only.

14. The NAEP uses a multistage sampling frame, and provides a set of weights to make the data representative. These weights were created for cross-sectional adjustments and we have revised them to be used in longitudinal analyses. This was done by dividing the original weight by the mean weight for that year, and then dividing the proportion of children sampled by the number of nine-year-olds in that year. Because we need to take into account

the complex weighting in the NAEP, we do not further weight our data to take into account the size of the states included in our analysis sample.

15. It is important to note that this will yield larger standard errors than implementing the recommended jackknife standard error corrections based on the survey sampling design, and thus our estimates are likely to be less precise than such estimates.

16. The estimated math gap in our sample is about 30 points in 1978 and 16 points in 2004 compared with 32 and 23 points respectively for the full sample of nine-year-olds in the NAEP LTT. The estimated reading gap in our sample is 31 points in 1975 and 18 points in 2004 compared with 35 and 26 points respectively for the full sample.

17. As noted earlier, we do not calculate these separately by race groups, as we think what is likely to matter to children is overall inequality rather than inequality within their race group.

18. This may be a function of measurement error because there are far more white children than black in the sample.

19. Indeed, close to 60 percent of children in this sample report that their mother has completed some college, most often a college degree.

20. We applied coefficients from our model 3 of regressions to the distribution of both the NAEP individual and CPS state-level parental education measures in both 1978 (1975) for math (reading) and 2004 to obtain estimates of the size of the gap at each of these points. We calculated convergence in the test scores by differencing the 1970s estimates from the 2004 estimates and confirmed them by considering the magnitude of the change in the coefficient of the black by 2004 interaction term that occurred with the introduction of parental education measures. We also found that estimates of the effects of CPS state-level characteristics were not sensitive to NAEP measures of parental education, and consequently that estimates of the convergence in test score gaps attributable to distribution of education within states were also not sensitive to whether students' reports of their parent's education were taken into account.

References

Campbell, Mary, Robert Haveman, Gary Sandefur, and Barbara Wolfe. 2005. "What Does Increased Economic Inequality Imply about the Future Level and Dispersion of Human Capital?" Project on Social Inequality Working Paper. New York: Russell Sage Foundation.

Cook, Michael D., and William N. Evans. 2000. "Families or Schools? Explaining the Convergence in White and Black Academic Performance." *Journal of Labor Economics* 18(4): 729–54.

Duncan, Greg J., and Jeanne Brooks-Gunn. 1997. *The Consequences of Growing Up Poor.* New York: Russell Sage Foundation.

Ellwood, David T., and Thomas J. Kane. 2000. "Who Is Getting a College Education: Family Background and the Growing Gap in Enrollment." In *Securing the Future: Investing in Children from Birth to Adulthood,* edited by Sheldon Danziger and Jane Waldfogel. New York: Russell Sage Foundation.

Evans, William N., Michael Hout, and Susan E. Mayer. 2004. "Assessing the Effect of Economic Inequality." In *Social Inequality*, edited by Kathryn M. Neckerman. New York: Russell Sage Foundation.

Freeman, Richard B., and Alexander M. Gelber. 2006. "Optimal Inequality/Optimal Incentives: Evidence from a Tournament." NBER Working Paper 12588. Cambridge, Mass.: National Bureau of Economic Research.

Fryer, Roland G., and Steven D. Levitt. 2006. "The Black-White Test Score Gap Through Third Grade." *American Law and Economics Review* 8(2): 249–81.

Grissmer, David, Ann Flanagan, and Stephanie Williamson. 1998. "Why Did the Black-White Test Score Gap Narrow in the 1970s and 1980s?" In *The Black-White Test Score Gap*, edited by Christopher Jencks and Meredith Phillips. Washington, D.C.: Brookings Institution Press.

Grodsky, Eric, Demetra Kalogrides, and Julie Siebens. 2007. "Virtuous Cycle or Perverse Openness? Race, Ethnicity and Social Class Reconsidered." Paper presented at the Annual Meeting of the American Educational Research Association. Chicago, Ill., April 11, 2007.

Haveman, Robert, and Barbara Wolfe. 1995. "The Determinants of Children's Attainments: A Review of Methods and Findings." *Journal of Economic Literature* 23(4): 1829–78.

Heckman, James J., and Paul A. LaFontaine. 2006. "Biased Corrected Estimates of GED Returns." *Journal of Labor Economics* 24(3): 661–700.

———. 2007. "The American High School Graduation Rate: Trends and Levels." NBER Working Paper 13670. Cambridge, Mass.: National Bureau of Economic Research.

Kane, Thomas J. 2004. "College-Going and Inequality." In *Social Inequality*, edited by Katherine M. Neckerman. New York: Russell Sage Foundation.

Magnuson, Katherine, and Greg Duncan. 2006. "The Role of Family Socioeconomic Resources in Racial Test Score Gaps." *Developmental Review* 26(4): 365–99.

Mayer, Susan E. 2001. "How Did the Increase in Economic Inequality Between 1970 and 1990 Affect Children's Educational Attainment?" *The American Journal of Sociology* 107(1): 1–32.

———. 2002. "How Economic Segregation Affects Children's Educational Attainment." *Social Forces* 81(1): 153–76.

Neckerman, Kathryn M., editor. 2004. *Social Inequality*. New York: Russell Sage Foundation.

Chapter 2

Changes in Families, Schools, and the Test Score Gap

Mark Berends and Roberto V. Peñaloza

Systematic empirical examination of the effects of changes between and within schools on student achievement has been of theoretical and empirical import for many years. Some researchers raise concerns that worsening family environments and schools have negative consequences for students' educational outcomes (Christensen 1990; Haveman and Wolfe 1994; Herrnstein and Murray 1994; Murray and Herrnstein 1992; Popenoe 1993; Uhlenberg and Eggebeen 1986). Not all research, however, supports the claims about the negative effects of changes in families and schools on student achievement (Berliner and Biddle 1995; Campbell, Hombo, and Mazzeo 2000; Cook and Evans 2000; Grissmer et al. 1994; Hedges and Nowell 1998; Koretz 1986, 1992; Lankford and Wyckoff 1995; Porter 2005; Tyack and Cuban 1995). The conventional wisdom about schools is that expenditures have doubled in real terms over the past few decades, but that achievement scores have declined (Hanushek 1986, 1989, 1994). This has led to continuing calls for educational reform, reflected in federal educational policy of No Child Left Behind Act of 2001 (NCLB), which places greater emphasis on high standards for student learning, testing, and accountability (see http://www.ed.gov/legislation/ESEA02/; on test-based accountability, see Hamilton, Stecher, and Klein 2002).

Current educational reformers stress raising the achievement of the entire population while reducing disparities among groups, which is certainly an important goal despite being a significant challenge (Berends, Bodilly, and Kirby 2002; Berends et al. 2005; Jencks and Phillips 1998). In part, the concern over some of these achievement gaps—for example, those between racial-ethnic groups—has been heightened by the growing diversity in the United States. The federal NCLB legislation, reauthorizing Title I, which is the largest federal funding program aimed at disadvantaged students, requires states to report achievement gaps between certain subgroups to help schools, districts, and states decrease achievement gaps over time. Specifically, NCLB states that the purpose of Title I

> is to ensure that all children have a fair, equal, and significant opportunity to obtain a high-quality education and reach, at a minimum, proficiency on challenging state academic achievement standards and state academic assessments. This purpose can be accomplished by . . . closing the achievement gap between high- and low-performing children, especially the achievement gaps between minority and nonminority students, and between disadvantaged children and their more advantaged peers. (1001 NCLB 3)

In this chapter, we empirically examine several family and school-based explanations for test score differences between African American and white students in mathematics over thirty years, using data available for several national cohorts of high school seniors between 1972 and 2004. We address the following four questions: How did the test scores of blacks and whites change between the early 1970s and 2004? How did selected family and school measures change over this period? To what extent were changes in these measures associated with the changes in the black-white test score gap that occurred? What are the policy implications that arise from our empirical analyses examining how changes in families and schools are related to trends in student gaps in mathematics achievement?

Because of the ongoing debates about families and schools, it is important to consider a more complete set of family and school changes than have so far been considered and to apply multivariate methods for estimating the net associations among changes in these measures and student achievement. In addition, researchers have infrequently assessed such associations among family and school measures and student achievement with several different longitudinal national cohorts. Additional empirical analyses need to be undertaken to place current student achievement scores in the context of long-term test score trends, to examine the relationships between these test score trends and changes in families and schools, and to address changes in educational policies (for example, school desegregation, tracking and ability grouping, standards-based reform, and the like).

Families, Schools, and the Black-White Test Score Gap

Data from the NAEP long-term trend assessment reveal that, when considering achievement proficiency in mathematics and reading, high school students in the United States were scoring about the same in 2004 as they were in the early 1970s (see figures I.1 and I.3, introduction, this volume). As discussed in the introduction, these overall trends mask significant progress among certain groups at certain points in time. For instance, between the early 1970s and early 1990s, when compared with their white counterparts, black students made substantial progress toward closing the test score gap in both mathematics and reading (see Campbell, Hombo, and Mazzeo 2000). Since that time, however, the NAEP black-white mathematics gap has increased somewhat, and that in reading did the same in the early 1990s but again decreased in the 2004 assessment.

Although many researchers have addressed possibilities for why the test score gaps closed between the early 1970s and early 1990s (for example, Ferguson 1998; Koretz 1986; Neal 2006; Porter 2005), only a few researchers have been able to empirically study how changes in family background and school factors related to the test score convergence that occurred (Berends et al. 2005; Cook and Evans 2000; Grissmer, Flanagan, and Williamson 1998; Grissmer et al. 1994; Hedges and Nowell 1998). The main reason for this is the lack of data for multiple student cohorts that would allow for the examination of relationships between family and school measures and student achievement gaps.

A few studies have been able to examine how changes in family background factors relate to student achievement gaps in national data. For example, RAND research was specifically interested in how changes in families related to the test score gaps among black and white students (Grissmer et al. 1994). In their analyses of the National Education Longitudinal Study of 1988 (NELS-88) and the National Longitudinal Survey of Youth (NLSY-80), David Grissmer and his colleagues described how students' family background (parents' educational attainment, family income, and mother's work status) and family structure (family size, age of mother at child's birth, and single-mother household) were related to mathematics and reading achievement.

The researchers also estimated the net effects on mathematics and reading scores of several important family changes occurring between the early 1970s and early 1990s and provided information about what nonfamily factors may have contributed to achievement trends (Grissmer et al. 1994). Specifically, the study examined how achievement scores would change for fourteen- to eighteen-year-olds raised in families of the 1950s and 1960s compared to families of the 1970s and 1980s. In addition to estimating the effects of family changes on overall test scores, the researchers estimated the effects for different racial-ethnic groups. They also compared actual changes in NAEP achievement to those predicted by changes in family characteristics. This approach produced residual estimates that provided indicators of the effects of factors operating outside the family. These residuals were obtained by comparing the predicted test score changes to actual changes in test scores based on the NAEP data during the period of the study.

These findings revealed that black and white students' academic achievement should have risen between the early 1970s and early 1990s. Overall, the researchers predicted a gain of about 0.20 standard deviation for fourteen- to eighteen-year-old youth in 1990 compared to similarly aged youth in 1970. They found that the major factors leading to higher predicted test scores were the markedly higher education levels for 1990 parents and smaller family size. Children in 1990 were living with better-educated parents, in smaller families, with more income per child. Grissmer and his colleagues concluded that the effect of these factors far outweighed the negative impact of more single-parent families, a small shift in births to younger mothers, and the changing racial-ethnic composition of the American population.

When estimating the effects of family changes for different racial-ethnic groups, Grissmer and his colleagues (1994) also predicted positive test score gains. Black students made sizable gains in test scores over and above the gains that family changes would predict, but white students did not. The Grissmer results suggested that changes in minority family characteristics—when considered together—were more supportive of student achievement in 1990 than in the early 1970s. Although their analyses fully accounted for the gains of white students, they concluded that changing family characteristics accounted for no more than about a third of the gain for black students.

Attempting to explain what factors outside the family were related to the achievement gains of black students, the RAND researchers suggested that changes in educational policies and public investment may have been influential. Because they did not have enough data to empirically examine these factors, they emphasized that additional research was needed (see Berends et al. 1999). In subsequent research, Grissmer, Ann Flanagan, and Stephanie Williamson (1998) extended the earlier Grissmer analysis by assessing what factors may have contributed to the test score gap convergence between black and white students by reviewing factors that may have changed between the early 1970s and early 1990s, such as desegregation, secondary school tracking, changes in the curriculum, per pupil expenditures, pupil-teacher ratios, teachers' educational background and experience, and school violence. Based on their review of extant research, they concluded that both social investment in the 1960s and 1970s (that is, the civil rights movement and the war on poverty programs) and the school-based changes (desegregation, secondary school tracking, and class size) were the likely factors behind the closing of the test score gap between black and white students. The researchers, however, were not able to conduct original empirical analyses of these factors, so the arguments remain speculative.

Building on the 1994 Grissmer research, Larry Hedges and Amy Nowell (1999) also addressed the achievement gaps among students over the past thirty years and how family background characteristics were related to any changes in those gaps. In their 1998 and 1999 studies of several national data sets from the early 1960s to the early 1990s, Hedges and Nowell pointed out several limitations of the 1994 Grissmer research. Their criticisms were aimed at assumptions that the effects of family characteristics on student achievement remained the same between the early 1970s and early 1990s and that all unexplained changes in the test score gaps were attributable to social and educational policies. Hedges and Nowell addressed some of these problems by analyzing all the national data that were available between 1965 and the early 1990s that included student test scores and family characteristics such as parents' educational attainment, family income, and mother's work status.[1]

Like Grissmer et al. (1994), however, Hedges and Nowell (1998, 1999) found when they examined changes in mean achievement levels that the black-white test score gap did narrow significantly over time. In addition, their analyses of family background characteristics accounted for roughly one-third of the achievement gap, which is also similar to the Grissmer et al. findings. However, in contrast to them, Hedges and Nowell found that the relationships between family characteristics and student achievement were not constant over time. Moreover, Hedges and Nowell argued that we need more direct measures of educational policies that may have contributed further to the closing of the gap.

Although they make a significant contribution to our understanding of black-white test score trends as they relate to family characteristics, the Hedges and Nowell studies (1998, 1999) are not without limitations. First, the measures of family characteristics (for example, family income and parents' education) were not operationalized the same way. For example, in the 1965 Equality of Educational Opportunity (EEO) data, Hedges and Nowell used possessions in the home as a proxy for family income because income data were not available in the EEO as they were in the other data they analyzed. Second, Hedges and Nowell were not able to examine changes in schools that occurred during the early 1960s and 1990s, and raised the importance of such analyses. Finally, although they allowed for the effects of family background to vary across cohorts, they did not systematically examine how changes in mean levels of family background measures or the effects (that is, coefficients) of those measures were related to the closing of the black-white test score gap.

Extending research to examine school quality, Michael Cook and William Evans (2000) were specifically interested in whether it was changes in family characteristics or changes in school quality (or both) that were associated with the narrowing of the black-white test score gap over time. Analyzing the NAEP long-term trend data, their research focused not only on how changes in mean levels of family and school characteristics were related to the black-white test score trends, but also on how the effects of family and school measures on achievement were related to black-white test score trends. They found that only about 25 percent of the overall convergence in black-white test scores can be attributed to changing family and school characteristics. They argued that the remainder is attributable to changes within schools.

There are several strengths of the Cook and Evans (2000) study. First, the researchers were able to make fewer assumptions than the studies just reviewed. For example, Cook and Evans—unlike Grissmer and his colleagues (1994, 1998) and Hedges and Nowell (1998, 1999)—examined tests that were stable over time. In addition, their methods allowed them to examine how changes in the relationships between their measures and student achievement differ over time, again in contrast to work by Grissmer and his colleagues (1994, 1998) that assumed stability of these relationships. Finally, Cook and Evans extended the critical work on changes in families to include changes in school quality when examining the black-white test score gap.

Their study, however, also has its limitations. Cook and Evans were limited to examining family background changes as measured by parent educational attainment. Unfortunately, the NAEP is very limited in terms of family background measures because it lacks other family measures such as parent income, occupational status, and other family characteristics (Berends and Koretz 1996; Grissmer, Flanagan, and Williamson 1998). In addition, Cook and Evans's measure of school quality was lacking in that they assume that "school quality is the effect that attending a given school has on student performance after controlling for the student's observable characteristics" (2000, 732). Their analyses lacked direct measures of schools, how these school measures changed, and how these changes (both means and effects) were associated with student test score gaps.

Thus, despite this important research, questions remain about achievement differences between black and white students and about what family and school factors are associated with achievement gaps over time. With data for four senior cohorts in 1972, 1982, 1992, and 2004, our analyses extend our knowledge about how changes in families and schools are related to black-white test score trends and builds on the work of Grissmer and colleagues (1994, 1998), Hedges and Nowell (1998, 1999), and Cook and Evans (2000).

Although decomposing the black-white achievement gaps into changes in families and schools is a complex exercise (Berends et al. 2005; Grissmer, Flanagan, and Williamson 1998), we believe our analyses make important contributions. For instance, like Cook and Evans, we use methods that allow for examination of changes in mean levels of family and school characteristics and changes in the relationships, or effects, of these characteristics with student achievement. However, our data have several direct measures of students' family and school characteristics, measured consistently over time. In addition, we extend the time frame of previous analyses to understand what happened between 1972 and 2004, because research has shown that the gap in the black-white test score gap stopped converging during the 1990s (Neal 2006; Porter 2005). The analyses that follow provide results about specific family and school factors that are related to student achievement trends, particularly the black-white mathematics scores for students in high schools. No study has comprehensively analyzed several family and school measures across nationally representative data for different cohorts of high school seniors with comparable achievement outcomes. Our study intends to fill this gap.

Data and Methods

In this study, we focus on student mathematics achievement and family and school measures that are consistently measured over time across nationally representative cohorts of high school seniors. We believe it is an important contribution to analyze family, school, and achievement measures between 1972 and 2004 that have been operationalized in the same way (for more details about variable justification and operationalization, see Berends et al. 2005). Moreover, the national data we analyze cover the same periods as the studies by Grissmer and his colleagues (1994), Hedges and Nowell (1998, 1999), and Cook and Evans (2000), and extend beyond those periods to 2004. Thus, our findings can not only be directly compared with their research but also extend our knowledge to encompass factors associated with more recent black-white test score trends.

In what follows, we analyze four cohorts of high school seniors in nationally representative data sets that cover the experiences of secondary school students in the United States between 1972, 1982, 1992, and 2004:

- NLS of the high school class of 1972 (NLS-72)
- HSB senior cohort of 1982 (HSB-82)
- LS senior cohort of 1992 (NELS-92)
- ELS senior cohort of 2004 (ELS-04)

These national data sets are part of the Longitudinal Studies program of the National Center for Education Statistics (NCES), so we refer to them as LS data, which we later compare to the long-term trend data of National Assessment of Educational Progress (NAEP). In what follows, we discuss the data sets analyzed, the operationalization of the individual, family, and school measures analyzed across the data sets, and our methodological approach.

National Longitudinal Study of the High School Class of 1972

NLS-72 was designed to produce representative data at the national level on a cohort of high school seniors who graduated in 1972. The base-year sample was a stratified, two-stage probability sample of students from all public and private schools in the United States, with schools as the first-stage units and students within schools as the second stage units. The result is a nationally representative sample of 19,000 seniors in 1,061 high schools (Riccobono et al. 1981). Student, school administrator, and test score data are available for measuring students' academic achievement and individual, family, and school characteristics. We analyzed data from student tests, student questionnaires, and information about the school. The student questionnaire was completed by 16,683 high school seniors. Because we wanted complete data from the questionnaires, the mathematics test, and information from the school information form, the sample for our analyses resulted in 14,469 students in 875 schools.

High School and Beyond

Similar to NLS-72, HSB is a two-stage stratified probability sample with schools as the first-stage units and students within schools as the second-stage units. In the first stage, 1,100 schools were selected, and in the second stage about thirty-six students were randomly selected within each school. Some types of schools were oversampled to ensure adequate numbers in subpopulations of interest. We analyzed the sample of about 26,000 students who were sophomores in the 1980 base year sample and were followed up on in 1982 when they were seniors. The follow-up sample retained the essential features of the base-year design—multistage, stratified, and clustered (see Jones et al. 1983).

HSB was unique in that it gathered data on two high school grade levels in 1980 (tenth and twelfth). Both the sophomore and senior cohorts in HSB have information on students, schools, and test scores. The sophomore cohort was followed up two years later when the students were seniors (HSB-82). Although we had previously analyzed the 1980 senior cohort (HSB-80), our descriptive and multivariate analyses of the effects of family and school measures on student achievement revealed no significant differences between it and the 1982 cohort (see Berends et al. 2005). For the sake of parsimony and presentation, we thus present the 1972, 1982, 1992, and 2004 comparisons when examining how the trends in the mathematics gap related to changes in family and school measures.

National Education Longitudinal Study

NELS is a nationally representative data set that includes detailed information from students, schools, and parents (Ingels et al. 1993). The 1988 base-year NELS included about 25,000 eighth grade students in 1,035 schools. Students in NELS were followed up in the tenth grade (1990), twelfth grade (1992), two years after high school (1994), and eight years after (2000). These data contain extensive information about the achievement and school experiences of students before they entered high school, data on school organization in middle and high school, students' family and demographic characteristics, and students' experiences after high school. In each of the first three waves of NELS, students were tested in various subject areas. When students were seniors, the sample was freshened so that the data could be examined as a nationally representative sample of high school seniors.

Educational Longitudinal Study

ELS tested achievement and educational perceptions and experiences of tenth grade students in a national, clustered probability sample of 15,362 students in 752 public, Catholic, and other private schools with tenth grades in the spring of 2002. The base-year data collection of ELS is the first wave of a new longitudinal study of high school students, and students were followed up in 2004 when they were seniors. The base-year study includes surveys of parents, teachers, school administrators, library media specialists, and tenth grade students in the spring term of the 2001–2002 school year. In 2004, during the first follow-up of the study, those base-year students remaining in the sample schools were surveyed and assessed again. The sample was freshened in the follow-up with 171 seniors to keep the sample representative of 2004 high school seniors. Base-year nonparticipants (n = 756) were also given a new opportunity to participate in the follow-up.

The ELS 2002 sampling design was a two-stage cluster sampling with stratification. The sampling frame of schools, which was obtained from the Common Core of Data (CCD) and the Private School Survey (PSS), was first divided into more than 350 strata, and then two or three schools were selected from each stratum with probability proportional to size. Finally, a random sample of students was selected from each of the selected schools' rosters. Some types of schools (for example private schools) and students from particular racial-ethnic groups (for example Asians) were oversampled.

For our analysis, we restricted the sample to the 2004 follow-up assessments, to only those students who were seniors in the spring of 2004 and enrolled in any of the base-year schools, and to those who had information on the measures examined. Some students were known to be seniors but had transferred to other schools, preventing us from knowing the characteristics of those schools; such students were excluded. After these restrictions, our sample contained a total of 12,267 students in 751 schools.

National Assessment of Educational Progress

When examining test score trends, we compare our estimates in the LS data sets to the NAEP long-term trend data, which contains information over time on the same set of test score items for nationally representative samples of students. Although NAEP asks the same items over time, NAEP data lack detailed information about individual, family, and school characteristics to examine family and school-based explanations over time (see Berends and Koretz 1996). NAEP does, however, provide a useful benchmark to compare the test score trends in NLS-72, HSB-82, NELS-92, and ELS-04 (Green, Dugoni, and Ingels 1995).

Dependent Measure: Mathematics Achievement

The dependent variable in our models is the individual student mathematics test scores, assumed to be a function of a set of independent individual, family, and school variables that are directly comparable in the senior cohort data sets. The group differences we focus on are those between black and white students during their senior year of high school.

To more accurately measure the extent of group differences within each of the senior cohorts, we linked the mathematics tests over time and calibrated them to be on the same scale so that it is as though students across cohorts had taken the same test (for details on linking procedures, see Berends et al. 2005). Because the reading, science, and social studies tests did not have items in common across the cohorts, we were limited to mathematics. However, because of the sensitivity of mathematics tests to school effects and variation in mathematics scores across schools (Sørensen and Morgan 2000), it is important to understand trends in mathematics achievement and how other family and school changes relate to them, particularly for students from different racial-ethnic groups.

Although the equating, or linking, methods provide accurate measures of student scores throughout the proficiency distribution, it is important to remain aware that the tests do differ; they are not identical across the different cohorts.[2] However, the tests are similar in structure and the domains tested, and do contain some common items to use for equating purposes. Moreover, research to date suggests the tests across these cohorts are reliable and valid measures of students' mathematics achievement in secondary school (see Berends et al. 2005; Koretz and Berends 2001; Rock et al. 1985; Rock and Pollack 1995). In addition, because we have not yet completed the linking to the 2004 mathematics test, we use the standardized measures in the analyses reported here.[3]

Family and School Measures

The definitions for the other measures in our models are matched across the data sets for the four senior cohorts. Our selection of variables was dictated by the necessity of comparable measures across the data sets (NLS-72,

HSB-82, NELS-92, and ELS-04). We analyzed a number of variables to extend previous research on student test score gaps with a particular emphasis on how changes in families and schools related to the black-white mathematics test score gap (Cook and Evans 2000; Grissmer et al. 1994, 1998; Hedges and Nowell 1998). The measures we analyze include individual characteristics (race-ethnicity and gender), family background (parents' educational attainment, occupational status, and family income), and school characteristics (socioeconomic and minority composition, sector, urban locale) (see the appendix; for a more detailed description and comparison of measures, see Berends et al. 2005).[4]

We also examine a self-reported measure of track placement (Gamoran 1989; Lucas 1999, Lucas and Gamoran 2001), a measure that deserves further comment. The survey question administered across the cohorts asked students to describe their high school program as being academic or college-bound, general, or vocational. We created a new variable that compared students in the college or academic track to those in the nonacademic track (that is, general or vocational). The structure of tracking has certainly changed between the early 1970s and the 1990s. Rather than taking a program of courses, students enter a hierarchy of subject-based ability group arrangements, such as honors, regular, or remedial (Oakes, Gamoran, and Page 1992; Lucas 1999; Lucas and Gamoran 2001). Whether such differentiation equates to or leads to differences in a program of courses is open to question.

Although there have been changes in tracking over the past several decades, several argue that the students' reports of their track placement are essential data. For example, Adam Gamoran (1987) suggested that because students have a great deal of choice in course selections in high school, perceived track placement may be a better predictor of achievement than school reports. Moreover, there is a long body of research that shows that self-reported track placement is one of the strongest and long-lasting school measures affecting long-term educational attainment (Lucas and Gamoran 2001; Gamoran and Berends 1987). Thus we suggest that student-reported track placement taps an important social-psychological dimension of tracking—revealing students' attitudes toward school, perceived opportunities within school, and their educational futures. Understanding changes in these perceptions of the school opportunity structures over time is important to understand whether students, who typically have been underserved by the education system, such as black and Latino students, have changed their social-psychological perceptions over time and whether these changes are related to trends in the test score gaps.

Because our models do not allow for estimating the conditions that are related to selection into certain track categories (for example, prior achievement, subject-area grades, teacher recommendations, motivation, and educational aspirations), this measure is a proxy for not only the social-psychological aspects of tracking but also these other factors, As such, we believe this measure remains useful to analyze because it provides an indication of changing educational opportunities, perceived and otherwise, within the school. If such opportunities are reported to be higher by black students relative to white students over time, this may be an important factor to analyze further if it is associated with the black-white test score gap. Nevertheless, because selection into a track may be affected by other variables of interest in the model, we estimated our models both with and without the control for track.

Methodology

Methods to assess the effects of individual, family, and school measures over time need to factor in both the changes in the characteristics of interest (means) and changes in the effects of these characteristics (coefficients) on achievement scores at different points in time. To decompose such effects, we rely on a technique widely used in labor economics called the Oaxaca decomposition (Oaxaca 1970; Cain 1986; Corcoran and Duncan 1979). Although attributed to Oaxaca, sociologists had used the technique for some time (Duncan 1967, 1968; Cancio, Evans, and Maume 1996; Sayer, Bianchi, and Robinson 2004). For the most part, the technique has been used to explain differences in wages across groups in cross-sectional data (Cain 1986; Corcoran and Duncan 1979) and the time-series pattern of wages in repeated cross-sections (Sahling and Smith 1983). More recently, it has been applied to education as well (Cook and Evans 2000; Goldhaber 1996; Gill and Michaels 1992). For example, as noted earlier, Cook and Evans (2000) used such methods to investigate how changes in the mean differences and changes in the coefficients of family and school measures were related to the convergence of the black-white test score gap; our analyses aim to build on their findings using a similar approach.

The first step in decomposing the effects of family background and school measures on the test score gap is to estimate a series of regressions for each senior cohort. These regressions estimate the relationship of mathematics achievement to mother's and father's educational attainment, the higher of mother's or father's occupational status (Duncan's SEI), the family income quintile dummies, academic track, minority and socioeconomic composition of the school, sector, and urban locale. Gender is also included in these regressions as a covariate.

Because students are nested in schools, we use multilevel regressions, fitting a hierarchical linear model to each cohort and estimating regression coefficients (Kreft and De Leeuw 1998; Raudenbush and Bryk 2002; Snijders and Bosker 1999). We then use the coefficients in the decomposition of the difference between the predicted means of white and black test scores (equation 2.1) (for example, Duncan 1967, 1968; Oaxaca 1970; Cain 1986; Sahling and Smith 1983; Gill and Michaels 1992; Cook and Evans 2000; Goldhaber 1996; Sayer, Bianchi, and Robinson 2004). The LS data allowed for this analysis over four time intervals, but here we focus mainly on the period between 1972 and 2004. By looking at the results of these decompositions, we can begin to understand how black students' mathematics scores changed relative to those of whites over this thirty-year span. Moreover, we examine two key subperiods: 1972 to 1982, and 1982 to 2004. Mathematically, for each of these intervals we employed the following decomposition:

$$\Delta \hat{y}_1 - \Delta \hat{y}_0 = \left(\Delta \overline{x}_1 - \Delta \overline{x}_0 \right) \cdot \hat{\beta}_0 + \Delta \overline{x}_1 \cdot \left(\hat{\beta}_1 - \hat{\beta}_0 \right) + \overline{x}_{1w} \cdot \left(\hat{\beta}_{1w} - \hat{\beta}_1 \right)$$
$$- \overline{x}_{0w} \cdot \left(\hat{\beta}_{0w} - \hat{\beta}_0 \right) + \overline{x}_{1b} \cdot \left(\hat{\beta}_1 - \hat{\beta}_{1b} \right) - \overline{x}_{0b} \cdot \left(\hat{\beta}_0 - \hat{\beta}_{0b} \right) \qquad (2.1)$$

where

- $\Delta \hat{y}_1 - \Delta \hat{y}_0 = \left(\hat{y}_{1w} - \hat{y}_{1b} \right) - \left(\hat{y}_{0w} - y_{0b} \right)$ is the change from time 0 to time 1 in the difference between the predicted means of white and black test scores,[5]
- $\Delta \overline{x}_i = \overline{x}_{iw} - \overline{x}_{ib}$ is the difference at time i between the means of black and white individual and school-level characteristics,
- $\overline{x}_{ib}$ and $\overline{x}_{iw}$ are the vectors of means at time i of individual and school-level characteristics for the black and white students, respectively,
- $\hat{\beta}_i$ is the estimated coefficient vector for a representative student at time i,
- $\hat{\beta}_{ib}$ and $\hat{\beta}_{iw}$ are the estimated coefficient vectors at time i for black and white students,
- $\left(\Delta \overline{x}_1 - \Delta \overline{x}_0 \right) \cdot \hat{\beta}_0$ is the explained portion of the achievement differentials, associated with changes from time 0 to time 1 in the differences between white and black seniors in the means of family and school characteristics, and
- $\Delta \overline{x}_1 \cdot \left(\hat{\beta}_1 - \hat{\beta}_0 \right) + x_{1w} \cdot \left(\hat{\beta}_{1w} - \hat{\beta}_1 \right) - x_{0w} \cdot \left(\hat{\beta}_{0w} - \hat{\beta}_0 \right) + x_{1b} \cdot \left(\hat{\beta}_1 - \hat{\beta}_{1b} \right) - x_{0b} \cdot \left(\hat{\beta}_0 - \hat{\beta}_{0b} \right)$ is the unexplained portion of the differentials attributable to variability in the effects (or coefficients) of family and school characteristics between representative students and black or white students, as well as differences in these effects from time 0 to time 1.

The explained component of this decomposition has two features of note. First, its magnitude will vary depending on which coefficients are used in the calculation. As indicated, we first weight the change in differences between white and black student means by the coefficient estimates from time 0 (or 1972). The explained component thus represents the change in the test score gap we would expect to see given the change in mean characteristics of black and white students between time 0 and time 1, holding everything else constant and assuming the returns to those characteristics were the same as they had been in 1972. The decomposition can also be calculated using estimated coefficients from the 2004 regression as weights, so we show the results from both the 1972 and 2004 estimations. Second, it uses the student cohort coefficient estimates, as opposed to white or black student estimates. Because black and white students in a given cohort were not schooled in total isolation from one another nor indeed from students of other ethnicities or races, they are not distinct populations. Thus, using a set of coefficient estimates for each student cohort seems more appropriate. This choice also avoids capriciously choosing either to weight the change in mean differences by the black or white student coefficient estimates, or estimating a set of coefficients for both and then attempting to mediate between the two sets of results generated. (The results from the regression models appear in tables 2.A1 and 2.A2; the first set of results does not include the track variable, but the second set does.)

Results

Before examining the results of this decomposition, it is important to understand trends in the black-white test score differences in the senior cohorts and compare them to other national achievement trends in the NAEP. Second, we examine the trends in family and school measures. Finally, we decompose the effects of family and school characteristics on the black-white achievement gap into changes in the levels of the family background and school measures and changes in their effects on achievement across cohorts.

Black-White Mathematics Test Score Trends

Consistent with other national data, black students have made considerable achievement gains in narrowing the black-white test score gap in mathematics when examining the senior cohorts of NLS-72, HSB-82, NELS-92, and ELS-04. The estimates for the black-white convergence in mathematics appear in figure 2.1. The estimates for the four LS senior cohorts are plotted against those in the NAEP long-term trend assessment because the NAEP provides the strongest trend assessment available in the United States and offers an important benchmark for the LS cohorts. In 1972, the black-white difference was greater than a standard deviation (SD = 1.01) in the NLS-72 data, but by the early 1990s, the gap narrowed by about 20 percent—to 0.81 standard deviation difference in NELS, and this gap remained stable until 2004 in the ELS-04.

In 1973, the black-white difference in NAEP was 1.14 standard deviation, narrowing to 0.89 standard deviation in 1996 (a 22 percent reduction) and 0.80 standard deviation in 2004. The decreased gap occurred in both

Figure 2.1   Black-White Mathematics Differences, Senior Cohorts Versus NAEP-LTT Assessment

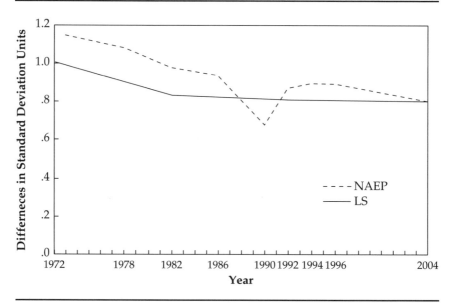

Source: Authors' compilation.

the NAEP and the LS, but the extent of the decrease was greater in NAEP than LS, although the overall patterns remain consistent. In short, the LS senior cohorts reveal a narrowing of the test score gap between blacks and whites, a convergence worthy of further examination.

Changes in Family Background Characteristics

In addition to the significant changes in the test score trends of black and white students, important changes have occurred in family background characteristics such as parents' educational attainment, occupational status, and income (see table 2.1).[6] Overall, compared to students' parents of the 1970s, high school seniors in 2004 are living with parents who are better educated and have higher occupational status. In 1972 parents' educational attainment levels in the LS data were 12.31 years for mothers and 12.54 for fathers. In both 1982 and 1992, parents' education levels increased, and by 2004 both mothers and fathers had more than an extra year of education: 13.65 years, on average, for mothers, and 13.76 for fathers.

Similarly, the occupational status of parents increased. In 1972 the Duncan's SEI was 42.00; in 1982 it was 48.46 and held steady at that level through 1992, when SEI was 47.21, and then increased to 56.16 in 2004, a 14.16 point increase from 1972 (or an increase of 0.53 standard deviation).

Table 2.1   Selected Differences in Family Background Characteristics in LS Data

	1972	1982	1992	2004	Change
Mother's education	12.31	12.65	13.29	13.65	+1.34
Whites	12.45	12.84	13.50	13.94	+1.49
Blacks	11.57	12.22	12.96	13.40	+1.83
Black-white difference	−0.88	−0.62	−0.54	−0.54	+0.34
Father's education	12.54	12.88	13.67	13.76	+1.22
Whites	12.73	13.19	13.92	14.06	+1.33
Blacks	11.27	11.76	12.96	13.30	+2.03
Black-white difference	−1.46	−1.43	−0.96	−0.76	+0.70
Occupational status					
(Duncan's SEI)	42.00	48.46	47.21	56.16	+14.16
Whites	43.68	51.00	49.58	59.60	+15.92
Blacks	31.06	40.39	40.64	51.24	+20.18
Black-white difference	−12.62	−10.61	−8.94	−8.36	+4.26

Source: Authors' compilation.

Black-White Family Background Trends

Examination of black-white differences in family background trends over time reveals that there have been important improvements in these conditions for black students. For example, black students made considerable progress relative to whites when considering parents' educational attainment and parent occupational status. As table 2.1 reveals, the black-white difference in 1972 for the educational attainment levels of students' mothers was almost one year of education. Specifically, the average black student's mother had 0.88 years less than the average white student's mother. This black-white gap in mothers' education levels decreased to 0.62 in 1982 and 0.54 in 1992, and stayed the same through 2004 (0.54). Similarly, the black-white gap in father's education narrowed between the time points measured in these data. In 1972, the black-white gap in father's education was about one and a half years (1.46). This declined slightly by 1982 (1.43), and then more dramatically by 1992 (0.96) and 2004 (0.76). The black-white gap in parent occupational status in 1972 was 12.62 points (or 0.47 standard deviation), and narrowed to 10.61 by 1982. The black-white gap in occupational status narrowed further by 1992, when it was 8.94 points, and remained relatively stable to 2004, when it was 8.36 points (or .31 standard deviation).

Changes in School Characteristics

Between 1972 and 2004, there have been increases in the proportion of students attending schools with a greater proportion of black and Latino students than white students. Table 2.2 shows the differences in school

Table 2.2   **Differences in School Conditions in LS Data**

	1972	1982	1992	2004	Change
Proportion minority					
composition	0.19	0.26	0.25	0.27	+0.08
Whites	0.17	0.21	0.18	0.14	−0.03
Blacks	0.36	0.37	0.42	0.60	+0.24
Black-white difference	+0.19	+0.16	+0.24	+0.46	+0.27
Mean socioeconomic					
composition	−0.05	−.05	0.05	0.06	+0.11
Whites	−0.03	0.04	0.13	0.15	+0.18
Blacks	−0.21	−0.04	−0.08	−0.11	+0.10
Black-white difference	−0.18	−0.08	−0.21	−0.26	−0.08
Proportion urban school	0.29	0.25	0.36	0.28	−0.01
Whites	0.27	0.21	0.30	0.20	−0.07
Blacks	0.44	0.36	0.44	0.47	+0.03
Black-white difference	+0.17	+0.15	+0.14	+0.27	+0.10
Proportion private school	0.07	0.12	0.16	0.08	+0.01
Whites	0.07	0.12	0.17	0.10	+0.03
Blacks	0.05	0.10	0.11	0.03	−0.02
Black-white difference	−0.02	−0.02	−0.06	−0.07	−0.05

Source: Authors' compilation.

conditions between 1972 and 2004 for the four cohorts overall and for black and white students. Although overall students in 1972 attended schools in which the proportion of the nonwhite student body was 0.19, this increased in 1982, when students attended schools in which the nonwhite proportion was 0.26, on average. Since 1982, the overall minority composition of schools has remained relatively stable (0.25 in 1992 and 0.27 in 2004).

Paralleling changes in students' families, schools tended to be somewhat higher in parent occupational status in 2004 than in 1972. For example, in 1972, students attended schools where the average socioeconomic status was −0.05, compared with 0.06 in 2004.

Examining changes in school characteristics in the data sets spanning 1972 to 2004, we see increases between 1972 and 1992 in the proportion of students across the nation who attended urban schools (from 0.29 to 0.36), but by 2004 a return to the 1972 levels (0.28).

Students in 2004 were also about as likely to attend private schools as their counterparts in 1972, at least as evident in these data sets. Whereas the proportion of students attending private schools in NLS-72 was 0.07, the proportion of seniors in the ELS attending private schools was 0.08, with slight increases in the intervening cohorts (0.12 in 1982 and 0.16 in 1992).

Black-White Differences in School Characteristics

When considering the types of schools that black and white students attended between 1972 and 2004, we see that some differences have remained over time. In 1972, black students were likely to attend schools for which the average proportion of schools classified as urban was 0.44 compared with white students, who attended schools for which the average proportion was 0.27. There were slight changes in the proportion of black students attending urban schools between 1972 and 2004, and the gap between blacks and whites increased from 0.17 in 1972 to 0.27 in 2004.

In reference to the socioeconomic composition of schools as measured by Duncan's SEI, the black-white difference in typical schools narrowed between 1972 (–0.18) and 1982 (–0.08) but increased by 1992 (–0.21) and even more by 2004 (–0.26). Apparently, the closing of the black-white socioeconomic circumstances among individuals was not reflected in the socioeconomic composition of schools that blacks and whites attended.

If a high minority composition is viewed as a proxy for schools that have historically been underserved by the education system in terms of providing high-quality resources, services, and instruction, then the increasing proportion of high-minority schools suggests a lack of progress for black students. In 1972, the average proportion of minority composition for schools attended by white students was 0.17, compared with 0.36 for schools attended by black students—a .19 gap. This gap actually declined somewhat by 1982 (0.16), but then increased to 0.24 by 1992 and to 0.46 by 2004. Although there were small changes in minority composition for schools attended by whites between 1972 and 2004, from 0.17 to 0.14, the average for schools attended by black students increased from 0.36 to 0.60, a .0.24 point change. Comparing minority composition in the typical schools between 1972 and 2004, there was actually an increase of the difference between blacks and whites (0.19 to 0.46).

When comparing the proportion of black and white students attending private schools, we find a slight increase for white students and a slight decrease for black students. In 1972, for example, the proportion of white students was 0.07, and that of black students 0.05. By 2004, the proportion of white students had risen to 0.10, and that of black students had dropped to 0.03. The black-white gap was –0.02 in 1972 and –0.07 in 2004, indicating that private school attendance is more prevalent among white students than among black and that the gap has increased over time.

Changes in Self-Reported Placement

The school organization characteristics just described are important because they have been related to student achievement, and because any changes over time for one racial-ethnic group in relation to another may suggest growing or declining inequities. Although school characteristics help describe elements of the organization, it is also important to consider schooling characteristics such as track placement, because these provide indicators of student perceptions of educational opportunities within the organization (Bidwell and Kasarda 1980; Gamoran 2004).

When considering student-reported track placement for the different national cohorts of high school seniors, we see an overall increase in the proportion of students reporting placement in the academic track. For example, in 1972 it was 0.47, dropping slightly in the early 1980s to 0.39, but increasing again to 0.47 in 1992 and to 0.55 in 2004 (see table 2.3).

Black-White Differences in Self-Reported Placement

When looking at black-white differences in student-reported track placement, we see a significant increase of the proportion of black students reporting academic-track placement, suggesting a closing of the tracking gap. In 1972, the figure was 0.28, but in 2004 was 0.53, a 0.25 point increase. Half of all white students in 1972 reported academic track placement and the proportion increased to 0.56 in 2004. Although the black-white difference was 0.22 in 1972, it declined significantly over the next decade so that by 1982 it was 0.07, where it held steady through 1992 (0.08), dropping to 0.03 by 2004. In short, the significant reduction between 1972 and 2004 suggests a possible benefit for black students in terms of perceived educational opportunities.

Although there were some changes in family and school characteristics that may contribute to the closing of the achievement gap, what are the relationships among these trends? How do the changes in the family background and school measures relate to black-white test score trends? By decomposing the effects of these measures on mathematics achievement, we can provide some answers to these questions.

Decomposing Gap Changes, 1972 to 2004

The methods we use allow us to disentangle the changes that have occurred for black and white students. First, we examine the changes between 1972 and 2004 in levels (means) of the individual, family background, and school measures. Scaling these changes by the 1972 and 2004 regression coefficients, we are able to examine how much family and school changes contributed to the changes that occurred in the test score gap between black and white students. In other words, we examine the results allowing for not only changes in the means of family and school measures but also their relationships to mathematics achievement as measured by the 1972 and 2004

Table 2.3   Differences in Self-Reported Track Placement in LS Data

	1972	1982	1992	2004	Change
Academic track	0.47	0.39	0.47	0.55	+0.08
Whites	0.50	0.42	0.49	0.56	+0.06
Blacks	0.28	0.35	0.41	0.53	+0.25
B-W difference	−0.22	−0.07	−0.08	−0.03	+0.19

Source: Authors' compilation.

coefficients. Second, when presenting the 1972 to 2004 results, we first focus on changes in family and school measures from a model not including academic track; we then reestimate our model and re-do the decomposition adding the measure for self-reported track. Third, we present additional decompositions between 1972 to 1982 and 1982 to 2004 because research has shown that the gap closed significantly during the 1970s and that since that time progress in the closing of the gap stalled, especially during the 1990s.

The results of the 1972 to 2004 decompositions for mathematics achievement scores appear in table 2.4. The column of Δ's in table 2.4 is the change in the black-white test score gap for the period being considered that is associated with the changes in the means for the variable (rows) being considered. The percent column is the percentage of the total black-white test score gap for the period being considered to which changes in that particular variable correspond. Positive percentages indicate that the predicted test score gaps would have decreased or converged. Negative percentages indicate that the black-white test score gap would have increased or diverged.

Between 1972 and 2004, relative to white students, black students' individual and family characteristics—parent education level, family income, and parent occupational status—improved. These changes were large, particularly when scaled by the 1972 regression coefficients; these relative changes corresponded to 62.37 percent of the change in the test score gap. If scaled by the 2004 coefficients, they corresponded to 36.24 percent of the change in the test score gap. Because the changes in scores range between 36.24 and 62.37 percent, it is likely that these scores are simply upper and lower bounds, and the real reduction likely falls between this range (that is, the average of 49.31 percent).

If one considers only changes in the mean school variables measured here when scaled by either the 1972 or 2004 regression coefficients, the changes would predict a corresponding substantial increase in the black-white test score gap between 1972 and 2004. Overall, changes in school-level means corresponded to a 76 to 81 percent increase in the black-white gap, depending on whether 1972 or 2004 coefficients were used. The

Table 2.4   Decomposition of the Relationships of Family Background, Perceived Track, and School Measures to the Convergence in Black-White Mathematics Scores, 1972 to 2004

	1972 Coefficients as Weights				2004 Coefficients as Weights			
	Δ	Percentage	Δ	Percentage	Δ	Percentage	Δ	Percentage
Individual and family measures total	-0.119	62.370	-0.074	39.410	-0.069	36.240	-0.067	35.190
Female	-0.015	7.730	-0.014	7.530	-0.007	3.680	-0.008	4.410
Family income	-0.021	11.140	-0.015	8.060	-0.004	2.290	-0.005	2.440
Parental education	-0.058	30.240	-0.030	15.760	-0.048	25.000	-0.044	23.110
Occupational status	-0.025	13.260	-0.015	8.060	-0.010	5.270	-0.010	5.230
School measures total	0.156	-81.950	0.158	-82.800	0.146	-76.510	0.144	-75.170
School mean socioeconomic status	0.011	-5.930	0.006	-3.070	0.025	-13.250	0.022	-11.460
School percent minority	0.119	-62.500	0.141	-73.830	0.116	-60.570	0.124	-64.830
Private school	0.010	-4.990	0.002	-0.980	0.004	-2.200	0.001	-0.330
Urban school	0.013	-6.780	0.002	-0.850	0.000	-0.160	-0.002	1.100
Rural school	0.003	-1.750	0.008	-4.070	0.001	-0.330	-0.001	0.350
Student-reported academic track			-0.169	88.510			-0.069	36.030
Total explained	0.037	-19.570	-0.086	45.110	0.077	-40.280	0.008	-3.960
Unexplained	-0.228	119.570	-0.105	54.890	-0.268	140.280	-0.199	103.960
Total change	-0.191		-0.191		-0.191		-0.191	

Source: Authors' compilation.

Note: The predicted change between 1972 and 2004 is the total change of –0.191. The negative sign means that estimated black-white test score gap decreased over this time period. The Δ column includes the estimated changes in means for the variable of interest scaled by either the 1972 or 2004 coefficients. For example, when considering the individual and family measures together, the estimated change due to changes in means evaluated using 1972 coefficients was –0.119, which divided by –0.191 is 62.37 percent.

increases in black students' likelihood of being segregated in high-minority schools corresponded to a 62.50 percent increase in the black-white mathematics gap when scaled by the 1972 coefficients and to a 60.57 percent increase when relying on the 2004 coefficients. In addition, increases in the gap of the average school SES attended by blacks and whites were associated with a 5.93 to 13.25 percent increase in the black-white mathematics gap, depending on whether scaling relied on the 1972 or 2004 coefficients, respectively.

Decomposing Gap Changes: Self-Reported Track Placement, 1972 to 2004

When including students' self-reported track placement and comparing the results to the previous results, a few patterns stand out. First, the corresponding changes in the black-white gap are similar whether the track placement measure is included (see figure 2.2).

Without the track variable, changes in school-level means corresponded to a 76 to 82 percent increase in the black-white gap, depending on whether 1972 or 2004 coefficients were used; with the track measure, there was a 75 to 83 percent increase. Second, for the family measures, including the track measure did not change the results much when using the 2004 coefficients, but did when using the 1972 coefficients. When using the 2004 coefficients for the family measures, changes in the black-white gap were associated with a 36.24 percent reduction without the track measure and a 35.19 percent reduction with it. When relying on the 1972 coefficients, changes in the family measures were associated with a 62.37 percent reduction in the gap without the track variable, and a 39.41 percent reduction with track placement included.

Considering the student self-reported track measure in these models, we find that the significant decrease of the mathematics test score gap between white and black students was connected to the change in black students' perceived schooling experiences. As discussed previously, the gaps in proportions between blacks and whites enrolled in the college track were −0.22 in 1972 and −0.03 in 2004. These differences indicate that although white students tended to report academic track placement more than black students, these differences decreased significantly between 1972 and 2004. In table 2.4, when this change is scaled to the 1972 regression coefficients, these changes in reported track placement between black and white students corresponded to an 88.51 percent change in the mathematics score gap. When relying on the 2004 coefficients, these changes were associated with a 36.03 percent change. The main reason for this is the large coefficient for track placement in 1972 compared with 2004 (see table 2A.2).

Figure 2.2   Changes in Measures Associated with Change in Black-White Mathematics Differences

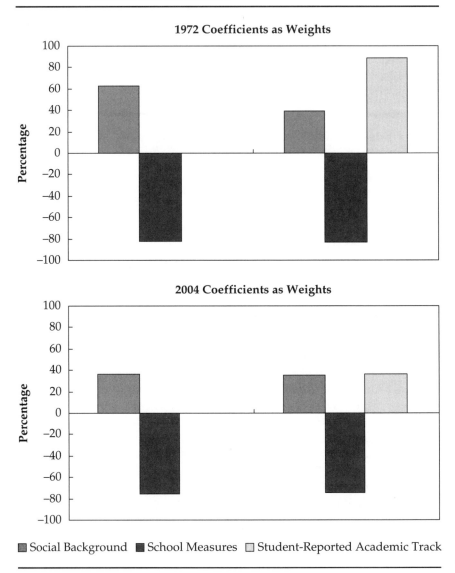

Source: Authors' compilation.

Decomposing Gap Changes, 1972 to 1982 and 1982 to 2004

Because of the significant progress of black students between 1972 and 1982, when the test score gap declined significantly, and the stalled progress between 1982 and 2004, we further decomposed the test score gap for these subperiods with our estimates from the models. The results are presented in table 2.5. We include the variable for self-reported track placement because other results for the family and school measures show consistency, with and without the track measure included.

Between 1972 and 1982, we noted that the black-white differences in family background measures improved for black students, but only slightly (see table 2.1). When scaling the changes, we see that they corresponded with a 2.1 percent increase in the test score gap when scaled with the 1972 coefficients and a 0.02 decrease with the 1982 (table 2.5). The slight improvement in the family background measures, then, resulted in little change in the predicted gap.

The school conditions for black students improved substantially compared with their white counterparts in this period, however, especially when considering school SES and minority composition. In table 2.2, we noted that the black-white gap in school mean SES declined from −0.18 to −0.08 and that minority composition declined from 0.19 to 0.16. These changes indicated that blacks were attending schools with higher socioeconomic conditions, and schools that were less segregated.

These positive changes in school characteristics for black students between 1972 and 1982 corresponded with a reduction in the test score gap. When scaling the changes in school SES composition with the 1972 and 1982 coefficients, we see that the gap declined by 6.66 and 13.26 percentage points, respectively. Moreover, when scaling the changes in minority school composition, we see that the mathematics gap decreased by 7.48 percentage points using the 1972 coefficients and by 8.11 points using the 1982 coefficients. Using all the school measures, we see an overall reduction of between 18.63 and 22.66 percentage points, depending on whether the 1972 or 1982 coefficients were used.

When examining the changes in the student self-reported track measure in these 1972–1982 models, we find that the significant decrease in the black-white gap for track placement (from −0.22 to −0.07 in table 2.3) was associated with a significant reduction in the black-white mathematics gap. As we can see in table 2.5, these changes—when scaled to the 1972 regression coefficients—corresponded to a 48.89 percent change in the mathematics score gap. When relying on the 1982 coefficients, the changes were associated with a 39.88 percent change.

Between 1982 and 2004, the black-white gap in mathematics changed only slightly in the data for these senior cohorts. In fact, changes in the pre-

Table 2.5   Decomposition of the Relationships of Variables to Convergence in Black-White Mathematics Scores

| | 1972 to 1982 | | | | 1982 to 2004 | | | |
| | 1972 as Weights | | 1982 as Weights | | 1982 as Weights | | 2004 as Weights | |
	Δ	Percentage	Δ	Percentage	Δ	Percentage	Δ	Percentage
Individual and family measures total	0.007	-2.100	-0.001	0.020	-0.070	-89.530	-0.036	-46.870
Female	-0.010	3.840	-0.005	1.810	-0.002	-2.400	-0.002	-2.990
Family income	-0.007	2.600	-0.002	0.600	-0.005	-6.640	0.003	3.340
Parental education	0.014	-5.010	0.008	-3.040	-0.045	-57.250	-0.032	-40.630
Occupational status	0.010	-3.530	-0.002	0.650	-0.018	-23.240	-0.005	-6.590
School measures total	-0.050	18.630	-0.061	22.660	0.227	288.270	0.228	290.190
School mean SES	-0.018	6.660	-0.036	13.260	0.047	60.350	0.089	113.010
School percent minority	-0.020	7.480	-0.022	8.110	0.175	222.240	0.141	179.500
Private school	0.000	0.000	0.000	0.000	0.000	-0.370	0.001	0.800
Urban school	0.001	-0.420	0.000	0.140	0.000	-0.210	-0.001	-0.820
Rural school	-0.013	4.910	-0.003	1.150	0.005	6.260	-0.002	-2.300
Student-reported academic track	-0.132	48.870	-0.108	39.880	-0.030	-38.550	-0.015	-19.230
Total explained	-0.177	65.410	-0.169	62.570	0.126	160.180	0.176	224.090
Unexplained	-0.093	34.590	-0.101	37.430	-0.047	-60.180	-0.097	-124.090
Total Change	-0.270		-0.270		0.079		0.079	

Source: Authors' compilation.
Note: The predicted change between 1972 and 1982 is the total change of -0.270. The negative sign means that estimated black-white test score gap decreased over this time period. Between 1982 and 2004, the estimated black-white difference was 0.079, indicating that the gap actually increased (positive sign). The Δ column includes the estimated changes in means for the variable of interest scaled by coefficients for the noted cohort (1972, 1982, or 2004). For example, when considering the individual and family measures together, the estimated change due to changes in means evaluated using 1972 coefficients was 0.007, which divided by -0.270 is -2.1 percent, suggesting that changes in family measures were associated with an increase in the gap by a very small amount.

dicted gap between 1982 and 2004 reveal that the gap widened slightly (total change of 0.079 in table 2.5). Thus the changes in the means and coefficients should be interpreted very cautiously given that they are explaining a change that is close to zero. Also, note that the estimated change is now positive (0.079) rather than negative, which it was in the results discussed previously. That said, the directions of the associations are consistent with our previous discussion: improvements in family measures for black students are associated with reductions in the predicted gap over the period, as are changes in the measure for track placement. Specifically, the improvements in family background measures are associated with a decrease in the gap by 89.53 percentage points using the 1982 coefficients and by 46.87 percent using the 2004 coefficients (or 68.20 percent if taking the average). It is significant that changes in school characteristics that did not benefit black students over this period are positively associated with increases in the gap in these models. Growing disparities in school percent minority and school mean SES are particularly consequential. For example, the changes in school minority composition are associated with a 288.27 percent increase using the 1982 coefficients and a 290.19 percent increase using the 2004 coefficients (289.23 percent average). However, as noted, overall these changes are small in an absolute sense, they appear large when expressed as a percentage only because the total change in the gap being explained during this time is so small.

Discussion

Our analyses examined several family and school factors related to black-white test score differences in mathematics. We set out to address certain limitations of past research by analyzing nationally representative data between 1972 and 2004 to address how selected family and school measures changed during this time and the correspondence of changes in these measures to the black-white mathematics gap. We end with a discussion of the policy implications that arise from our work.

Changes in Families and Score Gaps in Mathematics

When examining the relationships between family background measures and test score gaps among blacks and whites, researchers frequently analyze cross-sectional or panel data for a particular cohort of students to explain the percentage of the gap due to family or other social indicators (see Berends et al. 2005; Jencks and Phillips 1998; Phillips et al. 1998; Hedges and Nowell 1998, 1999; Brooks-Gunn, Klebanov, and Duncan 1996; Grissmer et al. 1994). In such analyses, family background explains about 25 to 30 percent of the cross-sectional black-white gap in scores for a particular cohort (see Hedges and Nowell 1998, 1999).

To further disentangle the relationships of family background to student achievement gaps, our analysis looks at the changes across cohorts in the levels of the background measures themselves and scaled these relationships to the 1972 and 2004 regression coefficients as well as those for sub-periods. For different senior cohorts between 1972 and 2004, our analyses reveal that the improved socioeconomic conditions of black students—such as parents' occupational status, educational attainments, and income— corresponded to a significant amount of convergence in black-white test scores. Changes in the family background measures we analyzed corresponded to a 35 to 62 percent decrease of the black-white mathematics gap between 1972 and 2004, depending on whether the 1972 or 2004 coefficients were used in the calculations. Because of the wide range in these percentage decreases, it is likely that the 1972 and 2004 coefficients provide upper and lower bounds, and the true decrease is closer to the average of 48.5 percent.

Changes in Schools and Score Gaps in Mathematics

Despite some of the positive changes in family circumstances for black students, the changes that occurred between schools corresponded to an increase of the black-white mathematics test score gap between 1972 and 2004. In our analyses, black students were more likely than white students to attend higher-minority schools in 2004 than in 1972, and these changes corresponded to an increase in the black-white mathematics achievement gap over the period. Several other authors have commented on the increasing segregation of minority students in recent years (Orfield and Yun 1999; Orfield 2001).

As our analyses suggest, changes in the minority composition of high schools did not correspond to a decrease of the black-white achievement gap during the period we analyzed. The increases in composition corresponded instead to an increase in test score gaps. Across the models that used the 1972 and 2004 coefficients and included or excluded the tracking measure, on average, minority school composition considered by itself was associated with a 65 percent increase in the black-white test score gap. Alternative measures of school desegregation, such as the dissimilarity index, yield slightly different estimates of how segregation may have affected the score gaps during the 1990s (see Vigdor and Ludwig, chapter 5, this volume). Nevertheless, both measurement approaches suggest that trends in desegregation were a factor in the stalled progress of those decades.

Compared with these between-school changes, changes in the perceived within-school experiences of black students over the thirty-year period were positive. Increases in the number of black students who report academic track placement (that is, increases in the social-psychological measure of perceived schooling opportunities) corresponded to a 36 to

40 percent decrease of the black-white mathematics gap between 1972 and 2004. Such significant changes are consistent with those in the organization of tracking that occurred over the same period (Lucas 1999). Certainly, deeper understanding of the changes and trends in the racial diversity of schools, academic tracking, and achievement is warranted (see Bankston and Caldas 2001; Lucas and Berends 2002).

Dropout Rates and Score Gap Trends

One issue that emerges when analyzing test score trends over time is that factors our models do not consider may have an influence. This type of omitted variables bias is important in any type of multivariate analyses and is worthy of critical reflection. Thus, when assessing the impact of changes in family background and school characteristics on student achievement trends over the past several decades, it is important consider three important issues: the direction and magnitude of the relationship (coefficient) of each characteristic, the average change (mean) that occurred for that characteristic across different cohorts and whether the mean changes were greater for black students compared with white students. For example, a family variable might have a strong, independent effect on achievement, but if the variable, on average, did not change more between two or more cohorts for black students than for white students, then it will not affect the average estimated black-white test score gap over time.

One such characteristic has to do with changes in dropout rates between the early 1970s and 2004. In examining national rates for the United States, we see a decrease for black students relative to their white counterparts. The U.S. Department of Education defines *status dropout* rates as "the percentage of individuals who are not enrolled in high school and who do not have a high school credential, irrespective of when they dropped out" (Laird, DeBell, and Chapman 2006, 6). We can see in figure 2.3 that, according to the U.S. Department of Education, dropout rates have decreased for the nation as a whole. The overall trend also indicates that the black-white dropout rate has converged. As a result, it can be argued that because students who are dropouts tend to have lower achievement scores (Berends 1995), those students who would have dropped out are now reflected in test score means, particularly the mean test score differences between black and white students.

However, when considering the cohorts analyzed in this chapter, it is important to note the dropout rate differences for 1972, 1982, 1992, and 2004. In 1972, the average gap between black and white students was 9 percent; in 1982, it narrowed to 7 percent; in 1992, to 6 percent; and in 2004 to 5 percent (see figure 2.3). Although an important convergence in the black-white dropout rate occurred overall between 1972 and 2004, the changes in the gap across the cohorts we analyze were not large. The largest conver-

Figure 2.3   Black-White Dropout Rates, Sixteen- to Twenty-Four-Year-Olds

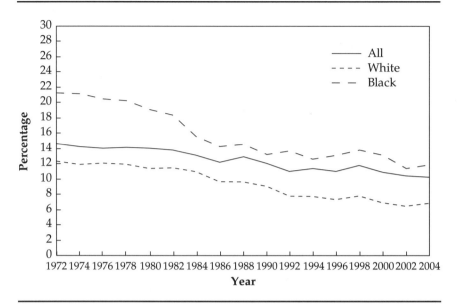

Source: Authors' compilation from Laird, DeBell, and Chapman (2006).

gence occurred between 1972 and 1982 (from a 9 to a 7 percentage point gap). In considering the test score trends observed across these LS cohorts, we see the largest convergence in the test score gap between 1972 and 1982 (nearly one-fifth of a standard deviation). Based on the argument about dropouts above, the gap should not have converged as much as it did over these ten years. Thus, we argue that though changes in dropout rates may be important, they likely would not have affected the results for the particular cohorts we examined.[7]

Persistent Inequality in the Mathematics Score Gaps

Our analysis reveals a mixed picture of the progress of black students relative to whites. On the one hand, individual, family, and some school circumstances have changed in ways that benefit blacks across cohorts, and this corresponds to the decrease of the black-white mathematics score gap that occurred between 1972 and 2004. However, significant test score disparities remain between blacks and whites, particularly in terms of their socioeconomic circumstances and achievement scores. Despite an approximate 20 percent reduction in the black-white mathematics test score gap in the LS databases we examine, the unadjusted differences remain about 0.81 of a standard deviation in mathematics—a large difference. Moreover, despite the large gains in the family background measures considered here, black students' continue to attend schools that are high minority and low SES, and indeed gaps on these measures widened from 1982 to 2004. Thus, though a great deal of progress has been made in improving some conditions of black students relative to whites, substantial inequalities remain (see Neal 2006).

Because of the positive changes in black families' socioeconomic circumstances that we found in our analyses, their correspondence with closing the achievement gaps, and the large gaps that remain, understanding what it would take to close remaining gaps is a policy exercise worth the difficult work and debate. As William Julius Wilson observed, "it could take several generations before adjustments in socioeconomic inequality produce their full benefits" (1998, 98; see also Neal 2006; Jencks and Phillips 1998).

Our analyses suggest that educational policy and reform need to be attentive to educational opportunities within schools and between schools by addressing issues related to secondary school tracking and the increasing isolation of minority students in predominately minority schools. Our analyses show significant advances for black students who reported academic-track placement in 2004 compared with the early 1970s. A large portion of the black-white mathematics score convergence corresponded to the increase over time of black students' social-psychological perceptions of their college-track opportunities compared with white students. Although our analyses cannot attribute cause to our tracking measure— especially given that our measure is a proxy not only for track placement but also for other schooling perceptions (such as motivation, educational expectations, and the like)—the correspondence we find in our analysis is consistent with those researchers who speculate that tracking and the resulting increased opportunities for minority and black students has played an important part in closing the achievement gaps (see Cook and Evans 2000; Grissmer et al. 1998; Porter 2005). Further attention to tracking in research and policy is therefore worth consideration.

In considering public policies that may contribute to the closing of the achievement gap—whether by providing more support to families, increasing educational opportunities within schools, or decreasing the racial isolation between schools—it is important to understand that family and welfare policies need to be coordinated with educational policies. This complex yet critical interplay is often ignored by policy makers, however. Unless such decision makers think about how educational policies complement or conflict with policies related to such spheres as welfare, work, and housing, the goal of narrowing achievement gaps will continue to face significant obstacles.

Appendix: Operationalization of Family and School Measures

Race-Ethnicity   All the surveys included items for students to report their racial-ethnic group. We include dummy variables to classify students into nonoverlapping categories for African American or black, Latino or Latina, non-Latino–white, and Other (mostly Asian and American Indian). In our analyses, we focus on the nonoverlapping student groups of blacks and whites; our overall sample estimates also include Latinos and the Other category.

Gender   In the analysis gender is included as a dummy variable equal to one if the student is female.

Parents' Education   Both mother's and father's educational attainment are included as separate variables in our analysis. Each senior cohort survey provided information to create a measure for parents' years of education, coded as ten years if the parent did not finish high school, twelve if the parent was a high school graduate, fourteen if the parent attended some college, sixteen if the parent received a four-year college degree, and eighteen if the parent received a graduate or professional degree. This variable included missing information when the father was not present in the household. We include a dummy variable for these missing data in our analyses, which is a proxy for single mother household as well as missing data for other reasons. (Because we did not have single parent variables in the 1972 data, we could not analyze this measure across cohorts.)

Parent Occupational Status   We included a measure of parent's SEI or occupational status measure, based on the maximum status reported for the father or mother (range in the data sets 7.33 through 70.21). On the surveys, respondents could select from a list of comparable occupations, which were then translated into Duncan's SEI (Duncan 1961) scores. NLS-72 through ELS-04 include a measure of Duncan's SEI (Duncan 1961), and this particular SEI measure is based on the 1960 census. Thus, the estimates of change provided use this earlier time frame for the SEI as a reference point.

Family Income   The income variable represents a particularly challenging problem due the fact that each survey used different intervals for students to select. Initially, we aimed to rescale all of the income variables to 1972 using the annual average consumer price index (CPI) value for each year. However, many categories in the upper tail of the income distribution for NELS-92 are not found in the other cohorts. As an alternative, we parsed each cohort's income values into five categories (five quintiles) by assigning the income category midpoints to the responses and then found the corresponding quintiles from the population as reported by the Census

Bureau. We created dummy variables for each quintile; the median income category in each cohort was the reference group.

School Socioeconomic Composition   The student-level measures for parent income and mother's education level were aggregated to the school level. Thus we were able to calculate the percentage of students within each school in the income quintiles as well as the average parent education level in the school.

School Minority Composition   School administrators NLS-72, HSB-82, and NELS-92 were asked about the percentage of various population groups that attended the school. Based on this information. we were able to create two school-level variables that measured the percentages of black and Latino students enrolled at each school. In ELS-04, the percentage minority was based on the combined student-level aggregate of black and Latino group reporting.

School Sector   Schools were classified as public or private. The categories were not directly comparable across NLS-72, HSB-82, NELS-92, and ELS-04, because NELS and ELS differentiated the private sector into additional categories. However, all the databases included a composite measure from which we were able to create a simple dummy variable for private schools (public schools as reference group).

School Urban Locale   Schools were located in urban, rural, or suburban locales.[8] We created dummy variables for each with rural as the reference category.

High School Track Placement   The data set included a question for measuring the students' perceptions of their secondary school track positions, either academic, general, or vocational. Although these measures are only general markers of students' positions within the educational stratification system (Lucas 1999; Gamoran and Berends 1987; Gamoran 1989), the academic group includes students who typically take courses for college-bound students (either an officially mandated program of courses or a more unofficial sequence within the curriculum). General track students refer to those who take neither courses oriented specifically toward college admission and acceptance, nor those focused on a specific vocation (such as vocational-track students). Dummy variables were created for track, with academic track coded as one and nonacademic track as zero for the reference group (see Gamoran 1987).

Missing Data   For our measures that had more than 3 percent missing data, we used multiple imputation procedures to replace missing data (see Little and Rubin 2002) and included a dummy variable in our analyses for measures and cases that relied on imputation of missing data.

Table 2.A1   Relationships of Variables (without Academic Track Measure) to Achievement, Weighted

	1972		1982		1992		2004	
Variable	Coefficient	Standard Error	Coefficient	Standard Error	Coefficient	Standard Error	Coefficient	Standard Error
Intercept	43.167*	0.592	37.076*	0.492	35.391*	0.711	37.668*	0.704
Female	−2.532*	0.149	−0.965*	0.118	−0.645*	0.162	−1.205*	0.160
Income quintile 1	−2.417*	0.264	−1.213*	0.182	−1.982*	0.280	−2.463*	0.302
Income quintile 2	−0.691**	0.235	−0.363	0.200	−1.139*	0.264	−1.382*	0.264
Income quintile 4	0.216	0.251	0.270	0.189	0.480*	0.243	1.058*	0.229
Income quintile 5	−0.237	0.276	−0.001	0.193	1.215**	0.297	2.817*	0.307
Missing income data	0.088	0.271	−0.835*	0.234	−0.035	0.285	—	—
Father's education	0.506*	0.039	0.619*	0.031	0.673*	0.045	0.457*	0.042
Missing father's education	−1.018	0.809	−0.447	0.251	−0.644**	0.281	—	—
Mother's education	0.401*	0.044	0.326*	0.035	0.423*	0.047	0.471*	0.045
Missing mother's education	−3.975*	0.916	−1.845*	0.311	−0.282	0.316	—	—
Parents' maximum SEI	0.027*	0.004	0.049*	0.003	0.037*	0.005	0.024*	0.005
Missing SEI data	−5.008*	0.202	−1.544*	0.390	−0.341	0.405	—	—
School mean socioeconomic status	1.334*	0.249	1.963*	0.241	1.078*	0.242	2.980*	0.391
School percent minority	−0.045*	0.005	−0.052*	0.004	−0.037*	0.005	−0.044*	0.005
Private school	1.874*	0.369	1.540*	0.357	0.739	0.453	0.828**	0.404
Urban school	−0.346	0.247	0.001	0.272	0.494	0.350	−0.008	0.297
Rural school	0.381	0.273	0.070	0.235	0.036	0.322	0.072	0.328

Source: Authors' compilation.
*$p < .001$; **$p < .05$

Table 2.A2   Relationships of Variables (with Academic Track Measure) to Seniors' Mathematics Achievement, Weighted

Variable	1972		1982		1992		2004	
	Coefficient	Standard Error	Coefficient	Standard Error	Coefficient	Standard Error	Coefficient	Standard Error
Intercept	44.812*	0.529	39.944*	0.457	37.103*	0.659	37.092*	0.689
Female	-2.465*	0.133	-1.161*	0.109	-1.011*	0.150	-1.443*	0.157
Academic track	8.992*	0.147	7.338*	0.122	7.236*	0.160	3.660*	0.163
Income quintile 1	-1.571*	0.235	-0.903*	0.168	-1.412*	0.258	-2.420*	0.295
Income quintile 2	-0.351*	0.209	-0.253	0.185	-0.788*	0.243	-1.373*	0.258
Income quintile 4	0.010	0.223	0.089	0.174	0.317	0.224	1.006*	0.224
Income quintile 5	-0.318	0.245	-0.093	0.178	0.876*	0.274	2.658*	0.300
Missing income data	-0.217	0.241	-0.583**	0.217	0.025	0.262	—	—
Father's education	0.265*	0.035	0.393*	0.029	0.495*	0.042	0.430*	0.041
Missing father's education	0.035	0.720	-0.404	0.231	-0.537**	0.259	—	—
Mother's education	0.182*	0.039	0.170*	0.033	0.276*	0.043	0.419*	0.044
Missing mother's education	-3.802*	0.815	-1.599*	0.287	-0.044	0.291	—	—
Parents' maximum SEI	0.012*	0.004	0.036*	0.003	0.026*	0.004	0.023*	0.005
Missing SEI data	-3.676*	0.181	-1.684*	0.361	-0.011	0.374	—	—
School mean socioeconomic status	0.691*	0.232	1.377*	0.222	1.272*	0.233	2.578*	0.380
School percent minority	-0.054*	0.005	-0.058*	0.004	-0.039*	0.005	-0.047*	0.005
Private school	0.367	0.349	-0.057	0.331	-0.647	0.440	0.123	0.394
Urban school	-0.043	0.232	0.015	0.251	0.400	0.340	0.056	0.288
Rural school	0.884*	0.256	0.207	0.217	0.023	0.315	-0.076	0.319

Source: Authors' compilation.
*p < .001; **p < .05

Table 2.A3   Variables for Longitudinal Studies High School Senior Populations, 1972

	All		Black		White	
	Mean	Standard Deviation	Mean	Standard Deviation	Mean	Standard Deviation
Number of students	14,469		1,719		11,370	
Math IRT	51.94	10.00	43.10	9.48	53.24	9.40
Female	0.50	0.50	0.57	0.50	0.50	0.50
Academic track	0.47	0.50	0.28	0.45	0.50	0.50
Income quintile 1	0.34	0.47	0.61	0.49	0.30	0.46
Income quintile 2	0.16	0.37	0.19	0.39	0.16	0.36
Income quintile 4	0.13	0.34	0.04	0.20	0.14	0.35
Income quintile 5	0.12	0.32	0.03	0.16	0.13	0.33
Missing income data	0.21	0.41	0.19	0.39	0.21	0.41
Father's education	12.54	2.43	11.27	1.83	12.73	2.44
Missing father's education	0.01	0.11	0.04	0.20	0.01	0.10
Mother's education	12.31	2.04	11.57	1.92	12.45	2.03
Missing mother's education	0.01	0.10	0.02	0.15	0.01	0.09
Parents' maximum SEI	36.93	26.81	19.72	24.07	39.55	26.23
Missing SEI data	0.19	0.40	0.44	0.50	0.16	0.37
School mean socioeconomic status	−0.05	0.51	−0.21	0.47	−0.03	0.50
School percent minority	19.08	25.94	36.21	28.01	16.60	22.13
Private school	0.07	0.25	0.05	0.21	0.07	0.25
Suburban school	0.48	0.50	0.38	0.48	0.49	0.50
Urban school	0.29	0.46	0.44	0.50	0.27	0.45

Source: Authors' compilation.

Table 2.A4   **Variables for Longitudinal Studies High School Senior Populations, 1982**

	All		Black		White	
	Mean	Standard Deviation	Mean	Standard Deviation	Mean	Standard Deviation
Number of students	20,888		2,593		14,255	
Math IRT	49.66	9.99	43.22	9.48	51.56	9.40
Female	0.51	0.50	0.54	0.50	0.52	0.50
Academic track	0.39	0.49	0.35	0.48	0.42	0.49
Income quintile 1	0.29	0.45	0.51	0.50	0.24	0.43
Income quintile 2	0.13	0.33	0.14	0.35	0.12	0.33
Income quintile 4	0.15	0.36	0.08	0.28	0.17	0.37
Income quintile 5	0.16	0.37	0.06	0.24	0.19	0.39
Missing income data	0.10	0.30	0.13	0.34	0.10	0.30
Father's education	12.88	2.51	11.76	2.04	13.19	2.53
Missing father's education	0.09	0.28	0.23	0.42	0.06	0.24
Mother's education	12.65	2.13	12.22	2.12	12.84	2.10
Missing mother's education	0.05	0.23	0.10	0.31	0.04	0.19
Parents' maximum SEI	47.79	22.26	38.47	24.72	50.64	20.77
Missing SEI data	0.03	0.16	0.07	0.26	0.01	0.12
School mean socioeconomic status	−0.05	0.56	−0.04	0.56	0.04	0.54
School percent minority	26.11	31.13	36.67	31.87	20.82	25.32
Private school	0.12	0.32	0.10	0.30	0.12	0.33
Suburban school	0.47	0.50	0.44	0.50	0.50	0.50
Urban school	0.25	0.43	0.36	0.48	0.21	0.41

Source: Authors' compilation.

Table 2.A5   Variables for Longitudinal Studies High School Senior Populations, 1992

	All		Black		White	
	Mean	Standard Deviation	Mean	Standard Deviation	Mean	Standard Deviation
Number of students	11,661		1,022		8,442	
Math IRT	50.50	9.88	43.94	8.66	51.92	9.55
Female	0.51	0.50	0.54	0.50	0.50	0.50
Academic track	0.47	0.50	0.41	0.49	0.49	0.50
Income quintile 1	0.25	0.43	0.41	0.49	0.19	0.39
Income quintile 2	0.14	0.34	0.18	0.39	0.13	0.33
Income quintile 4	0.19	0.39	0.11	0.32	0.21	0.41
Income quintile 5	0.13	0.33	0.04	0.19	0.15	0.36
Missing income data	0.16	0.37	0.14	0.35	0.14	0.35
Father's education	13.67	2.46	12.96	2.13	13.92	2.44
Missing father's education	0.14	0.35	0.25	0.43	0.11	0.31
Mother's education	13.29	2.30	12.96	2.26	13.50	2.25
Missing mother's education	0.11	0.31	0.12	0.32	0.09	0.28
Parents' maximum SEI	47.19	21.55	40.63	22.70	49.58	20.57
Missing SEI data	0.05	0.21	0.06	0.24	0.03	0.18
School mean socioeconomic status	0.05	0.76	−0.08	0.69	0.13	0.72
School percent minority	25.37	29.67	42.10	31.90	18.12	22.10
Private school	0.16	0.37	0.11	0.31	0.17	0.38
Suburban school	0.37	0.48	0.33	0.47	0.40	0.49
Urban school	0.36	0.48	0.44	0.50	0.30	0.46

Source: Authors' compilation.

Table 2.A6   **Variables for Longitudinal Studies High School Senior Populations, 2004**

	All		Black		White	
	Mean	Standard Deviation	Mean	Standard Deviation	Mean	Standard Deviation
Number of students	12,267		1,434		7,285	
Math IRT	50.51	9.97	43.90	8.27	51.93	9.38
Female	0.50	0.50	0.52	0.50	0.50	0.50
Academic track	0.55	0.50	0.53	0.50	0.56	0.50
Income quintile 1	0.12	0.33	0.26	0.44	0.07	0.25
Income quintile 2	0.17	0.38	0.24	0.43	0.14	0.34
Income quintile 4	0.37	0.48	0.24	0.43	0.42	0.49
Income quintile 5	0.14	0.35	0.06	0.24	0.18	0.38
Missing income data	n.a.	n.a.	n.a.	n.a.	n.a.	n.a.
Father's education	13.74	2.44	13.33	2.30	14.05	2.35
Missing father's education	n.a.	n.a.	n.a.	n.a.	n.a.	n.a.
Mother's education	13.62	2.24	13.40	2.11	13.93	2.14
Missing mother's education	n.a.	n.a.	n.a.	n.a.	n.a.	n.a.
Parents' maximum SEI	55.97	19.19	51.31	21.35	59.55	16.33
Missing SEI data	0.01	0.10	0.01	0.12	0.01	0.09
School mean socioeconomic status	0.06	0.41	−0.11	0.35	0.15	0.37
School percent minority	27.17	29.72	59.52	28.74	13.52	16.64
Private school	0.08	0.28	0.03	0.17	0.10	0.30
Suburban school	0.52	0.50	0.43	0.49	0.55	0.50
Urban school	0.28	0.45	0.47	0.50	0.20	0.40

Source: Authors compilation.

Acknowledgments

Please direct all correspondence to Mark Berends, University of Notre Dame, 810 Flanner Hall, Notre Dame, IN 46556 (mberends@nd.edu). We are grateful to Samuel Lucas, Thomas Sullivan, and R. J. Briggs, who collaborated on our previous research on test score gaps. We appreciated the generous cooperation of the National Center for Education Statistics in providing the restricted-use data, of Donald Rock and Judith Pollack of ETS, who shared with us their IRT expertise and data, and of Mathilde Dutoit of Scientific Software International, who provided technical support. Of course, this paper does not reflect the views of these agencies or individuals; any errors are the responsibility of the authors.

Notes

1. These data include the Equality of Educational Opportunity survey of 1965 (EEO), the National Longitudinal Study of the High School Class of 1972 (NLS-72), the High School and Beyond surveys (HSB), The National Longitudinal Surveys of Youth of 1980 (NLSY:80), the National Education Longitudinal Study of 1988 (NELS:88), and the National Assessment of Educational Progress (NAEP).
2. To measure a broader range of abilities and the extent of cognitive gains between eighth and twelfth grades, NELS included various forms of the tenth and twelfth grade tests to avoid floor and ceiling effects. For example, tenth graders in the first follow-up test administration were given different forms of the test depending on how they scored in the eighth grade base year. In mathematics, there were seven forms, and in reading there were five forms—all differing in difficulty to provide better estimates of achievement throughout the proficiency distribution (for further details on the psychometric properties of the NELS tests, see Rock and Pollack 1995). Specific test score information allowed us to link scores across all these NELS mathematics forms and the NLS and HSB cohorts. There were no common items to equate the reading scores in the senior NELS sample to the previous cohorts.
3. Equating the 2004 scores is unlikely to affect the results reported here. The equated 1972, 1982, and 1992 mathematics scores were very similar to the unequated scores (see Berends et al. 2005; see also Hedges and Nowell, 1998, 1999), so the 2004 are also likely to be similar, though we do not know for sure at this point. The equated black-white gaps in 1972, 1982, and 1992 were 1.01, 0.835, and 0.808, respectively (see figure 2.1), and the unequated scores for those time periods were 1.02, 0.850, and 0.820. In large part, we believe these equated and unequated scores are similar because of the nature of the items asked on the mathematics tests.
4. Although data on family structure (for example, single-parent family) are available for more recent cohorts of seniors, measures of family structure are not available for high school seniors in 1972. Other analyses have shown that the association between single-parent family and student achievement is mediated by family income (Grissmer et al. 1994). Thus, to make comparisons across cohorts, these measures are not included.

5. The predicted means used in the decompositions are not simple averages of the dependent variable. Given the nested nature of the data and the consequent need to employ a multilevel or hierarchical model (HLM), the cited equation would not necessarily hold if the change in the difference between simple averages $\Delta \bar{y}_{t1} - \Delta \bar{y}_{t0}$ were placed on the left-hand side since the estimates of β generated under HLM assumptions are not necessarily such that $\bar{y} = \bar{x} \cdot \hat{\beta}$. In fact, $\bar{y} = \bar{x} \cdot \hat{\beta}$ under HLM only if the HLM estimates of β are the same as the OLS estimates of β. Using the HLM estimates of β for our model, the dot product $\bar{x} \cdot \hat{\beta}$ equals $\hat{y}$, that is the predicted value of y given $\bar{x}$. Thus, we use $\hat{y}$ in each of our decompositions so that equality will hold between our manipulations of $\bar{x} \cdot \hat{\beta}$. The differences between $\hat{y}$ and $\bar{y}$ are slight in all cases.

6. The descriptive statistics and statistical models use the appropriate weights available in the data.

7. Others have called into question the way that the U.S. Department of Education measures dropout rates (Heckman and LaFontaine 2007; Swanson 2004; Warren and Halpern-Manners 2007). Because the U.S. Department of Education relies on the Current Population Survey which includes students who obtained a GED certificate, this makes the dropout rate seem less than it really is. James Heckman and Paul LaFontaine (2007) show that there was little convergence in the dropout rate between black and white students over the past several decades. This lack of convergence suggests that black dropouts, who tend to have lower test scores, would not affect the results presented in our analysis.

8. Locale is a seven-digit code on the CCD, defined as: (1) large city—a central city of a CMSA or MSA, with the city having a population greater than or equal to 250,000; (2) mid-size city—a central city of a CMSA or MSA, with the city having a population less than 250,000; (3) urban fringe of a large city—any incorporated place, census-designated place, or nonplace territory within a CMSA or MSA of a large city and defined as urban by the Census Bureau; (4) urban fringe of a mid-size city—any incorporated place, census-designated place, or nonplace territory within a CMSA or MSA of a mid-size city and defined as urban by the Census Bureau; (5) large town—an incorporated place or census-designated place with a population greater than or equal to 25,000 and located outside a CMSA or MSA; (6) small town—an incorporated place or census-designated place with population less than 25,000 and greater than or equal to 2,500 and located outside a CMSA or MSA; (7) rural—any incorporated place, census-designated place, or nonplace territory designated as rural by the Census Bureau. The usual practice is to combine these into three categories: urban = 1, 2; suburban–large town = 3, 4, 5; and rural–small town = 6, 7.

References

Bankston, Carl L., III, and Stephen J. Caldas. 2001. *A Troubled Dream: The Promise and Failure of School Desegregation in Louisiana.* Nashville, Tenn.: Vanderbilt University Press.

Berends, Mark. 1995. "Educational Stratification and Students' Social Bonding to School." *British Journal of Sociology of Education* 16(3): 327–51.

Berends, Mark, and Daniel Koretz. 1996. "Reporting Minority Students' Test Scores: How Well Can the National Assessment of Educational Progress

Account for Differences in Social Context?" *Educational Assessment* 3(3): 249–85.

Berends, Mark, Susan Bodilly, and Sheila Nataraj Kirby. 2002. *Facing the Challenges of Whole-School Reform: New American Schools After a Decade.* Santa Monica, Calif.: RAND Corporation.

Berends, Mark, David W. Grissmer, Sheila N. Kirby, and Stephanie Williamson. 1999. "The Changing American Family and Student Achievement Trends." *Research in Sociology of Education and Socialization* 12: 67–101.

Berends, Mark, Samuel R. Lucas, Thomas Sullivan, and R. J. Briggs. 2005. *Examining Gaps in Mathematics Achievement Among Racial-Ethnic Groups, 1972–1992.* Santa Monica, Calif.: RAND Corporation.

Berliner, David C., and Bruce J. Biddle. 1995. *The Manufactured Crisis: Myths, Fraud, and the Attack on America's Public Schools.* New York: Addison-Wesley.

Bidwell, Charles E., and James D. Kasarda. 1980. "Conceptualizing and Measuring the Effects of School and Schooling." *American Journal of Education* 88(4): 401–30.

Brooks-Gunn, Jeanne, Pamela Klebanov, and Greg J. Duncan. 1996. "Ethnic Differences in Children's Intelligence Test Scores: Role of Economic Deprivation, Home Environment, and Maternal Characteristics." *Child Development* 67(2): 396–408.

Cain, Glen G. 1986. "The Economic Analysis of Labor Market Discrimination: A Survey." In *Handbook of Labor Economics,* vol. I, edited by O. Ashenfelter and R. Layard. New York: Elsevier Science.

Campbell, Jay R., Catherine M. Hombo, and John Mazzeo. 2000. *NAEP 1999 Trends in Academic Progress: Three Decades of Student Performance.* Washington: U.S. Department of Education.

Cancio, A. Silvia, T. David Evans, and David J. Maume. 1996. "Reconsidering the Declining Significance of Race: Racial Difference in Early Career Wages." *American Sociological Review* 61(4): 541–56.

Christensen, Bryce J. 1990. *Utopia Against the Family.* San Francisco, Calif.: Ignatius Press.

Cook, Michael D., and William N. Evans. 2000. "Families or Schools? Explaining the Convergence in White and Black Academic Performance." *Journal of Labor Economics* 18(4): 729–54.

Corcoran, Mary E., and Greg J. Duncan. 1979. "Work History, Labor Force Attachment, and Earnings Differences between the Races and Sexes." *Journal of Human Resources* 14(1): 3–20.

Duncan, Otis Dudley. 1961. "A Socioeconomic Index for All Occupations." In *Occupations and Social Status,* edited by A. J. Reiss, Jr. New York: Free Press.

———. 1967. "Discrimination Against Negroes." *The Annals of the American Academy of Political and Social Science* 371(1): 85–103.

———. 1968. "Inheritance of Poverty or Inheritance of Race?" In *On Understanding Poverty: Perspectives from the Social Sciences,* edited by Daniel P. Moynihan. New York: Basic Books.

Ferguson, Ronald F. 1998. "Can Schools Narrow the Black-White Test Score Gap?" In *The Black-White Test Score Gap,* edited by Christopher Jencks and Meredith Phillips. Washington, D.C.: The Brookings Institution Press.

Gamoran, Adam. 1987. "The Stratification of High School Learning Opportunities." *Sociology of Education* 60(3): 135–55.

————. 1989. "Measuring Curriculum Differentiation." *American Journal of Education* 97(2): 129–43.

————. 2004. "Classroom Organization and Instructional Equity." In *Can Unlike Students Learn Together? Grade Retention, Tracking, and Grouping,* edited by M. C. Wang and H. J. Walberg. Greenwich, Conn.: Information Age Publishing.

Gamoran, Adam, and Mark Berends. 1987. "The Effects of Stratification in Secondary Schools: Synthesis of Survey and Ethnographic Research." *Review of Educational Research* 57(4): 415–35.

Gill, Andrew M., and Robert J. Michaels. 1992. "Does Drug Use Lower Wages?" *Industrial & Labor Relations Review* 45(3): 419–34.

Goldhaber, Dan D. 1996. "Public and Private High Schools: Is School Choice an Answer to the Productivity Problem?" *Economics of Education Review* 15(2): 93–109.

Green, Patricia J., Bernard L. Dugoni, and Steven J. Ingels. 1995. *Trends Among High School Seniors, 1972–1992.* NCES 95-380. Washington: National Center for Education Statistics.

Grissmer, David, Ann Flanagan, and Stephanie Williamson. 1998. "Why Did the Black-White Test Score Gap Narrow in the 1970s and 1980s?" In *The Black-White Test Score Gap,* edited by Christopher Jencks and Meredith Phillips. Washington, D.C.: Brookings Institution Press.

Grissmer, David W., Sheila N. Kirby, Mark Berends, and Stephanie Williamson. 1994. *Student Achievement and the Changing American Family.* Santa Monica, Calif.: RAND Corporation.

Hamilton, Laura S., Brian M. Stecher, and Steven P. Klein, editors. 2002. *Making Sense of Test-Based Accountability in Education.* Santa Monica, Calif.: RAND.

Hanushek, Eric A. 1986. "The Economics of Schooling: Production and Efficiency in Public Schools." *Journal of Economic Literature* 24(3): 1141–77.

————. 1989. "The Impact of Differential Expenditures on School Performance." *Educational Researcher* 18(4): 45–51.

————. 1994. *Making Schools Work: Improving Performance and Controlling Costs.* Washington, D.C.: Brookings Institution Press.

Haveman, Robert, and Barbara Wolfe. 1994. *Succeeding Generations: On the Effects of Investments in Children.* New York: Russell Sage Foundation.

Heckman, James J., and Paul A. LaFontaine. 2007. "The American High School Graduation Rate: Trends and Levels." NBER Working Paper 13670. Cambridge, Mass.: National Bureau of Economic Research.

Hedges, Larry V., and Amy Nowell. 1998. "Black-White Test Score Convergence since 1965." In *The Black-White Test Score Gap,* edited by Christopher Jencks and Meredith Phillips. Washington, D.C.: Brookings Institution Press.

————. 1999. "Changes in the Black-White Gap in Achievement Test Scores." *Sociology of Education* 72(2): 111–35.

Herrnstein, Richard J., and Charles Murray. 1994. *The Bell Curve: Intelligence and Class Structure in American Life.* New York: Free Press.

Ingels, Steven J., Kathryn L. Dowd, John D. Baldridge, James L. Stipe, Virginia H. Bartot, and Martin. R. Frankel. 1993. *NELS:88 Second Follow-Up Student Component Data File User's Manual.* Washington: National Center for Education Statistics.

Jencks, Christopher, and Meredith Phillips. 1998. *The Black-White Test Score Gap.* Washington, D.C.: Brookings Institution Press.

Jones, Calvin, Miriam Clark, Geraldine Mooney, Harold McWilliams, Ioanna Crawford, Bruce Stephenson, and Roger Tourangeau. 1983. *High School and*

Beyond. 1980 Sophomore Cohort First Follow-Up 1982 Data File User's Manual. Washington: National Center for Education Statistics.

Koretz, Daniel. 1986. *Trends in Educational Achievement.* Washington: Congressional Budget Office.

———. 1992. "What Happened to Test Scores, and Why?" *Educational Measurement: Issues and Practice* 11(4): 7–11.

Koretz, Daniel M., and Mark Berends. 2001. *Changes in High School Grading Standards in Mathematics, 1982–1992.* Santa Monica, Calif.: RAND.

Kreft, Ita G. G., and Jan De Leeuw. 1998. *Introducing Multilevel Modeling.* Thousand Oaks, Calif.: Sage Publications.

Laird, Jennifer, Matthew DeBell, and Chris Chapman. 2006. *Dropout Rates in the United States: 2004.* NCES 2007-024. Washington: National Center for Education Statistics.

Lankford, Hamilton, and James Wyckoff. 1995. "Where Has the Money Gone? An Analysis of School District Spending in New York." *Educational Evaluation and Policy Analysis* 17(2): 195–218.

Little, Roderick J. A., and Donald B. Rubin. 2002. *Statistical Analysis with Missing data.* New York: John Wiley & Sons.

Lucas, Samuel R. 1999. *Tracking Inequality: Stratification and Mobility in American High Schools.* New York: Teachers College Press.

Lucas, Samuel R., and Mark Berends. 2002. "Sociodemographic Diversity, Correlated Achievement and the Factor Tracking." *Sociology of Education* 75(4): 328–48.

Lucas, Samuel R., and Adam Gamoran. 2001. "Track Assignment and the Black-White Test Score Gap: Divergent and Convergent Evidence from 1980 and 1990 Sophomores." Paper presented to the Brown Center on Education Policy and Edison Schools Conference, Closing the Gap: Promising Strategies for Reducing the Achievement Gap. Washington, D.C., February 2, 2001. Accessed at http://www.brookings.edu/events/2001/0202education.aspx.

Murray, Charles, and Richard J. Herrnstein. 1992. "What's Really Behind the SAT-Score Decline?" *Public Interest* 106: 32–56.

Neal, Derek A. 2006. "Why Has Black-White Skill Convergence Stopped?" In *Handbook of Economics of Education,* edited by Eric Hanushek and Finis Welch. Amsterdam: North-Holland.

Oakes, Jeannie, Adam Gamoran, and Reba Page. 1992. "Curriculum Differentiation: Opportunities, Outcomes, and Meanings." In *Handbook of Research on Curriculum,* edited by Philip W. Jackson. New York: Macmillan.

Oaxaca, Ronald. 1970. "Male-Female Wage Differentials in Urban Labor Markets." *International Economic Review* 14(3): 693–709.

Orfield, Gary. 2001. *Schools More Separate: Consequences of a Decade of Resegregation.* Cambridge, Mass.: Harvard University, The Civil Rights Project.

Orfield, Gary, and John J. Yun. 1999. *Resegregation in American Schools.* Cambridge, Mass.: Harvard University, The Civil Rights Project.

Phillips, Meredith, Jeanne Brooks-Gunn, Greg J. Duncan, Pamela Klebanov, and Jonathan Crane. 1998. "Family Background, Parenting Practices, and the Black-White Test Score Gap." In *The Black-White Test Score Gap,* edited by Christopher Jencks and Meredith Phillips. Washington, D.C.: Brookings Institution Press.

Popenoe, David. 1993. "American Family Decline, 1960–1990: A Review and Appraisal." *Journal of Marriage and the Family* 55(1): 27–55.

Porter, Andrew C. 2005. "Prospects for School Reform and Closing the Achievement Gap." In *Measurement and Research in the Accountability Era,* edited by C. A. Dwyer. Mahway, N.J.: Lawrence Erlbaum.

Raudenbush, Stephen W., and Anthony S. Bryk. 2002. *Hierarchical Linear Models: Applications and Data Analysis Methods,* 2nd ed. Thousand Oaks, Calif.: Sage Publications.

Riccobono, John, Louise B. Henderson, Graham J. Burkheimer, Carol Place, and Jay R. Levinsohn. 1981. *National Longitudinal Study: Base Year (1972) Through Fourth Follow-Up (1979) Data File User's Manual.* Washington: National Center for Education Statistics.

Rock, Donald A., Thomas L. Hilton, Judith M. Pollack, Ruth B. Ekstrom, and Margaret E. Goertz. 1985. *Psychometric Analysis of the NLS and the High School and Beyond Test Batteries.* Washington: National Center for Education Statistics.

Rock, Donald A., and Judith M. Pollack. 1995. *NELS: 88 Base Year Through Second Follow-Up Psychometric Report.* Washington: National Center for Education Statistics.

Sahling, Leonard G., and Sharon P. Smith. 1983. "Regional Wage Differentials: Has the South Risen Again?" *Review of Economics and Statistics* 65(1): 131–35.

Sayer, Liana C., Suzanne M. Bianchi, and John P. Robinson. 2004. "Are Parents Investing Less in Children? Trends in Mothers' and Fathers' Time with Children." *American Journal of Sociology* 110(1): 1–43.

Snijders, Tom A. B., and Roel J. Bosker. 1999. *Multilevel Analysis.* London: Sage Publications.

Sørensen, Aage B., and Stephen L. Morgan. 2000. "School Effects: Theoretical and Methodological Issues." In *Handbook of Research in the Sociology of Education,* edited by M. T. Hallinan. New York: Kluwer Academic Press.

Swanson, Christopher B. 2004. "State Approaches for Calculating High School Graduation Rates." NCLB Implementation Report. Washington, D.C.: The Urban Institute, Education Policy Center. Accessed at http://www.urban.org/url.cfm?ID=410848.

Tyack, David, and Larry Cuban. 1995. *Tinkering Toward Utopia: A Century of Public School Reform.* Cambridge, Mass.: Harvard University Press.

Uhlenberg, Peter, and David Eggebeen. 1986. "The Declining Well-Being of American Adolescents." *The Public Interest* 82(1): 25–38.

Warren, John Robert, and Andrew Halpern-Manners. 2007. "Is the Glass Half Empty or Filling Up? Reconciling Divergent Trends in High School Completion and Dropout." *Educational Researcher* 36(6): 335–43.

Wilson, William Julius. 1998. "The Role of Environment in the Black-White Test Score Gap." In *The Black-White Test Score Gap,* edited by Christopher Jencks and Meredith Phillips. Washington, D.C.: Brookings Institution Press.

Chapter 3

Income Inequality and Racial Gaps in Test Scores

MARY E. CAMPBELL, ROBERT HAVEMAN,
TINA WILDHAGEN, AND BARBARA L. WOLFE

Income inequality among American families has grown steadily since the 1980s, as has the racial-ethnic income gap (Lichter and Eggebeen 1993). These trends are documented in table 3.1, which shows that the standard deviation of U.S. family income doubled from the 1980 to 2000 decennial censuses, and that the gaps between racial-ethnic groups also rose during this period. For example, the family income gap between blacks and whites rose by more than 50 percent over these two decades, and that between Latinos and whites almost doubled. Simultaneously, urban economic segregation grew, with particularly dramatic growth among African Americans and Latinos; the poor and the rich became increasingly isolated geographically (Jargowsky 1996).

Could this growth in income inequality, together with social factors related to the development, contribute to our understanding of trends in the black-white test score gap, and in particular the failure of this gap to narrow during the late 1980s and 1990s? In this chapter, we focus on the potential impact of changes in the level and distribution of family income and the larger context within which adolescents and young adults learn.

Family income is a powerful predictor of educational attainment, especially college attendance (Belley and Lochner 2007; Campbell et al. 2005). Although estimates of the impact of family income on test scores vary depending on the dataset used and the standardized test score analyzed, the results consistently show a small but statistically significant effect (see, for example, Phillips et al. 1998; Brooks-Gunn, Klebanov, and Duncan 1996). This literature implies that changes in income inequality between black and white families may also explain trends in the racial gap in test scores (Phillips et al. 1998). We build on this insight and study the relationship between the growth in the income advantage of white children relative to black and Latino children and recent trends

110

in the test score gap. Could this factor suggest why the gap has failed to narrow in recent years?

Racial and Ethnic Gaps in Test Scores

As we have noted, racial gaps in adolescent test scores declined significantly in the 1980s, but this progress stalled in the 1990s. Interestingly, the racial and ethnic gaps did not narrow consistently across the distribution of test scores. Although blacks and whites became more equal at the bottom and middle of the distribution, there was little improvement in the racial gap at the top for several types of standardized tests (Hedges and Nowell 1999). Significant test score gaps between Latinos and non-Latino whites also exist, and they too narrowed during the 1980s. Like blacks, Latinos are underrepresented at the top of the distribution. For example, "20% of whites, 3% of blacks [and] 7% of Mexican Americans . . . scored above a 600 on the SAT math section. . . . Eight percent of whites . . . 2% of blacks [and] 3% of Mexican Americans . . . scored above 600 on the SAT verbal section in 1990" (Kao and Thompson 2003, 421). These patterns have troubling implications in terms of future opportunities available to minorities, given that returns to standardized test scores are nonlinear, with greater rewards at the top of the distribution (Hedges and Nowell 1999).

The Effect of Income on Test Scores

A primary explanation for the narrowing of the black-white test score gap during the 1970s and 1980s focuses on changes in material deprivation and family characteristics over these decades. According to this argument, black parents' socioeconomic gains relative to whites since the 1970s account for much of the narrowing of the gap by increasing the relative scores of black students (see, for example, Armor 1992). For instance, the percentages of black parents who completed high school increased dramatically from 1974 to 1999 (Hoffman, Llagas, and Snyder 2003). Variation in parental education, income, and poverty status have been found to explain between 25 and 50 percent of the variation in the black-white test score gap (Brooks-Gunn, Klebanov, and Duncan 1996; Cook and Evans 2000; Grissmer, Flanagan, and Williamson 1998; Hedges and Nowell 1998); other research has indicated that convergence in socioeconomic status accounted for a large portion of the reduction in the gaps observed in the 1980s (Hedges and Nowell 1998).

Overall, most of the studies of the effects of income on vocabulary and reading test scores have suggested that the effect is statistically significant but often small (Blau 1999; Hill and O'Neill 1994; Mayer 1997; Parcel and Menaghan 1990; Phillips et al. 1998; Votruba-Drzal 2006; Yeung, Linver, and Brooks-Gunn 2002). Although some studies include enough information on the dependent and independent variables to allow quantitative estimates of the size of income effects, such comparisons are generally unsatisfactory because of substantial differences in control variables and estimation methods among the studies.[1]

Moreover, comparing estimates of the size of the effect of income on test scores is difficult because of the considerable variability in how income is measured and in the specification of the functional form of income. For instance, whereas some studies use measures of permanent income (such as averaging annual income over a period of years), others use measures of income at a given time. Several studies have shown that permanent income has a larger effect on test scores than a single year measure (Aughinbaugh and Gittleman 2003; Blau 1999; Korenman, Miller, and Sjaastad 1995; Mayer 1997, but see Dahl and Lochner 2005). One advantage of using permanent income is that it avoids the problem of transitory income fluctuations, but some have argued that it also reflects the "underlying educational quality of the home" (Hanushek 1992, 96).

Another issue complicating the comparison of income effects is that income is measured at different developmental stages, ranging from infancy to adolescence. Using NLSY data, David Blau (1999) found that the effect of mothers' permanent wages on vocabulary test scores was largest for six- to ten-year-olds. Similarly, Elizabeth Votruba-Drzal (2006) found that the effects of income during early childhood (birth to five or six years old) on Peabody Individual Achievement Test (PIAT) reading and math scores were larger than were those of income during middle childhood (from five or six years old to eleven or twelve years old). This complicates the question of how changing income distributions would impact changing test scores, given that the impact of the change would depend on the age of the child.

Additionally, some researchers have modeled the effects of income on test scores as linear and others have modeled them as nonlinear, allowing the effect of income to vary across levels of income. One would expect to find diminishing test score returns to income, with additional income having larger consequences for lower-income families, in part, because the proportion of family income reserved for children falls as income rises (Lazear and Michael 1988). Research, however, has produced mixed evidence on the diminishing effects of family income on vocabulary scores. For instance, Blau (1999) divided income into five categories and found that movement from the third to the fourth income category, which he likened to a move from the lower-middle class to the middle class, had the largest effect. However, using spline regression, Alison Aughinbaugh and Maury Gittleman (2003) found no difference in the effect of income on vocabulary test scores between those below and above one half of median family income.

Of course, test scores may be sensitive to not only the family's own income, but also other factors related to the family's socioeconomic status, such as neighborhood characteristics, peer characteristics, and characteristics of the schools children attend. The effects of racial gaps in wealth on the test score gap, for example, have been found to operate principally through racial differences in cultural capital (Orr 2003). The convergence of black and white test scores coincided with massive school desegregation, which is related to black students' gains from 1970 to 1990 (Grissmer, Flanagan, and Williamson 1998). Reviewing thirty-nine studies of mandatory desegregation policies, Robert Crain and Rita Mahard (1978) reported that twenty-four of them found positive effects of desegregation on black students' achievement gains. One test of the effect of school poverty on test scores determined, however, that the impact was "miniscule" (Myers, Kim, and Mandala 2004), and others have found that school policies do not usually advantage one group more than another (Bali and Alvarez 2003). Average neighborhood income is also positively related to test scores, though this relationship appears to be significant for whites across neighborhoods, and only significant for blacks who are living in neighborhoods with a large black population (Lopez Turley 2003).

How Has Income Inequality Changed?

Although income inequality, as measured by the Gini coefficient, was fairly stable in the 1970s, it rose rapidly during the 1980s and 1990s from 0.39 in 1970 to 0.46 in 2000 (DeNavas, Cleveland, and Webster 2003).[2] Over the same period, the 95:20 percentile household income ratio grew from 6.29 to 8.10 (DeNavas-Walt, Cleveland, and Webster 2003). Although both the upper and lower tails of the income distribution have diverged from the median over this period (Daly and Valletta 2006), most of the growth in income inequality has occurred in the top tail of the distribution (Autor, Katz, and Kearney 2005; Feenberg and Poterba 2000; Gottschalk and Danziger 2005, Piketty and Saez 2003; Schwabish 2006).

What happened to the black-white and Latino-white income gaps during this period of overall increases in individual and family income inequality? In spite of increases in mean family incomes of blacks and Latinos since the 1970s, the racial and ethnic gaps in mean family income have grown substantially between 1980 and 2000 (see table 3.1). Although racial and ethnic minorities have experienced income gains since 1970, the overall increase in family income inequality has contributed to growing black-white and Latino-white economic gaps over the same period.

Relating Trends in the Income Distribution to Test Score Inequality

The 1980s was the decade of both the largest increase in overall income inequality and the largest increase in blacks' test score gains relative to whites. On the basis of this, one might argue that the growth in overall income inequality in more recent years cannot be responsible for the

Table 3.1   Family Income by Race and Ethnicity, 1970 to 2000 Decennial Census

| | Mean Family Income, Total Population | Standard Deviation, Family Income | Mean Family Income | | | Racial Gaps | |
			Whites	Blacks	Latinos	White-Black	White-Latino
1970	$47,272	34,398	$50,780	$31,857	$38,641	$18,922	$12,138
1980	$45,361	31,659	$47,771	$32,567	$37,509	$15,204	$10,261
1990	$52,534	45,458	$55,841	$36,804	$40,166	$19,036	$15,675
2000	$59,015	60,589	$64,150	$40,628	$44,625	$23,522	$19,525

Source: IPUMS data, 1970 to 2000 Census.
Note: All income numbers are adjusted to 2000 dollars.

declining progress on the test score gap. However, the effect of increasing income inequality on the inequality of test scores may operate with a significant lag. For example, if experiences of inequality at a young age affect test scores at a later age, then the effects of income inequality on test scores would not be observed until years after the increase in income inequality. Mary Campbell and her colleagues, for example, found evidence that family income inequality experienced as a young child results in later inequality in years of education completed (2005). There may also have been countervailing forces in the 1980s that offset any deleterious effects of overall income inequality on the test score gap. For example, blacks' growing enrollment in college preparatory classes might have offset the negative effect of overall income inequality on the gap during the 1980s (Grissmer, Flanagan, and Williamson 1998).

There are three reasons that overall income inequality might increase racial and ethnic gaps in test scores. First, because black and Latino families are overrepresented in the lower half of the income distribution, overall income inequality may affect black and Latino students more than whites. In this case, an increase in overall inequality affects the test score gap because it widens racial-ethnic inequality. A second reason is that, regardless of whether overall inequality affects their own incomes, blacks and Latinos are more likely to live in neighborhoods and attend schools that are negatively affected by overall income inequality. For instance, because of residential segregation, middle-income black families are more likely than their white counterparts to live in neighborhoods with few resources and institutions that promote academic achievement (Massey and Denton 1993). Finally, black students may be more sensitive to certain contextual effects than whites, such as school quality and relationships with teachers (Oates 2003).

Data and Methods

Our data come from waves 1 and 3 of the National Longitudinal Study of Adolescent Health (Add Health), a nationally representative sample of adolescents. In the first wave, Add Health surveyed students in high schools and middle schools across the country between September 1994 and April 1995, collecting 20,746 detailed in-home interviews. The third wave of data was collected between 2001 and 2002, when 15,170 wave 1 respondents were reinterviewed in their homes (Udry 2003). At wave 3, the respondents were eighteen to twenty-eight years old, with most of them between ages nineteen and twenty-four (for more information on the design of the Add Health sample, see Harris et al. 2003). Because this chapter focuses on educational inequality between blacks, whites, and Latinos, we limit our sample to non-Latino whites, non-Latino blacks, and Latinos, excluding other racial-ethnic groups and individuals who selected more than one race. One of the strengths of these data is the time sequencing of the variables; the outcome is measured at wave 3, and the key independent variables of family income and experiences of inequality are measured at wave 1, when the respondents were still adolescents. Although this does not allow us to make definitive causal claims, it does reduce the possibility that reverse causality is at work; adults' test scores might affect their own earned income, but it is far less likely that the test score of the young adult impacted their parents' incomes.

Variables

We use the percentile rank on the Add Health Picture Vocabulary Test (PVT), an abbreviated version of the Peabody Picture Vocabulary Test Revised (PPVT-R), to measure vocabulary test score rank at wave 3. In the PVT, the tester asks the respondent to select which of four pictures best represents the meaning of a spoken word.[3] The PPVT is commonly used as a measure of the size of an English-speaking individual's vocabulary and verbal comprehension (Jencks and Phillips 1998; Phillips et al. 1998). Vocabulary tests tend to find larger black-white differences than reading and mathematics tests, but those gaps narrow with age (Phillips et al. 1998). Both racial gaps and social class gaps in vocabulary test scores are established early in life and remain somewhat constant during schooling (Farkas and Beron 2004).

The percentile rankings we use are constructed by Add Health as an "index of relative standing among same-age peers that is comparable across age groups" (Udry 2003). These rankings have a significant advantage in that all age groups have the same floor and ceiling values (0 and 100), allowing easy comparison across ages. Because the test is designed as a measure of an English-speaking person's vocabulary, we exclude from the sample children who primarily speak another language at home, as well as white and black respondents who were born abroad.[4] Excluding such respondents reduces our final sample size to N = 11,216.

The racial-ethnic gaps that we find in the Add Health picture vocabulary score are similar to the racial-ethnic gaps found in the reading NAEP scale scores for seventeen-year-olds. When expressed in units of the standard deviation of the test, the mean white-black and white-Latino gaps in vocabulary tests are 0.74 and 0.58, respectively, and the reading NAEP test has mean white-black and white-Latino gaps of 0.77 and 0.51, respectively.[5]

The key independent variables in our study are those related to family income and experiences of inequality in the local context. Our measure of family income is drawn from the parent's survey: "About how much total income before taxes did your family receive in 1994? Include your own income, the income of everyone else in your household, and income from welfare benefits, dividends, and all other sources." Total family income ranges from $0 to $999,000. It is best viewed as a one-year comprehensive measure of income.

Many studies of the impact of income on test scores include income in either linear or logged form, but a few use dummy variables or other nonlinear approaches (for example, Pungello et al. 1996). We tested for model fit using several functional forms of income and found that though complex nonlinear forms (such as quintiles) fit poorly, simpler nonlinear forms that allowed the effect of income above and below the poverty line to vary fit the data better than a log income specification. The best fit was achieved with a spline specification with two knots: at the poverty line and at twice the poverty line. We used the poverty line for the median family size in our data (four people, with a poverty line of $15,455) to calculate the knots.[6] A spline allows us to estimate the impact of changing income for individuals in each part of the income distribution (not possible with a simple dummy variable), and it allows for the possibility that income has a larger effect (greater slope) at some points in the income distribution than others. Accordingly, we include income in the model as three variables, all measured in $10,000 units: income below the poverty line for a median-sized family, income above the poverty line but below two times the poverty line, and income above that threshold.[7] The spline variables are constructed so that the coefficients measure the slope of income for that specific interval. We also include the number of years of parental education (measured as the number of completed years of education of the primary parent, usually the mother) which might be interpreted as an indicator of permanent income as well as parental human capital.

As resources in the local area are likely to be important for educational outcomes, we also include measures of resources available in the adolescent's school and friend network. We include measures of median family income in the school that the respondent attended as an adolescent and mean parental education level of the respondent's friends (calculated by matching the students to the ten friends they named on their in-school survey).[8] We also tested several other measures of local context, such as the average household income in the county, but the measures of income at the county level were not significant predictors of test scores.[9]

We also analyze how test scores are influenced by the experience of inequality in the local environment, as indicated by measures of inequality in the adolescent's school and friend network. We include the ratio of family incomes at the 90th and 10th percentile in the school (the 90:10 ratio) as a measure of inequality in the school the student attended at wave 1 (calculated by the authors for each school using the self-reported family incomes available for every student in the school). We also include a variable indicating the level of inequality in the friend network by calculating the standard deviation of parental education among the respondent's named friends.

We include controls for key demographic characteristics such as gender, age, two parents living at home at wave 1, and number of children in the home at wave 1. Finally, we also estimated change models, including vocabulary scores at wave 1 (seven years before the wave 3 test scores were collected) as an indicator of early academic achievement, giving us a conservative estimate of the effect of income that controls for other possible confounding socioeconomic factors. Because these results were not significantly different from the full models shown here, they are not included, but are available on request.

Missing data were replaced with multiple imputation, using the software NORM (Schafer 2000) to create five datasets with randomly drawn imputed values for the missing cases. The results were then combined using the method described in Paul Allison (2001), which results in unbiased estimates and revises the standard errors upwards due to the uncertainty added by the missing data. The descriptive statistics and models shown also control for Add Health's clustered probability sample design (Chantala and Tabor 1999).

Results

Descriptive statistics for the sample are presented in table 3.2. It shows that whites have the highest vocabulary scores, followed by Latinos and then by African Americans (with means at the 58th, 46th and 34th percentiles of the overall distribution of test scores, respectively). Both family income and the average income of the schools that students attend at wave 1 follow this pattern; again, whites rank highest in the distributions, followed by Latinos and then blacks. In these statistics, average family income among Latinos is 83 percent of whites' income and that of blacks is only 66 percent; for

Table 3.2　Unweighted Descriptives, National Longitudinal Study of Adolescent Health

	Whites		Blacks		Latinos		Range
	Mean	Standard Deviation	Mean	Standard Deviation	Mean	Standard Deviation	
Test scores							
Wave 3 percentile rank, PVT	58.2	26.9	34.36	28.41	46.21	28.61	0 to 100
Demographics							
Family income	$58,787	$88,408	$39,034	$59,801	$48,761	$74,274	$0 to 999k
Percent below poverty line	13		33		22		
Percent between poverty and 2× poverty	20		25		23		
Percent above 2× poverty	67		42		55		
Female	0.53		0.56		0.51		0/1
Age, wave 3	22.3	1.8	22.3	1.8	22.5	1.8	18–28
Number of children in the family, wave 1	1.18	1.08	1.50	1.44	1.57	1.36	0–10
Proportion with two parents at home, wave 1	0.59		0.34		0.51		0/1
Parent education, in years	13.9	2.7	13.7	2.9	12.7	3.0	0–20
Local and school context							
Median family income in the school	$41,036	$13,421	$32,854	$12,582	$36,487	$11,234	$14,000 to 110k
90:10 income ratio in the school	9.00	4.03	11.37	4.10	10.74	3.70	2.81 to 78,800
Mean of friends' parental education	14.11	1.78	14.08	1.78	13.30	2.04	0 to 20
Standard deviation of friends' parental education	1.99	0.93	2.00	1.00	2.23	1.15	0 to 12.73
Percent teachers with advanced degrees	50.86	25.69	45.17	25.59	43.93	30.04	0 to 100
Public school	0.93	0.27	0.96	0.21	0.96	0.20	0/1
Number of observations	7,303		2,757		1,156		

Source: Authors' compilation.
Note: All means are averaged across the five completed multiply imputed datasets, and all standard deviations are adjusted upwards to account for imputation.

Figure 3.1   Distribution of Vocabulary Test Score Percentile Rank (Wave 3)

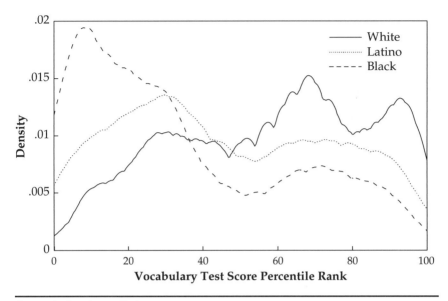

Source: Authors' compilation.

median school income, these percentages are 89 and 80 percent, respectively. Latinos are more disadvantaged than blacks in parental education, as well as the parental education of their friends, and attend schools with the fewest teachers with advanced degrees. It is important to remember that, because of our focus on an English vocabulary test, our sample excludes the 30 percent of Latinos in the overall sample who do not speak primarily English at home, so these numbers may underestimate the disadvantages facing the larger Latino community.

All three groups experience significant levels of inequality in their social contexts. Blacks attend schools with the greatest internal income inequality (a 90:10 ratio of 11 in the school), while whites attend schools with somewhat lower internal inequality (a ratio of 9). Whites also have somewhat lower inequality within their friend networks compared to Latinos (a standard deviation of friends' parental education of 2.0 compared to 2.2).

Test Score Inequality

Figure 3.1 shows how English vocabulary test scores vary across racial and ethnic groups. Blacks are the most overrepresented below the 20th national percentile, Latinos are slightly overrepresented, and whites are underrepresented. The opposite is true above the 80th percentile. Table 3.3 shows

Table 3.3   Proportion of Students Above and Below National Test Score Percentiles, by Race

	Unadjusted Scores	Adjusted for Family Income
Ratio of Proportion of Black Students to White Students		
Less than or equal to 5th	7.69	3.21
Less than or equal to 10th	6.01	2.99
Greater than or equal to 90th	0.24	0.50
Greater than or equal to 95th	0.20	0.50
Ratio of Proportion of Latino to White Students		
Less than or equal to 5th	6.34	1.55
Less than or equal to 10th	4.99	1.57
Greater than or equal to 90th	0.26	0.64
Greater than or equal to 95th	0.45	0.67

Source: Authors' compilation.

substantial racial-ethnic gaps in the tails of the distribution. The proportion of black young adults who score below the 5th national percentile on the vocabulary test is 7.7 times the proportion of white young adults who score that low, and the proportion of Latino young adults is 6.3 times the proportion of whites. At the very high end of the test score distribution, black and Latino young adults are underrepresented relative to whites; the proportion of blacks is one-fifth that of whites above the 95th percentile, and the proportion of Latinos is about one-half. This is particularly troubling because the returns to test scores are nonlinear, with the greatest returns concentrated among those with the highest scores (Hedges and Nowell 1999).

In the second column in table 3.3, we see that racial and ethnic differences in adolescent family income are related to these gaps. Adjusting for family income reduces the overrepresentation of blacks and Latinos at the bottom of the test score distribution and their underrepresentation at the top. If we were to equalize incomes across racial and ethnic groups, then, we would expect the test score distribution to equalize somewhat as well. For example, the proportion of blacks below the 5th percentile in their test scores is now estimated to be about three times the proportion of comparable whites, and the proportion of Latinos about 1.5 times.

The Relationship of Family Income to Vocabulary Test Scores

Table 3.4 presents a parsimonious model that can be viewed as indicating the maximum effect of income on test scores. It includes only two exogenous variables in addition to income—sex and age. We exclude any controls that might be related to family income to estimate the total

Table 3.4   **Model of the Maximum Effect of Income on Test Scores, by Race and Ethnicity**

	White	Black	Latino
Family income in adolescence (spline, in $10,000s)			
Below poverty line	0.532	4.940**	12.747*
	(3.007)	(1.730)	(6.129)
Above poverty line and	7.321**	4.658**	4.012
less than 2× poverty line	(1.406)	(1.532)	(3.192)
Above 2× poverty line	0.214**	0.239	0.144
	(0.077)	(0.317)	(0.211)
Female	−1.809*	−0.181	−0.678
	(0.883)	(1.732)	(2.723)
Age, wave 3	1.204**	−0.097	1.869**
	(0.368)	(0.638)	(0.706)
Constant	21.589*	23.050	−16.735
	(9.281)	(14.264)	(15.994)
Observations	7,303	2,757	1,156

Source: Authors' compilation.
Note: All models control for design effects and are averaged across the five completed multiply imputed datasets, and all standard deviations are adjusted upward to account for imputation.
Standard errors in parentheses.
*significant at $p < .05$ percent; **significant at $p < .01$

relationship between income and the respondent's percentile rank on the vocabulary test. The relationship is positive and significant for all three groups, but income, gender, and age explain very little of the variation in test scores for all three groups (R^2 between 0.03 and 0.07). For all three groups, increases in income just below or above the poverty line result in significant increase in test scores. Increases in the upper end of the income distribution have a significant (albeit small) positive effect only for whites. Consistent with David Blau's findings (1999), the largest income effect for whites occurs for those in the second income category, that is, between the poverty line and two times the poverty line. However, Blau's analysis did not test for racial differences in income effects. Our results suggest that the largest effect for blacks and Latinos occurs below the poverty line. Thus, increasing income is associated with increasing test scores, but the association is far greater at certain points in the income distribution, with the greatest impact just above or below the poverty line.[10]

The maximum effects of income presented in table 3.4 appear to be larger than those found in previous research. For instance, Blau found that, including no other regressors, a $10,000 increase in current annual income (in 1979 dollars) was associated with an increase in PPVT scores of 12 percent of a standard deviation (1999). Our results indicate that a

$10,000 increase in income for whites and blacks with incomes between the poverty line and two times the poverty line is associated with 27 percent (whites) and 16 percent (blacks) standard deviation increases in PPVT scores. The largest substantive income effect occurs for Latinos below the poverty line, with a $10,000 increase in income associated with a 45 percent standard deviation increase in scores. However, if these effects are averaged across the three income categories, they more closely match previous estimates. Treating nonsignificant effects as zero, the average increases, as a proportion of a standard deviation, associated with a $10,000 increase in income are 9 percent for whites, 11 percent for blacks, and 6 percent for Latinos.

Table 3.5 shows a more complete model of the relationships between income, social context, demographic factors, and vocabulary test scores. When controls for other key indicators of the broader social and school environment are included in the model, the relationship between income and vocabulary test scores becomes statistically nonsignificant for all three groups. Parental education, another important indicator of family resources and sometimes used as a proxy for the more permanent share of family income, remains a positive significant predictor for all three groups. Other indicators of family resources, however, such as family size and living with both parents, have significant influences on test scores only for black respondents, once other social context variables are controlled.

School and peer environments also have significant relationships with test score outcomes for all three groups. White and black youth who attend schools with higher median incomes have higher test scores, and a significant relationship between the parental education level of the peers' families and their own test scores exists for all three groups. The average socioeconomic status in school and peer environments, then, is positively related to test score outcomes. Experiencing inequality in schools, as measured by the 90:10 income ratio in the school, is positively related to test scores for whites, but negatively related to those for blacks, a finding that is robust across several different specifications of this model. The estimated effect is very small for whites but more sizable for blacks. This finding is interesting because black students encounter more inequality at school than either whites or Latinos, a finding that could have implications for school composition if a school district wishes to reduce the test score gap.

Family Income Inequality and Vocabulary Test Scores

The small and nonsignificant coefficients of family income in our test score models suggest that income inequality, as captured by changes in own family income during adolescence, is likely to have little effect on test scores, as would equalizing incomes across racial and ethnic groups. Table 3.6 illus-

Table 3.5   Full Model of Income on Test Scores

	White	Black	Latino
Family income in adolescence (spline, in $10,000s)			
Below poverty line	0.782	1.966	12.016
	(2.689)	(1.735)	(6.147)
Above poverty line and less	2.064	0.121	−0.679
than 2× poverty line	(1.355)	(1.334)	(3.304)
Above 2× poverty line	0.026	0.082	−0.027
	(0.060)	(0.234)	(0.176)
Female	−1.529*	0.966	−0.705
	(0.778)	(1.360)	(2.372)
Age, wave 3	1.170**	0.062	1.707*
	(0.316)	(0.487)	(0.714)
Number of children in the	−0.656	−1.124*	−0.511
family, wave 1	(0.404)	(0.490)	(0.800)
Two parents at home, wave 1	1.378	4.164*	0.975
	(0.947)	(1.825)	(2.598)
Parent education, in years	1.741**	1.612**	1.661**
	(0.189)	(0.393)	(0.546)
Median family income in the	0.183**	0.237*	0.101
school, divided by 1000	(0.050)	(0.119)	(0.112)
90:10 income ratio in the school,	.009**	−65.902*	−9.436
divided by 100	(.002)	(31.564)	(37.160)
Mean of friends'	2.824**	1.632**	2.432*
parental education	(0.388)	(0.485)	(0.955)
Standard deviation of friends'	−0.033	−0.161	−1.163
parental education	(0.804)	(0.958)	(1.401)
Percent teachers with	0.058**	0.082	0.065
advanced degrees	(0.022)	(0.050)	(0.049)
Public school	−4.542*	−8.734	−5.140
	(2.131)	(5.277)	(4.402)
Constant	−41.263**	−11.819	−58.057**
	(10.085)	(15.499)	(18.852)
Observations	7,303	2,757	1,156

Source: Authors' compilation.
Note: All models control for design effects and are averaged across the five completed multiply imputed datasets, and all standard deviations are adjusted upward to account for imputation.
Standard errors in parentheses.
*significant at p < .05 percent; **significant at p < .01

trates this. We simulate the effects on black and Latino mean test scores if black and Latino individuals in the xth percentile of their own income distribution were to be given the income of whites in the xth percentile of the white income distribution.[11] These simulations allow us to estimate the share of the racial-ethnic test score gap between 1970 and 2000 that results

Table 3.6   Predicted Test Scores By Racial Group

Predicted Scores Using Actual and Simulated Income for 1970 to 2000

	Predicted Scores Using Actual Income Values		Predicted Scores Using White Income Distribution		Simulated Mean- Actual Mean	Change in Gap/Size of Gap
	Mean	Standard Deviation	Mean	Standard Deviation		
Maximum Effects Model						
1970						
White	48.63	3.15				
Black	23.57	2.21	25.11	2.64	1.53	6%
Latino	33.38	6.12	35.58	6.22	2.20	15*
1980						
White	51.72	4.51				
Black	26.36	3.72	28.37	3.65	2.01	8*
Latino	38.51	6.89	40.39	6.39	1.88	14*
1990						
White	54.37	4.61				
Black	28.51	4.24	30.57	3.52	2.06	8*
Latino	41.15	6.63	42.86	5.73	1.71	13*
2000						
White	55.74	4.40				
Black	29.77	4.14	31.67	3.26	1.91	7*
Latino	42.57	6.11	44.00	5.30	1.43	11*
Full Model						
1970						
White	54.97	10.85				
Black	31.06	11.38	31.54	11.38	0.48	2
Latino	38.82	12.76	40.66	12.63	1.84	11*
1980						
White	55.94	11.12				
Black	31.69	11.42	32.06	11.29	0.38	2
Latino	42.23	12.41	43.21	11.78	0.98	7*
1990						
White	56.66	11.05				
Black	31.99	11.37	32.31	11.23	0.33	1
Latino	43.15	11.73	43.83	11.09	0.68	5
2000						
White	56.99	10.95				
Black	32.17	11.33	32.47	11.23	0.29	1
Latino	43.67	11.30	44.00	10.84	0.33	2

Source: Authors' compilation.
$N = 7303$ for whites; $N = 2757$ for blacks; $N = 1156$ for Latinos
Simulated values give each black and Latino respondent in the xth percentile of their own income distribution the income of whites at the xth percentile of the white income distribution.
*The change in the gap is significantly greater than zero, $p<.05$.

from income inequality between whites, blacks, and Latinos. Stated another way, they simulate the effect of equalizing income across all three racial-ethnic groups in each decade by simulating what would happen if each group had the same income distribution as whites.[12]

The results of this exercise, using the model that estimates the maximum effect of family income, indicate that only 6 to 15 percent of the racial-ethnic gap can be attributed to the racial-ethnic income gap. Assigning the white income distribution to black and Latino families would only shrink the gap between blacks and whites by 6 to 8 percent, and between Latinos and whites by 11 to 15 percent. Furthermore, for Latinos, the effect of equalizing income would have a declining effect over the decades. Using the more complete model that controls for other important contextual factors, equalizing income across the three groups would have an even smaller effect on the gaps in test scores.[13]

Income inequality within the white population also grew from 1970 to 2000; the standard deviation of family income for the white population (adjusted to 2000 dollars) grew from about $35,000 in 1970 to $64,000 in 2000. The predicted test scores of whites in the first column of table 3.6 shows the influence of this growing inequality, and the rising mean white family income, over time. Keeping other characteristics of the respondents the same, both the variance in test scores and the mean test scores of whites increased over these three decades as these changes in the family income distribution occurred. Had the white family income distribution remained the same as it was in 1970, and only the black and Latino family income distributions changed, our estimates suggest we would have seen a narrowing in the test score gap and smaller gaps in the tails of the distribution.

Why Does Growing Income Inequality Explain So Little?

The test score gains shown in table 3.6 are surprisingly small. Part of the reason for this nonfinding is the particular way in which income inequality has grown in the past twenty years. As table 3.4 shows, income gains near the poverty line are the most important for test scores. The largest growth in income inequality, however, has occurred at the very top of the income distribution, not evenly throughout. Table 3.7 shows the income advantage that whites in the bottom decile had over comparable blacks and Latinos, as well as the income advantage that whites in the top decile had over comparable blacks and Latinos. Although the income advantage of whites has grown at both ends of the income distribution, the steady growth at the bottom is dwarfed by the explosive growth among the very rich. Because there are no large gains in test scores associated with incomes at the very top of the distribution, the radical increase in racial-ethnic income inequality has much smaller effects on test scores than we

Table 3.7   Racial Income Gaps in the Lowest and Highest Deciles of the
             Income Distribution

	1970		1980	
	Lowest	Highest	Lowest	Highest
Gap between blacks and whites	$1,094	$7,950	$2,437	$13,646
Gap between Latinos and whites	$866	$5,645	$1,705	$9,750
	1990		2000	
	Lowest	Highest	Lowest	Highest
Gap between blacks and whites	$3,758	$34,744	$6,036	$114,053
Gap between Latinos and whites	$2,519	$34,309	$3,636	$60,317

Source: IPUMS data, 1970 to 2000 Census.
Note: All income numbers are adjusted to 2000 dollars.

would have seen had the increase in income inequality been found at the bottom. It appears there is a threshold effect; huge incomes do not appear to buy higher test scores, even if income can be used to buy other important educational outcomes, such as educational attainment. The explosion of income at the top of the distribution, then, does not suggest the need for intervention designed to offset adverse effects on the test score gap. Measurement issues could also affect these findings, however. As we noted earlier, we might also find greater effects of income on test scores if we measured income at an earlier stage of development rather than at adolescence (Blau 1999; Votruba-Drzal 2006) or if we used a measure of permanent income (Aughinbaugh and Gittleman 2003; Blau 1999; Korenman, Miller, and Sjaastad 1995; Mayer 1997, but see Dahl and Lochner 2005).

What Are the Effects of Inequality in Environment on Scores?

Another avenue through which growing inequality may influence test scores is environment, both school and peer. As table 3.5 indicates, after controlling for the qualifications of the teachers in the school and whether the school is public, the average family income of students in the school appears to have a significant effect on test scores. Black youths in schools with higher inequality (those with a greater 90:10 ratio) do have significantly lower test scores, whereas whites see a small boost in theirs. Blacks attend the most unequal schools in the sample. If the average black student were to experience the same level of income inequality at school as the average white student (a 90:10 ratio of 9.0 instead of 11.4), their test score rank would—in the full model prediction—increase by a statistically significant 1.6 percentage points (–66, the coefficient for blacks, times – .024, the drop in the 90:10 ratio divided by 100). This suggests, given that the overall gap is about 24 percentage points, an approximate 7 percent reduction. Tracking levels and changes in within-school income inequality, especially those schools attended by black students, seems warranted.

Friendship networks also appear to have a significant influence; the average level of parental education among the friends named by the respondent is significantly positively related to test scores. Comparing the three racial-ethnic groups, Latinos had networks with the lowest parental education levels, networks that could significantly depress the test scores of young Latinos. If the average Latino youth had a friendship network with a comparable level of parental education as that of their white counterparts, her or his test score would, in the full model prediction, increase by 1.7 percentage points, again about a 7 percent reduction in the overall test score gap.

From these estimates, we conclude that changes in family income alone in the last three decades have likely had very small direct effects on the vocabulary scores of young adults. Giving whites, blacks, and Latinos all the same income distribution during their adolescence would not substantially shrink the racial-ethnic gaps in vocabulary test scores, though changing the income distribution in schools might well influence the scores of black students and thus reduce such gaps. This conclusion should not, however, be interpreted to suggest that there are no effects on racial-ethnic gaps from unobserved factors that are related to family income.

Perhaps other factors related to inequality but not reflected in our model are more strongly associated with the racial-ethnic test score gap. Such factors could include unmeasured features of family structure and material deprivation, the extent of family nurture and support in early childhood, the quality of nonparental preschool care, the quality of nonschool time, unmeasured aspects of the schools children attend (for example, the extent of racial and ethnic segregation), or unmeasured characteristics of neighborhoods, peers and teachers. If these factors are significantly related to test scores or if changes in their levels or distribution differentially influence racial-ethnic groups, changes in either their level or in the inequality in their distribution could significantly influence the observed score gap.

A Puzzle: Effects of Changes in Income Distribution on Other Educational Outcomes

Although adolescent family income increases seem to have very little purchase in terms of securing percentile gains in vocabulary test scores, this does not appear to be the case with respect to gains in higher education attainment—an often used and perhaps more important predictor of ultimate economic and social success. Table 3.8 indicates the relative effects of moving from low to high positions in the income distribution—from the bottom to the top decile (or quartile)—on test scores and on indicators of educational success.

Consider first income increases within any of the income-test score distributions, shown in the bottom bank of the table. Regardless of the distribution (white, black, Latino, or total), relatively small percentile test score gains are observed as income increases. Going from the bottom to the top income decile reveals increases in average test score percentile ranging from 42 to 111 percent; moving from the bottom to the top quartile yields increases that range from 32 to 74 percent. In sum, within any relevant income distribution, test score values do not vary substantially with family income. Consistent with the findings in our models, then, income is not strongly associated with test scores, and hence changes in the distribution of income are unlikely to have large effects on test score differences.

Table 3.8 also shows the effects of family income on a few indicators of educational attainment. Except for the high school outcome, which is a weak indicator of educational success, given the pressures for school retention and the advent of the GED, gains in educational attainment in moving from the bottom to the top income percentile are substantially larger; they range from about 100 percent to nearly 500. Clearly, income increases are more strongly associated with educational attainment than they are with test scores. Presumably, ceteris paribus changes in income levels or the distribution of income are likely to be associated with substantial changes in college attainments and in racial-ethnic differences.

What social and institutional processes could account for the differences in the effects of family income on test scores relative to a variety of higher education outcomes? Several speculations seem relevant, including the role of success-related factors other than test scores, the difference in information regarding educational opportunities and payoffs between rich and poor families, the difference in family and school pressures for continued schooling and preparation for SAT-ACT examinations across income levels, the role of family income and wealth in the college admissions process, and the increasing financial burdens associated with tuition and fees and constrained borrowing (Belley and Lochner 2007).

Clearly, each of these speculations carries with it important clues regarding how society should intervene in equalizing the higher education attainments of children from high and low income families. Some focus on families, others on K–12 schools, and still others on the policies and practices of the nation's colleges and universities.

Conclusion

Our results have highlighted the puzzle but they have not resolved it. We have concluded that the observed increases in income inequality in the United States have not contributed directly to the nation's lack of progress

Table 3.8   Percentage Changes in Test Scores and Higher Education Outcomes Associated with Moving from Bottom to Top Decile (Quartile) in the Income Distribution

	Bottom Decile	Top Decile	Percentage Increase	Bottom Quartile	Top Quartile	Percentage Increase
Educational attainment						
Graduate high school	79	96	22%	81	95	17%
Attend college, conditional on being a high school graduate	31	77	150	36	74	107
Graduate college, conditional on attending college	4	23	497	5	20	296
Percentile test scores						
Black (Black income distribution)	21	44	111	25	43	74
Latino (Latino income distribution)	35	52	48	36	53	46
White (White income distribution)	46	68	47	50	66	32
Black (Total income distribution)	24	44	81	28	43	56
Latino (Total income distribution)	36	51	42	38	54	43
White (Total income distribution)	46	68	47	49	65	74
Total (Total income distribution)	35	63	80	39	61	55

Source: Authors' compilation.

in reducing racial-ethnic test score gaps. Whereas income appears to influence test scores at the bottom of the income distribution (especially for blacks), recent increases in income inequality are largely due to rapid income growth at the top. Decreases in low incomes may be related to increased nutritional deficiency, parental stress, lack of safety in neighborhoods and inadequate housing, all of which may hinder cognitive development and erode test scores, but increases in already adequate living standards do not appear to lead to sizable test score gains.

We have found that if the income distribution of English-speaking black and Latino students were to mimic that of English-speaking white students, the racial-ethnic test score gap would close only a small amount. However, we have also found evidence suggesting that within-school income inequality may influence test scores, especially for black students; policy makers should perhaps monitor developments in this pattern, especially within schools in which black students are concentrated. Of course, increasing the income of the family while the child is quite young or increasing family income over many years might also have a more substantial effect on test scores than we find here, if the small effects we note are in part because adolescence is too late in a child's development for income to have a sizable impact, or because we are not adequately measuring the long-term financial resources of the family (Blau 1999; Korenman, Miller, and Sjaastad 1995; Mayer 1997; Votruba-Drzal 2006).

Our comparison of the greater importance of income in explaining racial and ethnic differences in years of completed schooling is both a puzzle and avenue of progress. Although income does not appear to have an important direct effect on test score differences, it does appear to influence the number of years of schooling attained. Reducing income differences among individuals and racial-ethnic groups, then, may have a longer-term, indirect effect on racial-ethnic test score gaps. Such reduced income inequality could, by affecting differences in parental schooling levels (and the schooling levels of friends' parents), lead to reduced racial-ethnic test score gaps over the long run. However, reducing gaps in schooling attainments are surely easier to discuss than to accomplish.

Acknowledgments

Please direct correspondence to Mary E. Campbell, W140 Seashore Hall, Department of Sociology, University of Iowa, Iowa City, IA 52242; email mary-e-campbell@uiowa.edu, fax (319) 335-2509. The authors are listed in alphabetical order. We would like to thank the Russell Sage Foundation, Greg Duncan, Katherine Magnuson, Jane Waldfogel, and the Stalled Progress conference attendees. This research uses data from Add Health, a program project designed by J. Richard Udry, Peter S. Bearman, and Kathleen Mullan Harris, and funded by a grant P01-HD31921 from the National Institute of Child Health and Human Development, with cooperative funding from seventeen other agencies. Special acknowledgment is due Ronald R. Rindfuss and Barbara Entwisle for assistance in the original design. Persons interested in obtaining data files from Add Health should contact Add Health, Carolina Population Center, 123 W. Franklin Street, Chapel Hill, NC 27516-2524 (addhealth@unc.edu).

Notes

1. For instance, Toby Parcell and Elizabeth Menaghan (1990) found that a 1 standard deviation increase in spousal annual earnings (about $12,000 in 1985 dollars) corresponded to an increase of 12 percent of a standard deviation in the child's vocabulary score. Blau (1999) found that a $10,000 increase in current income predicted a 6 percent standard deviation increase in vocabulary scores.
2. Some of the observed increase in the 1990s may be an artifact of the change in the way the Current Population Survey measured income in 1993 (see DeNavas-Walt, Cleveland, and Webster 2003).
3. "For example, the word 'furry' has illustrations of a parrot, dolphin, frog, and cat from which to choose" (http://www.cpc.unc.edu/projects/addhealth/ design_focus/wave1#1188). The Add Health PVT uses half of the questions from the PPVT, for a total of eighty-seven items.
4. Eliminating those who primarily speak a language other than English at home reduced the Latino sample by 348 (30.1 percent).
5. However, the racial gaps at the top and bottom deciles of the PVT are larger than in the top and bottom deciles of the NAEP.
6. We used the poverty line for the median family size instead of the poverty line for each specific family size because using a spline variable for income requires that all of the respondents in the dataset have the same cutpoint, or "knot."
7. We also specified the spline function using the more traditional marginal approach, which constructs the categories so that each coefficient estimates the change in the slope from the preceding interval, again with knots at the poverty line and twice the poverty line. The results are consistent with those reported.
8. We matched each respondent to the (up to) ten friends they named on their in-school survey using Add Health identification codes, and then used the self-reports of the friends or the friends' parents as an indicator of each friend's parental education. We then averaged those reports for all matched friends. The standard deviation of parental education among the friends was also calculated from these data. We could not match friends who did not attend one of the schools in the sample.
9. We were also unable to resolve several apparent discrepancies in the data for county-level variables.
10. It is also interesting to note that white females have significantly lower vocabulary scores than white males. Meta-analyses have shown that there is no significant gender difference in verbal ability (Hyde and Linn 1988), but some studies have suggested a small male advantage in listening vocabulary tests (Boyle 1987).
11. We do this by first giving each respondent in the Add Health sample the amount of income that an individual in their own racial group and at the same percentile in that group's income distribution had in the census data for each decade, and then generating a predicted test score for each respondent. For example, a white respondent at the 10th percentile of the white income distri-

bution in Add Health is given the income of a white respondent at the 10th percentile of the white income distribution in the 1970 census data. This gives us predicted scores using actual income values for the group. We then assign a black or Latino respondent in, for example, the 10th percentile of the black or Latino income distribution the family income of whites at the 10th percentile in 1970, to calculate predicted scores using the white income distribution.

12. We also tested whether or not the change in the gap was significantly greater than zero by using the Stata macro CLARIFY (King, Tomz, and Wittenberg 2000) to estimate a confidence interval around the change in the average predicted value when the mean for blacks or Latinos was replaced with the mean for whites. Those changes where the 95 percent confidence interval did not contain zero are marked in table 3.6 with an asterisk.

13. These estimates may well underestimate the true effect of income. For example, if changing income inequality also changes the median family income in the school that the adolescent attends, simply changing the income characteristics of the family would underestimate the impact of income inequality shifts. For this reason, we prefer the top panel of table 3.6, based on the maximum effects model.

References

Allison, Paul D. 2001. *Missing Data.* Sage University Papers Series on Quantitative Applications in the Social Sciences 07-136. Thousand Oaks, Calif.: Sage Publications.

Armor, David J. 1992. "Why Is Black Educational Achievement Rising?" *Public Interest* 108(September): 65–80.

Aughinbaugh, Alison, and Maury Gittleman. 2003. "Does Money Matter? A Comparison of the Effect of Income on Child Development in the United States and Great Britain." *The Journal of Human Resources* 38(2): 416–40.

Autor, David, Lawrence Katz, and Melissa Kearney. 2005. "Trends in U.S. Wage Inequality: Re-Assessing the Revisionists." NBER Working Paper 11627. Cambridge, Mass: National Bureau of Economic Research.

Bali, Valentina A., and R. Michael Alvarez. 2003. "Schools and Educational Outcomes: What Causes the 'Race Gap' in Student Test Scores?" *Social Science Quarterly* 84(3): 485–507.

Belley, Philippe, and Lance Lochner. 2007. "The Changing Role of Family Income and Ability in Determining Educational Achievement." NBER Working Paper 13527. Cambridge, Mass.: National Bureau of Economic Research.

Blau, David. 1999. "The Effect of Income on Child Development." *Review of Economics and Statistics* 81(2): 261–76.

Boyle, Joseph P. 1987. "Sex Differences in Listening Vocabulary." *Language Learning* 37(2): 273–84.

Brooks-Gunn, Jeanne, Pamela K. Klebanov, and Greg J. Duncan. 1996. "Ethnic Differences in Children's Intelligence Test Scores: Role of Economic Deprivation, Home Environment, and Maternal Characteristics." *Child Development* 67(2): 396–408.

Campbell, Mary, Robert Haveman, Gary Sandefur, and Barbara Wolfe. 2005. "What Does Increased Economic Inequality Imply about the Future Level and

Dispersion of Human Capital?" *Project on Social Inequality* Working Paper. New York: Russell Sage Foundation.

Chantala, Kim, and Joyce Tabor. 1999. "Strategies to Perform a Design-Based Analysis Using the Add Health Data." Add Health Working Paper. Chapel Hill, N.C.: University of North Carolina, Carolina Population Center.

Cook, Michael D., and William N. Evans. 2000. "Families or Schools? Explaining the Convergence in White and Black Academic Performance." *Journal of Labor Economics* 18(4): 729–54.

Crain, Robert, and Rita Mahard. 1978. "Desegregation and Black Achievement: Review of the Research." *Law and Contemporary Problems* 42(1): 17–56.

Dahl, Gordon B., and Lance Lochner. 2005. "The Impact of Family Income on Child Achievement." *Institute for Research on Poverty* Discussion Paper 1305-05. Madison, Wisc.: University of Wisconsin. Accessed at http://www.irp.wisc.edu/publications/dps/pdfs/dp130505.pdf.

Daly, Mary C., and Robert G. Valletta. 2006. "Inequality and Poverty in the United States: The Effects of Rising Dispersion of Men's Earnings and Changing Family Behavior." *Economica* 73(289): 75–98.

DeNavas-Walt, Carmen, Robert W. Cleveland, and Bruce H. Webster, Jr. 2003. "Income in the United States: 2002." *Current Population Reports* P60-221. Washington: U.S. Census Bureau.

Farkas, George, and Kurt Beron. 2004. "The Detailed Age Trajectory of Oral Vocabulary Knowledge: Differences by Class and Race." *Social Science Research* 33(3): 464–97.

Feenberg, Daniel, and James Poterba. 2000. "The Income and Tax Share of Very High Income Households, 1960–1995." NBER Working Paper 7525. Cambridge, Mass.: National Bureau of Economic Research.

Gottschalk, Peter, and Sheldon Danziger. 2005. "Inequality of Wage Rates, Earnings and Family Income in the United States, 1975–2002." *Review of Income and Wealth* 51(2): 231–54.

Grissmer, David, Ann Flanagan, and Stephanie Williamson. 1998. "Why Did the Black-White Test Score Gap Narrow in the 1970s and 1980s?" In *The Black-White Test Score Gap*, edited by Christopher Jencks and Meredith Phillips. Washington, D.C.: Brookings Institution Press.

Hanushek, Eric A. 1992. "The Trade-Off Between Child Quality and Quantity." *Journal of Political Economy* 100(1): 84–117.

Harris, Kathleen Mullan, Francesca Florey, Joyce Tabor, Peter S. Bearman, Jo Jones, and J. Richard Udry. 2003. *The National Longitudinal Study of Adolescent Health: Research Design.* Accessed at http://www.cpc.unc.edu/projects/addhealth/design.

Hedges, Larry V., and Amy Nowell. 1998. "Black-White Test Score Convergence since 1965." In *The Black-White Test Score Gap*, edited by Christopher Jencks and Meredith Phillips. Washington, D.C.: Brookings Institution Press.

———. 1999. "Changes in the Black-White Gap in Achievement Test Scores." *Sociology of Education* 72(2): 111–35.

Hill, M. Anne, and June O'Neill. 1994. "Family Endowments and the Achievement of Young Children with Special Reference to the Underclass." *Journal of Human Resources* 29(4): 1064–1100.

Hoffman, Kathryn, Charmaine Llagas, and Thomas D. Snyder. 2003. *Status and Trends in the Education of Blacks.* NCES 2003-034. Washington: National Center for Education Statistics. Accessed at http://nces.ed.gov/pubs2003/2003034.pdf.

Hyde, Janet Shibley, and Marcia C. Lynn. 1988. "Gender Differences in Verbal Ability: A Meta-Analysis." *Psychological Bulletin* 104(1): 53–69.

Jargowsky, Paul A. 1996. "Take the Money and Run: Economic Segregation in U.S. Metropolitan Areas." *American Sociological Review* 61(6): 984–98.

Jencks, Christopher, and Meredith Phillips. 1998. "The Black-White Test Score Gap: An Introduction." In *The Black-White Test Score Gap,* edited by Christopher Jencks and Meredith Phillips. Washington, D.C.: Brookings Institution Press.

Kao, Grace, and Jennifer S. Thompson. 2003. "Racial and Ethnic Stratification in Educational Achievement and Attainment." *Annual Review of Sociology* 29(2003): 417–42.

King, Gary, Michael Tomz, and Jason Wittenberg. 2000. "Making the Most of Statistical Analyses: Improving Interpretation and Presentation." *American Journal of Political Science* 44(2): 347–61.

Korenman, Sanders, Jane Miller, and John Sjaastad. 1995. "Long-Term Poverty and Child Development in the United States: Results from the NLSY." *Children and Youth Services Review.* 17(1–2): 127–55.

Lazear, Edward, and Robert T. Michael. 1988. *Allocation of Income Within the Household.* Chicago: University of Chicago Press.

Lichter, Daniel T., and David J. Eggebeen. 1993. "Rich Kids, Poor Kids: Changing Income Inequality Among American Children." *Social Forces* 71(3): 761–80.

Lopez Turley, Ruth N. 2003. "When Do Neighborhoods Matter? The Role of Race and Neighborhood Peers." *Social Science Research* 32(1): 61–79.

Massey, Douglas S., and Nancy Denton. 1993. *American Apartheid.* Cambridge, Mass.: Harvard University Press.

Mayer, Susan E. 1997. *What Money Can't Buy: Family Income and Children's Life Chances.* Cambridge, Mass.: Harvard University Press.

Myers, Samuel L., Hyeoneui Kim, and Cheryl Mandala. 2004. "The Effect of School Poverty on Racial Gaps in Test Scores: The Case of the Minnesota Basic Standards Tests." *Journal of Negro Education* 73(1): 81–98.

Oates, Gary L. 2003. "Teacher-Student Racial Congruence, Teacher Perceptions, and Test Performance." *Social Science Quarterly* 84(3): 508–25.

Orr, Amy J. 2003. "Black-White Differences in Achievement: The Importance of Wealth." *Sociology of Education* 76(4): 281–304.

Parcel, Toby, and Elizabeth Menaghan. 1990. "Maternal Working Conditions and Children's Verbal Facility: Studying the Intergenerational Transmission of Inequality from Mothers to Young Children." *Social Psychology Quarterly* 53(2): 132–47.

Phillips, Meredith, Jeanne Brooks-Gunn, Greg J. Duncan, Pamela Klebanov, and Jonathan Crane. 1998. "Family Background, Parenting Practices, and the Black-White Test Score Gap." In *The Black-White Test Score Gap,* edited by Christopher Jencks and Meredith Phillips. Washington, D.C.: Brookings Institution Press.

Piketty, Thomas, and Emmanuel Saez. 2003. "Income Inequality in the United States, 1913–1998." *The Quarterly Journal of Economics* 118(1): 1–39.

Pungello, Elizabeth, Janis Kupersmidt, Margaret Burchinal, and Charlotte Patterson. 1996. "Environmental Risk Factors and Children's Achievement from Middle Childhood to Early Adolescence." *Developmental Psychology* 32(4): 755–67.

Schafer, Joe L. 2000. *NORM: Multiple Imputation of Incomplete Multivariate Data Under a Normal Model*, Version 2.03. Accessed at http://www.stat.psu.edu/~jls/misoftwa.html.

Schwabish, Jonathan A. 2006. "Earnings Inequality and High Earners: Changes During and After the Stock Market Boom of the 1990s." Working Paper Series 2006-06. Washington: Congressional Budget Office. Accessed at http://www.cbo.gov/ftpdocs/71xx/doc7164/2006-06.pdf.

Udry, J. Richard. 2003. *The National Longitudinal Study of Adolescent Health (Add Health), Waves I & II, 1994–1996; Wave III, 2001–2002* [machine-readable data file and documentation]. Chapel Hill, N.C.: Carolina Population Center, University of North Carolina.

Votruba-Drzal, Elizabeth. 2006. "Economic Disparities in Middle Childhood Development: Does Income Matter?" *Developmental Psychology* 42(6): 1154–67.

Yeung, W. Jean, Miriam Linver, and Jeanne Brooks-Gunn. 2002. "How Money Matters for Young Children's Development: Parental Investment and Family Processes." *Child Development* 73(6): 1861–79.

PART II

EXPLAINING GAPS AT SCHOOL
ENTRY AND DURING SCHOOL

Chapter 4

Can Gaps in the Quality of Early Environments and Noncognitive Skills Help Explain Persisting Black-White Achievement Gaps?

DAVID GRISSMER AND ELIZABETH EISEMAN

A large body of research in social science has been directed toward addressing the causes of and solutions to continuing inequality of outcomes between black and white Americans (for recent summaries, see Neckerman 2004; Jencks and Phillips 1998). Historically, this research has created an expectation that such gaps would close over generations in a competitive economy if educational and labor market opportunities were equalized. The research, however, has been unable to account for several key aspects of the empirical data—specifically, to explain why progress is so slow, why there can be periods of either rapid or no progress, and why substantial gaps might remain. In this chapter, we examine three factors that might help explain these more complex dynamics in the empirical data:

- Recognizing that early childhood environments create much of the achievement gap and may set limits on later achievement, educational attainment and labor force outcomes

- Recognizing that the behavior and proximal processes that underlie early cognitive development may be different for racial-ethnic groups, and these differences may not be strongly linked to differences in commonly used surrogate variables (income, parent education), and may not change even as social and economic equality improves

- Recognizing that a narrow focus on cognitive achievement measures rather than a broader focus on noncognitive skills such as behavioral, emotional, social and motor skills can leave persisting gaps because:

139

- long-term educational attainment and labor force outcomes depend not only on cognitive skills, but also on noncognitive skills
- some of these noncognitive skills may be implicit cognitive skills,[1] that is, linked to the development or performance of cognitive skills

The identification of these factors is done through reviews of recent literature and empirical estimations with the Early Childhood Longitudinal Survey of Kindergartners (ECLS-K). The major contributions from the literature are related to the interactive genetic and environmental mechanisms driving development from conception to kindergarten entrance, the emerging importance of noncognitive skills in explaining educational and labor market outcomes, and identifying implicit cognitive skills.

Historically, researchers assumed that achievement gaps emerge during schooling through inequality of schools and family characteristics, and looked to the equalization of schooling opportunity as a major policy lever. However, research now shows that a substantial share of the gap is present at school entry, and that school equalization may therefore not fully close score gaps (Lee and Burkam 2002; Fryer and Levitt 2004, 2006).[2] Research also suggests that closing these gaps may be more difficult at later ages (Heckman and Masterov 2007; Cunha et al. 2006) and that some intense early environments may limit later cognitive development even in the best of later circumstances (O'Connor, Rutter, and Beckett 2000; Beckett et al. 2006).

Eliminating gaps before school entrance now appears to be critical to achieving social and economic equality in adulthood. This task may be even more challenging than equalizing schooling, given the numerous, diverse, and complex influences on child development in the early years. The behaviors and proximal processes that underlie the causative mechanisms in early cognitive development may not be adequately captured by the traditional surrogate variables focusing on family and neighborhood characteristics. Research suggests that interactions between genes and these behaviors and processes may account for much variance making their identification and measurement difficult (Rutter 2002; Shonkoff and Phillips 2000). Yet it will likely be in the discovery of these behaviors and processes and the possible differences across groups that will lead to the knowledge required for efficient early interventions to eliminate gaps.

Finally, an implicit assumption in achieving social equality has been that cognitive development plays the dominant role in predicting gaps in later, long-term outcomes. However, noncognitive skills such as social, motor, emotional, and behavioral skills are now also known to affect educational attainment and other long-term outcomes and are receiving increasing attention in early development (Bowles, Gintis, and Osborne 2001, 2002; Heckman and Rubinstein 2001; Heckman, Stixrud, and Urzua 2006; Borghaus, Duckworth, and Heckman forthcoming). In fact, such noncognitive skills may directly affect more than longer-term outcomes. Developmental research and the evidence in this chapter suggest that some noncognitive skills may also be implicitly linked to development and cognitive skills at kindergarten entrance (Diamond 2000; Duncan et al. 2007; Raver, Garner, and Smith-Donald 2007; Snow 2007; Blair et al. 2007; Diamond et al. 2007). Historically, educational policy makers and researchers who have studied schooling effects have focused on cognitive skills as measured by achievement scores as the most important and often as their sole measure of interest. Such focus might help explain persisting score gaps if noncognitive skills also influence later, long-term outcomes. Developmental researchers studying early childhood have included both cognitive and noncognitive skills in their research, but the specific links between cognitive and noncognitive skills are not yet well understood, and persisting score gaps are possible until these links become better known.

Incorporating Recent Research

The two traditional explanations for persisting gaps in achievement between black and white children are genetic differences and continuing discrimination. Recent research suggests that measurable cognitive differences between black and white children do not exist at about nine months of age, and much of the cognitive gaps present during schooling develop between birth and the start of kindergarten rather than after the start of schooling (Lee and Burkham 2002; Fryer and Levitt 2006).[3] These results, if accurate, would suggest no differences in those genes responsible for prenatal and very early cognitive development between black and white children, and suggest that environments, perhaps interacting with genes, between birth and kindergarten entrance, may account for the emergence of gaps (Dickens 2005). This evidence also suggests that schools are not the source of a significant proportion of the score gap, and it is social and economic inequality in family characteristics and environments in the preschool years together with differences in preschooling opportunities that seem critical to the origination and formation of substantial parts of the score gaps.[4]

The continuing presence of discrimination is still a possible explanation for current gaps, and even for persistent gaps. New legislation and court decisions can eliminate some forms of discrimination supported by previous legislation or court decisions, and create stronger sanctions for certain forms of discriminatory behavior. The effects, however, may be limited. Evidence suggests that discrimination legislation may have had a role in improving black wages between 1965 and 1975, but the impacts appear to have diminished considerably (Heckman and Verkerke 1990). The ongoing existence of extensive housing segregation, which is partly responsible for unequal schools, also illustrates the limitations of legislation and court decisions. Research suggests that the roots of some forms of discrimination may be hard to change because they lie in behaviors that are discriminatory but not consciously chosen (see, for instance, the literature review in Blank, Dabady, and Citro 2004). The presence of continuing discrimination needs to be included in any explanation of continuing gaps, but will not be a focus of this chapter. Our focus is the three factors mentioned and their possible role in persisting gaps.

The Primacy of Early Childhood Environments

The primacy of early childhood environments over schooling in the formation of cognitive gaps changes the dynamics inherent in the predictions from traditional research. The traditional framework implicitly assumes that a continuing, iterative, generational process occurs to fully close score gaps. An examination of this process reveals conditions that would predict periods of either more rapid or slower progress as well as persisting gaps.

In the simplest case, an assumption would be made that unequal schooling and labor markets account for all of the variance in outcomes between blacks and whites. Then, providing an equal quality education and ensuring no future job discrimination could theoretically achieve social equality within a generation. However, the Coleman report significantly changed this model by showing that common family characteristics accounted for much more variance than schooling variables in schooling outcomes and racial gaps (Coleman et al. 1966). If family characteristics during schooling years account for a significant part of the outcome variance, then a longer iterative, generational process is needed to close gaps.

The first generation after all discrimination was removed would improve only the part of educational and labor market outcomes that discrimination in schools and labor markets accounted for. The first generation's improvement in education and income would then improve the family characteristics somewhat for the second generation. These characteristics would in turn improve the children's cognitive development, educational attainment, income, and so on. The duration of the process in this model depends on the proportion of variance in outcomes accounted for by school and labor market discrimination compared to family characteristics. The much greater role of family characteristics compared with school and labor market factors makes the generational process much longer.

Gaps are predicted to close only to the extent that the common family variables (parental education, family income, family size, age of mother at child's birth, etc.) that predict higher youth achievement actually change for the higher achievers as they move into adulthood. That is, higher youth achievement in one generation produces, for instance, higher parent education and income, smaller family size and fewer young parents in a succeeding generation, and these incrementally better characteristics produce higher achievement in the following generation of children. While a more detailed dynamic quantitative model could more fully explore this process, there is a strong implicit assumption in this iterative process that is needed for *full* gap closure. The black-white gap in *every* variable that predicts higher achievement for white students will eventually close for black students when they become adults *solely* as a result of their higher achievement.

In this chapter, we explore two conditions under which this assumption fails to hold, and gaps would not fully close. The first is differences in behaviors and proximal processes in early environments that predict later achievement, but would not change as factors like parental education and income improve. For instance, practices in parenting and raising children that raise achievement, but are primarily culturally based, may not change as parental education and income improve and may stop the convergence of the iterative gap-closing process. Second, parental education and income and other factors that predict youth achievement may depend on learning non-cognitive skills as well as cognitive skills. Thus, a sole focus on cognitive skills would leave gaps in parental education and income that would also stop the convergence of the iterative gap-closing process.

Differences in Behaviors and Proximal Processes Affecting Achievement

The primacy of early childhood environments over schools in determining gaps produces more vulnerability to the effects of specific early behaviors and proximal processes that may vary by race-ethnicity and may be resistant to change even if parental education and income improve. Derek Neal (2006) suggested several examples that would fit within this framework and lead to permanent gaps. One example is parenting behaviors that do not depend on the parents' education or income (Brooks-Gunn, Duncan, and Klebanov 1996) but do affect early cognitive development. Ferguson, in this volume, provides evidence of culture specific black practices such as "fear of acting white," lack of working together on homework, and styles of music that may be more immune to progress in social equality. Neal (2006) also suggested the possibility of different cultural attitudes and norms toward marriage and being single parents, and that blacks striving for higher achievement may face social sanctions from other black students. Complete gap closure would not occur over generations if these type of behaviors, norms, and proximal processes are present, but would require interventions targeted to such practices and norms, or other compensating interventions, for these differences.

Identifying more precisely the circumstances under which permanent gaps could occur will require explaining more of the variance in child and adult outcomes, less dependence on the use of surrogate variables, and identifying the separate and joint genetic and environmental influences that underlie effects measured from surrogate variables. Models that predict achievement and education outcomes have consistently accounted for no more than about one-third of the variance, so most of the variance remains unknown, and these missing variables may include ones that help explain more complex patterns in progress toward social equality. Surrogate variables—rather than those reflecting actual behaviors and proximal processes within families, schools, and neighborhoods that are closer to the causative mechanisms that create differences in outcomes— still account for a significant portion of the explained variance.[5] Until most of these other variables are identified, it is unclear precisely what part of the variance is in fact due to the surrogate variables. Also, part of the effect measured for surrogate variables is due to genetic effects that cannot explain black-white group differences. Thus, equations that suggest that black-white score gaps at kindergarten entrance can be accounted for by family characteristics may overstate the influence of these variables (Lee and Burkam 2002; Fryer and Levitt 2004). If the joint and separate innate and environmental components of the effects are identified, such equations may predict persisting gaps.[6]

Cognitive Skills as the Primary Predictor of Outcomes

An underlying assumption in the literature until recently is that cognitive development as measured by achievement scores rather than noncognitive skills will capture the important skills that predict later educational attainment and labor force behavior. Evidence is accumulating, however, that would suggest that noncognitive skills also account for a significant part of this variance (Bowles, Gintis, and Osborne 2001, 2002; Heckman and Rubinstein 2002; Heckman, Stixrud, and Uzrua 2006; Knudsen et al. 2006). If noncognitive skills do play a role in accounting for long-term outcomes for adults, then closing the achievement gap may not eliminate gaps in long-term outcomes.

Noncognitive skills may impact more than long-term outcomes. Research and this chapter suggest that certain noncognitive skills may play an implicit role in the development and performance of cognitive skills (Diamond 2000; Snow 2007; Raver et al. 2007; Blair et al. 2007). These links have long been made in the developmental literature (see, for example, Meltzoff 1993; Rosenbaum, Carlson, and Gilmore 2001). Such associations could reflect common tasks or subskills that need to be mastered to develop or perform cognitive functions that in turn have or are developed as noncognitive skills develop. Another possibility is that both types of skills share common regulatory functions whose development is critical to developmental progress in both cognitive and noncognitive skills.

Possibly one of the most important implicit cognitive skills, called executive function—a cognitive regulatory capacity that develops prior to and parallel with more explicit cognitive skills—encompasses skills that have traditionally been classified as noncognitive, such as sustaining attention and inhibitory control. Developing executive function may depend on many earlier processes, and it has been suggested that practice of any complex activity (physical, emotional, cognitive) may help develop this regulatory function. Executive function has been linked to working memory and ability to sustain attention and inhibition of other stimuli (Engle 2002; Zelazo et al. 2003).[7] Research suggests that executive function coordinates complex activities that require the use and communication among several parts of the brain regardless of whether the task is motor, emotional, behavioral or cognitive (Diamond 2000; Blair et al. 2007). It is possible that complex behavior in any developmental area can strengthen this function and have positive crossover effects for complex activity in other domains.

Some empirical evidence suggests a link between executive function and academic achievement. An analysis of six nationally representative longitudinal data sets found that an executive function-related ability—an early measure of attention—was an important indicator of school performance at later grades after controlling for earlier cognitive performance measures (Duncan et al. 2007). Studies conducted with preschoolers (McClelland et al. 2007) and kindergarteners (Blair and Razza 2007) reveal executive function predicts growth in reading, writing, and math. Executive function at kindergarten entry predicts academic outcomes in second grade after controlling for prior achievement and sociodemographic risk (McClelland, Morrison, and Holmes 2000). In middle childhood, executive function is related to achievement in reading, math, and science (St. Clair-Thompson and Gathercole 2006).

We have so far suggested that the phenomenon of very slowly narrowing and persisting score gaps might be related to the implicit dynamic assumptions of the prior literature as well as the primary focus on schools and cognitive characteristics rather than early environments and noncognitive characteristics. The research needed to explore the role of dynamic assumptions would, ideally, require longitudinal data over generations, though simulation models built on long-term cross-sectional data could be useful. The research presented here, however, focuses only on the role of early environments and noncognitive characteristics that can be explored using data collected at kindergarten entrance.

Data and Methods

In this study, we use the Early Childhood Longitudinal Survey (ECLS-K) of beginning kindergarten students to develop models for reading readiness at the beginning of kindergarten. The ECLS-K is a longitudinal study of a nationally representative sample of approximately 20,000 entering kindergarten students in the 1998–1999 school year. A comprehensive set of data was collected from parents, teachers, principals, and children at the beginning of kindergarten to better understand what skills and knowledge children bring to kindergarten and to determine what explains differences among children in their level of skills. Of particular interest for this study, the data are able to measure achievement gaps before school entry and contain a unique set of measures of an array of noncognitive developmental characteristics that might be linked to achievement.

Sample Design and Characteristics

The sample of kindergarten students in the 1998–1999 school year was chosen using a multistage probability sample. The number of children successfully sampled was 19,173, which was an overall response rate of 90 percent. The parent response rate for sampled children was 85 percent.

Cognitive Assessments

Children's skills were assessed in language and literacy (reading), mathematical thinking (math), and knowledge of the physical and social world (general knowledge) using an untimed one-on-one assessment lasting between fifty and seventy minutes. The tests included both multiple-choice and open-ended items and consisted of a set of two-stage assessments. The first stage consisted of twelve to twenty items with a broad range of difficulty administered to each child. The second stage assessed two or three levels of more difficult skills and the child's performance on the first stage determined which second stage assessments were administered.

The reading assessment had questions designed to measure basic skills (print familiarity, letter recognition, beginning and ending sounds, rhyming sounds, and word recognition), vocabulary and comprehension (listening and words in context). The reading assessment was designed to have five proficiency levels in which mastery of a higher level implied mastery of lower levels. The five levels were naming letters, associating letters with sounds at the beginning of words, associating letters with sounds at the end of words, recognizing common words by sight, and reading words in context.

The aggregate reading assessment measure was scaled using item response theory (IRT) that enabled scores to be estimated as if all children had taken all items in stage one and two. Standardized scores were estimated and scaled to have a mean score of 50 with a standard deviation of 10.

Physical Assessments

The child's height and weight were recorded. Two measures of psychomotor assessment were obtained—gross and fine motor skills. Fine motor skills were assessed by having each child use building blocks to replicate a model, copy figures on paper, and draw a person. Gross motor skills were assessed by asking the child to skip, hop on one foot, walk backward, and stand on one foot.

Socioemotional Measures

Parents and teachers were asked a number of items related to a child's social and emotional development on a four point scale based on the frequency of observing specific behavior (never to most of the time). The items were combined to obtain five overall developmental measures plausibly linked to achievement: approaches to learning, self-control, social interactions, impulsive-overactive, and sad-lonely. Each item assessed how often specific behaviors were observed by the parent or teacher.

The approaches to learning scale was formed from items that rate how often children show eagerness to learn, interest and curiosity, creativity, attention, persistence, concentration, and responsibility. The self-control scale was formed from items that asked frequencies of behavior such as fighting, argues, gets angry, and throws temper tantrums. The social interaction scale was formed from items that assessed the ease of a child's entering into play, making and keeping friends, and positive peer interactions. The impulsive-overactive scale was formed from items about the child's impulsivity and activity level. The sad-/lonely scale was formed from items that assessed a child's being accepted and liked by others and levels of sadness and loneliness.

Methodology

We predict reading scores for first-time kindergarten entrants as a function of the usual family, parent, home, and community characteristics, adding measures for several of the child's noncognitive characteristics.

$$t_i = a + dy_i + bx_i + e_i \qquad (4.1)$$

where
t_i is the scaled test score (mean = 50, standard deviation = 10) of student i, y_i represent a set of characteristics of the family, parent or home of student i, x_i is a collection of noncognitive characteristics of student i, a, b and d are parameters estimated by the regression, and e_i is the assumed normally distributed random error. Equation 4.1 is estimated using ordinary least squares with standard errors estimated by replicate weights that incorporate design effects. Missing data was handled by missing data dummy variables.

Estimates made with nonexperimental data, even comprehensive longitudinal data like the ECLS-K, pose threats of bias from missing variables causing selectivity or omitted variable bias. Three important sources of omitted variables in previous studies have been missing family variables (partly because they are expensive to collect), information on the child's environment and experience from birth to school entry, and measurement of the child's noncognitive skills. Much cognitive development occurs in early childhood, and the absence of variables from this period posed a significant missing variables threat. Developmental research has also suggested links between the development of cognitive and noncognitive skills. Thus the absence of measures of noncognitive skills may also account for missing variance and pose bias threats. The ECLS-K due to its comprehensive data collection may significantly reduce the threat from missing variables and selectivity bias.

Another source of possible omitted variable bias has been the absence of nonlinear terms. A missing interaction or squared term is essentially a variable missing from the model with the potential for bias. The large sample of the ECLS-K allows nonlinear terms to be included and more accurately estimated, and the models estimated here include many variables with nonlinear terms.

A final issue in these models is endogenous variables. This problem can occur when the contextual or explanatory variables used to explain the skill levels of individuals are influenced by the actions of the individuals or of the parents or teachers of the individual (Duncan et al. 2004). For instance, the selectivity of environments by a child or parents or schools may implicitly reflect a child's abilities. Smarter children may thus be read to more or play more games rather than children who are read to or play games more will become smarter. Likewise, children selected into special education, though such designations should be made based on specific developmental problems, may be screened or selected more often when cognitive measures are lower. Greg Duncan, Katherine Magnuson, and Jens Ludwig (2004) suggested that developmental phenomena may be particularly susceptible to this problem, and even more comprehensive data collections may not fully address the issue because of the absence of information about how environments are shaped. We have estimated models that both include and leave out several of the variables judged to be potentially endogenous (reading to children, activities with children, special education status, and attendance at prekindergarten, preschool, daycare, or Head Start), but the results for noncognitive variables of interest change little. We discuss later the possibility of the noncognitive variables themselves being endogenous.

We estimate five models by adding additional variables to all previous variables. Model 1 is meant to measure score gaps at kindergarten entrance for similarly aged children. A number of variables are included to account for selectivity into kindergarten and different times of testing. The test was not administered to children on the same day but was spread out from September through December. Different learning during these months would be expected depending on whether kindergarten was a half or a full day. We construct a set of dummy variables that specify the month of testing and length of kindergarten day to control for differential learning from school attendance to the time of testing. To control for selectivity, we use the parents' report of whether the child started kindergarten on time, earlier, or later than peers.

Model 2 adds the most commonly available family characteristics used in models in prior research. They include education of each parent or caretaker, current family income, age of mother at child's birth, number of siblings, the number and relationship of caretakers to the child, language spoken at home, whether born in the United States, gender and labor force status of mother. Education of mother and father is measured in five categories. Family income, age of mother at child's birth, and number of siblings are also included along with their squared terms. The relationship of the child to primary caregiver includes eight categories that specify the biological relationship of caregivers and the presence of caregivers who are not biologically related.

Model 3 adds parental and child characteristics that are less commonly available in educational research. Home environment for learning is captured by books in the home (and a squared term) and frequency of reading to child. Home emotional environment that has also been linked to achievement is captured by measures of depression of caretaker and measures of parent reported emotional warmth between caretaker and child. Family mobility is captured by number of places lived since birth. Child's health status is captured by birth weight and an overall parent reported health status. Finally a measure of economic well being from birth is captured by an item of money problems from birth.

Model 4 adds variables that capture activities of the child or parent. It includes the frequency that parents reported of sports, games and building activities, and number of hours watching television. It includes a parent assessment of whether the child spends free time in more or less active pursuits. It includes whether the child was in Head Start, daycare, preschool, or prekindergarten in the year before starting kindergarten, and whether the child had been in Head Start in earlier years. The variables corresponding to attendance at daycare, Head Start, and preschool and prekindergarten take into account the number of months of attendance and the number of hours per week of attendance. The weekly hours of attendance also include a squared term to account for developmental limits in learning and possible risk from long attendance at daycare.

Model 5 adds variables that indicate the level of child noncognitive skills and disabilities. The noncognitive skills are teacher reported or directly measured. Five noncognitive characteristics were assessed by teachers and include a variable that attempts to measure the child's approaches to learning (attention span, curiosity, and so on), social skills, internalizing (shy, withdrawn) and externalizing behavior (disruptive and the like) and self control. We also consider here measures of the child's gross motor skills and fine motor skills. The disabilities include learning, speech and hearing, and an indication of special education status.[8]

The models described show a potential strong linkage between cognitive and two noncognitive variables—fine motor skills and approaches to learning—that we refer to as implicit cognitive skills. An important question is how these noncognitive skills develop. Specifically, does there appear to be significant genetic influence? An analysis of twins in the ECLS-K can provide one estimate of the extent of genetic influence. The key test for genetic influence is that identical twins will have less variance on a given characteristic than same-sex fraternal twins because fraternal twins have half the genetic similarity of identical twins.

The ECLS-K includes about fifty pairs of identical twins and about the same number of same-sex fraternal twins. We use this sample to test the extent of genetic influence. We also generate a sample of random pairs of individuals from different families by choosing a single same-sex twin from different twin families that took the test at approximately the same age. We chose the random pairs from twin families to control for the influence of being in families with at least two children identically aged. Thus the random sample is comprised of pairs of twins who live in different families that took the test at the same age but are not biologically related.

As a measure of similarity of pairs, we use the average across pairs of the absolute value of the difference between pairs on a given characteristic. This measure allows a statistical test for the differences between sets of fraternal and identical twins and between twins and random pairs. For instance, for height, we note the difference in height between each pair, take the absolute value, and estimate the average across all pairs. We include in our list of characteristics those that have been shown in previous research to have a biological influence. We use these to validate the methodology and contrast with the characteristics of interest in this study. The characteristics that have shown biological influence from previous research on twins include height, weight, reading and math scores, child health, and internalizing behavior.

Results

We present two sets of results. The first is for estimates using the entire sample of first-time kindergarten students, and the second presents results for comparisons of characteristics of identical and fraternal twins to estimate genetic influence for noncognitive characteristics.

Estimation for All Students

The means and standard deviation of the variables are given in table 4A.1, and the results of the estimation for all students for reading scores are in table 4A.2. We first discuss the effects of the specific variables in the models and then the implication for black-white reading gaps.

In model 1, chronological age shows a very strong effect with about a 0.5 standard deviation difference between children one year apart, other things equal (because the standard deviation is 10, the effect size is obtained for each variable by dividing the coefficient by 10). Children entering kindergarten early score about 0.2 standard deviation higher than those entering on time, and children entering late score about 0.14 lower. The interaction variables that control for month of testing and half- and full-day attendance suggest that learning does occur in the early months. By December, children in full-day kindergarten have gained about 0.45 of a standard deviation compared to those tested in September, and those in half-day kindergarten have gained 0.40 standard deviation.

Results from model 2 show almost all family variables are strongly associated with achievement in the expected direction. The estimated effects of mother's education appear somewhat stronger than the father's education. Family income, age of mother at birth, and number of siblings show strong effects and all have statistically significant nonlinear terms. These terms indicate that an additional increment of income is more important at lower levels of income, an additional year of age of the mother is more important at younger ages, and an additional sibling has a stronger effect at fewer siblings. Speaking another language at home and not being born in the United States each have moderate negative effects on reading readiness skills. Males—other things equal—have lower reading skills than females. All family types other than two biological parents show negative effects that are almost always statistically significant. Children with working mothers show an insignificant negative effect.

Model 3 shows statistically significant and positive associations between achievement and a greater number of books in the home, high birth weight, more places lived since birth, a nondepressed mother, better child health, and absence of long-term money problems since birth. Books in the home and birth-weight have significant nonlinear terms indicating the effect of another book is higher at lower numbers of books and the effect of another pound at birth is more important at lower birth weights. More reading activity is not significant, possibly due to the strong significance of books in the home. The sign of the number of places lived is surprising—indicating more places lived before kindergarten entrance is associated with higher readiness. High mobility during school has typically been associated with lower scores, partly because of learning gaps that can occur when switching schools. However, mobility before kindergarten may indicate movement either into better school districts or linked to job changes that are linked to higher wages, and does not risk learning gaps from changing schools. The addition of the less commonly available set of family characteristics has lowered the associations of almost all commonly available characteristics with achievement, suggesting that the more proximal family processes and child characteristics are mediating the effects of surrogate variables.

Model 4 suggests that some parent-child activities may be more valuable than others in improving reading readiness. Playing games shows positive impact, but sports and building activities show little effect. Children who are more active in free time—other factors equal—score lower than those who are less active. Watching more hours of television is associated with a negative impact on reading readiness. Attendance at Head Start either full- or part-time in the previous year or in earlier years shows no positive association with reading readiness. However, attendance at prekindergarten or preschool shows very strong positive and nonlinear effects, while day care shows no negative effect. Prekindergarten shows strong diminishing returns as hours of attendance per week increase. The data show that increasing from fifteen to twenty hours brings an estimated increment of 0.038 standard deviation in reading, but further additional hours bring minimal gains. The marginally diminishing returns may be due to the developmental limits of the child within a day or week, or to curriculum differences between half- and full-day prekindergarten.

Finally, model 5 shows unusually strong significance from two noncognitive characteristics—fine motor skills and approaches to learning. The other noncognitive characteristics show statistical significance, but markedly smaller effects than fine motor skills and approaches to learning.[9] The signs of social skills (negative) and self-control (negative) are unexpected, though the correlations among the noncognitive characteristics (such as between self-control and externalizing behavior) as well as the strength of the two implicit cognitive characteristics—fine motor skills and approaches to learning—can make predictions difficult. The disability variables show appropriate signs, but only special education status and learning disabilities are significant. We have also estimated the models for math skills with similar results.[10]

Figure 4.1 shows the black-white achievement gap as measured by the ECLS-K in 1999, the fourth grade reading National Assessment of Educational Progress (NAEP) test in 2003 and the eighth grade reading NAEP test in 2007. The black-white reading score gap at kindergarten entrance is about one-half that at fourth grade and the gap at eighth grade is approximately the same as at fourth grade. This suggests that much of the gap is present at entering kindergarten, but significant growth in the gap occurs from kindergarten to fourth grade, but changes little from fourth to eighth grade. This result suggesting expanding black-white gaps in

Figure 4.1   Comparison of Black-White Score Gaps

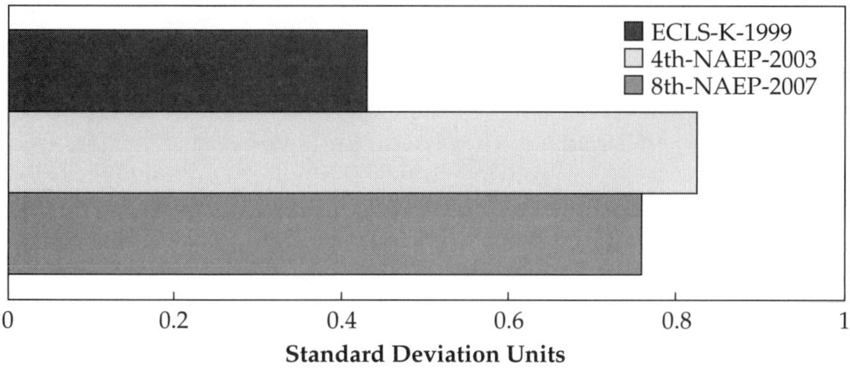

Legend:
- ECLS-K-1999
- 4th-NAEP-2003
- 8th-NAEP-2007

X-axis: 0   0.2   0.4   0.6   0.8   1

Standard Deviation Units

Source: Authors comp ilation.

early grades is consistent with evidence in Ronald Fryer's and Steven Levitt's findings (2006).[11] This evidence suggests that addressing black-white gaps may need to address both interventions and policies before school entry as well as in early grades.

Similar to other reported results, black reading score gaps are substantially reduced in model 2 and disappear in model 3. The common interpretation of this result is that if family characteristics were equalized between black and white families, the gaps would disappear. However, as discussed earlier, the estimated effects from equalizing family characteristics from model 3 may be biased upward, due to failure to separate the genetic and environmental components in variables like parental education and income. It is possible that unbiased models would still show significant gaps even if family characteristics were equalized. If so, unbiased estimates would suggest that persisting gaps are possible, and support the search for other explanations of persisting gaps.

The results are consistent with an interpretation that models 3, 4, and 5 contain variables that could be considered to represent behavioral and proximal processes that mediate the effects of the more common family characteristics. As we proceed from model 2 to model 5, a shift occurs from stronger to weaker influence of most common family characteristics such as parental education, income and family type as the more specific variables are added in models 3, 4, and 5. The coefficient of family income declines about 60 percent, and those of parental education and family type typically by between 30 and 60 percent. The added variables from model 2 to model 4 do not add greatly to explained variance, but rather shift those explaining variance from the surrogate to more proximal variables.

Another interesting feature of the parental coefficients is that the mother's education predicts more strongly than the father's in model 2, but by model 5 the influence of education is about the same for mother and father. The proximal processes appear to be more linked to the mother's than father's education, perhaps indicating a stronger role for the mother's than father's behavior.

The lack of significant additional variance explained by variables from model 2 to model 4 is in contrast to model 5, which shows a 33 percent increase in variance explained from 0.32 to 0.43 along with further reduction in the magnitude of the common variables. This may suggest that a prime source of missing variables in equations predicting achievement has been noncognitive characteristics, and it is possible that additional noncognitive skills need exploration

The surprising strength of fine motor skills and approaches to learning could have several explanations. Two would be somewhat spurious. First, their strength could reflect a simultaneous development of skills at a given age range that are causally unrelated. Second, their strength could reflect an artifact of the measurement process. The first suggests that cognitive and certain noncognitive skills are developing independently at about the same age. However, the control for age in the regression should remove any effects attributable to simultaneous development, provided children follow similar developmental paths.[12] It should be noted that the coefficient of age holds steady in models 1 through 4, but declines from 6.0 to 3.6 when noncognitive variables are inserted, indicating a not surprising correlation between these skills and age. Age may draw part of its significance as a proxy for implicit cognitive skills missing from the equation.

The method of measurement of each of these variables could also introduce bias. The fine motor skills test requires the performance of several tasks by the child with ratings given for each task. However, the instructions for the task are given orally, and it is possible that performance is linked to a student's ability to understand the instructions and understanding the instructions, in turn, is linked to cognitive skills. The teacher provides the assessment of approaches to learning, which involves separate judgments of four skills including attention span, curiosity, persistence, and eagerness to learn. The teacher's assessment might in fact be affected by a more global impression linked to reading readiness skills. The results, however, are essentially the same regardless of whether the teacher assessment at the beginning or the end of the year, or parental assessments are used. Assessments done at the beginning of the year would have much less experience with the child and possibly less knowledge of reading performance.

A third explanation for the strength of the noncognitive skills is that their development is implicitly linked to the development or use of cognitive skills—which is why we refer to them as implicit cognitive skills. As discussed earlier, there is a long empirical trail in the developmental liter-

Figure 4.2   Average Level of Two Noncognitive Characteristics

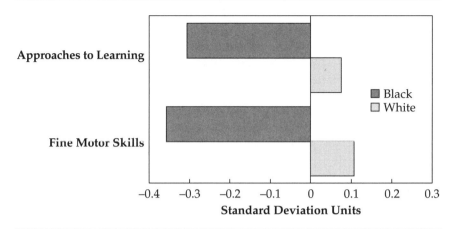

Source: Authors' compilation.

ature suggesting links between motor and cognitive skills and between emotional and attention regulation and cognitive skills (Meltzoff 1993; Rosenbaum, Carlson, and Gilmore 2001; Johnson 2001). More recent links are suggested by both empirical evidence and neural linkages in the brain (Diamond 2000; Blair et al. 2007; Raver, Garner, and Smith-Donald 2007, Duncan et al. 2007; Diamond et al. 2007).

A final possibility is that these variables are endogenous. Better cognitive development may partly boost noncognitive development. Clancy Blair and his colleagues suggested such interdependency (2007). However, fine motor skills and approaches to learning seem to have earlier developmental trajectories than the skills measured in reading readiness, and suggest that any relationship is not entirely from cognitive to noncognitive skills.

The level of noncognitive skills varies by racial-ethnic group and gender. Figure 4.2 shows the differences in fine motor skills and approaches to learning for black and white students. The black-white gap in fine motor skills and approaches to learning is approximately 0.4 standard deviation. Each of these characteristics continues to develop, and the rate of development can be estimated by the differences between children whose ages are one year apart. We estimate the annual growth rate by regressing each characteristic as a function of age, and a set of control variables indicating the time of testing and whether the child entered kindergarten at the appropriate time. Figure 4.3 shows the black gap with white students in years of development for fine motor skills and approaches to learning— approximately eight to nine months.

Figure 4.3   Black-White Developmental Gap in Two Noncognitive Skills

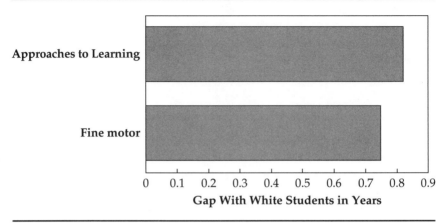

Source: Authors' compilation.

It is also important to take account of gender differences in noncognitive skills that show girls of each race having better skills than boys. Figure 4.4 shows the combined race and gender gaps with white girls. Black boys of similar ages to white girls enter kindergarten with gaps in approaches to learning of about nineteen months and in fine motor skills of about fifteen months.[13] Separate estimates that add the noncognitive characteristics only to model 1 show that equalizing these characteristics reduces the reading black-white gap by 40 percent.

A key question is the extent to which the noncognitive characteristics have genetic influence. If fine motor skills and approaches to learning have little genetic influence, then the predicted effects from closing the gaps in these skills will suggest the possibility of viable interventions.

Analysis of Twin Data

We used the sample of twins on the ECLS-K to test for the genetic influence of several cognitive and noncognitive characteristics. Table 4.1 shows the characteristics tested. The first three columns show the average of the absolute value of differences for identical, fraternal and random pairs. The units are in standard deviation units across the whole sample. Thus the average height difference for identical twins is 0.389 standard deviation, 0.796 for fraternal twins, and 0.995 for random pairs in different families. We test for the statistical difference of the measures by replicate weights. The t-values are given for each comparison in columns 4 through 6. For height, the difference in the average of height of identical and fraternal twins is highly statistically significant. Identical twins also have more height sim-

Figure 4.4   Gaps in Two Noncognitive Skills by Gender

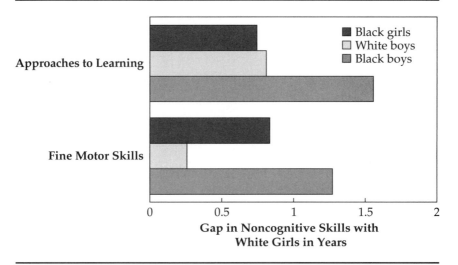

Gap in Noncognitive Skills with
White Girls in Years

Source: Authors' compilation.

ilarity than random pairs and the difference is also statistically significant. Fraternal twins have more similarity in height than random pairs and the difference is statistically significant at the 10 percent level.

We have sorted the results according to those characteristics that show the highest level of genetic influence as measured by the t-value of the identical-fraternal difference. Thus height shows the highest level of genetic influence. Reading and math scores also show significant genetic influence consistent with results from much larger samples of twins. Child health status, weight and internalizing behavior all show some genetic influence that is statistically significant at least at the 10 percent level. None of the other characteristics tested have statistically significant differences between identical and fraternal twins, suggesting little genetic influence.

Children from different twin families (random pairs) nearly always have statistically significant differences with both identical and fraternal twins raised in the same family. The differences between identical and random pairs are more significant than between random and fraternal pairs for characteristics with genetic influence because both genetic influence and differences across families are present. Where no genetic influence is indicated, the differences between identical and random pairs have similar significance levels to fraternal and random pairs, indicating mainly interfamily differences.

Fine motor skills and approaches to learning appear to have little genetic influence and mainly a between family influence. It should be noted that

Table 4.1   **Comparison of Average Differences for Identical, Fraternal and Random Pairs**

	Average of Absolute Value of Pair Differences (Standard Deviation Units)			T-Values		
	Identical	Fraternal	Random	Identical Versus Fraternal	Identical Versus Random	Fraternal Versus Random
Height	0.389	0.796	0.995	3.1	5.7	1.7
Math score	0.396	0.574	1.100	2.2	6.2	4.5
Reading score	0.405	0.618	1.093	2.2	5.5	3.8
Child health	0.268	0.622	1.134	2.1	5.8	3.3
Weight	0.349	0.514	0.896	2.3	4.2	2.7
Internalizing behavior	0.490	0.745	1.098	1.8	4.2	2.4
Fine motor skills	0.810	0.895	1.120	0.6	2.7	1.9
General knowledge	0.442	0.545	1.130	1.2	5.7	4.8
Gross motor skills	0.817	0.817	1.006	0	1.5	1.4
Interpersonal skills	0.717	0.783	1.083	0.4	2.9	2.3
Approaches to learning	0.692	0.646	1.123	−0.2	3.7	3.8
Externalizing behavior	0.516	0.500	0.875	−0.1	3.1	3
Self-control	0.712	0.627	1.017	−0.6	2.7	3.2
Birth weight	0.478	0.358	1.194	−1.3	5.2	5.8

Source: Authors' compilation.

the lack of genetic influence for the measures used in this test and for this age group does not rule out that later development of such skills can be genetically mediated. Finally, fine and gross motor skills show the lowest levels of significant differences between random pairs and either identical or fraternal twins. This evidence may indicate that the measures include a lot of noise and may lack discriminatory power to show differences.

Discussion

Empirical data on gaps in black-white achievement, educational attainment, and income show periods of rapid progress, slow progress, and sustained gaps. Historically, inequality in schools was viewed as the primary agent causing achievement gaps, and equalizing schools was the primary instrument to remedy such gaps. The research presented here suggests that early childhood environments play a critical role in creating significant black-white score gaps before schooling.

The primacy of early childhood environments in causing achievement gaps, and a part of later gaps in educational attainment and income, has introduced new factors that might help explain why progress toward social equality can be rapid or slow, and can stagnate for long periods. Until the last ten or fifteen years, little attention has been given to addressing inequality in early environments, and thus sustained gaps may simply reflect that inequality in early environments has not changed much, and gaps will remain until this inequality is addressed.

Addressing this inequality in early environments will likely not involve focusing on a few family characteristics. Although family characteristics are still linked to early cognitive outcomes, these variables are considered as surrogates for a numerous, diverse, and complex set of behaviors and proximal processes linked to early cognitive development. A possible explanation for persisting gaps is that these behaviors and processes are different for black and white children and families, and the differences may not change as gaps in parental education and income narrow. Much work is still required to identify such variables and processes. At the same time, evidence from this chapter suggests that roughly one-third to one-half of the variance accounted for by the major surrogate variables might be accounted for by more proximal variables, such as birth weight, health status of child and mother, preschool attendance, home environments, household migration, and the incidence of certain activities between parent and child. Gaps may persist until we identify the behaviors and processes and determine the extent to which differences are present between racial-ethnic groups and whether such differences are linked to SES differences or are perhaps more culturally determined. Gaps are likely to persist unless interventions address the behaviors and processes or can otherwise compensate for remaining differences.

Another likely candidate for some portion of the persisting gaps is the almost exclusive focus on cognitive development as measured by achievement tests as the key to improving later educational and labor force achievement. This focus ignores evidence that noncognitive skills are as important in explaining variance as cognitive skills. Thus, even if cognitive skills were equalized, the gaps in later outcomes may not close if gaps still exist in noncognitive skills.

This chapter suggests that noncognitive skills may also contribute to shaping early cognitive outcomes. The possible dual function of noncognitive skills—in contributing to building early cognitive skills as well as independently to later educational attainment and income—would appear to give noncognitive skills as much, if not more, primacy in families, schools, and research. Fine motor skills and approaches to learning, then, but not social skills, would seem to be much more strongly linked to cognitive measures of reading readiness at kindergarten entrance than any single family characteristic. Black children have large gaps in these implicit cognitive skills compared to white children, and the differences would predict up to 40 percent of the reading gap at kindergarten entrance. The evidence provided here suggests that these skills have little or no genetic influence, and are likely almost entirely shaped by differential environments from birth to school entrance. Understanding how these skills develop differently in black and white children and exploring interventions to strengthen such skills appear to be good targets for research.

Including noncognitive skill variables in the estimates of reading readiness increases the explained variance by 33 percent—from 0.32 to 0.43. This might suggest that a key source of missing variables in previous estimates is implicit cognitive skills. Other such skills might explain even more variance. Research suggests that one explanation of the link between implicit and explicit cognitive skills is a cognitive regulatory function, often referred to as executive function, that may be common to the development or performance of many complex skills requiring coordination of different functional parts of the brain. The path to explaining more variance in cognitive outcomes may be in better measurements of such a function and in a search for other skills also linked to cognitive development and performance.

Recently, a political and research consensus has emerged on the need for high quality preschool. Underlying this consensus are decades of research on the effects of early intervention. Four small-scale studies that were quasi or fully experimental suggest that such interventions can have large positive effects on several important long-term outcome measures, and that the benefits exceed the investment costs (Karoly et al. 1998; Karoly, Kilburn, and Cannon 2006; Lynch 2004; Masse and Barnett 2002; Reynolds et al. 2002; Schweinhart 2004).

These interventions, however, were small-scale and targeted on high-risk children where large effect sizes might be expected. It is uncertain whether effect sizes or cost-benefit ratios could be maintained in large-scale, publicly funded programs. One challenge is to design large-scale programs, like Head Start and state prekindergarten, that can also produce significant long-term effects and favorable cost-benefit ratios. Lynn Karoly and James Bigelow (2005) suggested that state universal pre-K programs may have favorable cost-benefit ratios even assuming smaller effect sizes compared with the larger ones measured in the small-scale programs for high-risk children. It is still uncertain, however, what the effect sizes will be for such programs, and what factors underlie higher effect sizes.

Empirical evidence generally supports the assumption that exposure to large-scale preschool helps prepare children for kindergarten. Specifically, several studies—most based on natural or planned experimental designs—corroborate the link between preschool attendance and higher scores on preliteracy and math tests (Gormley et al. 2005; Loeb et al. 2007; Ludwig and Phillips 2007; Magnuson, Ruhm, and Waldfogel 2007). State-funded preschool programs typically show effect sizes around 0.25, with notable exceptions (Gilliam and Zigler 2001), and it is unclear whether differential quality or biased estimates account for the exceptions.

What constitutes high quality preschool or pre-K is still the subject of debate. Many common measures—such as teacher credentials, pupil-teacher ratios, facility and equipment quality, curriculum content, emphasis and length of day—are used for accreditation purposes. However, the empirical evidence to support many of these factors is often thin. Evidence from an eleven-state study of preschool that focused on the characteristics of preschool and teachers and included extensive structured observations suggested that the quality of interactions between students and teachers best predicted skill gains during preschool. More commonly used measures for accreditation had little predictive power for skills gains or for predicting effective student teacher interactions (Mashburn et al. 2007; Pianta et al. 2005).

An important question is the extent to which the curriculum in preschool matters and whether noncognitive skills can be taught. In a recent randomized-controlled experiment, the focus was improving executive function skills. In this study, low-income preschoolers were exposed either to a curriculum, called Tools of the Mind, that emphasized the development of executive function or a literacy curriculum that was more didactic (Diamond et al. 2007). Adele Diamond and her colleagues found that children in Tools classrooms outperformed those in the didactic literacy curriculum and were twice as likely to pass (more than 75 percent correct) the most challenging executive function task. Other direct assessments measured skills that were not taught or practiced in the classroom. These skills also increased, highlighting how executive function skills can transfer to other contexts. These findings are particularly relevant given the strong correlation between preschoolers' executive function task performance and scores on standardized math tests (Blair and Razza 2007).

The evidence presented here suggests that high quality preschool or pre-K will be necessary, but not enough, to close gaps. Providing universal access to high quality preschool will close gaps to the extent that blacks currently have more limited access to such programs or that effect sizes of such programs are larger for black children. But gaps continue to expand from kindergarten to fourth grade, and a series of interventions starting at pre-K and extending into K-4 seems essential. For instance, a reconceptualization is under way for what is now fragmented and poorly aligned public education for children between the ages of three and eight (Bogard and Takanishi 2005; Gilliam and Zigler 2001).

It will probably be essential to identify the early causative mechanisms from conception to preschool that create both implicit and explicit cognitive gaps as well as those in other noncognitive characteristics that predict long-term educational and labor market success. Earlier family-oriented interventions that might impact such gaps also need to be explored.

Finally, the current chronological age entrance criteria place children in kindergarten with significant developmental gaps that will unlikely close. This variance suggests exploring more tailored entrance channels into kindergarten, with up to two years of pre-K curriculum directed to lagging developmental skills.

There is much to be pessimistic about in closing score gaps—the substantial remaining gaps, the lack of progress over the last twenty years, the lack of viable explanations for the lack of progress, and little compelling evidence that might be used to significantly reduce these gaps. However, there is also much to be optimistic about. The combined pace of research in genetics, cognitive science, human capital economics, developmental psychology, and development science has fueled the process of understanding the causative mechanisms creating the gaps. There is good reason to believe that the quality of the research will improve given better available data, more focus on natural and planned experimentation, more variance being explained, continuing improvement in technology in genetics and cognitive research, and greater integration across disciplinary areas. The efficiency and power of interventions to solve problems usually increases dramatically, the closer research comes to understanding causative mechanisms. Such knowledge also can help develop whatever political will may be needed. The beginning of the end of score gaps—possibly.

Appendix

Appendix tables appear on the following pages.

Table 4.A1   Definitions of Variables

Variable Name	Brief Definition	Means	SD
Reading t-score	Reading t-score	50.7	10.02
Math t-score	Math t-score	50.73	10.02
White (reference group)	Race/ethnicity marked as white	0.61	0.49
Black	Race/ethnicity is marked as black only	0.15	0.36
Hispanic	Race/ethnicity is marked as Hispanic only or Hispanic and another category	0.18	0.39
Asian	Race/ethnicity is marked as Asian only	0.04	0.21
Native American	Race is marked as Native American only	0.02	0.13
Age in years	Age of child at time of testing	5.69	0.34
Entered school early	Child entered school before normal cutoff date	0.02	0.14
Entered school on time (reference group)	Child entered school during year after normal cutoff date		
Waited to enter school	Child entered school a year after normal cutoff date	0.07	0.26
September*halfday (reference group)	Test taken in September at a half-day kindergarten		
September*fullday	Test taken in September at a full-day kindergarten	0.03	0.17
October*halfday	Test taken in October at a half-day kindergarten	0.2	0.4
October*fullday	Test taken in October at a full-day kindergarten	0.27	0.44
November*halfday	Test taken in November at a half-day kindergarten	0.2	0.4
November*fullday	Test taken in November at a full-day kindergarten	0.23	0.42
December*halfday	Test taken in December at a half-day kindergarten	0.03	0.16
December*fullday	Test taken in December at a full-day kindergarten	0.02	0.13
Father ed: some HS SHS (reference group)	Father education—not a high school graduate	0.07	0.25
Father ed: HS degree	Father education—high school graduate, but no postsecondary	0.26	0.44

Father ed: some college	0.21	0.41
Father education—high school graduate and some postsecondary, but not a college graduate		
Father ed: college degree	0.15	0.35
Father education—a college degree, but no postcollege		
Father ed: postcollege	0.08	0.27
Father education—college degree and postcollege education		
Mother ed: Some HS	0.09	0.29
Mother education—not a high school graduate		
(reference group)		
Mother ed: HS degree	0.3	0.46
Mother education—high school grad, but no postsecondary		
Mother ed: some college	0.32	0.47
Mother education—high school graduate and some postsecondary education, but not a college graduate		
Mother ed: college degree	0.17	0.38
Mother education—college degree, but no postcollege		
Mother ed: postcollege	0.06	0.23
Mother education—a college degree and postcollege		
Family income	52.47	54.23
Estimated annual family income		
Family income squared	5,694	28,079
Square of family income		
Mother's age at birth	26.42	7.84
Mother's age at child's birth		
Mother's age at birth squared	760	419
Square of mother's age at child's birth		
Number of siblings	1.44	1.13
Number of siblings living at home		
Number of siblings squared	3.36	5.74
Square of number of siblings		
English spoken at home		
Parent response to main language spoken at home—English		
(reference group)		
Non-English at home	0.11	0.31
Non-English main language spoken at home		
Not born in U.S. (reference group)		
Child not born in United States		
Born here	0.92	0.27
Child born in United States		
Gender = female (reference group)		
Gender is female		
Gender = male	0.5	0.5
Gender is male		
Two biological parents	0.5	0.5
Child lives with two biological parents		
(reference group)		
Bio mother other father	0.08	0.27
Child lives with biological mother and nonbiological father		
Other mother bio father	0.01	0.09
Child lives with biological father and nonbiological mother		
Biological mother only	0.21	0.41
Child lives with biological mother only		

(continued)

Table 4.A1   Definitions of Variables (Continued)

Variable Name	Brief Definition	Means	SD
Biological father only	Child lives with biological father only	0.02	0.13
1 or 2 adoptive parents	Child lives with one or two adoptive parents	0.01	0.11
Related guardian	Child lives with a related guardian	0.02	0.13
Unrelated guardian	Child lives with a nonrelated guardian	0.01	0.07
Mom did not work outside home (reference group)	Mom did not work outside home		
Mother worked outside home	Mother was employed outside home	0.72	0.45
How often read: <once a week (reference group)	Child read to less than once a week		
How often read: 1–2×/week	Child was read to one to two times weekly	0.18	0.39
How often read: 3–4×/week	Child was read to three to four times weekly	0.35	0.48
How often read: every day	Child was read to every day	0.45	0.5
Number of books	Number of children's books in home	75.04	59.65
Number of books squared	Square of number of books	9189	12752
Birthweight, lbs	Estimated birth weight of child	6.94	1.33
Birthweight squared	Square of birth weight	49.98	17.87
Lived in same place since birth (reference group)	Lived in same place since birth		
Num places lived: 2	Lived in two places since birth	0.33	0.47
Num places lived: 3	Lived in three places since birth	0.17	0.38
Num places lived: 4+	Lived in four or more places since birth	0.07	0.26
Num places lived: 5+	Lived in five or more places since birth	0.05	0.23
Warmth to child: not hard (reference group)	Hard to feel warm to child—never true		
Warmth to child: sometimes hard	Hard to feel warm to child—sometime true	0.17	0.37

Warmth to child: mostly hard	Hard to feel warm to child—mostly true	0.03	0.18
Warmth to child: completely hard	Hard to feel warm to child—completely true	0.02	0.15
Caretaker not depressed (reference group)	Caretaker not depressed		
Depressed: some of time	Caretaker depressed some of the time	0.21	0.41
Depressed: mod amt of time	Caretaker depressed moderate or most of the time	0.05	0.22
1–5 scale: child's health	Child health status (1 = poor, 5 = excellent)	4.33	0.82
No money problems from birth (reference group)	Family had no money problems since child's birth		
Money problems from birth	Family had money problems since child's birth	0.24	0.43
Freq of sports: < once a week (reference group)	Played sports less than once a week		
Freq of sports: 1–2 times week	Played sports one to two times a week	0.36	0.48
Freq of sports: 3–6 times week	Played sports three to six times a week	0.33	0.47
Freq of playing sports: all the time	Played sports all the time	0.21	0.41
Freq of games: < once a week (reference group)	Played games less than once a week		
Freq of games: 1–2 times week	Played games one to two times a week	0.35	0.48
Freq of games: 3–6 times week	Played games three to six times a week	0.39	0.49
Freq of playing games: all the time	Played games all the time	0.22	0.42
Freq of building: < once a week (reference group)	Played with building toys less than once a week		
Freq of building: 1–2 times week	Played with building toys one to two times a week	0.44	0.5
Freq of building: 3–6 times week	Played with building toys three to six times a week	0.25	0.43
Freq of building toys: all the time	Played with building toys all the time	0.14	0.34
More active in free time	More active in free time	0.26	0.44
Normal activity in free time (reference group)	Normally active in free time		

(continued)

Table 4.A1 Definitions of Variables (Continued)

Variable Name	Brief Definition	Means	SD
Less active in free time	Less active in free time	0.05	0.21
Number of hours of television	Number of hours television	1.79	1.01
Did not attend Head Start (reference group)	Did not attend Head Start in previous year		
Head Start less than 20 hours week	Head Start less than twenty hours a week for preschool	0.08	0.27
Head Start more than 20 hours week	Head Start more than twenty hours a week for preschool	0.06	0.24
Did not attend preschool/ kindergarten or in daycare in previous year (reference group)	Child in home care in previous year		
Hours of preschool/kindergarten: 7 months or more	Weekly hours preschool/prekindergarten—more than seven months in previous year	7.31	12.15
Hours of preschool/kindergarten: less than 7 months	Weekly hours preschool/prekindergarten—less than seven months in previous year	1.19	0.05
Hours of daycare: 7 months or more	Weekly hours daycare—more than seven months in previous year	2.65	9.1
Hours of daycare: less than 7 months	Weekly hours of daycare—less than seven months in previous year	0.53	4.12
Pre hvy hrs squared	Pre heavy hours squared	201.2	437.9
Pre lt hrs squared	Pre light hours squared	29.4	172.9
Day hvy hrs squared	Day heavy hours squared	89.9	340.6
Day lt hrs squared	Day light hours squared	17.3	150.8
No attendance in Head Start more than a year ago (reference group)	No attendance in Head Start more than one year ago		

Attended Head Start more than 1 year ago	Attended Head Start more than one year ago		
Attended Head Start more than 1 year ago	Attended Head Start more than one year ago	0.02	0.13
Approaches to learning	Teacher estimate of child's learning approach-spring	3.13	0.65
Externalizing behavior	Teacher estimate of child's self control-spring	3.18	0.6
Social skills	Teacher estimate of child's social skills-spring	3.13	0.61
Internalizing behavior	Teacher estimates of whether child is sad and lonely-spring	1.56	0.49
Self-control	Teacher estimate of impulsivity or overactiveness-spring	1.66	0.61
Gross motor skills	Test of child's gross motor skills	6.35	1.84
Fine motor skills	Test of child's fine motor skills	5.82	2.04
No learning disability (reference group)	No learning disability		
Learning disability	A learning disability has been diagnosed	0.02	0.15
No speech problem (reference group)	No speech problem		
Speech problem	A speech problem has been diagnosed	0.07	0.26
No hearing problem (reference group)	No hearing problem		
Hearing problem	A hearing problem has been diagnosed	0.01	0.11
Not designated special education (reference group)	Not designated special education		
Designated special education	Child designated to be eligible for special education	0.09	0.29

Source: Authors' compilation.

Table 4.A2 Regression Results for Beginning Kindergarten Reading Readiness Scores

Variable	Model 1		Model 2	
	Coefficient	T.	Coefficient	T.
Black	−4.3	(−9.09)	−0.80	(−2.20)
Hispanic	−4.95	(−11.7)	−1.52	(−4.33)
Asian	3.22	(5.07)	2.67	(5.03)
Native American	−8.84	(−5.09)	−5.12	(−3.47)
Age in years	5.29	(17.81)	6.11	(24.13)
Entered school early	2.14	(2.68)	1.67	(2.65)
Waited to enter school	−1.44	(−3.16)	−1.62	(−3.93)
September*fullday	1.42	(0.9)	0.81	(0.91)
October*halfday	−0.2	(−0.16)	−0.49	(−0.96)
October*fullday	0.9	(0.69)	0.87	(1.54)
November*halfday	1.01	(0.75)	0.74	(1.24)
November*fullday	2.19	(1.63)	2.19	(3.35)
December*halfday	4.01	(2.65)	2.55	(3.29)
December*fullday	4.48	(2.78)	3.85	(3.96)
Father ed: HS degree			1.61	(5.11)
Father ed: some college			3.11	(9.63)
Father ed: college degree			4.37	(10.61)
Father ed: postcollege			5.81	(12.46)
Mother ed: HS degree			2.30	(8.21)
Mother ed: some college			3.95	(13.52)
Mother ed: college degree			5.48	(14.78)
Mother ed: postcollege			6.70	(12.48)
Family income			2.48	(7.89)
Family income squared			−0.24	(−4.23)
Mother's age at birth			0.33	(5.07)
Mother's age at birth squared			−0.004	(−3.78)
Number of siblings			−1.63	(−10.27)
Number of siblings squared			0.084	(3.01)
Non-English at home			−1.75	(−4.47)
Born here			1.57	(2.36)
Gender = male			−1.90	(−11.37)
Bio mother other father			−1.11	(−3.60)
Other mother bio father			−2.04	(−4.17)
Biological mother only			−2.06	(−4.04)
Biological father only			−1.66	(−0.76)
1 or 2 adoptive parents			−2.06	(−2.77)
Related guardian			−3.01	(−3.97)
Unrelated guardian			−4.22	(−3.45)
Mother worked outside home			−0.28	(−1.57)
How often read: 1–2×/week				
How often read: 3–4×/week				
Number of books				
Number of books squared				
Birthweight, lbs				
Birthweight squared				
Num places lived: 2				

Model 3		Model 4		Model 5	
Coefficient	T.	Coefficient	T.	Coefficient	T.
0.57	(1.53)	0.79	(2.23)	0.62	(1.87)
−0.89	(−2.64)	−0.82	(−2.59)	−1.21	(−4.09)
3.73	(7.09)	3.93	(7.72)	2.44	(5.06)
−4.08	(−3.33)	−3.53	(−3.54)	−4.02	(−4.20)
6.08	(23.65)	5.99	(22.98)	3.56	(14.46)
1.48	(2.44)	1.31	(2.14)	1.56	(2.84)
−1.49	(−3.57)	−1.46	(−3.59)	−0.98	(−2.70)
1.06	(1.25)	0.66	(0.82)	1.57	(2.00)
−0.43	(−0.91)	−0.57	(−1.24)	0.02	(0.03)
1.06	(2.02)	0.59	(1.19)	1.28	(2.24)
0.80	(1.48)	0.67	(1.30)	1.40	(2.43)
2.34	(3.89)	1.84	(3.26)	2.39	(3.91)
2.56	(3.48)	2.42	(3.48)	3.14	(4.41)
3.96	(4.29)	3.64	(3.95)	4.20	(4.41)
1.19	(3.76)	1.00	(3.22)	0.85	(3.08)
2.44	(7.46)	2.12	(6.50)	1.83	(6.04)
3.61	(8.66)	3.21	(7.92)	2.79	(7.48)
4.98	(10.54)	4.55	(9.33)	4.07	(8.86)
1.72	(6.03)	1.46	(5.27)	0.95	(3.56)
3.02	(10.18)	2.56	(8.60)	1.82	(6.04)
4.35	(12.08)	3.69	(10.41)	2.87	(8.51)
5.58	(10.58)	4.79	(9.44)	3.81	(8.08)
1.92	(6.14)	1.26	(4.45)	1.00	(3.17)
−0.18	(−3.30)	−0.11	(−2.20)	−.07	(−1.70)
0.30	(4.80)	0.24	(3.80)	0.20	(3.85)
−0.004	(−3.42)	−0.003	(−2.56)	−.002	(−2.65)
−1.60	(−10.22)	−1.31	(−8.37)	−1.25	(−8.22)
0.086	(3.09)	0.064	(2.27)	0.080	(2.78)
−1.09	(−2.76)	−1.16	(−3.01)	−1.55	(−4.00)
1.43	(2.17)	1.32	(1.98)	1.91	(2.88)
−1.80	(−10.70)	−1.66	(−9.90)	−0.33	(−2.11)
−0.89	(−2.77)	−0.79	(−2.42)	−0.45	(−1.62)
−1.70	(−3.71)	−1.59	(−3.35)	−1.18	(−2.32)
−1.71	(−3.45)	−1.69	(−3.53)	−0.92	(−2.08)
−1.69	(−0.81)	−1.80	(−0.89)	−0.03	(−0.02)
−2.24	(−3.21)	−2.28	(−3.38)	−0.54	(−0.84)
−2.59	(−3.61)	−2.41	(−3.33)	−1.38	(−2.12)
−3.89	(−3.28)	−3.81	(−3.33)	−2.12	(−2.21)
−0.24	(−1.26)	−0.48	(−2.52)	−0.49	(−2.66)
0.28	(0.30)	0.20	(0.23)	−0.39	(−0.47)
1.08	(1.17)	0.90	(1.02)	0.19	(0.24)
6.16	(11.10)	5.58	(9.98)	4.57	(8.66)
−2.19	(−8.62)	−1.97	(−7.82)	−1.59	(−6.76)
1.01	(2.99)	0.96	(2.89)	0.08	(0.26)
−0.052	(−2.07)	−0.049	(−1.98)	−.003	(−0.12)
0.11	(0.56)	0.10	(0.53)	0.22	(1.22)

(*continued*)

Table 4.A2   Regression Results for Beginning Kindergarten Reading Readiness Scores (*Continued*)

Variable	Model 1		Model 2	
	Coefficient	T.	Coefficient	T.
Num places lived: 3				
Num places lived: 4+				
Warmth to child: sometimes hard				
Warmth to child: mostly hard				
Depressed: some of time				
Depressed: mod amt of				
Child's health: 1–5 scale				
Money problems from birth				
Freq of sports: 1–2 times/wk				
Freq of sports: 3–6 times/wk				
Freq of playing sports: all the time				
Freq of games: 1–2 times week				
Freq of games: 3–6 times week				
Freq of playing games: all the time				
Freq of building: 1–2 times week				
Freq of building: 3–6 times week				
Freq of building toys: all the time				
More active in free time				
Less active in free time				
Number of hours of television				
Head Start < 20 hours				
Head Start > 20 hours				
Hours of preschool/kindergarten: 7 months or more				
Hours of preschool/kindergarten: less than 7 months				
Hours of daycare: 7 months or more				
Hours of daycare: less than 7 months				
Pre hvy hrs squared				
Pre lt hrs squared				
Day hvy hrs squared				
Day lt hrs squared				
Attended Head Start > 1 year ago				
Approaches to learning				
Externalizing behavior				
Social skills				
Internalizing behavior				
Self-control				
Gross motor skills				
Fine motor skills				
Learning disability				
Speech problem				
Hearing problem				
Designated special education				
Constant	20.55	(9.64)	4.18	(2.09)
R-Squared	.11		.29	
N	14955		1495	

Source: Authors' compilation.

Model 3		Model 4		Model 5	
Coefficient	T.	Coefficient	T.	Coefficient	T.
0.40	(1.59)	0.40	(1.62)	0.49	(2.21)
0.82	(2.49)	0.84	(2.63)	0.78	(2.60)
0.30	(1.51)	0.29	(1.52)	0.35	(1.99)
−0.47	(−1.34)	−0.38	(−1.14)	−0.43	(−1.36)
−0.45	(−2.69)	−0.38	(−2.11)	−0.27	(−1.70)
−0.99	(−2.31)	−0.82	(−1.83)	−0.36	(−0.92)
0.55	(5.59)	0.54	(5.79)	0.21	(2.52)
−0.65	(−4.03)	−0.57	(−3.50)	−0.29	(−1.82)
		−0.07	(−0.28)	−0.24	(−0.93)
		−0.15	(−0.55)	−0.45	(−1.70)
		−0.88	(−2.51)	−0.93	(−2.90)
		0.86	(1.94)	0.44	(1.05)
		1.55	(3.61)	0.99	(2.45)
		1.67	(3.47)	1.24	(2.64)
		0.28	(1.29)	0.19	(0.96)
		−0.13	(−0.59)	−0.25	(−1.21)
		−1.19	(−4.87)	−1.09	(−4.40)
		−0.41	(−2.57)	−0.22	(−1.54)
		0.99	(2.50)	1.46	(3.84)
		−0.35	(−3.65)	−0.26	(−2.88)
		−1.12	(−3.70)	−0.63	(−2.23)
		−0.63	(−1.59)	−0.33	(−1.00)
		0.207	(9.32)	0.19	(8.55)
		0.158	(3.72)	0.14	(4.20)
		0.076	(1.70)	0.08	(1.81)
		−0.017	(−0.17)	0.03	(0.35)
		−0.004	(−5.69)	−.003	(−5.21)
		−0.004	(−3.49)	−.004	(−3.80)
		−0.001	(−0.83)	−.001	(−1.16)
		0.000	(0.11)	−.001	(−0.41)
		0.02	(0.04)	0.20	(0.33)
				4.54	(30.45)
				0.37	(2.17)
				−0.46	(−2.81)
				−0.85	(−4.05)
				−0.78	(−2.95)
				0.15	(3.68)
				0.72	(16.77)
				−1.21	(−2.15)
				−0.36	(−1.34)
				−0.83	(−1.39)
				−2.05	(−9.54)
−4.78	(−1.81)	−2.59	(−1.01)	3.98	(1.54)
.30		.32		.43	
14955		14953		14953	

Acknowledgments

This research was partly supported by the Institute for Educational Sciences, U.S. Department of Education, through grant R305A60021 to the University of Virginia. The opinions expressed are those of the authors and do not represent views of the U.S. Department of Education. We are also grateful for funding support from the Russell Sage Foundation.

Notes

1. The term now used in the economic literature, *noncognitive,* to describe skills like social, emotional, motor and behavioral is unsatisfactory because it is based on a simple model of development that assumes independence and separability among skill domains as they are developed or performed. A major thrust of brain and developmental research, by contrast, is the interconnection and interdependence among skills. A more complex nomenclature is needed to reflect this possible interdependence. In this chapter, we keep the term *noncognitive* to reflect the historical distinction between skills that were thought to be involved in cognitive performance and skills in other domains like social, emotional, behavioral and motor. However, we adopt the term *implicit* cognitive skills to define those noncognitive skills used in developing or performing cognitive skills. One definition of *implicit* is "involved in the nature or essence of something though not revealed, expressed, or developed." *Implicit* suggests a non-obvious dependence during the development or performance of cognitive skills on other skill domains. This chapter and other research suggests that fine motor skills and measures linked to attention are implicit cognitive skills.
2. There is also evidence that learning gaps can widen during the summer months when children are not in school (Downey, von Hippel, and Broh 2004; Fryer and Levitt 2004; Alexander, Entwisle, and Olson 2007). These summer effects might also help explain persisting gaps to the extent that differential learning occurs between black and white students during the summer.
3. The evidence of no racial differences in the cognitive skill measurements at nine months may also indicate the lack of sensitivity and comprehensiveness of the measurements.
4. The equations in Lee and Burkam (2002) and Fryer and Levitt (2004) suggest that black-white reading gaps would be predicted to disappear if family characteristics were equalized. Although we later argue that such results may overstate the effects of family characteristics, the evidence is still strong that differences in family characteristics between black and white families are still large, and can explain part of the persisting gap. Magnuson, Ruhm, and Waldfogel suggested that the effects of preschool are larger and longer lasting for disadvantaged children (2007). Bridget Hamre and Robert Pianta suggested that high quality preschool programs have larger effects on disadvantaged children, but that these children have less access to such high quality programs (2007).

5. There has been much progress in identifying such behavior and proximal processes. These include, for instance, reading to children, types of parenting behavior, depression in mothers, birth weight, the amount and quality of verbal interactions between mother and child, and the emotional relationship between parents and between parents and children.

6. Some research suggests that the effects of parental education are partly genetic, and, for instance, the effect of higher parental education on adopted children is much smaller than for biological children (see, for example, Rowe, Jacobson, and van der Oord 1999; Neiss and Rowe 2000; Van-Ijzendoorn, Juffer, and Poelhuis 2005).

7. One definition is "cognitive or supervisory processes associated with the active maintenance of information in working memory, the appropriate shifting and sustaining of attention among goal-relevant aspects of a given task or problem, and the inhibition of prepotent or extraneous information and responding within a given task context" (Blair et al. 2007, 151).

8. We also estimated models leaving out the special education and disability status variables, and these did not significantly diminish the effects of the remaining noncognitive skills.

9. The results for fine motor skills and approaches to learning are insensitive to the removal of the other noncognitive characteristics or to inclusion of any combination of them or to removal of either fine motor skills or approaches to learning.

10. One important difference for math results is that gross motor skills becomes highly significant (t-value of 9.6) as well as fine motor skills and approaches to learning.

11. Fryer and Levitt (2006) compared score gaps across grades with the longitudinal ECLS-K sample that may be vulnerable to nonrandom attrition—especially given that attrition is higher for lower scoring groups. The NAEP samples at fourth and eighth grade are very large, nationally representative samples for the same cohort and may provide better estimates of differences in score gaps by grade. Of course, both the ECLS-K and NAEP use different tests at later grades, and caution may be necessary to the extent that the size of gaps are dependent on particular tests. Greg Duncan and Katherine Magnuson (2005) pointed out the black score gap in the ECLS-K was smaller than the gaps reported for two other data sets collected on similar aged children using somewhat different tests.

12. We have introduced squared and cubed terms for age to check for more complex age dependent development growth with little effect on the noncognitive variables.

13. These gaps are measured for children at the same age. In kindergarten, children's age range usually spans a full year and differences in age would be added to the gaps in figure 4.4.

References

Alexander, Karl L., Doris R. Entwisle, and Linda S. Olson. 2007. "Lasting Consequences of the Summer Learning Gap." *American Sociological Review* 72(April): 167–80.

Beckett, Celia, Barbara Maughan, Michael Rutter, Jenny Castle, Emma Colvert, Christine Groothues, Jana Kreppner, Suzanne Stevens, Thomas G. O'Connor, and Edmund J. S. Sonuga-Barke. 2006. "Do the Effects of Severe Deprivation on Cognition Persist into Early Adolescence? Findings from the English and Romanian Adoptees Study." *Child Development* 77(3): 696–711.

Blair, Clancy, Hilary Knipe, Eric Cummings, David P. Baker, David Gamson, Paul Eslinger, and Steven L. Thorne. 2007. "A Developmental Neuroscience Approach to the Study of School Readiness." In *School Readiness and the Transition to Kindergarten,* edited by Robert Pianta, Martha J. Cox, and Kyle L. Snow. Baltimore, Md.: Paul H. Brookes Publishing.

Blair, Clancy, and Rachel Peters Razza. 2007. "Relating Effortful Control, Executive Function, and False-Belief Understanding to Emerging Math and Literacy Ability in Kindergarten." *Child Development* 78(2): 647–63.

Blank, Rebecca M., Marilyn Dabady, and Constance F. Citro, editors. 2004. *Measuring Racial Discrimination.* Washington, D.C.: The National Academies Press.

Bogard, Kimber, and Ruby Takanishi. 2005. "PK-3: An Aligned and Coordinated Approach to Education for Children 3 to 8." *Social Policy Report* 19(3): 3–24. Accessed at http://www.fcd-us.org/usr_doc/PK-3AnAlignedandCoordinated Approach.pdf.

Borghaus, Lex, Angela Lee Duckworth, and James J. Heckman. Forthcoming. "The Economics of Noncognitive Skills." *Journal of Human Resources.*

Bowles, Samuel, Herbert Gintis, and Melissa Osborne. 2001. "Incentive-Enhancing Preferences: Personality, Behavior, and Earnings." *American Economic Review* 91(2): 155–58.

———. 2002. "The Determinants of Individual Earnings: Skills, Preferences, and Schooling." *Journal of Economic Literature* 39(4): 1137–76.

Brooks-Gunn, Jeanne, Greg J. Duncan, and Pamela K. Klebanov. 1996. "Ethnic Differences in Children's Intelligence Scores: Role of Economic Deprivation, Home Environment and Maternal Characteristics." *Child Development* 67(2): 396–408.

Coleman, James S., Ernest Q. Campbell, Carol J. Hobson, James McPartland, Alexander M. Mood, Frederic D. Weinfeld, and Robert L. York. 1966. *Equality of Educational Opportunity.* Washington: U.S. Government Printing Office.

Cunha, Flavio, James J. Heckman, Lance Lochner, and Dimitry V. Masterov. 2006. "Evidence on Life Cycle Skill Formation." In *Handbook of the Economics of Education,* edited by Erik Hanushek and Finis Welch. Amsterdam: North-Holland.

Diamond, Adele. 2000. "Close Interaction of Motor Development and Cognitive Development and of the Cerebellum and Prefrontal Cortex." *Child Development* 71(1): 44–56.

Diamond, Adele, Steven Barnett, Jessica Thomas, and Sarah Munro. 2007. "Preschool Program Improves Cognitive Control." *Science* 318(5855): 1387–88.

Dickens, William T. 2005. "School Readiness and Genetic Differences." *The Future of Children* 15(1): 55–69.

Downey, Douglas B., Paul T. von Hippel, and Beckett A. Broh. 2004. "Are Schools the Great Equalizer? Cognitive Inequality During the Summer Months and the School Year." *American Sociological Review* 69(October): 613–35.

Duncan, Greg J., Chantelle J. Dowsett, Amy Claessens, Katherine A. Magnuson, Aletha C. Huston, Pamela Klebanov, Linda S. Pagani, Leon Feinstein, Mimi Engel, Jeanne Brooks-Gunn, Holly Sexton, Kathryn Duckworth, and Crista Japeli. 2007. "School Readiness and Later Achievement." *Developmental Psychology* 43(6): 1428–46.

Duncan, Greg J., and Katherine A. Magnuson. 2005. "Can Family Socioeconomic Resources Account for Racial and Ethnic Test Score Gaps?" *Future of Children* 15(1): 35–54.

Duncan, Greg J., Katherine A. Magnuson, and Jens Ludwig. 2004. "The Endogeneity Problem in Developmental Studies." *Research in Human Development* 1(1–2): 59–80.

Engle, Randall W. 2002. "Working Memory Capacity as Executive Attention." *Current Directions in Psychological Science* 11(1): 19–23.

Fryer, Roland G., and Steven D. Levitt. 2004. "Understanding the Black-White Test Score Gap in the First Two Years of School" *Review of Economics and Statistics* 86(2): 447–64.

———. 2006. "The Black-White Test Score Gap Through Third Grade." *American Law and Economics Review* 8(2): 249–81.

Gilliam, Walter S., and Edward F. Zigler. 2001. "A Critical Meta-Analysis of All Evaluations of State-Funded Preschool from 1977 to 1998: Implications for Policy, Service Delivery and Program Evaluation." *Early Childhood Research Quarterly* 15(4): 441–73.

Gormley, William T., Jr., Ted Gayer, Deborah Phillips, and Brittany Dawson. 2005. "The Effects of Universal Pre-K on Cognitive Development." *Developmental Psychology* 41(6): 872–84.

Hamre, Bridget K., and Robert C. Pianta. 2007. "Learning Opportunities in Preschool and Early Elementary Classrooms." In *School Readiness and the Transition to Kindergarten in the Era of Accountability,* edited by Robert C. Pianta, Martha J. Cox, and Kyle Snow. Baltimore, Md.: Paul H. Brookes Publishing.

Heckman, James J., and Dimitry V. Masterov. 2007. "The Productivity Argument for Investing in Young Children." NBER Working Paper 13016. Cambridge, Mass.: National Bureau of Economic Research.

Heckman, James J., and Yona Rubinstein. 2001. "The Importance of Noncognitive Skills: Lessons from the GED Testing Program." *American Economic Review* 91(2): 145–49.

Heckman, James J., Jora Stixrud, and Sergio Urzua. 2006. "The Effects of Cognitive And Noncognitive Abilities on Labor Market Outcomes and Social Behavior." NBER Working Paper 12006. Cambridge, Mass.: National Bureau of Economic Research.

Heckman, James J., and J. H. Verkerke. 1990. "Racial Disparity and Employment Discrimination Law: An Economic Perspective." *Yale Law and Policy Review* 8(1): 276–98.

Jencks, Christopher, and Meredith Phillips, editors. 1998. *The Black-White Test Score Gap.* Washington, D.C.: Brookings Institution Press.

Johnson, Mark H. 2001. "Functional Brain Development in Humans." *Nature Reviews Neuroscience* 2(7): 475–83.

Karoly, Lynn A., and James H. Bigelow. 2005. *The Economics of Investing in Pre-kindergarten in California.* MG 349. Santa Monica, Calif.: RAND Corporation.

Karoly, Lynn A., Peter W. Greenwood, Susan S. Everingham, Jill Hoube, M. Rebecca Kilburn, C. Peter Rydell, Matthew Sanders, and James Chiesa. 1998. *Investing in Our Children: What We Know and Don't Know About the Costs and Benefits of Early Childhood Interventions.* MR-898-TCWF. Santa Monica, Calif.: RAND Corporation.

Karoly, Lynn A., M. Rebecca Kilburn, and Jill S. Cannon. 2006. *Early Childhood Interventions: Proven Results, Future Promise.* MG 341. Santa Monica, Calif.: RAND Corporation.

Knudsen, Eric I., James J. Heckman, Judy Cameron, and Jack P. Shonkoff. 2006. "Economic, Neurobiological and Behavioral Perspectives on Building America's Future Workforce." *Proceedings of the National Academy of Science* 103(27): 10155–62.

Lee, Valerie E., and David T. Burkam. 2002. *Inequality at the Starting Gate: Social Background Differences in Achievement as Children Begin School.* Washington, D.C.: Economic Policy Institute.

Loeb, Susanna, Margaret Bridges, Daphna Bassok, Bruce Fuller, B., and Russell W. Rumberger. 2007. "How Much Is Too Much? The Influence of Preschool Centers on Children's Social and Cognitive Development." *Economics of Education* 26(1): 52–66.

Lynch, R. G. 2004. Exceptional Returns: Economic, Fiscal, and Social Benefits of Investment in Early Childhood Development. Washington, D.C.: Economic Policy Institute.

Ludwig, Jens, and Deborah Phillips. 2007. "The Benefits and Costs of Head Start." *SRCD Social Policy Report* 21(3): 1–18.

Magnuson, Katherine A., Christopher J. Ruhm, and Jane Waldfogel. 2007. "Does Prekindergarten Improve School Preparation and Performance?" *Economics of Education Review* 26(1): 33–51.

Mashburn, Andrew J., Robert C. Pianta, Bridget K. Hamre, Jason T. Downer, O. Barbarin, and D. Bryant. 2007. "Pre-K Program Standards and Children's Development of Academic, Language and Social Skills." Manuscript under review. University of Virginia.

Masse, Leonard N., and W. Steven Barnett. 2002. *A Benefit Cost Analysis of the Abecedarian Early Childhood Intervention.* New Brunswick, N.J.: National Institute for Early Education Research, Rutgers University.

McClelland, Megan M., Claire E. Cameron, Carol McDonald Connor, Carrie L. Farris, Abigail M. Jewkes, and Frederick J. Morrison. 2007. "Links Between Early Self-Regulation and Preschoolers' Literacy, Vocabulary, and Math Skills." *Developmental Psychology* 43(4): 947–59.

McClelland, Megan M., Frederick J. Morrison, and Deborah L. Holmes. 2000. "Children at Risk for Early Academic Problems: The Role of Learning-Related Social Skills." *Early Childhood Research Quarterly* 15(3): 307–29.

Meltzoff, Andrew N. 1993. "The Centrality of Motor Coordination and Proprioception in Social and Cognitive Development: From Shared Actions to Shared Minds." In *The Development of Coordination in Infancy,* edited by G. J. P. Savelsbergh. Amsterdam: Elsevier Science.

Neal, Derek A. 2006. Why Has Black-White Skill Convergence Stopped? In *The Economics of Education*, edited by Eric Hanushek, and Finis Welch. Amsterdam: North-Holland.

Neckerman, Kathryn M., editor. 2004. *Social Inequality*. New York: Russell Sage Foundation.

Neiss, Michelle, and David C. Rowe. 2000. "Parental Education and Children's Verbal IQ in Adoptive and Biological Families." *Behavioral Genetics* 30(6): 487–95.

O'Connor, Thomas G., Michael L. Rutter, and Chris Beckett. 2000. "The Effects of Global Severe Deprivation on Cognitive Competence: Extension and Longitudinal Follow-up." *Child Development* 71(2): 376–90.

Pianta, Robert C., Carollee Howes, Margaret Burchinal, Donna Bryant, Richard Clifford, Diane Early, and Oscar Barbarin. 2005. "Features of Pre-Kindergarten Programs, Classrooms, and Teachers: Do They Predict Observed Classroom Quality and Child-Teacher Interactions?" *Applied Developmental Science* 9(3): 144–159.

Raver, Cybele C., Pamela W. Garner, and Radiah Smith-Donald. 2007. "The Roles of Emotion Regulation and Emotion Knowledge for Children's Academic Readiness: Are the Links Causal?" In *School Readiness and the Transition to Kindergarten in the Era of Accountability*, edited by Robert C. Pianta, Martha J. Cox, and Kyle L. Snow. Baltimore, Md.: Paul H. Brookes Publishing.

Reynolds, Arthur J., Judy A. Temple, Dylan L. Robertson, and Emily A. Mann. 2002. "Age 21 Cost-Benefit Analysis of the Title I Chicago Child-Parent Centers." *Educational Evaluation and Policy Analysis* 24(4): 267–303.

Rosenbaum, David A., Richard A. Carlson, and Rick O. Gilmore. 2001. "Acquisition of Intellectual and Perceptual-Motor Skills." *Annual Review of Psychology* 52(2001): 453–70.

Rowe, David C., Kristen C. Jacobson, and Edwin J. C. G. Van der Oord. 1999. "Genetic and Environmental Influences on Vocabulary IQ: Parental Education as Moderator." *Child Development* 70(5): 1151–62.

Rutter, Michael. 2002. "Nature, Nurture, and Development: From Evangelism Through Science Toward Policy and Practice." *Child Development* 73(1): 1–21.

Schweinhart, Lawrence J. 2004. *The High/Scope Perry Preschool Study Through Age 40*. Ypsilanti, Mich.: High/Scope Educational Research Foundation.

Shonkoff, Jack P., and Deborah A. Phillips, editors. 2000. *From Neurons to Neighborhoods: The Science of Early Childhood Development*. Washington, D.C.: National Academies Press.

Snow, Kyle L. 2007. "Integrative Views of the Domain of Child Functions." In *School Readiness and the Transition to Kindergarten in the Era of Accountability*, edited by Robert C. Pianta, Martha J. Cox, and Kyle L. Snow. Baltimore, Md.: Paul H. Brookes Publishing.

St. Clair-Thompson, Helen L., and Susan E. Gathercole. 2006. "Executive Functions and Achievements in School: Shifting, Updating, Inhibition, and Working Memory." *The Quarterly Journal of Experimental Psychology* 59(4): 745–59.

Van-Ijzendoorn, Marinus H., Femmie Juffer, and Caroline W. Poelhuis. 2005. "Adoption and Cognitive Development: A Meta-Analytic Comparison of Adopted and Non-Adopted Children's IQ and School Performance." *Psychological Bulletin* 131(2): 301–16.

Zelazo, Philip D., Ulrich Mueller, Douglas Frye, and Stuart Marcovitch. 2003. *The Development of Executive Function in Early Childhood.* Monographs of the Society for Research in Child Development, 63 (3, Serial No. 274). New York: Blackwell Publishing.

Chapter 5

Segregation and the Test Score Gap

JACOB L. VIGDOR AND JENS LUDWIG

Disparities in educational outcomes between African Americans and whites declined steadily for most of the twentieth century, but this progress has halted or even reversed in recent years (Neal 2006). Understanding why the black-white test score gap narrowed over time, and why this progress stalled during the 1990s, is critical if we are to design policies capable of further reducing inequality in schooling outcomes in the United States. Given the widely documented association between educational outcomes and earnings, health and crime, successful efforts to further reduce the gap would undoubtedly have far-reaching consequences for society as a whole.

This chapter considers the role of school and neighborhood segregation in explaining trends in the black-white schooling gap. As we will discuss, provocative time-series and cross-sectional evidence points to strong associations between segregation and achievement gaps. The break in trend toward narrower test score gaps coincided with another toward greater school integration. Cross-sectionally, states with more segregated schools also tend to have wider gaps. It is not clear, however, whether causal interpretations should be attached to these correlations.

Social science has struggled mightily to produce definitive proof that segregation and racial disparities are causally linked, and the available evidence—backed by eminently plausible theoretical arguments and proposed mechanisms—has influenced policy debates for decades. Key to the Supreme Court's transformational decision fifty years ago in *Brown v. Board of Education* is the assumption that racial segregation within the public schools contributes to black-white inequality in schooling outcomes. Attending a disproportionately minority school might affect both the motivation of students and their perceptions of the larger opportunity structure they face in society and their exposure to high-quality school resources or even the academic climate in the school.

It is possible that the race-ethnicity of one's schoolmates might simply be a stand-in for their academic achievement level, which could affect the way or rate at which teachers present material or the productivity of student study groups, or as a stand-in for their socioeconomic status (SES). In fact, the influential report by James Coleman in the mid-1960s argued that a school's SES composition was at least as important in explaining inequality in student achievement as is school racial composition (Coleman et al. 1966). Understanding the distinct influences of school racial versus social class composition is relevant because some policies focused on reducing school racial segregation may not have very large impacts on school socioeconomic composition, and vice versa.

Measures of school segregation by either race or social class could matter in largest part because they are proxies for the racial or class composition of the local neighborhood. Because most children attend local public schools, in national data there will be a great deal of cross-sectional correlation between school and neighborhood measures of race or SES segregation. The neighborhood social environment could matter above and beyond the composition of the local public school by shaping the youth social norms that help shape children's behavior, particularly given that so much socializing and exposure to local role models occur outside of school (Wilson 1987). Understanding the distinct influences of school versus neighborhood environments is important for policy because policies such as public or private school choice have the potential to change school but not neighborhood social compositions, and some housing mobility interventions might generate larger changes in neighborhood than school characteristics (see, for example, Sanbonmatsu et al. 2006).

Figure 5.1 presents a basic conceptual framework outlining the potential causal mechanisms linking segregation to test score gaps. Neighborhood segregation could affect these outcomes directly or through its influence on school segregation. Direct links between neighborhood and test scores might be through neighborhood-level deviant peer influence, role model effects, or impacts on parental income derived from spatial mismatch-type effects. Direct links between school segregation and test scores could be mediated by differences in school input quality, or by peer influence operating at the school or classroom level.

Thinking carefully about the particular mechanism through which social environment affects children is also important in understanding patterns in black-white student outcomes because different measures of segregation have been following different trajectories in recent years. Neighborhood racial and economic segregation actually declined during the 1990s, though these national trends mask important differences by region and so do not necessarily imply that neighborhood segregation is not relevant for understanding the slowdown in narrowing of the black-white test score gap (Glaeser and Vigdor 2003; Jargowsky 2003).

Figure 5.1   Conceptual Framework

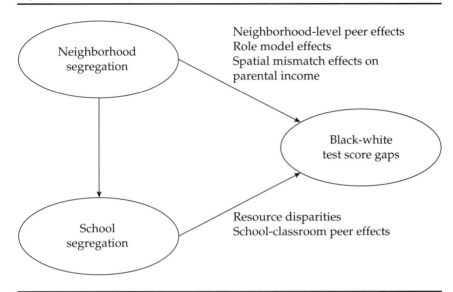

Source: Authors comp ilation.

Controversy continues about whether school segregation has increased or decreased over this same period. Increases reported in some studies (for example, Clotfelter 2004; Orfield and Eaton 1996) confound the increasing diversity of the student body in American public schools with increases in the separation of blacks from students of other races (Logan 2004). Measures more commonly accepted in the sociological and economic literature on segregation indicate very slight decreases in the degree of segregation over the past two decades. Regardless of measure, it is clear that school segregation has declined more slowly than neighborhood segregation over the same time period. The failure of school segregation to track neighborhood segregation reflects a broad decline in governmental efforts to integrate public schools (Orfield and Eaton 1996; Clotfelter, Ladd, and Vigdor 2005).

In our judgment, the evidence linking school segregation to student achievement is stronger than evidence supporting a direct causal role for neighborhood segregation. The current evidence implicating school race segregation certainly outweighs the available research on the effects of school segregation by social class, though the specific mechanisms through which racial composition affects student outcomes remain poorly understood.

The best available evidence suggests that a 10 percent increase in the black share of a school's student body would reduce achievement test scores for black students by between 0.025 and around 0.08 standard deviations, and reduce test scores for whites by perhaps one-quarter to two-fifths as much. Thus, if school segregation had displayed a decrease in the 1990s commensurate with the observed decrease in neighborhood segregation, our best estimate is that the black-white test score gap would be roughly 0.01 to 0.02 standard deviation narrower.

Basic Facts

The factors that determine the degree of interracial exposure witnessed by students of a given race, or the degree of economic diversity experienced by individuals of a given socioeconomic status, are a complex set. Residential segregation has a direct impact on the characteristics of a student's neighbors, and indirectly influences classmate and schoolmate characteristics by affecting the cost to a school district of achieving racial balance across campuses. Beyond this residential component, the structure of local government in a local area, particularly whether school districts serve large or small geographic areas, and a number of other policies implemented by districts themselves can influence classroom racial composition.

Between 1970 and the late 1980s, several factors converged to produce historic declines in school segregation. As we will discuss in more detail, residential segregation declined during this period. Moreover, under court direction, many school districts either increased their integration efforts or merged in ways that reduced the potential for across-district segregation. In the mid-1960s, many districts were making no efforts whatsoever to integrate their schools; the average black public school student attended a school that was almost entirely black. Integration occurred rapidly in the wake of a series of major court rulings in the late 1960s; in the South, the proportion of black students attending schools where 90 percent or more of the students were black declined from 75 to 25 percent in just four years, from 1968 to 1972 (Clotfelter 2004). The fifteen years after 1972 witnessed additional progress toward integration, albeit at a much slower rate.

Although residential segregation has continued to decline over the past decade, school districts have broadly decreased integration efforts. On net, these two effects led to a modest increase in interracial contact among the nation's black students. In 1987, the average black public school student attended a campus that was 51.5 percent black. By 2003, this number had declined to 48.3 percent. The exposure of non-Hispanic white students to black students remained nearly constant over the same period, thus much of the change in the racial composition of the typical black student's school can be attributed to increasing Asian and Hispanic enrollments. As noted in the introduction, the policy-driven slowdown in school integration occurred at roughly the same time as the slowdown in black-white test score convergence. This potentially causal coincidence leads us to discuss

Figure 5.2   Mean Residential Dissimilarity for U.S. Metropolitan Areas

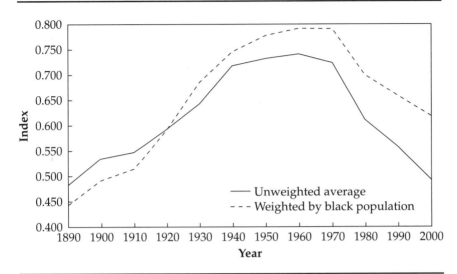

Source: Glaeser and Vigdor 2003.

trends in residential and school segregation in greater detail. Black-nonblack residential segregation in the United States peaked around 1970 and has been declining ever since (Cutler, Glaeser, and Vigdor 1999; Glaeser and Vigdor 2003). Figure 5.2 illustrates the time-series pattern of residential segregation over the twentieth century, using perhaps the most common measure of segregation, the dissimilarity index. This is defined as follows:

$$D = \frac{1}{2} \sum_i \left| \frac{black_i}{black_{total}} - \frac{nonblack_i}{nonblack_{total}} \right|, \tag{5.1}$$

where i indexes all the neighborhoods within a metropolitan area, or all the schools within a district, $black_i$ represents the black population in a neighborhood or enrollment in a school, $black_{total}$ represents the overall black population of the metropolitan area or black enrollment in the district, and $nonblack_i$ and $nonblack_{total}$ represent analogous counts for individuals who are not black. The dissimilarity index can be interpreted as the fraction of black individuals who would have to be moved between neighborhoods or schools to achieve a perfectly even balance across the metropolitan area or district.[1] In 1970, the average black lived in a metropolitan area where nearly 80 percent of the group would have to switch neighborhoods to achieve that balance. By 2000, that proportion had declined to just over 60 percent. In 2000, the average black resided in a neighborhood where 51 percent of the residents were black. This average proportion was 56 percent in 1990 (Glaeser and Vigdor 2003). This downward trend was accompanied by a modest increase in the percentage black in the neighborhood occupied by the average white.

The decline in residential segregation since 1970 has generally been attributed to the enactment and enforcement of fair housing laws in the 1960s, along with other measures that reduced the severity of discrimination in the housing and mortgage markets. For the most part, the decline in segregation came about with the entry of modest numbers of black families into new suburban developments or into existing neighborhoods that had been entirely white (Cutler, Glaeser, and Vigdor 1999). Declines in segregation have been steepest in growing metropolitan areas, where new developments make up a larger proportion of the housing stock. The vast majority of neighborhoods that were predominantly black in 1970 remain predominantly minority; in many areas these neighborhoods have depopulated substantially over the past thirty years.

Declines in racial residential segregation since 1970 are particularly noteworthy because they have occurred in periods of both increasing and decreasing economic inequality. The coexistence of decreasing segregation and increasing inequality may seem paradoxical at first, but it is important to note that the racial segregation that existed before the civil rights movement was pervasive along all levels of socioeconomic status. As of 1970, black high school dropouts and blacks with at least some postsecondary education experienced nearly identical dissimilarity levels (Cutler, Glaeser, and Vigdor 1999, table 2). Reductions in segregation after this time period were most rapid for the most educated group of blacks—consistent with the notion that black suburbanization explains most of the decline in segregation. Less-educated blacks, who presumably have been harmed the most by broad increases in inequality, witnessed more modest declines in segregation after 1970.

The decline in residential segregation has been accompanied, for a good part of the same period, by an increase in similar measures of socioeconomic segregation. Segregation by household income increased between 1970 and 1990 and fell slightly between 1990 and 2000 (Jargowsky 1996, 2003; Watson 2006). Trends in economic segregation thus track changes in the income distribution much more closely than trends in racial segregation.

The literature on school segregation has developed independently from the literature on residential segregation. One consequence of this disconnect is a general tendency for studies of school segregation to use measures and indices that are relatively uncommon elsewhere in the literature. Although increases in school segregation have been reported for twenty years, most of the reported increases are unique to a single segregation measure, the fraction of black students attending majority nonwhite schools (Clotfelter 2004). Because of the nation's increased racial diversity, students of all races now find themselves attending schools with a high fraction of nonblack nonwhites (Logan 2004; Clotfelter, Ladd, and Vigdor 2005). Other measures of segregation show little or no time trend over this period. There is at least some evidence that the retreat from court-ordered busing in the 1990s led to segregation levels higher than they would have been, which can possibly explain why school segregation remained effectively constant even while residential segregation was declining.

Which is the "right" method of measuring segregation? Although there have been some attempts to ground segregation indices in economic or other social scientific models of behavior (see, for example, Echenique and Fryer 2005), there is surprisingly little guidance in the existing research literature on the relative merits of different measures. The dissimilarity index is clearly superior in evaluating the degree of effort a district undertakes to achieve integration in its schools and classrooms; it measures the proportion of the black (or nonblack) members of the student body that would need to be moved to achieve perfect evenness. It can be criticized, however, because it does not map directly into implications for the composition of classrooms and schools occupied by typical students of any race. For a school district experiencing no trend in racial enrollment patterns, increases in dissimilarity imply that percentage black in the average black student's school is increasing relative to the average white's school. Such implications cannot be drawn when comparing across districts or over time in a district undergoing demographic change.

At first glance, a measure of peer percentage nonwhite, such as those commonly used in the school segregation literature, might seem to be the best measure to use in an analysis of the impact of segregation on racial test score disparities. A brief example casts doubt on this supposition. Suppose district A is 75 percent black, and all schools within it are 75 percent black. Dissimilarity equals zero, and measures of peer percentage nonwhite will be high. District B is 5 percent black, but all the blacks are concentrated in one school, where they form 25 percent of the student body. The dissimilarity index will be much higher in B, and the peer percentage nonwhite measure will be lower. In which district would we expect wider black-white disparities in test scores? The potential is clearly higher in district B, given that in that district students of different races systematically attend different schools.

As we will see, the majority of empirical studies of the effects of racial composition on student achievement look for evidence that the impact of peer racial composition on individual test scores is different for blacks and whites. If increases in peer percentage black are detrimental for black students but inconsequential for white students, then the aggregate achievement-maximizing distribution of students would involve integration rather than segregation. The traditional measure of percentage nonwhite is inadequate for using results such as these to infer the impact of segregation on black-white gaps, because it incorporates no mechanism for contrasting the experience of white students. Making such an inference requires incorporating information on the average experience of white students. The dissimilarity index captures exactly such a contrast in experiences by race.

Another caution regarding the use of a peer percentage nonwhite measure is that much of the time-series variation in it has been driven by increases in the share of nonblack nonwhites in the population. Cross-sectional studies of the impact of peer composition on achievement, by contrast, are driven largely by variation in percentage black. To accurately judge whether increases in peer percentage nonwhite might account for stalled progress in the black-white test score gap, it would be necessary to identify differential impacts of peer percentage Asian and Hispanic on test scores for black and white students.

The strongest arguments in favor of using a measure of peer percentage nonwhite focus on broader mechanisms that might not explain black-white disparities within a district or community, but could explain broad differences across communities. In the cited example, suppose that districts A and B serve the same metropolitan area, and that no black-white test score gap exists in either one, at least conditional on observed characteristics. An across-district gap could still easily arise for any of several reasons. Teachers often exhibit preferences to work in schools with lower concentrations of minority students. The broad correlation of race with family income implies that the district with higher minority concentration may have fewer educational resources at the school, neighborhood, or family levels.

In summary, the dissimilarity index is most useful for analyzing variation in the effort required to achieve perfect integration in school districts or states, and for assessing the potential for racial disparities in school-level conditions within a school district. Peer percentage nonwhite measures provide a better idea of the classroom composition actually faced by typical students in a district or state, and may be more useful when considering mechanisms influenced by absolute rather than relative racial composition.

Table 5.1 presents basic information on school segregation levels in the United States as a whole and for a selection of large urban school districts, based on school membership counts found in the Common Core of Data for the 1987–1988 and 2003–2004 school years. This table uses the dissimilarity index as a measure of segregation, thus these values are quite comparable to the neighborhood-level segregation indices summarized in figure 5.2. Several patterns in the data on school segregation are striking. First, dissimilarity levels are generally much lower at the school level than at the neighborhood level, which reflects the fact that many districts take at least some action to counteract neighborhood segregation in the manner

Table 5.1   School-level Black-Nonblack Dissimilarity, United States and Selected School Districts

Geographic Entity	1987 to 1988	2003 to 2004	Change
United States, LEAs weighted by enrollment	0.306 (0.177) (N=7,939)	0.286 (0.172) (N=13,416)	−0.02
United States, LEAs weighted by black enrollment	0.358 (0.193) (N=7,939)	0.357 (0.202) (N=13,416)	−0.001
Los Angeles Unified	0.603	0.554	−0.049
City of Chicago	0.561	0.698	+0.137
Dade County, Florida	0.604	0.656	+0.052
Houston ISD	0.599	0.564	−0.035
Philadelphia	0.617	0.618	+0.001
Detroit	0.611	0.734	+0.121
Broward County, Florida	0.544	0.522	−0.022
Dallas ISD	0.584	0.531	−0.053
San Diego City	0.359	0.298	−0.061
Clark County, Nevada	0.267	0.260	−0.007
Jefferson County, Kentucky	0.157	0.204	+0.047
Milwaukee	0.303	0.596	+0.293
Palm Beach County, Florida	0.546	0.502	−0.044
Orange County, Florida	0.462	0.480	+0.018
Pinellas County, Florida	0.270	0.384	+0.114
Charlotte-Mecklenburg	0.217	0.418	+0.211
Cleveland City	0.277	0.723	+0.446

Source: Authors' compilation from U.S. Department of Education (1988, 2004).
Note: Indices are reported for the largest school districts with data on school racial composition available for both school years.

they assign students to schools.[2] Second, there has been virtually no change in the segregation level experienced by the average black student over the sixteen years covered here. The stability of this mean masks several dramatic changes in the patterns in individual school districts over time. Among the nation's largest school districts, there are several examples with double-digit increases in dissimilarity over the period. Although we lack comprehensive data on official district busing policies, it is clear that segregation increases in some of these districts, such as Charlotte-Mecklenburg, directly reflect the decisions of federal courts.

The relatively low dissimilarity indices within districts do not necessarily imply that schools are integrated by any objective standard. In many parts of the country, a high degree of school segregation results from between-district differences in racial composition. Table 5.2 documents this

Table 5.2   District-Level Black-Nonblack Dissimilarity, by State

State	1987 to 1988	2003 to 2004	Change
Arizona	0.438	0.302	−0.136
Arkansas	0.607	0.675	+0.068
California	0.487	0.406	−0.081
Colorado	0.621	0.547	−0.074
Connecticut	0.609	0.572	−0.037
Delaware	0.079	0.219	+0.140
Florida	0.222	0.246	+0.024
Illinois	0.626	0.639	+0.013
Indiana	0.673	0.680	+0.007
Iowa	0.644	0.533	−0.111
Kansas	0.600	0.536	−0.064
Kentucky	0.574	0.576	+0.002
Massachusetts	0.620	0.586	−0.034
Michigan	0.819	0.758	−0.061
Minnesota	0.705	0.571	−0.134
Nebraska	0.728	0.602	−0.126
Nevada	0.292	0.254	−0.048
New Jersey	0.653	0.597	−0.056
North Carolina	0.354	0.335	−0.019
North Dakota	0.672	0.408	−0.264
Ohio	0.717	0.717	−
Oklahoma	0.576	0.551	−0.025
Oregon	0.650	0.470	−0.180
Pennsylvania	0.746	0.687	−0.059
Rhode Island	0.577	0.503	−0.074
South Carolina	0.357	0.353	−0.004
Texas	0.489	0.459	−0.030
Utah	0.508	0.285	−0.223
Washington	0.536	0.465	−0.071
Wisconsin	0.717	0.725	+0.008

Source: Authors' compilation from U.S. Department of Education (1988, 2004).
Note: Indices are reported for those states reporting racial composition of schools reliably in both years.

pattern by reporting the degree of dissimilarity between school districts for a set of states reporting comprehensive data on racial enrollment patterns in 1987 and 2003. Dissimilarity values tend to be quite high for northeastern and midwestern states. This can be explained by the relatively high degrees of residential segregation in those states, coupled with the general tendency for school districts to serve single municipalities rather than larger areas. These dissimilarity levels are high, but some evidence does suggest that they have been decreasing over time in most states, consistent with the general decline in residential segregation witnessed during the same period.

In the appendix, we provide analogous tables documenting the degree of dissimilarity experienced by students eligible for the federal free lunch program. These data reveal trends quite similar to racial segregation in schools: within-district dissimilarity shows little overall trend between 1987 and 2003 even though some districts post large increases. Across-district dissimilarity shows evidence of a decline in many states.

Could the relative stability of school segregation in the 1990s, which contrasts with periods of rapid integration in preceding decades, explain the stalled progress in closing the black-white test score gap in the same period? As discussed earlier, the two time series mesh well. Cross-sectional evidence is also consistent with a causal link between school segregation and the black-white test score gap, as is evident in figure 5.3, which plots the state-level black-white gap in fourth grade NAEP mathematics test scores against state-level across-district dissimilarity for 2003. There is an unmistakable positive association between the two variables; the plotted least-squares regression line indicates that the predicted black-white test score gap is nearly 50 percent larger in states with the highest levels of across-district dissimilarity as in states with the lowest levels.

Of course, it is inappropriate to assign a causal interpretation to simple time-series or cross-sectional correlations. Segregation levels are the outcome of a large number of choices, made by households in their residential location decisions and by public school officials. These decisions are quite likely correlated with a number of underlying variables that could easily exert their own influence on test scores. In the sections that follow, we discuss the proposed causal mechanisms linking segregation levels to educational outcomes, and the most reliable attempts to disentangle such causal channels from other processes.

Effects of Neighborhoods

Whether or how neighborhood context affects the long-term life chances of poor families independently of school context remains somewhat unclear. The best evidence currently available suggests that moving into a neighborhood that is relatively less segregated by race or social class has at most very modest effects on children's test scores or other schooling outcomes, at least through the first five years or so following the neighborhood change. These findings, together with the fact that on average neighborhood class and race segregation declined somewhat during the 1990s, lead us to conclude that changes in neighborhood conditions are unlikely to have contributed much to the halt in narrowing of the black-white test score gap.

Decades of research throughout the social sciences have documented substantial variation across neighborhoods in adult or child outcomes,

Figure 5.3   District-level Segregation and Black-White Test Score Gap, 2003

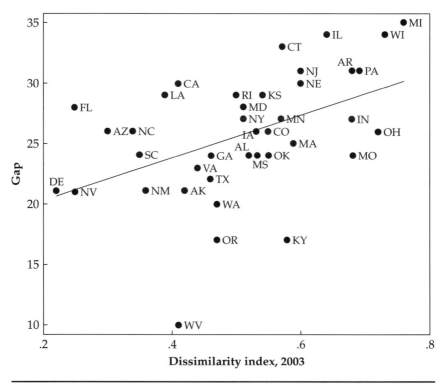

Source: Authors' compilation from U.S. Department of Education (2004).
r = 0.47, significant at 1 percent level

even after conditioning on observable individual or family attributes (Sampson, Morenoff, and Gannon-Rowley 2002; Kawachi and Berkman 2003; Leventhal and Brooks-Gunn 2000; Ellen and Turner 2003; for a review of numerous recent nonexperimental studies of neighborhoods and youth outcomes, see Vigdor 2006a). A number of causal pathways have been proposed to explain these correlational patterns, including spatial mismatch effects, whereby adults suffer from living in a neighborhood with few job opportunities, peer contagion at the neighborhood level, and the importance of local role models on the goal orientation of youth. Neighborhoods have also been hypothesized to matter because they partially determine school characteristics. We examine these proposed pathways more exclusively in the next section. Yet these studies, by and large, fail to provide convincing evidence in favor of any of these pathways because they cannot separate the effects of neighborhoods from those of unmeasured individual attributes associated with residential selection.

The most compelling evidence for neighborhood effects on youth outcomes has come from quasi-experimental studies that exploit neighborhood changes induced by housing programs. One of the best known is Chicago's Gautreaux residential mobility program (Rubinowitz and Rosenbaum 2001), which resulted from a 1976 Supreme Court decree finding that the Chicago Housing Authority and HUD had engaged in systematic and illegal segregation. Follow-up interviews with Gautreaux families suggested improved outcomes for those who moved to the suburbs rather than other parts of Chicago, particularly for youth. For example only 5 percent of suburban movers, compared to 20 percent of city movers, dropped out of high school, with an impressively large suburban advantage in college attendance as well, 54 percent versus 21 percent (Rubinowitz and Rosenbaum 2001, 163). In principle, these findings are relevant for present purposes because suburban communities are relatively more affluent and have a higher proportion of white families. More recent studies of Gautreaux show smaller impacts, however (Mendenhall, Duncan, and Deluca 2004; Keels, Rosenbaum, and Duncan 2004). Furthermore, Gautreaux has important limitations. The degree to which the program breaks the link between family preferences and mobility outcomes is unclear because convincing documentation of the voucher-offer and acceptance process remains difficult to reconstruct. In addition, Gautreaux studies cannot compare outcomes for program movers versus nonmovers or nonparticipants.

Motivated by the encouraging findings from Gautreaux, the U.S. Department of Housing and Urban Development (HUD) launched the Moving to Opportunity (MTO) randomized housing-mobility intervention to identify the causal effects of residential mobility interventions on families. MTO has been in operation since 1994 in five cities—Baltimore, Boston, Chicago, Los Angeles, and New York. Eligibility for the voluntary MTO program was limited to low-income families with children living in public housing or Section 8 project-based housing located within designated high-poverty census tracts in these cities, with poverty rates of 40 percent or more. Families were recruited through fliers, tenant associations, and other means. Almost all of the 4,600 households that signed up were headed by a female, nearly two-thirds African American and most of the rest Hispanic. Three-quarters of household heads were on welfare at baseline, and fewer than half had graduated from high school. Although we do not know the immigration status of MTO participants, most speak English.

By random lottery, some families were assigned to a Section 8 group that was offered unrestricted Section 8 subsidies (vouchers)[3] that they could use to move to a new private-market apartment of their choice. Other families were assigned to an experimental group that was offered housing search assistance and Section 8 subsidies that could only be used to relocate to a low-poverty census tract, that is, those with a 1990 poverty rate below 10 percent. After one year in a low-poverty tract, experimental families could use their subsidies to move elsewhere. Families in both groups were given four to six months (depending on the site) to submit a request for approval of an eligible apartment they would like to lease, and the apartment then had to pass a quality inspection. Families could continue to receive rental subsidies so long as they remained income eligible. A third, control group received no special assistance from MTO but remained eligible for public or project-based housing and other social programs.

Of those households assigned to the experimental group 47 percent used a MTO voucher to relocate to a low-poverty census tract, and 62 percent of those assigned to the Section 8 group relocated through MTO. That the compliance rate is higher for the Section 8 group is presumably attributable in large part to the fact that the vouchers available through MTO were not geographically restricted. In both treatment groups, compared to non-compliers, the compliers tended to be younger, relatively more dissatisfied with their baseline neighborhoods, and to have had fewer children (for details, see Shroder 2002; Feins and Shroder 2005).

The explicit goal of MTO was to help move families into less economically distressed communities. As shown in table 5.3, by this measure MTO was successful. One year after random assignment families in the two MTO treatment groups live in census tracts with average poverty rates 11 to 13 percentage points (25 to 30 percent) below those of the control group. The gap declined somewhat over time in part because of subsequent mobility among all groups. Even six years out, however, the treatment-control differences in tract poverty came to 7 to 8 percentage points (20 percent of the control mean), and the differences in cumulative exposure to neighborhood poverty (duration weighted averages) were 9 to 10 percentage points (20 to 25 percent). The MTO experimental treatment in particular also increased households' exposure to affluent college-educated neighbors, which Greg Duncan, Jeanne Brooks-Gunn, and P. K. Klebanov (1994) suggested have distinct effects from exposure to poor neighbors. Unlike Gautreaux, though, MTO generated surprisingly modest changes in neighborhood racial integration. Evidence also suggests that the treatment-control differences in the characteristics of public schools attended were also very modest. Thus, evidence of such differences in youth outcomes from a study such as MTO would point more clearly to causal pathways that did not involve school characteristics.

Although the postrandomization mobility of control families somewhat reduces MTO's treatment dose on neighborhood characteristics, these patterns may also make the demonstration results somewhat more policy relevant: The counterfactual neighborhood conditions for families in the MTO experimental and Section 8 groups were no longer restricted to the highest-

Table 5.3   Mobility Characteristics of MTO Households

	Controls	Experimental Group		S8-Only Group	
	All	All	Program Movers Only	All	Program Movers Only
Number of moves since RA	1.345	1.741	2.290	1.864	2.416
	(.060)	(.050)	(.061)	(.087)	(.099)
Tract share poor					
One year	.454	.328	.194	.344	.286
	(.007)	(.008)	(.009)	(.011)	(.011)
Six years	.376	.296	.206	.307	.283
	(.008)	(.007)	(.007)	(.010)	(.010)
Average through six years*	.422	.316	.203	.335	.293
	(.006)	(.007)	(.005)	(.008)	(.008)
Tract share college ed.					
One year	.147	.211	.278	.169	.178
	(.006)	(.006)	(.008)	(.007)	(.009)
Six years	.156	.197	.236	.176	.176
	(.006)	(.005)	(.007)	(.007)	(.009)
Average through six years*	.144	.196	.246	.167	.173
	(.004)	(.004)	(.006)	(.006)	(.007)
Tract share minority					
One year	.889	.800	.676	.875	.841
	(.009)	(.011)	(.017)	(.013)	(.017)
Six years	.885	.821	.744	.859	.859
	(.010)	(.010)	(.015)	(.015)	(.015)
Average through six years*	.886	.801	.700	.855	.832
	(.008)	(.009)	(.013)	(.012)	(.015)
N	426	701	361	263	172

Source: Authors' compilation.
Note: RA = random assignment. Mean values shown with standard errors in parentheses. Sample consists of adults interviewed during the MTO interim evaluation and randomized by 12/31/1995 (results one and four years post RA are similar for full sample of MTO adults). Tract characteristics are from the 2000 Census. Number of moves was calculated using the adult's address history.
* = Duration-weighted postrandomization neighborhood averages

poverty census tracts, in which a relatively small set of public housing families lived.

Short-term findings for MTO (two to three years after assignment) were generally consistent with the predictions of previous research suggesting that moving to a less distressed community will on net improve adult and child outcomes (Katz, Kling, and Liebman 2001; Ludwig, Duncan, and

Table 5.4   Impact of MTO on Selected Child and Youth Outcomes, Interim Evaluation

	Females		Males	
	C Mean	ITT	Controls	ITT
Experimental versus control group				
Reading test z-scores [6–20]	.103	.060 (.038)	−.096	−.002 (.045)
Graduated or still enrolled [15–20]	.772	.064 (.036)	.759	−.044 (.037)
Used pot last thirty days [15–20]	.131	−.059* (.028)	.118	.053 (.030)
Number arrests violent crime [15–25]	.241	−.077* (.031)	.537	−.045 (.051)
Number arrests property crime [15–25]	.164	−.057* (.026)	.474	.150* (.055)
Psych distress K6, z-score [15–20]	.268	−.246* (.091)	−.162	.069 (.091)
Has fair or poor health [15–20]	.101	.021 (.027)	.045	.033 (.019)
Section 8 versus control group				
Reading test z-scores [6–20]	.103	.012 (.043)	−.096	.033 (.046)
Graduated or still enrolled [15–20]	.772	.049 (.037)	.759	−.040 (.041)
Used pot last thirty days [15–20]	.131	−.052 (.030)	.118	.075* (.035)
Number arrests violent crime [15–25]	.241	−.079* (.036)	.537	.024 (.062)
Number arrests property crime [15–25]	.164	.031 (.039)	.474	.072 (.059)
Psych distress K6, z-score [15–20]	.268	−.133 (.104)	−.162	−.027 (.096)
Has fair or poor health [15–20]	.101	−.003 (.027)	.045	.033 (.023)

Source: Authors' compilation.
Note: Age range of analytic sample as of December 31, 2001, is reported in parentheses next to each variable. For more details, see Kling, Ludwig, and Katz (2005), Kling, Liebman, and Katz (2006) and Sanbonmatsu et al. (2006).

Hirschfield 2001; Ludwig, Ladd, and Duncan 2001; Leventhal and Brooks-Gunn 2004).

However, the interim MTO evaluation conducted four to seven years after random assignment found a pattern of results more complicated than less segregated neighborhoods, better youth outcomes. Table 5.4 summarizes results for MTO youth, drawing on the results of four studies between 2003 and 2007 (Orr et al. 2003; Sanbonmatsu et al. 2006; Kling, Ludwig, and

Katz 2005; Kling, Liebman, and Katz 2007). These data yield no evidence for statistically significant differences across MTO-assigned groups in reading or math achievement scores measured using the Woodcock-Johnson-Revised (WJ-R) tests. We might expect MTO's impacts on achievement scores to be more pronounced for relatively younger children, in part because of limitations of these tests with teens in the interim MTO study sample,[4] and in part because a growing body of research in developmental psychology, neuroscience, and economics suggests that children may be more sensitive to environmental changes early in life (Shonkoff and Phillips 2000; Carniero and Heckman 2003; Knudsen et al. 2006). Yet Lisa Sanbonmatsu and her colleagues (2006) found no evidence that treatment-control differences in test scores vary by age at random assignment, at least within the range of ages found among those MTO children who were administered tests. Those MTO participants who were very young children at baseline were not tested as part of the interim study, and so it remains possible that MTO effects on their achievement may be more pronounced.

There is a hint in the MTO data that female youth assigned to the experimental group were somewhat more likely to graduate from high school than those assigned to the control group, though the point estimate is not statistically significant and the estimated experimental-treatment effect on graduation for male youth is negative and not statistically significant. More generally, the interim MTO evaluation found that treatment-group assignment improved a variety of behavioral outcomes for female youth but on balance had detrimental effects on behavior for male youth.

One way to reconcile the MTO and Gautreaux findings is to consider that the latter engendered more neighborhood racial segregation than the former, and so perhaps it is the racial rather than social class composition of a community that matters for youth schooling outcomes. In fact, one recent study suggested that exposure to more affluent neighbors may actually have deleterious effects on happiness (Luttmer 2005), which raises the possibility that any beneficial effects from MTO moves on behavior attributable to reductions in neighborhood racial segregation could be masked in the overall program impact estimates by offsetting deleterious effects from reductions in class segregation.

This possibility can be tested by exploiting variation across MTO sites in treatment effects on mobility outcomes to use site-treatment group interactions as instruments for specific neighborhood characteristics (see Kling, Liebman, and Katz 2007). Jens Ludwig and Jeffrey Kling (2007) found that census tract minority composition was a stronger predictor of youth violent criminal behavior than either the tract poverty rate or local-area crime rate. In unpublished results, they found no evidence for an association between tract minority composition and children's achievement test scores.

MTO offers in our view perhaps the best evidence available to date about neighborhood effects on youth outcomes, but it is important to keep in mind that the MTO program population consisted of those very low-income minority families living in some of the nation's worst housing projects who volunteered to participate in this mobility demonstration. In principle, neighborhood effects may be different on other populations. But there is a plausible case to be made that the MTO families were those who expected to benefit the most from moving, which might suggest that MTO estimates are an upper bound for the effects of neighborhood change on other, similarly disadvantaged families.[5]

An alternative concern about the MTO findings is that the demonstration examined the effects of neighborhood change, and so in principle might have confounded the effects of mobility with those of neighborhood composition. Jeffrey Kling, Jeffrey Liebman, and Lawrence Katz provided one argument against this concern, exploiting variation across MTO demonstration sites in treatment effects on neighborhood poverty rates and found evidence of a "treatment dose-response" relationship between changes in tract poverty and MTO participant outcomes (2007).

Kling, Ludwig, and Katz provided another data point against the moving hypothesis (2005). They examined longitudinal arrest histories for MTO youth and found that, in the near term, assignment to the experimental rather than the control group reduced male arrests for violent crime, and led to a detrimental experimental effect on property crime arrests only, beginning about three or four years after random assignment. This temporal pattern in MTO impacts runs contrary to what we would expect if the disruption of moving were driving behavioral problems among experimental group males. More generally, given that the U.S. population became only modestly less poor during the 1990s and experienced an increase in the share minority, national declines in neighborhood racial and class segregation must be driven more by resorting families across neighborhoods than by changes in the characteristics of persistent residents of a given neighborhood. In this case, any consequences of social churning and the difficulties of developing new social ties among neighborhood residents that is at play in the MTO data would seem to be relevant for understanding the consequences for the black-white gap from changes in neighborhood segregation in the United States as a whole.

Perhaps the most important qualification to the MTO findings is that the interim evaluation measures outcomes four to seven years after random assignment, and in principle the effects of neighborhood changes on children, could increase over time as the children become more socially integrated in their new communities, or as their exposure to more developmentally productive inputs accumulates. The interim MTO evaluation did find positive effects on some family inputs, particularly parent mental health, that could in principle improve student learning over the long term. However, even if there are long-term effects of neighborhood mobility on youth outcomes that cannot be detected by MTO, the puzzling fact remains that the black-white test score gap stopped closing during a period when neighborhood racial segregation steadily declined, and neighborhood economic segregation rose at most slightly before declining.

Evidence of at most a small role for neighborhood socioeconomic characteristics from the MTO study is corroborated by recent quasi-experimental studies of families randomly assigned to public housing units in Toronto (Oreopoulos 2003) and families displaced by public housing demolition in Chicago (Jacob 2004). Some studies, notably Daniel Aaronson's (1998) of siblings in the Panel Study of Income Dynamics, and David Harding's (2003) propensity score-matching model using the same dataset, did report significant associations between neighborhood characteristics and youth outcomes. David Cutler and Edward Glaeser, using various instrumental variables for segregation, found significant cross-sectional associations between segregation levels and black-white outcome disparities at the metropolitan level (1997). But each of these methodologies is subject to criticism, and none can exclude the possibility that schools are the main causal pathway between neighborhood characteristics and outcomes (for further discussion, see Vigdor 2006a). The next section focuses more exclusively on arguments that racial disparities in school characteristics, made possible by school segregation, influence the magnitude of the black-white test score gap.

Effects of Schools

The methodological equivalent of conducting an MTO-style experiment to assess the importance of school segregation in perpetuating black-white test score gaps would involve randomly assigning students to schools—or even school districts—of varying racial composition, for potentially varying periods. To our knowledge, no such experiment has ever taken place. Some efforts have been made to exploit variation in the timing of school desegregation orders in the 1960s and 1970s, as well as unitary status declarations in a later time period, to infer the impact of racial composition on outcomes. These studies rest on the assumption that variation in the timing of such court orders is idiosyncratic from the perspective of the individual student. Jonathan Guryan (2004) found evidence suggesting that court-ordered school desegregation plans reduce black dropout rates by 2 to 3 percentage points, with no detectable effect on whites. Byron Lutz (2005) found qualitatively similar effects when he examined the impacts of termination of many of these desegregation plans during the 1990s. These court-ordered desegregation plans may also reduce violent crime victimizations among both white and black youth (Weiner, Lutz, and Ludwig 2007).

Jacob Vigdor (2006b) used data from the U.S. Census and the National Longitudinal Survey of Youth 1979 cohort to document that the black-white earnings gap was generally larger in the South than in the North for cohorts born before 1950, but displayed no association with region for cohorts born after that date. Cohorts born in the South after 1950 would have witnessed at least some effective school integration before their eighteenth birthday as the South made its transition from having the nation's most segregated schools to having the most integrated. The NLSY evidence shows that the black-white gap among a group born between 1958 and 1965 is significantly narrower for those who lived in the South at age fourteen, controlling independently for region of birth and region of residence. This group would have reached age fourteen between 1972 and 1979, a period when school segregation levels were significantly lower in the South than in other regions of the country.

To date, these studies of the impact of broad policy changes provide perhaps the most convincing evidence linking school segregation to changes in outcomes. None of them, however, considers the potential impact of segregation on test scores. An ideal study would couple comprehensive test score data with information on the timing and extent of school desegregation orders. To our knowledge, no such study has been conducted.

Nonexperimental studies of the potential impact of segregation on test score gaps follow one of two methodologies. The first examines longitudinal patterns. If trends in the gap between blacks and whites who attend the same school are identical to the overall trend, it is difficult to argue that differential assignment to schools explains the overall gap. The second method directly relates individual test scores to measures of school or classroom composition. Studies using this second method are often referred to as peer effects studies.

Prominent studies of between- and within-school growth in the achievement gap include those by Roland Fryer and Steven Levitt (2004) and by Eric Hanushek and Steven Rivkin (2006). These studies used the same data—the Early Childhood Longitudinal Survey—but came to conflicting conclusions. Fryer and Levitt reported that most of the growth in the black-white test score gap between kindergarten and third grade occurs within rather than between schools, which in turn limits the potential explanatory power of across-school segregation. Hanushek and Rivkin found fault with Fryer and Levitt's decomposition strategy, and report that "virtually all of the grade-to-grade increases in the overall gap occur between schools" (2006, 10).

Even accepting the finding that black-white gaps grow because blacks disproportionately attend schools where all students fare worse over time, it is not necessarily true that altering attendance patterns would reduce the gap. Students predisposed to poor growth in test scores for reasons unrelated to school quality might tend to congregate in schools serving a predominantly black population. This weakness with the first nonexperimental methodology is addressed to some extent by the second method, which generally introduces at least some controls for student background characteristics when attempting to infer the impact of school or classroom composition on achievement.

The greatest weakness in these studies is the inherently imperfect nature of controlling for student background. Many studies go beyond controlling for student characteristics, adding classroom- or school-level covariates in a hierarchical framework. Some go so far as to use classroom-level variation in peer composition and employ school fixed-effects. This strategy has the advantage of eliminating omitted variable bias associated with nonrandom sorting into schools, but it has the disadvantage of eliminating several potential causal mechanisms linking racial composition to achievement. Predominantly black schools may find it more difficult to recruit high-quality teachers, for example, but the variation in teacher quality across classrooms within a school is probably smaller and less correlated with race. Classroom racial composition in year t may also be poorly correlated with classroom racial composition in prior years. Studies that use school fixed-effects are thus ill-suited to test dose response hypotheses.

Keeping these caveats in mind, it is worthwhile surveying studies linking school or classroom composition to achievement. Among studies examining school-level variation, which are subject to concerns regarding nonrandom sorting across schools, the Coleman report of 1966 is perhaps the best known. This study found that a school's socioeconomic class composition was among the more important predictors of individual student achievement levels, certainly much more important than racial composition. Recent studies that use cross-sectional variation in school segregation often generate similar findings—school racial composition seems to be weakly if at all related to student outcomes, and SES of the school's student body may have a stronger association with student achievement (Rivkin 2000; Cook and Evans 2000; Rumberger and Palardy 2005).

David Card and Jesse Rothstein (2006) documented a correlation similar to that in figure 5.3, substituting SAT scores for NAEP test scores. In a contrast with much of the existing literature, the authors attributed much of the apparent relationship to causal mechanisms other than those involving school quality or school segregation. The pattern of reported results is consistent with a model in which long-term rather than instantaneous measures of segregation matter more for test score outcomes, and long-term school segregation is more highly correlated with neighborhood segregation than with instantaneous measures of school segregation.

Eric Hanushek, John Kain, and Steven Rivkin (2004) exploited a rich panel dataset of student-level observations from Texas public schools, which enabled them to infer the impact of racial composition by comparing variation across cohorts of students who attend the same school.

Because their preferred specifications used school fixed effects to address concerns about endogenous sorting into schools, the results are subject to the criticism that they excluded some potential causal mechanisms and rendered inferences about nonlinear dose response difficult. The study found that a 10 percent reduction in percentage black in school would increase test scores for blacks by sbout 0.025 standard deviation and increase those for whites by about 0.01 standard deviation (not statistically significant). These effects are about twice as large for black students at the top of the achievement distribution as for those at the bottom. That their finding holds even after controlling for either the average achievement level or social class composition of other students in the school is significant. These authors controlled for a variety of potential confounding factors, including student-specific rates of change in achievement test scores and hard-to-measure factors that vary at the level of the school-by-grade or even attendance zone-by-year. They argued that the magnitude of their estimates suggests that equalizing the racial composition of all schools in Texas would reduce achievement gaps in that state by roughly 25 percent. In the end, it is difficult to assess whether the estimates understated or overstated the true impact of segregation on test score gaps.

Caroline Hoxby (2000) used plausibly random variation across cohorts in student demographic composition in Texas and found that a 10 percent increase in the proportion of black students reduces achievement test scores for blacks by about 0.1 standard deviation in reading and about 0.06 in math. She found some evidence that the effects of changes in segregation are strongest in schools that are composed of at least one-third black students already. The mean effect of increases in the proportion of black students on white students is of the same sign as for black students but only around one-quarter as large in magnitude. As with the Hanushek, Kain, and Rivkin study, these effects may understate the impact of segregation because they excluded school-level causal mechanisms, or overstated them if the restriction to cross-cohort variation in peer group composition failed to eliminate all potential sources of omitted variable bias.

Jacob Vigdor and Thomas Nechyba (2007) used administrative data on North Carolina public schools to examine the relationship between peer composition and test scores at both the school and classroom levels. Unlike the Texas studies, their results fail to show any negative association between peer percentage black and the relative performance of black students. Relative to the Texas administrative data, the North Carolina data included more detailed family background information and permitted the matching of students to classrooms and teachers in elementary grades. The authors also analyzed variation in peer composition associated with the opening of new schools in rapidly growing districts, by examining how achievement scores change for students that have a substantial change in peer group composition (without moving schools themselves).

The absence of peer effects could be attributed to differences in methodology, including the focus on elementary rather than middle school grades.

Jane Cooley (2006) used the same North Carolina data to estimate a structural model of the relationship between peer effort and achievement. She allowed the impact of peer effort on individual achievement to vary by race of the individual and the peer. The results were used to forecast the potential impact of integrating two neighboring school districts with varying racial composition, and eliminating within-district segregation in each. In this simulation, the black-white achievement gap was reduced by roughly .03 standard deviations.

Overall, the literature on school segregation and the black-white test score gap, though clearly not unanimous, provides more substantial support than the complementary literature on the impact of neighborhood-level segregation on comparable outcomes. By several estimates, the impact of segregation is modest. Extrapolations of even the most supportive studies would imply a black-white gap of sizable magnitude in the absence of any school segregation. There are several unexplored questions within this literature as well, which seem ripe for further explanation. First, it is plausible that the cumulative effect of spending several years in a segregated environment is greater than the linear extrapolation of short-term effects. Few, if any, studies have examined the impact of past peer racial composition on current outcomes. Second, as discussed earlier, the most striking change in school racial composition patterns has been the increase in students who are neither black nor white, and few if any studies have documented whether black students fare particularly poorly in schools with higher shares of Hispanic or Asian students. Finally, the further exploitation of true experiments or quasi-experiments creating exogenous variation in school racial composition also seems like a promising avenue for further research.

How do we reconcile evidence that school racial composition matters for student outcomes with findings from MTO of no detectable impacts on achievement test scores, dropout, or other outcomes? As noted, MTO had relatively modest effects on neighborhood racial segregation, and even more modest impacts on school racial segregation—in part because a fair number of children assigned to the MTO treatment groups remained in their old schools. For MTO participants assigned to the experimental group, the average change in the proportion of minority students at a school was about 3 or 4 percentage points, half as large as the average change in the proportion of minority residents in their neighborhood (Sanbonmatsu et al. 2006, table 2). The results from Hanushek, Kain, and Rivkin (2004) and Hoxby (2000) suggested the result should be an increase in student achievement test scores on the order of 0.01 to 0.03 standard deviation, which would be too small to be detected in the MTO data.

Conclusion

Can segregation explain the stalled progress toward closing the black-white test score gap since 1990? If so, is there some reason for hope that progress will resume in the near future? As discussed, there are a number of reasons to think that segregation influences black-white test score gaps. Some incorporate school-specific characteristics as a mediating factor, others do not. The most reliable empirical evidence, derived from the MTO demonstration program and other quasi-experimental studies, indicates that any links between neighborhood and outcomes not mediated by school factors must be small. This conclusion is supported by general evidence on the downward trend in residential segregation, which continued unabated in the 1990s.

The downward trend in residential segregation in the 1990s was not matched by a commensurate downward trend in school segregation. Percentage black in the neighborhood occupied by the average black declined 5 percentage points in the 1990s, but percentage black in the public school attended by the average black student declined only 3 points between 1987 and 2003. Percentage nonwhite in the public school attended by the average black student actually increased over this time period (see Berends and Peñaloza, chapter 2, this volume). Seen either as an increase or a more modest decline, the post-1980s trend in school segregation can be explained largely as the result of declining efforts to integrate public schools. Although schools remain more integrated than the communities they serve, school segregation is clearly converging toward the degree of neighborhood segregation. Moreover, the reduction in the rate of school segregation occurred at roughly the same time that the black-white test score gap stalled. The circumstantial case linking school segregation to the test score gap is compelling. The period of rapid school integration beginning in the late 1960s immediately preceded a period of rapid narrowing in the black-white test score gap, most apparent in contrasts between the high school graduating classes of 1981 and 1989.

The literature on the impact of school segregation suffers from the lack of a school-level analogue to the MTO experiment. That said, a number of studies do offer evidence to support some causal component to the basic correlational relationship documented in figure 5.3. Studies have documented relative gains to black students associated with discrete changes in school segregation, both at the regional and local levels. The gaps between black and white students who attend the same school tend to be small relative to the overall gap. Some additional studies exploiting idiosyncratic variation in racial composition apparent in administrative public school data have found a significant link with achievement test scores, in spite of the fact that they frequently use school fixed effects, which eliminate potentially important causal mechanisms linking racial composition to outcomes. These studies, significantly, do not estimate the impact of changes in percentage Hispanic or Asian on the black-white test score gap.

To be sure, the magnitude of the estimated school racial composition effects, coupled with the slight increase in school segregation relative to residential segregation, imply that the relationships identified here can explain only a small portion of what occurred in the 1990s. Accepting the largest available point estimate, the additional 2 percent reduction in percentage black that would have transpired if school segregation exactly tracked residential segregation would have resulted in a narrowing of the black-white test score gap by about .02 standard deviations—an effect too small to be detected except in samples of extraordinary size. This is our best guess of the impact of reductions in desegregation effort, but we readily admit that it is a poor guess. There are simply not any reliable causal estimates of the effect of school racial composition on the black-white test score gap that incorporate potential between- and within-school mechanisms.

It is also clear, however, that even the limited estimates at our disposal suggest that the future trend of school segregation could have a larger impact on the gap. A complete elimination in district efforts to integrate public schools could raise gaps significantly in some cases. In others, school integration is moot at the district level because entire school systems are nearly 100 percent nonwhite. Should the long-term trend toward lower levels of residential segregation continue in the twenty-first century, however, we might expect to see renewed progress towards closing the gap. Indeed, one reading of the evidence during the 1990s is that school segregation levels eased upward in response to court rulings, but that future trends will be dominated by the secular trend toward greater neighborhood integration that is now nearing its fifth decade.

If society's only goal were to eliminate racial disparities in test scores, setting aside the various concerns that have led courts to move away from school integration over time, the literature points to some clear remedies. Busing, or other measures to reduce segregation across schools within a district, appears to have a modest narrowing effect on the black-white test score gap. Two recent 5–4 decisions handed down by the Supreme Court struck down voluntary racial desegregation plans in Louisville and Seattle. Justice Kennedy, however, siding with the majority, nonetheless seemed to leave the door open to more narrowly targeted race-conscious plans, which might include siting schools in areas that would draw more racially mixed student bodies, or implementing magnet school programs.[6] In 1974 the Supreme Court in *Milliken v. Bradley* (418 US 717) struck down an inter-district desegregation plan in Detroit, and set stringent conditions for when the approach would be allowed. Given existing differences in the racial composition of cities versus suburbs in America, though, it seems clear that desegregation efforts that worked across district lines could accomplish much more than an order to integrate schools within districts in some parts of the country.

An alternative approach to remedying the negative effects of school segregation, such that they exist, would be to directly address the causal mechanisms producing the effects. For example, if teachers were to systematically avoid taking jobs in schools serving minority students, then a policy of equalized funding would result in unequal opportunity. Because the mechanisms linking racial composition to achievement are still poorly understood, society may be better served by a program of experimentation and pilot studies, rather than a full-fledged acceptance of an untested hypothesis. Such a program would serve both the social scientist's need for rigor and the policy maker's desire for action.

Table 5.A1   School-Level Free Lunch Eligible-Ineligible Dissimilarity, U.S. and Large School Districts

Geographic Entity	1987 to 1988	2003 to 2004	Change
United States, LEAs weighted by enrollment	0.269 (0.143) (N=3,198)	0.279 (0.131) (N=12,976)	+0.010
United States, LEAs weighted by free lunch-eligible enrollment	0.294 (0.131) (N=3,198)	0.291 (0.127) (N=12,976)	−0.003
Dade County, Florida	0.474	0.418	−0.056
Broward County, Florida	0.477	0.448	−0.029
Hillsborough County, Florida	0.352	0.372	+0.020
Duval County, Florida	0.385	0.381	−0.004
Palm Beach County, Florida	0.510	0.509	−0.001
Orange County, Florida	0.409	0.343	−0.066
Pinellas County, Florida	0.331	0.386	+0.055
District of Columbia	0.522	0.387	−0.135
Orleans Parish	0.411	0.447	+0.036
Charlotte-Mecklenburg	0.297	0.460	+0.163
DeKalb County, Georgia	0.455	0.383	−0.072
Atlanta City	0.443	0.409	−0.034
Cobb County, Georgia	0.523	0.511	−0.012
Polk County, Florida	0.345	0.333	−0.012
Wake County, North Carolina	0.257	0.286	+0.029
Gwinnett County, Georgia	0.369	0.407	+0.038
Jefferson Parish	0.379	0.325	−0.054

Source: Authors' compilation from U.S. Department of Education (1988, 2004).

Table 5.A2   District-Level Free Lunch Eligible-Ineligible Dissimilarity, by State

State	1987 to 1988	2003 to 2004	Change
Alaska	0.310	0.252	−0.058
Delaware	0.101	0.170	+0.069
Florida	0.132	0.176	+0.044
Georgia	0.365	0.298	−0.067
Idaho	0.327	0.195	−0.132
Indiana	0.327	0.326	−0.001
Iowa	0.212	0.263	+0.051
Louisiana	0.276	0.230	−0.046
Minnesota	0.374	0.359	−0.015
Nebraska	0.347	0.288	−0.059
New Hampshire	0.289	0.313	+0.024
North Carolina	0.262	0.191	−0.071
Oregon	0.210	0.203	−0.007
Rhode Island	0.421	0.564	+0.143
Vermont	0.370	0.324	−0.046

Source: Authors' compilation from U.S. Department of Education (1988, 2004).

Acknowledgments

Paper prepared for the conference "Stalled Progress: Inequality and the Black-White Test Score Gap," Russell Sage Foundation, November 16–17, 2006. We are grateful to conference participants and especially Adam Gamoran, Katherine Magnuson, and Jane Waldfogel for helpful comments on an earlier draft. Any errors and all opinions are of course our own.

Notes

1. The dissimilarity index has been criticized along a number of dimensions. It is preferred here primarily for its ease of computation and of interpretation (for a more complete discussion of segregation measures and their relative advantages, see Massey and Denton 1988; Echenique and Fryer 2005).
2. Direct comparison between segregation levels at the school and neighborhood level should be undertaken with caution, as segregation indices tend to rise as the size of the neighborhood or other unit of observation decreases. In this comparison, neighborhoods are proxied by census tracts, which have an average of 4,000 residents each, implying roughly 800 school-age children per tract. The average school in the CCD data serves about 500 children. Thus the direct comparison between neighborhood and school segregation likely understates the impact of school district efforts on segregation levels.
3. The Section 8 program provides housing assistance through rental certificates or vouchers. Income eligibility is usually set to 50 percent of local median income, with subsidies equal to the difference between 30 percent of tenant income and

an area-wide threshold established by HUD. Since MTO got under way, the voucher program has been renamed the Housing Choice Voucher (HCV) program, but we will use the terminology in effect at the start of MTO.

4. Larry Orr and his colleagues (2003, 107, Exhibit 6.2) noted that there is very little variation in mean WJ-R scores on the reading test by age for youth age twelve to nineteen at the end of 2001, the year before the surveys were conducted. For example, children who were five at the end of 2001 had a mean scale score of 433 versus that of 507 for those who were twelve, a difference of 75 points. In contrast, the mean scale score for nineteen-year-olds in the interim MTO sample was 517, just 10 points higher than that for twelve-year-olds. This could indicate that the WJ-R tests are not very strongly related to what children learn in school during their adolescent years, so that the WJ-R tests do not well capture MTO impacts on adolescent learning environments.

5. In addition, Marianne Page, Gary Solon, and Greg Duncan (2000) found relatively modest correlations in outcomes for youth living in the same primary sampling unit within the Panel Study of Income Dynamics (PSID).

6. The two cases announced on June 28, 2007, were *Meredith v. Jefferson Co. Board of Ed* and *Parents Involved in the Community Schools v. Seattle School District No. 1.*

References

Aaronson, Daniel. 1998. "Using Sibling Data to Estimate the Impact of Neighborhoods on Children's Educational Outcomes." *Journal of Human Resources* 33(4): 915–46.

Card, David and Jesse Rothstein. 2006. "Racial Segregation and the Black-White Test Score Gap." NBER Working Paper 12078. Cambridge, Mass.: National Bureau of Economic Research.

Clotfelter, Charles T. 2004. *After Brown: The Rise and Retreat of School Desegregation.* Princeton, N.J.: Princeton University Press.

Clotfelter, Charles T., Helen F. Ladd, and Jacob L. Vigdor. 2005. "Federal Oversight, Local Control, and the Specter of 'Resegregation' in Southern Schools." NBER Working Paper 11086. Cambridge, Mass.: National Bureau for Economic Research.

Coleman, James, E. Q. Campbell, C. J. Hobson, J. McPartland, A. M. Mood, F. D. Weinfeld, and R. L. York. 1966. *Equality of Educational Opportunity.* Washington: Government Printing Office.

Cook, Michael D., and William N. Evans. 2000. "Families or Schools? Explaining the Convergence in White and Black Academic Performance." *Journal of Labor Economics* 18(4): 729–54.

Cooley, Jane. 2006. "Desegregation and the Achievement Gap: Do Diverse Peers Help?" Unpublished manuscript. University of Wisconsin, Madison.

Cutler, David M., and Edward L. Glaeser. 1997. "Are Ghettos Good or Bad?" *Quarterly Journal of Economics* 112(3): 827–72.

Cutler, David M., Edward L. Glaeser, and Jacob L. Vigdor. 1999. "The Rise and Decline of the American Ghetto." *Journal of Political Economy* 107(3): 455–506.

Duncan, Greg J., Jeanne Brooks-Gunn, and Pamela Klebanov. 1994. "Economic Deprivation and Early Childhood Development." *Child Development* 65(2): 296–318.

Echenique, Federico, and Roland Fryer. 2005. "On the Measurement of Segregation." NBER Working Paper 11258. Cambridge, Mass.: National Bureau of Economic Research.

Ellen, Ingrid Gould, and Margery Austin Turner. 2003. "Do Neighborhoods Matter and Why?" In *Choosing a Better Life? Evaluating the Moving to Opportunity Social Experiment*, edited by John Goering and Judith D. Feins. Washington, D.C.: Urban Institute Press.

Feins, Judith D., and Mark D. Shroder. 2005. "Moving to Opportunity: The Demonstration's Design and Its Effects on Mobility." *Urban Studies* 42(8): 1275–99.

Fryer, Roland G., and Steven D. Levitt. 2004. "Understanding the Black-White Test Score Gap in the First Two Years of School." *Review of Economics and Statistics* 86(2): 447–64.

Glaeser, Edward L., and Jacob L. Vigdor. 2003. "Racial Segregation: Promising News." In *Redefining Urban and Suburban America: Evidence from Census 2000*, vol. 1, edited by Bruce Katz and Robert E. Lang. Washington, D.C.: Brookings Institution Press.

Guryan, Jonathan. 2004. "Desegregation and Black Dropout Rates." *American Economic Review* 94(4): 919–43.

Hanushek, Eric A., John F. Kain, and Steven G. Rivkin. 2004. "New Evidence about Brown v. Board of Education: The Complex Effects of School Racial Composition on Achievement." Hoover Institution Working Paper. Stanford, Calif.: Stanford University Press.

Hanushek, Eric A., and Steven G. Rivkin. 2006. "School Quality and the Black-White Achievement Gap." NBER Working Paper 12651. Cambridge, Mass.: National Bureau of Economic Research.

Harding, David J. 2003. "Counterfactual Models of Neighborhood Effects: The Effect of Neighborhood Poverty on Dropping Out and Teenage Pregnancy." *American Journal of Sociology* 109(3): 676–719.

Hoxby, Caroline. 2000. "Peer Effects in the Classroom: Learning from Gender and Race Variation." NBER Working Paper 7867. Cambridge, Mass.: National Bureau of Economic Research.

Jacob, Brian A. 2004. "Public Housing, Housing Vouchers, and Student Achievement: Evidence from Public Housing Demolitions in Chicago." *American Economic Review* 94(1): 233–58.

Jargowsky, Paul A. 1996. "Take the Money and Run: Economic Segregation in U.S. Metropolitan Areas." *American Sociological Review* 61(6): 984–98.

———. 2003. "Stunning Progress, Hidden Problems: The Dramatic Decline of Concentrated Poverty in the 1990s." *Living Cities Census Series.* Washington, D.C.: Brookings Institution, Center on Urban and Metropolitan Policy.

Katz, Lawrence F., Jeffrey R. Kling, and Jeffrey B. Liebman. 2001. "Moving to Opportunity in Boston: Early Results of a Randomized Mobility Experiment." *Quarterly Journal of Economics.* 116(2): 607–54.

Kawachi, Ichiro, and Lisa F. Berkman, editors. 2003. *Neighborhoods and Health.* New York: Oxford University Press.

Keels, Micere, Jim Rosenbaum, and Greg Duncan. 2004. "Second Generation Effects of Chicago's Gautreaux Residential Mobility Program on Crime." Paper presented at the Annual APPAM Research Conference on Creating and Using

Evidence in Public Policy Analysis and Management. Atlanta, Ga., October 28–30, 2004.

Kling, Jeffrey R., Jeffrey B. Liebman, and Lawrence F. Katz. 2007. "Experimental Analysis of Neighborhood Effects." *Econometrica* 75(1): 83–119.

Kling, Jeffrey R., Jens Ludwig, and Lawrence F. Katz. 2005. "Neighborhood Effects on Crime for Female and Male Youth: Evidence from a Randomized Housing Voucher Experiment." *Quarterly Journal of Economics* 120(1): 87–130.

Knudsen, Eric I., James J. Heckman, Judy Cameron, and Jack P. Shonkoff. 2006. "Building America's Future Workforce: Economic, Neurobiological and Behavioral Perspectives on Investment in Human Skill Development." *Proceedings of the National Academy of Sciences* 103(27): 10155–62.

Leventhal, Tama, and Jeanne Brooks-Gunn. 2000. "The Neighborhoods They Live In: The Effects of Neighborhood Residence on Child and Adolescent Outcomes." *Psychological Bulletin* 126(2): 309–37.

———. 2004. "A Randomized Study of Neighborhood Effects on Low-Income Children's Educational Outcomes." *Developmental Psychology* 40(4): 488–507.

Logan, John. 2004. "Resegregation in American Public Schools? Not in the 1990s." Albany, N.Y.: Mumford Center for Comparative Urban and Regional Research. Accessed at http://mumford.albany.edu/census/noresegregation/noresegregation01.htm

Ludwig, Jens, Greg J. Duncan, and Paul Hirschfield. 2001. "Urban Poverty and Juvenile Crime: Evidence from a Randomized Housing-mobility Experiment." *Quarterly Journal of Economics.* 116(2): 655–80.

Ludwig, Jens, and Jeffrey R. Kling. 2007. "Is Crime Contagious?" *Journal of Law and Economics* 50(3): 491–518.

Ludwig, Jens, Helen F. Ladd, and Greg J. Duncan. 2001. "The Effects of Urban Poverty on Educational Outcomes: Evidence from a Randomized Experiment." In *Urban Poverty and Educational Outcomes,* edited by William Gale and Janet Rothenberg Pack. Washington, D.C.: Brookings Institution Press.

Luttmer, Erzo F. P. 2005. "Neighbors as Negatives: Relative Earnings and Well-Being." *Quarterly Journal of Economics* 120(3): 963–1002.

Lutz, Byron F. 2005. "Post Brown vs. the Board of Education: The Effects of the End of Court-Ordered Desegregation." Finance and Economics Discussion Series Working Paper 2005-64. Washington: Federal Reserve Board.

Massey, Douglas S., and Nancy Denton. 1988. "The Dimensions of Residential Segregation." *Social Forces* 67(2): 281–315.

Mendenhall, Ruby, Greg J. Duncan, and Stefanie DeLuca. 2004. "Neighborhood Resources and Economic Mobility: Results from the Gautreaux Program." Unpublished paper. Presented at the annual meeting of the American Sociological Association. Atlanta, Ga., August 16, 2003. Accessed at http://www.allacademic.com/meta/p_mla_apa_research_citation/1/0/6/7/4/p106749_index.html.

Oreopoulos, Philip. 2003. "The Long-Run Consequences of Living in a Poor Neighborhood." *Quarterly Journal of Economics* 118(4): 1533–75.

Orfield, Gary, and Susan Eaton. 1996. *Dismantling Desegregation: The Quiet Reversal of Brown v. Board of Education.* New York: The New Press.

Orr, Larry, Judith D. Feins, Robin Jacob, Erik Beecroft, Lisa Sanbonmatsu, Lawrence F. Katz, Jeffrey B. Liebman, and Jeffrey R. Kling. 2003. *Moving to*

Opportunity Interim Impacts Evaluation. Washington: U.S. Department of Housing and Urban Development, Office of Policy Development and Research.

Page, Marianne, Gary Solon, and Greg J. Duncan. 2000. "Correlations Between Neighboring Children in Their Subsequent Educational Attainment." *The Review of Economics and Statistics* 82(3): 383–92.

Rivkin, Steven G. 2000. "School Desegregation, Academic Attainment and Earnings." *Journal of Human Resources* 35(2): 333–46.

Rubinowitz, Leonard S., and James E. Rosenbaum. 2001. *Crossing the Class and Color Lines: From Public Housing to White Suburbia.* Chicago: University of Chicago Press.

Rumberger, Russell W., and Gregory J. Palardy. 2005. "Does Segregation Still Matter? The Impact of Student Composition on Academic Achievement in High School." *Teachers College Record* 107(9): 1999–2045.

Sampson, Robert J., Jeffrey D. Morenoff, and Thomas Gannon-Rowley. 2002. "Assessing 'Neighborhood Effects': Social Processes and New Directions in Research." *Annual Review of Sociology* 28(2002): 443–78.

Sanbonmatsu, Lisa, Jeffrey R. Kling, Greg J. Duncan, and Jeanne Brooks-Gunn. 2006. "Neighborhoods and Academic Achievement: Results from the Moving to Opportunity Experiment." *Journal of Human Resources* 41(4): 649–91.

Shonkoff, Jack P, and Deborah A. Phillips, editors. 2000. *From Neurons to Neighborhoods: The Science of Early Childhood Development.* Washington, D.C.: National Academies Press.

Shroder, Mark. 2002. "Locational Constraint, Housing Counseling, and Successful Lease-Up in a Randomized Housing Voucher Experiment." *Journal of Urban Economics* 51(2): 315–38.

U.S. Department of Education. 1988. Common Core of Data: Public School Universe Data, 1987–88.

———. 2004. Common Core of Data: Public School Universe Data, 2003–04.

Vigdor, Jacob L. 2006a. "Peer Effects in Neighborhoods and Housing." In *Deviant Peer Influences in Programs for Youth: Problems and Solutions,* edited by Kenneth A. Dodge, Thomas J. Dishion and Jennifer E. Lansford. New York: Guilford Press.

———. 2006b. "The new promised land: Black-white convergence in the American South, 1960–2000." NBER Working Paper 12143. Cambridge, Mass.: National Bureau of Economic Research.

Vigdor, Jacob L., and Thomas Nechyba. 2007. "Peer Effects in North Carolina Public Schools." In *Schools and the Equal Opportunity Problem,* edited by P. E. Peterson and L. Woessmann. Cambridge, Mass.: MIT Press.

Watson, Tara. 2006. "Metropolitan Growth, Inequality, and Neighborhood Segregation by Income." Unpublished manuscript. Williams College.

Weiner, David A., Byron F. Lutz, and Jens Ludwig. 2007. "The Effects of School Desegregation on Crime." Paper presented at the annual meetings of the American Economic Association. Chicago, Ill., January 7, 2007.

Wilson, William Julius. 1987. *The Truly Disadvantaged: The Inner City, the Underclass, and Public Policy.* Chicago: University of Chicago Press.

Chapter 6

The Role of Inequality in Teacher Quality

Sean P. Corcoran and William N. Evans

In January 2002, the federal government enacted No Child Left Behind (NCLB), an aggressive effort to hold schools and state education agencies accountable for "clos[ing] the achievement gap between high- and low-performing children, especially the achievement gap between minority and non-minority students."[1] After decades of progress, the achievement gap between African American and white children in reading and mathematics had begun to stagnate—or in many cases widen—and lawmakers viewed this legislation as a critical response to growing inequalities in basic skills (for a comprehensive overview, see the introduction).

One principal component of NCLB is the requirement that all core academic subject teachers be highly qualified.[2] When states fall short of this mandate, the law requires documentation of actions that will be taken "to ensure that poor and minority children are not taught at higher rates than other children by inexperienced, unqualified, or out-of-field teachers."[3] Though much debate remains over what constitutes a highly qualified teacher, the legislation's emphasis on teachers is well founded. Nearly all recent research on the subject has demonstrated that teacher quality ranks among the most important inputs that schools contribute to educational outcomes (for a review, see Hanushek and Rivkin 2006).

The central role of teacher quality in educational outcomes has led many researchers and policy analysts to point to differential exposure of white and black students to effective teachers as a possible contributor to the black-white achievement gap (Ferguson 1998). Recent research has shown that teachers are unevenly distributed across districts and schools, with less-qualified teachers disproportionately located in schools with students from predominately low-income families or racial and ethnic minorities (Lankford, Loeb, and Wyckoff 2002; Clotfelter, Ladd, and Vigdor 2005, 2006). What is less clear, however, is whether changes in black-white exposure to high quality teachers can explain observed trends in the black-white test score gap.[4] As the introduction to this volume demonstrates, the achievement gap in reading and mathematics steadily narrowed at all grade levels for more than a decade through the 1980s (1975 to 1986), only to come to an abrupt halt and reverse course in the 1990s. Growth in the gap was especially pronounced in middle school (age thirteen) and high school (age seventeen), where the gap in reading achievement grew 54.8 and 51.3 percent (respectively) between 1988 and 1999, and the math gap rose 31.8 and 8.8 percent.[5] By contrast, the elementary school (age nine) gap in reading achievement ended the decade 21.2 percent larger in 1999, masking a general reduction in the gap between 1990 and 1996. The gap in elementary math achievement rose only marginally in the 1990s. This variation at the elementary and secondary levels suggests that differences in exposure to effective teachers may have evolved differently by schooling level.

There is reason to believe that little has changed in recent years with respect to the distribution of teacher quality across black and white students. School enrollment has not become more racially integrated. Charles Clotfelter (2004) and Gary Orfield and Chungmei Lee (2006) found that, after a long period of desegregation, black students in most regions of the country became more racially isolated during the 1990s (see also Vigdor and Ludwig, chapter 5, this volume). Teacher decisions about where to work depend on the class and racial composition of students as much or more as on relative salaries (Hanushek, Kain, and Rivkin 2004; Scafidi, Sjoquist, and Stinebrickner 2007), and teacher labor markets are remarkably local.[6] Teacher placement continues to depend on the seniority privileges and preferences of individual teachers, in addition to parental voice and action. Absent any aggressive policies on the part of states, districts, and schools to more equitably distribute teachers—of which there are few examples—the existing pattern of student enrollment and teacher placement is likely to persist.[7]

We draw on several large surveys of teachers and high school sophomores to assess how the exposure of white and black students to high quality teachers has changed over fifteen years. We begin by briefly reviewing the evidence on teacher effectiveness, highlighting specific teacher attributes that have been shown to have a consistent relationship with student achievement. Then in our own analysis, we examine the distribution of teacher characteristics over students, focusing in particular on teaching experience, advanced degrees, subject-matter preparation, certification, race, gender, and self-reported attitudes and effort. Although observable qualities of teachers have admittedly been found to matter less than unobservable dimensions of quality (Rivkin, Hanushek, and Kain 2005), attributes such as teaching experience and content knowledge do have important effects on student learning and in select cases appear to play a more powerful role for black students than for whites.

Our analysis produces several key results. First, in annual cross-sections, the observed characteristics of teachers teaching black students are for the most part similar to those teaching white students, with a few important exceptions, such as teacher race, certification and experience. Where differences exist, they tend to be small. Second, time-series comparisons demonstrate that the gap in qualifications, characteristics, and attitudes between teachers of the average black and average white student widened during the 1990s. These differences are much more pronounced when comparing teachers in predominately black schools to teachers in predominately nonblack schools. Third, almost all of the growing inequality in exposure to experienced or qualified teachers during the 1990s can be explained by changes occurring at the elementary level. The observed characteristics of teachers teaching black students at the secondary level mostly improved relative to those of white students over this period. Fourth, we find no evidence that overall improvement at the secondary level masks important changes in teacher-student matching within schools (through ability tracking, for example).

Our findings suggest that differential changes in exposure to qualified teachers are an unlikely explanation for stalled progress in the achievement gap. The racial gap in student exposure to qualified teachers grew during the 1990s, but almost entirely at the elementary level. In middle and high schools—where the achievement gap widened the most—exposure to qualified teachers remain quite stable, and in some cases improved. Our cursory look at trends in class size over this period suggests that contrasting findings at the elementary and secondary level may be a by-product of state class size reduction efforts in the early grades. Pupil-teacher ratios in elementary schools plummeted during the 1990s but class sizes in high school fell only nominally. As other researchers have shown, large-scale class size reduction policies can have the unintended consequence of lowering teacher quality in hard-to-staff schools (Jepsen and Rivkin 2002).

We conclude—at least at the secondary level, where most of the growth in the black-white achievement gap has occurred—that changes in the mean quality of teachers is unlikely to have negatively affected the achievement gap. If anything, trends at the secondary level during the 1990s suggest that the changing distribution of teacher quality may have prevented further worsening of the test score gap.

Dimensions of Teacher Quality

That a set of individual characteristics one can collectively call teacher quality or effectiveness exists is rarely disputed. This will come as no surprise to any of us who recall a particularly masterful or inspirational teacher in our own education. However, despite intense interest in raising the quality of teachers, consensus is scant over what teacher attributes contribute most to the academic and social progress of students (for recent reviews, see Rice 2003; Wayne and Youngs 2003; Hanushek and Rivkin 2006). Complicating matters is the likelihood that many important traits in promoting educational outcomes—such as patience, dedication, creativity, and communication—are largely immeasurable.

One empirical approach to measuring teacher effectiveness that remains agnostic with respect to teacher attributes uses indirect "teacher effect" estimates to calculate the fraction of overall variation in achievement gains that can be attributed to individual teachers (see Nye, Konstantopoulos, and Hedges 2004; Rockoff 2004; Rivkin, Hanushek, and Kain 2005; Boyd et al. 2006; Kane, Rockoff, and Staiger 2006; Aaronson, Barrow, and Sander 2007). In a survey of the literature, Barbara Nye, Spyros Konstantopoulos, and Larry Hedges (2004) concluded that as much as 21 percent of the variance in student achievement gains can be explained by such variation. Taking advantage of the random assignment design of the Tennessee STAR experiment, the same authors confirm that teacher effects cannot be attributed solely to a systematic matching of students to teachers based on unobservable characteristics.

Evidence of large teacher effects demonstrates the importance of individual teachers but does little to help researchers, policy makers, and practitioners identify observable metrics of teacher quality. Thus, in an attempt to identify observable correlates with teaching effectiveness, the literature often goes further to examine the relationship between teacher value-added and specific teacher attributes. For the most part, traditional measures of teacher qualifications seem to explain little of the variation in teacher value-added (Rockoff 2004; Rivkin, Hanushek, and Kain 2005; Kane, Rockoff, and Staiger 2006; Aaronson, Barrow, and Sander 2007). Yet several characteristics—such as experience and content knowledge—are important exceptions.[8]

When researchers have attempted to quantify the importance of specific teacher qualities, they have focused on those traditionally tied to compensation (education and subject matter preparation, years of teaching experience, certification), direct or indirect measures of aptitude and intelligence (licensure or standardized test scores, college selectivity), or immutable characteristics (such as race and gender). In the remainder of this section, we motivate the selection of teacher characteristics in our own analysis by briefly reviewing the evidence on teacher attributes and teaching effectiveness.

Education and Content Knowledge

The fraction of teachers holding Masters' degrees has skyrocketed in recent decades (Larsen 2006), yet evidence from the teacher-effects literature finds little if any relationship between teacher value-added and advanced degrees (Nye, Konstantopoulos, and Hedges 2004; Rivkin, Hanushek, and Kain 2005; Aaronson, Barrow, and Sander 2007). More direct estimates of the effects of advanced degrees draw similar conclusions (Goldhaber and Brewer 1996, 2000; Clotfelter, Ladd, and Vigdor 2007; Croninger et al. 2007).

The finding that advanced degrees are unrelated to teacher effectiveness is not universal, however. Several authors have found differential effects of Masters' degrees by race and gender of the student. For example, Ronald Ehrenberg and Dominic Brewer (1994, 1995) found that teachers' education had beneficial effects on the achievement gains and high school completion rates of black students, but not for white students. In an experimental context, Thomas Dee (2004) found that in the early grades, girls performed at a statistically significant higher level in mathematics when taught by teachers with an advanced degree, though no beneficial effects were found in reading for either gender.

The evidence on college major and subject matter preparation is more robust, particularly for science and mathematics. Of a large set of observed teacher characteristics, Daniel Aaronson, Lisa Barrow, and William Sander (2007) found that preparation in mathematics was the most important characteristic in explaining variation in teacher value-added in ninth grade math. Likewise, Dan Goldhaber and Dominic Brewer (1996, 2000) and David Monk and Jennifer King (1994) uncovered evidence that undergraduate or graduate preparation in math and science yields higher test score gains in those subjects among secondary students. No such effects are found for English or history.[9]

Teaching Experience

The teacher effectiveness literature provides conflicting evidence on the relationship between teaching experience and achievement gains. Although both Steven Rivkin, Eric Hanushek, and John Kain (2005) and Donald Boyd and his colleagues (2006) found no additional returns to experience after the first three years in elementary math and reading, Jonah Rockoff (2004) uncovered persistent returns in elementary reading and Aaronson, Barrow, and Sander (2007) found no return to experience in ninth grade mathematics. In the Tennessee STAR experiment, Nye, Konstantopoulos, and Hedges (2004) detected only a weak relationship between K–3 teacher value-added and experience. In their analysis of the NELS cohort, however, Goldhaber and Brewer (1996, 2000) found no evidence of returns to teaching experience.[10] Several subsequent studies, on the other hand, all found sustained improvements in teacher productivity with experience in both the early and later grades (Clotfelter, Ladd, and Vigdor 2007; Croninger et al. 2007; Harris and Sass 2007).

Aptitude and College Selectivity

Where such measures are available, empirical evidence strongly suggests that teachers who score higher in a distribution of standardized test takers produce more favorable academic outcomes than those who score lower (Ferguson 1991; Ferguson and Ladd 1996; Ehrenberg and Brewer 1995; Clotfelter, Ladd, and Vigdor 2006, 2007). Unfortunately, few large-scale databases contain this particular metric of teacher quality.

Undergraduate college selectivity—perhaps serving as a proxy for aptitude—has been found to have a qualitatively similar relationship with teacher effectiveness as teacher test scores. Ehrenberg and Brewer (1994) and Clotfelter, Ladd, and Vigdor (2007), for example, found higher gain scores among students whose teachers attended more selective institutions, though in the former case selectivity was more strongly related to achievement among black students than whites. In one prominent exception, Aaronson, Barrow, and Sander (2007) found no relationship between teacher aptitude or college selectivity and high school mathematics scores.

Professional Licensure and Certification

One of the more consistent results in the literature is the finding that state-licensed teachers are rarely more responsible for superior academic outcomes than unlicensed teachers (Goldhaber and Brewer 1996; Ballou and Podgursky 2000; Hanushek et al. 2005; Kane, Rockoff, and Staiger 2006; Aaronson, Barrow, and Sander 2007; Croninger et al. 2007). Here again, this finding is not universal, given that other recent studies have found returns to standard state licensure (Clotfelter, Ladd, and Vigdor 2007). Other authors have explored the effects of alternative pathways into teaching (Teach for America and the New York City Teaching Fellows program are prominent examples) and typically find that teachers who enter the profession through nontraditional routes produce smaller test score gains in their early years of teaching, but soon catch up to traditionally certified teachers (Boyd et al. 2006; Decker, Mayer, and Glazerman 2004).

An exception to the literature on professional licensure concerns the more rigorous National Board for Professional Teaching Standards (NBPTS) certification. In this case, research has shown that teachers with National Board certification are demonstrably more effective in raising student achievement than those without such credentials, although there is nothing about the credentialing process per se that enhances teacher productivity (Goldhaber and Anthony 2007; Harris and Sass 2007; Clotfelter, Ladd, and Vigdor 2007).

Teacher Race and Gender

Student exposure to teachers of the same gender, race, or ethnic background is often cited as a possible avenue for closing the achievement gap between minority and nonminority students or between boys and girls in science and mathematics. As such, the underrepresentation of African Americans and Hispanics in the teacher workforce compared to the student population leads to frequent calls for greater minority recruitment into teaching. The argument that students may perform better when exposed to a teacher of the same race or gender is rooted in the idea that teacher expectations, interactions, or assumptions regarding ability can vary, whether consciously or not, by the race and gender of the student (Ferguson 1998; Ehrenberg, Goldhaber, and Brewer 1995). Students' enthusiasm, behavior, or interest in academic work may in turn vary with teacher characteristics.

In fact, there is a fair amount of evidence that supports this hypothesis. Under random assignment of students to teachers, Dee found that both black and white students score higher in math and reading when they share the same race with their teacher (2004).[11] Similarly, he also showed that middle school girls scored higher (and boys lower) in science, social studies, and English when their teacher was female (2005). Dee offers further evidence that gender differences in scores may be due to the kinds of behaviors cited—for example, teacher perceptions are found to vary with the gender of the student, as do student attitudes about learning.[12]

Summary

Taken together, there are few observable teacher characteristics that have consistently shown evidence of large and systematic effects on student achievement on standardized tests. The metric offering the most compelling evidence—a teacher's academic aptitude—is seldom available to researchers, particularly those interested in drawing inferences about changes in teacher quality over time.[13] Yet each of the attributes cited has been found in at least one rigorous empirical study to have an important effect—if sometimes small—on student achievement. Several observable qualifications or traits—such as teaching experience, content knowledge, NBPTS certification, and race—more often than not show systematic effects on student outcomes. Other qualifications such as advanced degrees may matter more for the academic achievement of black students than for white.

Beyond the independent effects of individual teacher characteristics on student learning, there is only limited evidence on how teacher attributes interact or cumulate in the production of education. It may be that students exposed to teachers lacking along multiple dimensions fall behind more than those whose teachers fall short on only one qualification. Further, repeated exposure to inexperienced or underqualified teachers may have cumulative effects, where differences that appear small in any one year of achievement growth compound into a much larger inequalities in acquired skills over time (Sanders and Rivers 1996). In the following section, we consider how a wide range of teacher attributes varies across schools and classrooms of varying racial compositions, and how the distribution of teachers over students has changed over time.

Trends in Exposure to Quality Teachers

A number of recent studies have documented the extent to which teacher qualifications are unevenly distributed across schools and students (Lankford, Loeb, and Wyckoff 2002; Clotfelter, Ladd, and Vigdor 2005, 2006). Most of this work shows that teachers in predominately urban, low-income, and high-minority schools have less experience, are less likely to be licensed or hold National Board certification, come from less selective colleges, and have lower academic aptitude overall than other teachers.[14] The role of nonpecuniary factors such as working conditions and the "draw of home" that Boyd and his colleagues documented (2005) has important ramifications for the distribution of teachers across schools; as net importers of teachers, urban districts face persistent difficulties attracting teachers from other regions of the state.

Less is known about how differential black-white exposure to high quality teachers has changed over time. The persistence of teacher sorting patterns and school segregation by race suggest that considerable change is unexpected. Indeed, in an analysis of teacher sorting in New York State, Hamilton Lankford, Susanna Loeb, and James Wyckoff (2002) found little to no change in the distribution of teacher attributes across school districts between 1985 and 1999.[15] In another study similar to our own, Meredith Phillips and Tiffani Chin (2004) noted very few changes in the qualifications of teachers by school minority enrollment composition.

Evidence from the Schools and Staffing Survey

We begin with an analysis of the Schools and Staffing Survey (SASS) series, five large cross-sectional surveys of teachers, schools, and administrators conducted by the National Center for Education Statistics (NCES) in the school years ending 1988, 1991, 1994, 2000, and 2004.[16] In each of these survey years, we compare average teacher qualifications and attributes in schools attended by the typical white and black student. We do this by first averaging teacher characteristics within schools and then computing a weighted average over schools using total white or black enrollment as weights.[17] Such measures indicate the average exposure of white and black students to particular teacher characteristics or qualifications, allowing us to compute an exposure gap for each characteristic in each survey year.

Tables 6.1 and 6.2 summarize our results. During the 1990s, teachers of the average white and black student differ in several notable ways. The average black student is more likely to have a female teacher and much more likely to have an African American teacher. For example, in the 2003 to 2004 school year, the fraction of black teachers in the average black student's school exceeded that in the average white student's school by more than 22 percentage points (25.7 percent versus 3.0), though black teachers were still considerably underrepresented relative to enrollment in these schools.[18] Teachers teaching black students were consistently less likely to be state certified, more likely to hold emergency or temporary certification, and had fewer years of experience working at the same school. These differences are statistically significant in almost all cases, but many are small in magnitude. For example, during the 1990s, teachers of the average black student consistently had lower mean teaching experience than teachers of the average white student. However, in the 1999 to 2000 sample, this difference amounted to little more than nine months.

Of greater interest to this volume is how differences in exposure to teacher characteristics changed during the 1990s. In table 6.2, we present the black-white gap in mean teacher characteristics in each of the five SASS surveys, with a calculated change in this gap for the 1990s (1991 to 2000) and for the entire length of the SASS (1988 to 2004). Gaps in exposure to male or black teachers fell consistently through the 1990s, with the gap in exposure to male teachers falling nearly in half from 1988 and 2004—a statistically significant change. The gap in exposure to black teachers also narrowed over the same period, though, as table 6.1 indicates, this occurred via an overall decline in black teachers, with a disproportionate decline among teachers teaching black students.

By contrast, the black-white gap in exposure to qualified teachers—as measured by experience, education, and certification—steadily expanded in the 1990s. Average teaching experience and rates of new and novice (first-year) teaching were generally comparable across students in 1988 and 1991, but by the end of the decade, the black-white gap in these metrics had risen markedly. In 2000, exposure to first-year teachers was 27 percent higher for black students than for white (6.2 versus 4.9 percent) and exposure to teachers with three or fewer years of teaching experience 23 percent higher (17.7 versus 14.4). Mean teaching experience was 3.4 percent lower in the average black student's school. Average tenure at the same school fell from 1988 to 2000 among teachers of the typical black student but rose for the typical white student.[19] Every gap in exposure to experienced teachers widened even more between 2000 and the 2003 to 2004 wave of the SASS.

Table 6.1   Characteristics, Qualifications, and Attitudes of Teachers

Teacher Characteristics:	Average White Student					Average Black Student				
	1988	1991	1994	2000	2004	1988	1991	1994	2000	2004
Percent male	28.6	27.4	26.9	25.5	25.7	23.4	23.5	23.4	22.4	22.9
Percent white	94.3	93.0	93.1	93.0	93.7	69.2	68.9	70.6	67.5	69.6
Percent black	3.9	4.2	3.6	3.5	3.0	29.1	27.4	25.6	27.6	25.7
Percent first-year teacher	3.5	3.6	4.1	4.9	4.2	3.5	4.0	4.5	6.2	6.0
Percent three or fewer										
years experience	10.1	10.1	10.7	14.4	12.6	10.9	11.2	13.1	17.7	17.5
Years of experience	14.6	15.2	15.3	14.9	14.7	14.8	15.1	14.9	14.2	13.2
Years at current school	8.2	8.6	8.8	8.6	8.4	7.4	7.6	7.5	7.2	6.7
Percent with MA or higher	47.5	46.8	46.2	47.9	48.4	49.9	49.1	47.6	46.4	44.6
Percent with BA in education	73.5	77.1	74.1	69.3	81.4	72.8	76.0	71.7	67.0	77.8
Percent of MAs in education	86.4	85.1	84.9	83.4	90.3	87.6	85.0	85.0	82.3	89.4
Secondary math: percent with										
math degree	39.3	24.3	26.9	32.6	—	39.8	26.2	25.5	29.0	—
Secondary science: percent with										
science degree	58.3	56.0	54.3	54.1	—	59.8	50.3	49.5	53.7	—
Secondary English: percent with										
English degree	27.9	26.6	26.1	31.3	—	31.0	24.3	24.3	30.4	—

(continued)

Table 6.1   Characteristics, Qualifications, and Attitudes of Teachers (Continued)

Teacher Characteristics:	Average White Student					Average Black Student				
	1988	1991	1994	2000	2004	1988	1991	1994	2000	2004
Percent with traditional state certification	97.8	97.8	97.1	95.0	89.3	95.3	96.5	95.2	91.7	83.5
Percent with emergency or temporary certification	5.0	3.4	1.1	5.0	6.2	5.7	4.6	1.8	6.9	11.3
Percent would teach again	58.5	65.3	65.3	68.2	69.2	53.3	60.3	59.4	63.6	67.0
Percent that plan to exit teaching as soon as possible	3.8	2.8	3.9	2.8	2.0	5.0	3.5	6.0	5.0	2.5
Percent that agree student behavior interferes	40.1	32.8	41.2	37.1	32.3	52.5	47.7	55.8	55.0	50.2
Percent that do not believe principal supports them	16.3	12.3	18.0	16.4	11.4	17.6	15.2	21.6	23.3	14.7
Hours required to be at school per week	32.2	35.4	32.0	36.4	37.0	31.3	35.2	31.8	36.7	37.0
Hours spent on school work outside of school	9.4	11.2	12.1	11.9	—	8.6	10.3	10.3	11.1	—

Source: Authors' calculations.
Note: Mean teacher responses within schools averaged over schools using white or black enrollment as weights. Schools and Staffing Surveys, 1987 to 1988, 1990 to 1991, 1993 to 1994, 1999 to 2000, and 2003 to 2004. Degree codes in the 2003 to 2004 survey are not directly comparable with those used in the other survey waves. The measurement of required work hours in 1987 to 1988 differs from the remaining surveys.

Table 6.2   Black-White Differences in Exposure to Teacher Attributes

	1988	1991	1994	2000	2004	Change 1991 to 2000	Change 1987 to 2004
Percent male	−5.1 (0.8)*	−3.9 (0.7)*	−3.5 (0.7)*	−3.0 (0.8)*	−2.8 (0.7)*	0.9 (1.1)	2.3 (1.1)*
Percent black	25.2 (0.6)*	23.3 (0.6)*	22.1 (0.6)*	24.1 (0.6)*	22.7 (0.6)*	0.9 (0.9)	−2.5 (0.9)*
Percent first-year teacher	0.0 (0.3)	0.4 (0.3)	0.4 (0.3)	1.3 (0.4)*	1.8 (0.4)*	0.9 (0.5)	1.8 (0.5)*
Percent three or fewer years experience	0.7 (0.5)	1.1 (0.5)*	2.4 (0.6)*	3.3 (0.7)*	5.0 (0.6)*	2.2 (0.8)*	4.2 (0.8)*
Years of experience	0.23 (0.09)*	−0.10 (0.08)	−0.43 (0.09)*	−0.75 (0.10)*	−1.45 (0.09)*	−0.65 (0.13)*	−1.68 (0.13)*
Years at current school	−0.82 (0.08)*	−0.99 (0.08)*	−1.31 (0.08)*	−1.38 (0.09)*	−1.65 (0.08)*	−0.39 (0.12)*	−0.83 (0.11)*
Percent with MA or higher	2.5 (0.9)*	2.3 (0.9)*	1.4 (0.9)	−1.5 (0.9)	−3.8 (0.9)*	−3.8 (1.2)*	−6.3 (1.2)*
Percent with BA in education	−0.8 (0.8)	−1.0 (0.7)	−2.4 (0.8)*	−2.3 (0.8)*	−3.6 (0.7)*	−1.2 (1.1)	−2.9 (1.1)*
Percent of MAs in education	1.2 (0.7)	−0.1 (0.7)	0.1 (0.7)	−1.1 (0.7)	−0.9 (0.6)	−1.1 (1.0)	−2.2 (0.9)*
Secondary math: percent with math degree	0.5 (1.6)	1.9 (1.3)	−1.3 (1.2)	−3.6 (1.4)*	—	−5.5 (1.9)*	—
Secondary science: percent with science degree	1.5 (1.7)	−5.7 (1.6)*	−4.7 (1.5)*	−0.4 (1.6)	—	5.3 (2.2)*	—
Secondary English: percent with English degree	3.1 (1.5)*	−2.2 (1.2)	−1.8 (1.1)	−0.9 (1.3)	—	1.4 (1.8)	—
Percent with traditional state certification	−2.5 (0.3)*	−1.4 (0.3)*	−1.9 (0.3)*	−3.4 (0.5)*	−5.8 (0.6)*	−2.0 (0.5)*	−3.3 (0.7)*
Percent with emergency or temporary certification	0.8 (0.4)*	1.2 (0.3)*	0.7 (0.2)*	2.0 (0.4)*	5.1 (0.5)*	0.8 (0.5)	4.3 (0.6)*

(continued)

Table 6.2   Black-White Differences in Exposure to Teacher Attributes (*Continued*)

	1988	1991	1994	2000	2004	Change 1991 to 2000	Change 1987 to 2004
Percent would teach again	−5.2 (0.9)*	−5.0 (0.8)*	−5.9 (0.8)*	−4.6 (0.9)*	−2.3 (0.8)*	0.4 (1.2)	3.0 (1.2)*
Percent that plan to exit teaching as soon as possible	1.2 (0.4)*	0.7 (0.3)*	2.0 (0.4)*	2.2 (0.4)*	0.5 (0.3)*	1.5 (0.5)*	−0.6 (0.5)
Percent that agree student behavior interferes	12.4 (0.9)*	14.9 (0.8)*	14.7 (0.8)*	17.9 (0.9)*	17.8 (0.8)*	3.0 (1.2)*	5.5 (1.2)*
Percent that do not believe principal supports them	1.4 (0.7)*	2.9 (0.6)*	3.5 (0.7)*	6.9 (0.7)*	3.4 (0.6)*	4.0 (0.9)*	2.0 (0.9)*
Hours required to be at school per week	−0.82 (0.09)*	−0.19 (0.07)*	−0.17 (0.11)	0.34 (0.07)*	0.00 (0.05)	0.53 (0.10)*	0.87 (0.10)*
Hours spent working outside of school	−0.77 (0.07)*	−0.86 (0.07)*	−0.96 (0.08)*	−0.74 (0.08)*	—	0.13 (0.11)	—

Source: Authors' calculations using Schools and Staffing Surveys, 1990 to 1991, 1993 to 1994, 1999 to 2000, and 2003 to 2004.
Note: Standard errors in parentheses. Exposure gap calculated as black − white difference in means from Table 1. *denotes difference is statistically significant at the 5 percent level. Degree codes in the 2003 to 2004 survey are not directly comparable with those used in the other survey waves. The measurement of required work hours in 1987 to 1988 differs from the remaining surveys.

Gaps in exposure to teachers with high levels of training and state certification also widened during the 1990s. In 1988, the fraction of teachers holding Masters' degrees was more than 2.5 percentage points higher for the average black student; by 2000, this proportion had dropped 1.5 points below that for the typical white student.[20] The average black student was statistically significantly less likely in most years to be taught by a teacher with a Bachelor's degree in education—a difference that grew steadily between 1988 and 2004—although rates of exposure to teachers holding Master's degrees in education were roughly the same.[21] Subject matter preparation of secondary teachers also varied across the average white and black student. Among math teachers, the proportion with a degree in mathematics rose for both groups between 1991 and 2000.[22] The increase, however, was considerably larger among teachers of the average white student. As a result, the gap in math teacher preparation widened to 3.6 percentage points by 2000.[23] The opposite trend occurred for teachers of science and English, though only the former change was statistically significant. The black-white gap in exposure to state-certified teachers more than doubled between 1991 and 2000, from a 1.4 percentage point gap in 1991 to 3.4 point gap in 2000, and quadrupled between 1991 and 2004, from a 1.4 point gap to 5.8. By 2004, more than 16 percent of teachers in the average black student's school did not have full state certification, compared with 11 percent in the average white student's school. Similarly, 11.3 percent of teachers in the average black student's school held emergency or temporary certification but only 6.2 percent of teachers in white students' schools did so.

The picture emerging from tables 6.1 and 6.2 is that teacher characteristics differed between black and white students in every survey year, but that trends in teacher sorting during the 1990s appear to have worked to the relative disadvantage of black students. That is, the likelihood that a teacher in the average black student's school was inexperienced, in his or her first year, uncertified, or lacking an advanced degree all rose relative to that for teachers of the average white student. This said, in many cases the magnitude of the change in these disparities was small.

The staffing patterns reflected here may be indicative of differences in job satisfaction among teachers across schools. The SASS teacher questionnaire included several questions pertaining to attitudes toward teaching, students and school leadership. Mean responses to a few of these questions are included in table 6.1. Teachers of the average black student were persistently less likely to state that they would choose to become a teacher again if given the chance to start over, though this gap was mostly unchanged between 1991 and 2000. This gap fell in half between 2000 and 2004.[24] On the other hand, black-white differences in the proportion of teachers who indicated a desire to leave the profession as soon as possible rose during the 1990s. Among teachers teaching black students, the proportion with such plans was approximately 5 to 6 percent.[25] Teachers of the average black student also held a much more negative view of the school environment and administration during this period. For example, in 2000, more than half affirmed that "the level of student misbehavior . . . interferes with my teaching," and more than 23 percent felt their principal was not supportive of their efforts. The black-white gap in these teacher sentiments grew substantially during the 1990s—with the gap in perceptions of the work environment growing 3.0 percentage points between 1991 and 2000, 5.5 points between 1987 and 2004, and the gap in views about school administration growing four points between 1991 and 2000, 2 points over the full survey period.

We also examined differences in the weekly work hours and earnings of teachers (the latter results are not presented here). While required hours of work did not vary much with the racial composition of the school—and the gap in these work hours narrowed—hours spent working outside of the classroom did vary considerably. Altogether, average weekly hours outside of the classroom on school-related activities, either with or without students present, were almost an hour lower for the average black student's teacher (see table 6.2). This gap improved only slightly, and statistically insignificantly, during the 1990s.[26] Compensation was higher among teachers of the average black student, partly due to differences in location and urbanicity, and these teachers were less likely to hold a second job outside of school, a propensity that changed little over this period.

Table 6.3 disaggregates black-white gaps in teacher quality by school level, presenting only the differences in 1991 and 2000 and the changes in these gaps over time.[27] The results in table 6.3 show that most of the time series changes observed in table 6.2 between 1991 and 2000 occurred at the elementary level. For example, we find a statistically significant drop in the relative experience of teachers at schools attended by the average black elementary student, but virtually no change in relative teacher experience at the secondary level. On the other hand, the gap in exposure to traditionally certified teachers widened more in secondary schools (2.3 percentage points) than at the elementary level (1.5 points). Differences in teacher satisfaction with the teaching environment and level of principal support grew much more at the elementary level than at the secondary level, where the 1991 to 2000 change was statistically insignificant.

Given the evidence linking teacher sorting patterns to student race and socioeconomic status (Hanushek, Kain, and Rivkin 2004; Scafidi, Sjoquist, and Stinebrickner 2007; Lankford, Loeb, and Wyckoff 2002) there is good reason to believe that schools with particularly high minority or low-income student populations were affected disproportionately by changes in the distribution of teachers across schools. Black students experience a high rate of racial isolation in U.S. public schools, and there is no evidence that school segregation by race diminished during the 1990s (see Vigdor and Ludwig, chapter 5, this volume).

Table 6.4 uses the Common Core of Data Public Schools Universe to illustrate the extent to which black students were in racially isolated schools in 1990 and 2000. In both years, 23 percent of all black students in public schools attended schools that were more than 90 percent black, and an additional 28 percent attended schools that were at least majority black. By contrast, three-quarters of all white public school students were in schools where 10 percent or fewer students were African American. Fewer than 3 percent of all white students attended schools where blacks were in the

Table 6.3   Black-White Differences in Exposure to Teacher Attributes

	Elementary Teachers			Secondary Teachers		
	1991	2000	Change 1991 to 2000	1991	2000	Change 1991 to 2000
Percent male	−0.4 (0.8)	0.9 (0.8)	1.3 (1.2)	−5.7 (1.3)*	−3.5 (1.4)*	2.2 (1.9)
Percent black	25.2 (0.9)*	24.3 (0.9)*	−0.9 (1.3)	20.5 (0.9)*	24.1 (1.0)*	3.5 (1.3)*
Percent first-year teacher	0.7 (0.5)	2.1 (0.6)*	1.4 (0.8)	−0.6 (0.4)	0.0 (0.6)	0.6 (0.8)
Percent three or fewer years experience	1.9 (0.8)*	5.4 (1.0)*	3.5 (1.3)*	−0.7 (0.7)	0.5 (1.0)	1.3 (1.2)
Years of experience	−0.36 (0.14)*	−1.41 (0.17)*	−1.05 (0.22)*	0.37 (0.11)*	0.34 (0.13)*	−0.03 (0.17)
Years at current school	−0.91 (0.12)*	−1.71 (0.14)*	−0.80 (0.18)*	−0.73 (0.10)*	−0.67 (0.12)*	0.06 (0.16)
Percent with MA or higher	2.5 (1.3)*	−1.4 (1.3)	−3.9 (1.8)*	3.4 (1.3)*	−0.4 (1.4)	−3.8 (1.9)*
Percent with BA in education	−1.9 (0.9)	−4.4 (1.1)*	−2.6 (1.4)*	−3.1 (1.2)*	−2.6 (1.4)	0.5 (1.8)
Percent of MAs in education	−2.0 (0.8)*	−2.7 (0.9)*	−0.6 (1.2)	−0.4 (1.2)	−1.9 (1.3)	−1.5 (1.7)
Percent with traditional state certification	−1.7 (0.4)*	−3.2 (0.6)*	−1.5 (0.7)*	−0.8 (0.4)	−3.0 (0.7)*	−2.3 (0.8)*
Percent with emergency or temporary certification	1.0 (0.5)*	2.6 (0.6)*	1.6 (0.8)	0.3 (0.5)	1.7 (0.7)*	1.4 (0.8)
Percent would teach again	−5.2 (1.2)*	−5.3 (1.2)*	−0.1 (1.7)	−6.0 (1.3)*	−4.2 (1.3)*	1.8 (1.8)
Percent that plan to exit teaching as soon as possible	1.0 (0.4)*	2.3 (0.5)*	1.3 (0.6)*	0.9 (0.5)	2.4 (0.6)*	1.5 (0.8)
Percent that agree student behavior interferes	15.4 (1.2)*	20.0 (1.3)*	4.6 (1.8)*	14.6 (1.3)*	14.1 (1.4)*	−0.5 (1.8)

(continued)

Table 6.3   Black-White Differences in Exposure to Teacher Attributes (*Continued*)

	Elementary Teachers			Secondary Teachers		
	1991	2000	Change 1991 to 2000	1991	2000	Change 1991 to 2000
Percent that do not believe principal supports them	2.8 (0.8)*	8.5 (1.0)*	5.7 (1.3)*	3.5 (0.9)*	5.1 (1.1)*	1.6 (1.5)

Source: Authors' calculations using Schools and Staffing Surveys, 1990 to 1991, 1993 to 1994, 1999 to 2000, and 2003 to 2004.
Note: Standard errors in parentheses. Exposure gap calculated as black–white difference in means (computed separately for elementary and secondary teachers). *denotes difference is statistically significant at the 5 percent level.

Table 6.4   Integrated Within-District School Segregation and the Racial Composition of Schools

	1990	2000
Percent of white students in schools		
0 to 10 percent black	75.5	74.6
11 to 50 percent black	22.1	22.9
51 to 90 percent black	2.3	2.4
More than 90 percent black	0.001	0.001
Percent of black students in schools		
0 to 10 percent black	8.7	9.2
11 to 50 percent black	40.5	39.7
51 to 90 percent black	28.1	28.4
More than 90 percent black	22.8	22.8
Mean school district segregation index (weighted by student enrollment)	0.087	0.090
Elementary students only	0.097	0.104
Secondary students only	0.052	0.055
Distribution of school district segregation index (weighted by student enrollment)		
10th centile	0.002	0.001
25th centile	0.006	0.004
50th centile	0.034	0.017
75th centile	0.122	0.110
90th centile	0.258	0.321

Source: Authors' compilation using the Common Core of Data Public Schools Universe 1989 to 1990 and 1999 to 2000.

majority. If students had been randomly distributed across schools the average school would have been comprised of approximately 16 to 17 percent non-Hispanic blacks.[28] Average within-district school segregation grew slightly over this period, mostly attributable to increased segregation among the most highly segregated districts (the median and 75th percentile student—when sorted by the extent of their district's segregation—were in less segregated districts in 2000 than in 1990, while the 90th percentile student was in a much more racially segregated district).[29]

Given these patterns, we examined how the characteristics of teachers differed between predominately black (greater than 90 percent black), majority black (50 to 90 percent) and predominately nonblack (0 to 10 percent) schools. Our results are provided in table 6.5. Here we see more pronounced disparities in teacher characteristics between high- and low-percentage black schools as well as notable nonlinearities in exposure to teacher attributes.[30] In any given year, the black-white gap in exposure to male or black teachers is twice as large when comparing predominately black and predominately nonblack schools, though this gap narrowed slightly between 1991 and 2000. In each year, the gaps in teaching experience and tenure are similar in magnitude or sometimes smaller than in table 6.2. The growth in the gap between low- and high-percent black schools, however, is larger. For example, the growth in the gap in exposure to inexperienced teachers, less than or equal to three years, is 45 percent larger (3.2 points versus 2.2), and the increased gap in mean experience more than twice as large as at the mean. Differences in teacher satisfaction and views of their work environment were much more pronounced when comparing predominately black schools with predominately nonblack schools than at the mean (table 6.2). For example, the black-white gap in exposure to teachers affirming that student behavior is disruptive was 24.4 percentage points in 1991 and 25.8 points in 2000 when comparing these categories, versus 14.9 and 17.9 points at the mean.

Differences in teacher satisfaction and views of their work environment are also more pronounced when comparing predominately black schools with predominately nonblack schools and low-percent black schools, and the growth in these gaps mirrored those at the mean. One notable gap is in the proportion of teachers whose principal does not support of their work efforts. This rose to 15 percentage points in 2000, with 31 percent of teachers in predominately black schools holding this view, compared with 16 percent in predominately nonblack schools. Differences in teacher work effort outside of school hours are larger when comparing mostly black and mostly nonblack schools, though this gap improved by almost half in the 1990s. Altogether, the gap between these groups in teacher hours outside of class narrowed from 2.1 hours per week to 1.2.[31]

Comparing the extremes of the distribution masks a few interesting nonlinearities in exposure to certain teacher characteristics. In many

Table 6.5   Characteristics, Qualifications, and Attitudes of Teachers by Percentage Black Enrollment

	1991				2000				Difference-in-Difference
	0 to 10%	51 to 90%	More than 90%	Difference	0 to 10%	51 to 90%	More than 90%	Difference	
Percent male	29.3	24.6	21.6	-7.7 (1.4)*	27.1	20.4	20.5	-6.6 (1.3)*	1.1 (1.9)
Percent black	1.5	32.6	61.2	59.6 (1.6)*	1.6	32.3	56.6	55.0 (1.5)*	-4.6 (2.2)*
Percent first-year teacher	3.7	4.8	4.0	0.4 (0.7)	4.7	7.0	6.4	1.7 (0.8)*	1.3 (1.0)
Percent three or fewer years experience	10.0	12.9	9.9	-0.1 (1.0)	14.3	17.0	17.4	3.0 (1.2)*	3.2 (1.5)*
Years of experience	15.2	14.7	16.3	1.1 (0.3)*	15.0	14.0	14.7	-0.3 (0.3)	-1.4 (0.5)*
Years at current school	8.8	7.2	8.0	-0.8 (0.3)*	8.8	7.2	7.0	-1.8 (0.3)*	-1.0 (0.4)*
Percent with MA or higher	45.7	48.4	51.1	5.5 (1.7)*	47.8	47.1	47.3	-0.5 (1.6)	-6.0 (2.3)*
Percent with BA in education	76.3	77.8	79.6	3.2 (1.3)*	68.2	70.5	72.1	3.9 (1.4)*	0.7 (1.9)

Percent of MAs in education	84.6	84.1	86.0	1.4 (1.6)	83.9	85.7	83.3	-0.6 (1.6)	-2.0 (2.3)
Percent with traditional state certification	98.0	95.9	96.3	-1.6 (0.6)*	95.4	91.0	91.1	-4.3 (0.9)*	-2.6 (1.1)*
Percent with emergency or temporary certification	3.2	4.7	2.9	-0.3 (0.6)	5.5	7.2	7.4	2.0 (0.8)*	2.3 (1.0)*
Percent would teach again	66.3	60.7	58.8	-7.6 (1.6)*	69.4	63.3	65.1	-4.3 (1.5)*	3.3 (2.2)
Percent that plan to exit teaching as soon as possible	2.6	3.2	4.5	1.9 (0.7)*	2.7	4.7	6.4	3.7 (0.8)*	1.8 (1.0)
Percent that agree student behavior interferes	30.7	51.5	55.1	24.4 (1.7)*	34.9	59.9	60.8	25.8 (1.5)*	1.4 (2.2)
Percent that do not believe principal supports them	12.4	16.8	17.8	5.4 (1.3)*	16.3	21.0	31.0	14.6 (1.4)*	9.2 (1.9)*
Hours spent working outside of school	11.3	10.6	9.2	-2.1 (0.2)*	12.0	10.4	10.8	-1.2 (0.2)*	0.9 (0.3)*

Source: Authors' calculations using Schools and Staffing Surveys, 1990 to 1991 and 1999 to 2000.
Note: Standard errors in parentheses. *denotes difference is statistically significant at the 5 percent level.

cases—as with mean teaching experience, tenure, and certification—black-white differences in teacher qualities are larger when comparing predominately nonblack schools to schools where black students constitute 50 to 90 percent of enrollment. We do not explore the hypothesis here, but these nonlinearities might suggest some effects of student heterogeneity (or at least, student heterogeneity when the majority of enrollment is black) on teacher turnover and job satisfaction.

Evidence from Matched Teacher-Student Data

A disadvantage of using the Schools and Staffing Survey to estimate average exposure to teacher qualifications and characteristics is its reliance on school-level teacher and student attributes. As Clotfelter, Ladd, and Vigdor (2005) and others have shown, there are likely to be differences in the matching of students to teachers within schools as well as between them. Average teacher characteristics at the school level may thus underestimate the differences in teachers that white and black students experience. To investigate this possibility, we turn to two nationally representative longitudinal surveys of high school sophomores—the National Education Longitudinal Survey (NELS-88) and the Education Longitudinal Study of 2002 (ELS)—that explicitly match students to teachers in several subjects.[32] The set of teacher attributes captured in these two surveys is smaller than that in the SASS, and we will be able to examine only the characteristics of mathematics and English teachers of high school sophomores. Still, using these surveys does allow us to avoid the potential measurement error issue encountered when using school-level data. For comparability with our SASS results, we restrict our attention to non-Hispanic black and white students who are enrolled in math or English and whose teacher also participated in the survey.[33]

Tables 6.6 and 6.7 present the average exposure of black and white sophomores to English and mathematics teachers with various attributes in 1990 and 2002, along with the gaps in those years and a difference-in-difference estimate that measures the change in the black-white gap between 1990 and 2002. Among students in tenth grade English classes, we find that black students are less likely to have male or white teachers in every year than the average white student; teacher experience is systematically lower among teachers of black students, as is experience working at the same school (see table 6.6). Consistent with our findings in the SASS for secondary teachers, we find only minor changes in the black-white gap in teacher characteristics, and in many cases the gap decreased. For example, we observe a more than 50 percent reduction in the black-white gap in teacher experience and smaller differences in exposure to new or inexperienced teachers. The race gap in the proportion of teachers with advanced degrees and degrees in-subject also narrowed, from a deficit (in favor of

Table 6.6   Characteristics of Tenth Grade English Teachers in Matched Teacher-Student Data

	NELS 1st Follow-up, 1990			ELS Base Year, 2002			
	Average White Student	Average Black Student	Black-White Difference	Average White Student	Average Black Student	Black-White Difference	Difference-in-Difference
Percent male	30.2	20.8	-9.5	23.3	18.0	-5.3	4.1
	(0.6)	(1.4)	(1.6)*	(0.6)	(1.1)	(1.3)*	(2.1)
Percent black	3.6	24.3	20.7	3.0	24.3	21.3	0.5
	(0.3)	(1.5)	(0.8)*	(0.2)	(1.1)	(0.8)*	(1.2)
Percent same-gender teacher	49.3	52.7	3.4	50.0	50.9	0.9	-2.5
	(0.7)	(1.7)	(1.8)	(0.7)	(1.4)	(1.6)	(2.5)
Percent same-race teacher	95.2	24.2	-70.9	93.8	24.3	-69.5	1.4
	(0.3)	(1.5)	(0.9)*	(0.3)	(1.2)	(0.9)*	(1.4)
Years of teaching experience	16.6	15.0	-1.6	14.7	14.1	-0.6	1.0
	(0.1)	(0.3)	(0.3)*	(0.2)	(0.3)	(0.3)	(0.5)*
Years of secondary teaching experience	15.9	14.0	-1.9	14.0	13.4	-0.6	1.3
	(0.1)	(0.3)	(0.3)*	(0.2)	(0.3)	(0.3)	(0.5)*
Percent two or fewer years experience	6.3	8.5	2.2	12.9	14.6	1.7	-0.4
	(0.3)	(0.9)	(0.9)*	(0.5)	(1.0)	(1.1)	(1.5)
Years at current school	11.5	8.9	-2.7	10.1	8.8	-1.7	0.9
	(0.1)	(0.2)	(0.3)*	(0.1)	(0.2)	(0.3)*	(0.4)*
Percent with MA or higher	52.9	49.5	-3.3	46.8	50.9	4.1	7.4
	(0.7)	(1.7)	(1.7)	(0.7)	(1.7)	(1.6)*	(2.4)*
Percent with degree in field	79.4	76.6	-2.8	81.9	84.4	2.5	5.3
	(0.6)	(1.5)	(1.5)	(0.6)	(1.0)	(1.3)	(2.0)*
Percent that would teach again	55.6	52.1	-3.6	69.6	63.1	-6.4	-2.8
	(0.7)	(1.7)	(1.7)*	(0.6)	(1.3)	(1.5)*	(2.4)

Source: Authors' calculations using NELS-88 first follow-up survey (1990) and ELS base year survey (2002).
Note: Standard errors in parentheses. *denotes statistically significant difference at the 5 percent level. Base-year student weights are used in all calculations.

Table 6.7 Characteristics of Tenth Grade Math Teachers in Matched Teacher-Student Data

	NELS 1st Follow-up, 1990			ELS Base Year, 2002			
	Average White Student	Average Black Student	Black-White Difference	Average White Student	Average Black Student	Black-White Difference	Difference-in-Difference
Percent male	55.8	36.8	−18.9	43.7	42.9	−0.9	18.0
	(0.7)	(1.9)	(1.9)*	(0.7)	(1.3)	(1.5)	(2.7)
Percent black	2.1	27.6	25.5	2.1	21.2	19.1	−6.4
	(0.2)	(1.7)	(0.9)*	(0.2)	(1.1)	(0.7)*	(1.2)*
Percent same-gender teacher	50.7	50.5	−0.2	51.6	49.9	−1.7	−1.5
	(0.7)	(0.2)	(1.9)	(0.7)	(1.4)	(1.6)	(2.7)
Percent same-race teacher	96.1	27.6	−68.4	93.4	21.2	−72.3	−3.9
	(0.3)	(1.7)	(1.0)*	(0.3)	(1.1)	(0.9)*	(1.4)*
Years of teaching experience	16.4	15.1	−1.1	15.0	15.6	0.6	1.7
	(0.1)	(0.3)	(0.4)*	(0.1)	(0.3)	(0.3)	(0.6)*
Years of secondary teaching experience	15.7	14.4	−1.2	14.7	15.1	0.4	1.7
	(0.1)	(0.3)	(0.3)*	(0.2)	(0.3)	(0.3)	(0.6)*
Percent two or fewer years experience	7.8	9.0	1.2	10.1	9.4	−0.7	−1.9
	(0.4)	(1.1)	(1.1)	(0.4)	(0.8)	(1.0)	(1.6)
Years at current school	11.2	8.5	−2.7	10.0	8.1	−1.9	0.8
	(0.1)	(0.3)	(0.3)*	(0.1)	(0.2)	(0.3)*	(0.5)
Percent with MA or higher	50.9	45.3	−5.6	50.7	49.1	−1.5	4.1
	(0.7)	(1.9)	(2.0)*	(0.7)	(1.4)	(1.6)	(2.7)
Percent with degree in field	77.4	66.4	−11.0	82.0	78.8	−5.5	5.5
	(0.6)	(1.9)	(1.7)*	(0.5)	(1.2)	(1.3)*	(2.3)*
Percent that would teach again	55.5	49.6	−5.9	66.7	64.0	−2.7	3.2
	(0.7)	(2.0)	(1.9)*	(0.6)	(1.3)	(1.5)	(2.6)

Source: Authors' calculations using NELS-88 first follow-up survey (1990) and ELS base year survey (2002).
Note: Standard errors in parentheses. *denotes statistically significant difference at the 5 percent level. Base-year student weights are used in all calculations.

white students) to an advantage for the typical black sophomore. The only adverse change observed here is in the gap in the proportion of teachers who believed they would choose to teach again, which nearly doubled between 1990 and 2002 (though the change is not statistically significant).

For mathematics teachers, we find black-white differences in teacher gender, race, experience, tenure, educational attainment, and job satisfaction similar to those for English teachers (see table 6.7). The gap in the fraction of teachers who are male, white, or black narrowed during the 1990s, as did the black-white gap in teaching experience. Likewise, the gap in the fraction of mathematics teachers who held a degree in math narrowed considerably, from a deficit of 11 percentage points in 1990 to 5.5 points in 2002, a result that contrasts with a growing gap in exposure to secondary math teachers with math degrees found in table 6.3 using the SASS. Changes in the black-white gap in novice teaching, teacher tenure, advanced degree attainment, and job satisfaction were not statistically significant but in all cases the point estimate of the change suggests a narrowing of the gap.

Another advantage of teacher-student matched data is the ability to examine teacher-student matching on the basis of race or gender. In English, we find that black students are more likely to have a same-gender English teacher but significantly less likely to have a teacher of the same race; only 24 percent of black sophomores had an English teacher who was also black, a propensity that was unchanged over the 1990s. In mathematics, the average black sophomore was again much less likely to have an African American teacher, and somewhat less likely to have a math teacher of the same gender. In contrast to English, we observe a widening of the black-white gap in exposure to same-race teachers (a statistically significant change).

Do Teacher Sorting Patterns Reflect Concentrations of Student Poverty or Race?

Our tabulations from the Schools and Staffing Surveys, NELS, and ELS find that teacher attributes and qualifications are unevenly distributed across schools, in most cases to the relative disadvantage of black students. This evidence mirrors that found in recent studies relying on state personnel data (in New York, Lankford, Loeb, and Wyckoff 2002; in North Carolina, Clotfelter, Ladd, and Vigdor 2005; in California, Jepsen and Rivkin 2002). At face value, however, it is unclear whether these differences can be attributed to the racial composition of schools, or whether they in fact reflect some other school characteristic, such as student poverty. This distinction is important. Given recent black-white convergence in family income (Campbell et al., chapter 3, this volume), if teachers are selecting into schools based on student income rather than to race, income convergence would imply an eventual convergence in exposure to qualified teachers. On the other hand, if teacher sorting depends at least in part on the racial composition of schools, these gaps are likely to persist as long as there is persistent school segregation.

Existing research on teacher sorting across schools suggests that a school's minority concentration has a substantial negative impact on teacher recruitment and retention, over and above that explained by student income. For example, Benjamin Scafidi, David Sjoquist, and Todd Stinebrickner (2007) find using Georgia administrative data that a school's racial composition is a stronger predictor of teacher attrition than student poverty. Likewise, Marigee Bacolod (2007) and Hanushek, Kain, and Rivkin (2004) found that both new and experienced teachers are more likely to leave or avoid schools with a high concentration of minority students, controlling for a wide array of individual teacher and school characteristics, including poverty.

As a rough test of this hypothesis in our own data, we return to the Schools and Staffing Survey and regress school-level teacher characteristics—those summarized in tables 6.1 and 6.2—on the black percentage of school enrollment, the percent of enrollment eligible for free or reduced price lunch, and dummy variables for census region, school level (elementary, secondary, or combined), and urbanicity. The results are displayed in table 6.8, which shows our estimated coefficients on percentage black and percentage free lunch eligible from a series of regressions from the 1987 to 1988 and 2003 to 2004 SASS data. Region, level, and urbanicity coefficients are not shown.

Controlling for a limited set of covariates, teacher attributes and qualifications measured at the school level tend to be related to both the racial composition of the school and student poverty. This finding is particularly strong in our most recent set of data (2004), where a school's percentage black is in many cases a stronger predictor of average school teacher characteristics than student income is. For example, in 2003 and 2004, holding constant the percentage eligible for free lunch, a 1 standard deviation rise in the percentage black (0.252) is associated with a 0.5 percentage point higher rate of first-year teaching (on a baseline of 4.4 percent). By contrast, a 1 standard deviation higher rate of poverty (0.281) is associated with a 0.4 percentage point higher rate of novice teaching. This pattern holds for many other teacher attributes in 2004, including inexperienced teaching, tenure at the same school, certification, and intent to leave. The same regressions in 1987 and 1988 present a much more mixed picture, in which the racial composition of the school is associated with teacher characteristics when controlling for student poverty in only a few cases.

Taken together, our results in table 6.8 suggest that observed correlations between student race and teacher qualifications are not merely a

Table 6.8 Relationship Between Teacher Characteristics, School Racial Composition, and School Poverty

	1987 to 1988 SASS (7,288 Observations)			2003 to 2004 SASS (7,050 Observations)		
	Mean of Dependent Variable	Percent Black	Percent Free Lunch	Mean of Dependent Variable	Percent Black	Percent Free Lunch
Dependent variable						
Percent first-year teacher	0.0376	−0.0120	0.0210	0.0441	0.0214	0.0136
		(0.0064)	(0.0059)*		(0.0061)*	(0.0055)*
Percent three or fewer years experience	0.1112	−0.0341	0.0425	0.1355	0.0534	0.0450
		(0.0104)*	(0.0095)*		(0.0101)*	(0.0090)*
Years of experience	14.313	2.347	−1.461	14.400	−1.566	−1.824
		(0.288)*	(0.263)*		(0.3287)*	(0.2941)*
Years at current school	7.808	0.4681	−0.6424	8.095	−1.987	−0.3912
		(0.2576)	(0.2353)*		(0.2745)*	(0.2456)
Percent with MA or higher	0.4339	0.0904	−0.0598	0.4869	0.0164	−0.0750
		(0.0296)*	(0.0271)*		(0.0287)	(0.0257)*
Percent with traditional state certification	0.9737	−0.0036	−0.0429	0.8877	−0.0847	−0.0256
		(0.0058)	(0.0053)*		(0.0103)*	(0.0093)*
						(continued)

Table 6.8 Relationship Between Teacher Characteristics, School Racial Composition, and School Poverty (*Continued*)

	1987 to 1988 SASS (7,288 Observations)			2003 to 2004 SASS (7,050 Observations)		
	Mean of Dependent Variable	Percent Black	Percent Free Lunch	Mean of Dependent Variable	Percent Black	Percent Free Lunch
Percent with emergency or temporary certification	0.0539	0.0034 (0.0081)	0.0229 (0.0074)*	0.0665	0.0753 (0.0083)*	0.0212 (0.0074)*
Percent would teach again	0.5884	−0.0715 (0.0298)*	−0.0104 (0.0272)	0.6744	0.0354 (0.0269)	−0.0293 (0.0241)
Percent that plan to exit teaching as soon as possible	0.0368	0.0091 (0.0114)	0.0173 (0.0104)	0.0187	0.0175 (0.0078)*	−0.0096 (0.0070)
Percent that agree student behavior interferes	0.4047	0.1423 (0.0295)*	0.1446 (0.0269)*	0.3362	0.1939 (0.0267)*	0.1943 (0.0240)*
Percent that do not believe principal supports them	0.1576	−0.0033 (0.0220)	0.0819 (0.0201)*	0.1171	0.0104 (0.0186)	0.0505 (0.0166)*

Source: Authors' calculations using Schools and Staffing Surveys, 1987 to 1988 and 2003 to 2004.

Note: Each row-year combination presents the coefficient estimates from a separate OLS regression in which the listed dependent variable (measured at the school level) is regressed on the percent black enrollment, percent free lunch eligible enrollment, four census region dummies, three school level dummies (elementary, secondary and combined), and three urbanicity dummies (large or mid-size central city, urban fringe, and small town/rural). Only estimated coefficients on percent black and percent free lunch eligible are shown, and standard errors are in parentheses.
*denotes coefficient estimate is statistically significant at the 5 percent level.

reflection of the effects of concentrated poverty. Rather, the racial composition of student enrollment appears to matter for the distribution of teachers over schools as much or more as student income, a result broadly consistent with the existing literature. This relationship if anything appears to have strengthened over the 1988–2004 period.

Can Class Size Explain Trends in the Teacher Quality Gap?

Our analysis suggests that most of the changes in black-white exposure to qualified and experienced teachers occurred in elementary rather than secondary schools. One hypothesis for the growing teacher quality gap at the elementary level is the wave of class size reduction policies that occurred during this decade.[34] The much-publicized benefits of class size reduction in the early grades in Tennessee's Project STAR led to a widespread movement to cut already-shrinking class sizes in other states. California's 1996 initiative to cut K-3 class sizes by 30 percent is the most prominent example of this movement, though similar policies were enacted earlier in Nevada (1989), Utah (1990), and North Carolina (1991).[35]

Sweeping class size reduction initiatives that require large increases in the teacher workforce have the potential to shift the level and distribution of teacher quality within and between schools. The large number of new hires required to accommodate smaller classes is likely to lower the overall experience level of teachers in affected grades (and perhaps in other grades to the extent teachers move between grades). Further, the growing demand for teachers across all schools may lead to a movement of experienced and well-qualified teachers toward opportunities in more desirable schools and away from hard-to-staff classrooms, compounding the challenges faced by already disadvantaged schools and school districts. Indeed, Christopher Jepsen and Steven Rivkin found that predominately black schools in California suffered a significant deterioration in teacher quality after that state's class size reduction initiative (2002).

As figure 6.1 shows, pupil-teacher ratios fell slowly in the late 1980s but began an accelerated decline in the mid-1990s.[36] The average black student in every year of this series was enrolled in a school with a lower pupil-teacher ratio than the average white student. The two groups converged in the mid-1990s, only to diverge again at the end of the decade. Figures 6.2 and 6.3 illustrate the trend in ratios separately for elementary and secondary schools. It is clear that the vast majority of the declining ratio in the United States can be explained by changes at the elementary level. Between 1995 and 2000, pupil-teacher ratios dropped from approximately 19:1 to 17:1 in elementary schools—a drop of 10.5 percent in five years—but less than 5 percent at the high school level. Class sizes continued to fall in elementary schools after the turn of the century but turned

Figure 6.1   Average Pupil-Teacher Ratio, All U.S. Schools

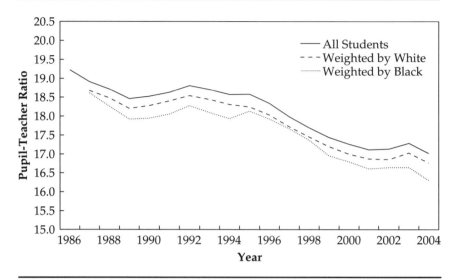

Source: Authors calc ulations, using the NCES Common Core of Data School Universe Survey Longitudinal Data File (1986 to 1998) and annual Public School Universe files 1999 to 2000 through 2004 to 2005.
Note: Pupil-teacher ratios are calculated as: fall membership/full-time equivalent teachers. Each series is a weighted average over schools using total ("all students" series), African American, or white enrollment as weights.

up again at the secondary level. Of course, more research is needed to establish a causal link between changes in class size and black-white exposure to teacher quality, but the trends observed here are fully consistent with our divergent findings on teacher quality at the elementary and secondary level.

Differential trends in class size may have independently contributed to changes in the black-white achievement gap in the 1990s. Class size itself has been shown to have modest impacts on student achievement, and may matter more for the academic success of African American students than for whites (Krueger 1999). At the elementary level (figure 6.2), average class sizes converged between these groups in the 1990s, with pupil-teacher ratios falling faster for white students than for black at the beginning of the decade. The opposite was true at the end of the decade. In secondary schools (figure 6.3), where the black-white achievement gap worsened, pupil-teacher ratios mostly moved in tandem through the 1990s. Thus a cursory look at resource intensity in schools attended by white and black students does not reveal any differential experiences of class size that are likely to explain changes in the achievement gap.

Figure 6.2   Average Pupil-Teacher Ratio, U.S. Elementary Schools

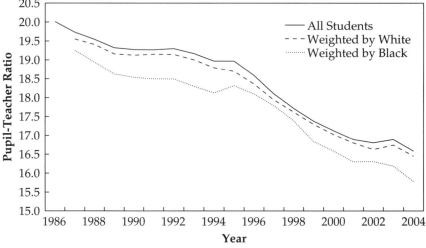

Source: Authors' calculations, using the NCES Common Core of Data School Universe Survey Longitudinal Data File (1986 to 1998) and annual Public School Universe files 1999 to 2000 through 2004 to 2005.
Note: Pupil-teacher ratios are calculated as: fall membership/full-time equivalent teachers. Each series is a weighted average over elementary schools using total ("all students" series), African American, or white enrollment as weights.

Conclusion

Evidence on the role of observed teacher qualifications in students' academic achievement remains inconclusive. It is also clear that unobserved dimensions of teaching effectiveness matter as much or more than the acquisition of any advanced degree or state licensure. Yet—as our brief review of the literature indicated—there are a number of characteristics and qualifications that have been found empirically to have large and important effects on student learning. Attributes such as teaching experience and subject matter preparation are important in the short term for student achievement, and may have cumulative effects over time. Repeated exposure to inexperienced or underqualified teachers may eventually yield adverse outcomes considerably larger than those observed in any cross-sectional study.

The importance of teacher quality in the academic success of children has led many to point to differential exposure to qualified teachers as a possible explanation for the black-white achievement gap. Our analysis in this chapter cannot rule out this possibility. In fact, our results reveal that teach-

Figure 6.3   Average Pupil-Teacher Ratio, U.S. Secondary Schools

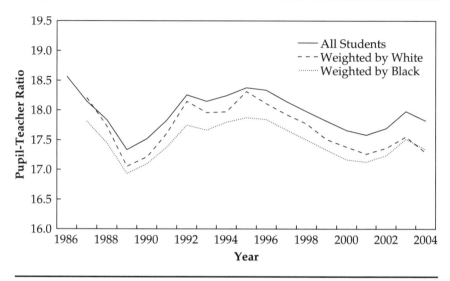

Source: Authors' calculations, using the NCES Common Core of Data School Universe Survey Longitudinal Data File (1986 to 1998) and annual Public School Universe files 1999 to 2000 through 2004 to 2005.
Note: Pupil-teacher ratios are calculated as: fall membership/full-time equivalent teachers. Each series is a weighted average over secondary schools using total ("all students" series), African American, or white enrollment as weights.

ers of the average black student are consistently more likely to be inexperienced, uncertified, and unhappy with their career choice and work environment than teachers of the average white student. However, we have no evidence to suggest that changes in exposure to qualified teachers adversely affected the black-white achievement gap during the 1990s. We find that black-white differences in exposure to quality teachers grew most at the elementary level, though the achievement gap suffered most at the secondary level. In fact, our analysis of teacher-student matched data at the high school level suggests that the exposure gap to high-quality teachers actually narrowed in secondary schools.

The lack of change in the relative quality of teachers for black and white students is not altogether surprising. Teacher labor markets are rigid, local, and as responsive to student demographics as to salary. If anything, public schools in the United States became more racially segregated during the 1990s. Only through significant changes in teacher sorting behavior would the race gap in teacher characteristics be likely to close. Policy makers should be cognizant of the links between the quality of a school's teaching staff, its student composition, and working conditions, and then tailor policies that recognize these links. Policies offering additional compensation to teachers working in hard-to-staff schools have shown promise (Clotfelter, Ladd, and Vigdor 2006), but it is unclear whether such policies are enough to overcome the powerful effects of residential and school segregation.

Perhaps of some concern is our finding that the gap in exposure to experienced and qualified teachers grew significantly in elementary schools over this period. Our cursory look at trends in pupil-teacher ratios during the 1990s suggests that efforts to reduce class sizes in the early grades may have had a deleterious effect on teacher quality in hard-to-staff schools. Additional research on this question is needed.

Acknowledgments

Prepared for the Russell Sage Foundation conference on "Stalled Progress: Inequality and the Black-White Test Score Gap," November 2006. The authors would like to thank Joydeep Roy for providing tabulations from the 2003–2004 Schools and Staffing Survey, Timothy Moore and Erin Cocke for research assistance, Deborah Reed and participants at the 2006 APPAM conference for their comments, and the National Center for Education Statistics for granting access to the restricted-use Schools and Staffing Surveys.

Notes

1. Elementary and Secondary Education Act (ESEA) Section 1001(3), Public Law 107-110, 107th Congress, accessed at http://www.ed.gov/policy/elsec/leg/esea02/107-110.pdf.
2. NCLB defines *highly qualified* as meeting three conditions: possession of a bachelor's degree, full certification by the state, and demonstrated competence in the subject matter taught (§9101(23)(a)-(c)).
3. ESEA §1119(a)(1) and §1111(b)(8)(c).
4. Christopher Jencks and Meredith Phillips (1998) hinted at the possibility of a convergence in teacher quality across black and white students (see, for example, chapter 6, "Why Did the Black-White Test Score Gap Narrow in the 1970s and 1980s?" by Grissmer, Flanagan, and Williamson) but provided little data to support any definitive conclusions.
5. Based on authors' calculations from the National Assessment of Educational Progress (NAEP) Long-Run Trend Assessments. The long-run trend assessments in reading and math were initially administered in different years—mathematics in 1986, and reading in 1988.
6. Donald Boyd and his colleagues (2005) found in New York State that an extraordinarily high proportion of teachers accept their first teaching position in the same district in which they attended high school.
7. Unfortunately, it is too early to tell whether No Child Left Behind has reduced inequities in teacher qualifications. Not until 2005 was the teacher quality provision enforced by the federal government, and even then only weakly.
8. It is important to keep in mind that the teacher effects literature has focused almost exclusively on student achievement gains on standardized tests.

Teacher aptitudes that yield gains in math and reading are not necessarily the same skills that promote social development, high school completion, or many of the other educational outcomes commonly expected of schools (on the indirect estimates of teacher effects on the social development of students, see Booher-Jennings and DiPrete 2007).

9. Contrary to most findings, two recent studies found no evidence that pre-service preparation such as undergraduate major affects student outcomes (Harris and Sass 2007; Betts, Zau, and Rice 2003).

10. Thomas Dee's (2004) analysis of the Tennessee STAR data provided similar results in the aggregate, but with variation by race and gender. He showed that teaching experience had greater returns for white males in mathematics than for black males or (all) females, and greater returns in reading for (all) whites and black females in reading than for black males.

11. Dee's estimates relied on within-school variation in student-teacher race assignment, and thus unlikely to have been driven by between-school differences in teacher quality. Ehrenberg and Brewer (1995) and Clotfelter, Ladd, and Vigdor (2007) found similar results.

12. For example, girls are more likely to report that they do not look forward to a subject, or that they are afraid to ask questions in class, if their teacher is male (especially true in science). Ehrenberg and his colleagues (1995) and Ferguson (1998) offered evidence that the subjective evaluations of students made by teachers vary by race, gender, and ethnicity.

13. General evidence on the quality of teachers entering the teaching profession can be found in Corcoran, Evans, and Schwab (2004) and Bacolod (2007). Unfortunately, data on the academic proficiency of teachers in those studies cannot be matched to the students of those teachers.

14. For example, in North Carolina, Clotfelter, Ladd, and Vigdor showed that the average black student in 2000 and 2001 was 54 percent more likely to face a novice teacher than the average white student, and that two-thirds of the overall black-white difference in exposure to novice teachers can be attributed to within- rather than between-district differences (2005, 2006). As in New York, teachers with better qualifications, more experience, degrees from more selective colleges and universities, National Board Certification, and high licensure test scores, were more likely to work in school with fewer nonwhite students and students eligible for free or reduced price lunch (see also Lankford, Loeb, and Wyckoff 2002).

15. These authors find that the composition of new and all teachers in both urban and rural areas remained approximately the same along almost every dimension over these fifteen years, with one exception—the fraction of teachers who failed a test of general knowledge rose in New York City relative to suburban areas, though this may have been due to changes in the exam itself.

16. More information on the SASS is available at http://nces.ed.gov/surveys/sass.

17. SASS sampling weights are used where appropriate. We use the restricted use versions of the Schools and Staffing Surveys, which provide the exact racial composition of teachers' schools. Given this information, we are able to examine mean characteristics of teachers in overwhelmingly black or overwhelmingly white schools. Meredith Phillips and Tiffani Chin (2004) summarized

teacher characteristics by four categories of minority enrollment shares (where the top category is 50 or more percent).

18. For example, the average black student in 2000 attended a school where 54.6 percent of students were also black, yet only 27.6 percent of the teachers in these schools were African American.

19. We are not aware of any evidence that tenure at the same school has beneficial effects on student outcomes. In fact, estimating the effect of tenure on student achievement would be difficult in practice due to the nonrandom assignment of teachers to schools. Nonetheless, this measure might be thought of as a broader indicator of teacher turnover or long-term job satisfaction at individual schools.

20. The last section noted that empirical evidence on the effectiveness of advanced degrees in teaching is weak; yet where the evidence tilted in favor of advanced degrees it tended to be most beneficial for black students.

21. Unfortunately, the degree codes used in the 2003 to 2004 wave of the SASS do not appear to be comparable to earlier waves, with the proportion of teachers with a BA in education falling by an implausible amount.

22. Both the 1987 to 1988 and the 2003 to 2004 waves of the SASS included questions related to college major. Teacher responses to these questions, however, differed markedly from responses in the intervening years (particularly in 2003 and 2004). We have elected to omit results from 2003 and 2004 in tables 6.1 and 6.2; results from 1987 and 1988 results should be taken with caution.

23. In subjects other than math, the black-white gap in subject-matter preparation is typically negative, but rarely statistically significant at conventional levels. One area in which the black-white gap in teacher preparation appears to have narrowed during the 1990s is in English and reading, where the difference in the fraction of teachers who majored in English fell in half, from −0.026 to −0.013. Most likely because of the small sample size, this change is not statistically significant.

24. The question reads, "if you could go back to your college days and start over again, would you become a teacher or not?" Table 6.1 shows the percent of teachers that responded "certainly would" or "probably would."

25. A question posed in the 1991 and 1994 survey that was unfortunately discontinued showed a similar trend—a growing gap in teachers' intentions to remain in the same school, with 13.5 percent of the average black student's teachers indicating they did not plan to return to the same school in 1994.

26. Assuming a 180-day school year (thirty-six weeks), 0.86 hours per week—the black-white gap in 1991—amounts to thirty-one fewer hours each school year, nearly equivalent to a week's worth of classroom instruction. Unfortunately, the measurement of teacher work hours outside of the classroom differed considerably in 2003 and 2004. As such, we have not presented averages for that year.

27. Teachers are included in the elementary averages if they predominately taught students in kindergarten through sixth grade. Teachers are included in the secondary average if they predominately taught students in grades seven through twelve. As in tables 6.1 and 6.2, these averages are taken over schools, where schools are included in the elementary average if they are designated as elementary (or combined elementary-secondary) schools, and schools are included in the secondary average if they are designated as secondary (or combined elementary-secondary) schools.

28. These extrapolations are based on Fall 1991 and 1999 tabulations of public K-12 enrollment (National Center for Education Statistics 1991, 1992).
29. Our segregation measure is the average (student-weighted) difference between a school's exposure rate of white students to black students and the district-wide proportion black (on this, see Clotfelter 2004).
30. We use the predominately black (greater than 90 percent) and predominately nonblack (less than 10 percent black) categories as our basis for comparison here. In a number of cases the gaps in teacher characteristics are larger when comparing predominately nonblack schools to schools with 51 to 90 percent black enrollment.
31. The remaining gap still appears to be a sizable difference. Assuming thirty-six weeks in the school year, this amounts to 42.8 fewer hours devoted to school work over one year.
32. NELS-88 is a nationally representative, multistage probability sample of eighth graders who were first surveyed in the spring of 1988. A subsample of respondents were then surveyed again in 1990, 1992, 1994, and 2000. Questionnaires were also sent to parents, math and English teachers, and school administrators. ELS is similar in design to NELS-88, but the base-year survey was conducted of a nationally representative sample of high school sophomores in 2002. We use the first follow-up survey from NELS and the base-year survey from ELS as our sample of high school sophomores in 1990 and 2002. Base year student weights are used in all calculations.
33. After appropriate sample restrictions we have similarly sized samples for students taking English classes in the two surveys, but there are approximately 1,700 fewer students with valid data on their math teachers in the NELS than the ELS.
34. Other authors have pointed out that the economics of teacher quality in recent decades may have resulted in a substitution away from teacher quality (highly skilled teachers) and toward teacher quantity, that is, smaller class sizes. (see Lakdawalla 2006).
35. On the California Class Size Reduction Initiative, see the archived research plan at http://www.classize.org. For other examples, see WestEd's 1998 *Policy Brief* 23 (August) at http://www.wested.org/policy/pubs/full_text/pb_ft_csr23.htm.
36. The reader should keep in mind that pupil-teacher ratios are not the same as class size. The ratios include more than full-time classroom teachers in the denominator and thus tend to be smaller than actual class sizes. The two statistics do tend to move together over time, however (Lewitt and Baker 1997).

References

Aaronson, Daniel, Lisa Barrow, and William Sander. 2007. "Teachers and Student Achievement in the Chicago Public High Schools." *Journal of Labor Economics* 25(1): 95–135.

Bacolod, Marigee. 2007. "Do Alternative Opportunities Matter? The Role of Female Labor Markets in the Decline of Teacher Quality." *Review of Economics and Statistics* 89(4): 737–51.

Ballou, Dale, and Michael Podgursky. 2000. "Reforming Teacher Preparation and Licensing: What is the Evidence?" *Teachers College Record* 102(1): 5–27.

Betts, Julian R., Andrew C. Zau, and Lorien A. Rice. 2003. *Determinants of Student Achievement: New Evidence from San Diego.* San Francisco, Calif.: Public Policy Institute of California.

Booher-Jennings, Jennifer, and Thomas A. DiPrete. 2007. "Teacher Effects on Academic and Social Outcomes in Elementary School." Mimeo. Department of Sociology, Columbia University.

Boyd, Donald, Pamela Grossman, Hamilton Lankford, Susanna Loeb, and James Wyckoff. 2006. "How Changes in Entry Requirements Alter the Teacher Workforce and Affect Student Achievement." *Education Finance and Policy* 1(2): 176–216.

Boyd, Donald, Hamilton Lankford, Susanna Loeb, and James Wyckoff. 2005. "The Draw of Home: How Teachers' Preferences for Proximity Disadvantage Urban Schools." *Journal of Policy Analysis and Management* 24(1): 113–32.

Clotfelter, Charles T. 2004. *After Brown: The Rise and Retreat of School Desegregation.* Princeton, N.J.: Princeton University Press.

Clotfelter, Charles T., Helen F. Ladd, and Jacob L. Vigdor. 2005. "Who Teaches Whom? Race and the Distribution of Novice Teachers." *Economics of Education Review* 24(4): 377–92.

———. 2006. "Teacher-Student Matching and the Assessment of Teacher Effectiveness." NBER Working Paper 11936. Cambridge, Mass.: National Bureau of Economic Research.

———. 2007. "How and Why Do Teacher Credentials Matter for Student Achievement?" CALDER Working Paper 2. Washington, D.C.: The Urban Institute.

Corcoran, Sean P., William N. Evans, and Robert M. Schwab. 2004. "Women, the Labor Market, and the Declining Relative Quality of Teachers." *Journal of Policy Analysis and Management* 23(3): 449–70.

Croninger, Robert G., Jennifer King Rice, Amy Rathbun, and Masako Nishio. 2007. "Teacher Qualifications and Early Learning: Effects of Certification, Degree, and Experience on First-Grade Student Achievement." *Economics of Education Review* 26(3): 312–24.

Decker, Paul T., Daniel P. Mayer, and Steven Glazerman. 2004. *The Effects of Teach for America on Students: Findings from a National Evaluation.* Princeton, N.J.: Mathematica Policy Research.

Dee, Thomas S. 2004. "Teachers, Race, and Student Achievement in a Randomized Experiment." *Review of Economics & Statistics* 86(1): 195–210.

———. 2005. "A Teacher Like Me: Does Race, Ethnicity, or Gender Matter?" *American Economic Review* 95(2): 158–65.

Ehrenberg, Ronald G., and Dominic J. Brewer. 1994. "Do School and Teacher Characteristics Matter? Evidence from High School and Beyond?" *Economics of Education Review* 13(1): 1–17.

———. 1995. "Did Teachers' Verbal Ability and Race Matter in the 1960s? Coleman Revisited." *Economics of Education Review* 14(1): 1–21.

Ehrenberg, Ronald G., Daniel D. Goldhaber, and Dominic J. Brewer. 1995. "Do Teachers' Race, Gender, and Ethnicity Matter? Evidence from the National Educational Longitudinal Study of 1988." *Industrial and Labor Relations Review* 48(3): 547–61.

Ferguson, Ronald F. 1991. "Paying for Public Education: New Evidence on How and Why Money Matters." *Harvard Journal on Legislation* 28(2): 465–98.

———. 1998. "Teachers' Perceptions and Expectations and the Black-White Test Score Gap." In *The Black-White Test Score Gap,* edited by Christopher Jencks and Meredith Phillips. Washington, D.C.: Brookings Institution Press.

Ferguson, Ronald F., and Helen F. Ladd. 1996. "How and Why Money Matters: An Analysis of Alabama Schools." In *Holding Schools Accountable: Performance-Based Reform in Education,* edited by Helen F. Ladd. Washington, D.C.: Brookings Institution Press.

Goldhaber, Dan D., and Emily Anthony. 2007. "Can Teacher Quality Be Effectively Assessed? National Board Certification as a Signal of Effective Teaching." *Review of Economics and Statistics* 89(1): 134–50.

Goldhaber, Dan D., and Dominic J. Brewer. 1996. "Evaluating the Effect of Teacher Degree Level on Educational Performance." In *Developments in School Finance, 1996,* edited by William J. Fowler, Jr. NCES 97-535. Washington: National Center for Education Statistics.

———. 2000. "Does Teacher Certification Matter? High School Teacher Certification Status and Student Achievement." *Educational Evaluation and Policy Analysis* 22(2): 129–45.

Grissmer, David, Ann Flanagan, and Stephanie Williamson. 1998. "Why Did the Black-White Test Score Gap Narrow in the 1970s and 1980s?" In *The Black-White Test Score Gap,* edited by Christopher Jencks and Meredith Phillips. Washington, D.C.: The Brookings Institution Press.

Hanushek, Eric A., John F. Kain, and Steven G. Rivkin. 2004. "Why Public Schools Lose Teachers." *Journal of Human Resources* 39(20): 326–54.

Hanushek, Eric A., John F. Kain, Daniel M. O'Brien, and Steven G. Rivkin. 2005. "The Market for Teacher Quality." NBER Working Paper 11154. Cambridge, Mass.: National Bureau of Economic Research.

Hanushek, Eric A., and Steven G. Rivkin. 2006. "Teacher Quality." In *Handbook of the Economics of Education,* edited by Eric A. Hanushek and Finis Welch. Amsterdam: North-Holland.

Harris, Douglas N., and Tim R. Sass. 2007. "Teacher Training, Teacher Quality and Student Achievement." CALDER Working Paper 3. Washington, D.C.: The Urban Institute.

Jencks, Christopher, and Meredith Phillips. 1998. *The Black-White Test Score Gap.* Washington, D.C.: Brookings Institution Press.

Jepsen, Christopher, and Steven G. Rivkin. 2002. "What Is the Trade-off Between Smaller Classes and Teacher Quality?" NBER Working Paper 9205. Cambridge, Mass.: National Bureau of Economic Research.

Kane, Thomas J., Jonah E. Rockoff, and Douglas O. Staiger. 2006. "What Does Certification Tell Us About Teacher Effectiveness? Evidence from New York City." NBER Working Paper 12155. Cambridge, Mass.: National Bureau of Economic Research.

Krueger, Alan B. 1999. "Experimental Estimates of Education Production Functions." *The Quarterly Journal of Economics* 114(2): 497–532.

Lakdawalla, Darius. 2006. "The Economics of Teacher Quality." *Journal of Law and Economics* 49(1): 285–329.

Lankford, Hamilton, Susanna Loeb, and James Wyckoff. 2002. "Teacher Sorting and the Plight of Urban Schools: A Descriptive Analysis." *Educational Evaluation and Policy Analysis* 24(1): 37–62.

Larsen, S. Eric. 2006. "The Race to the Top: Increases in Teacher Education Levels, 1960–2000." Mimeo. Department of Economics, University of California, Davis.

Lewitt, Eugene M., and Linda S. Baker. 1997. "Class Size." *The Future of Children* 7(3): 112–21.

Monk, David H., and Jennifer King. 1994. "Multi-level Teacher Resource Effects on Pupil Performance in Secondary Mathematics and Science: The Role of Teacher Subject Matter Preparation." In *Contemporary Policy Issues: Choices and Consequences in Education,* edited by Ronald G. Ehrenberg. Ithaca, N.Y.: ILR Press.

National Center for Education Statistics. 1991. *Digest of Education Statistics, 1991.* NCES 91697 (November). Washington: U.S. Department of Education. Accessed at http://nces.ed.gov/pubs91/91697.pdf.

———. 1992. *Digest of Education Statistics, 1992.* NCES 92097 (November). Washington: U.S. Department of Education. Accessed at http://nces.ed.gov/pubs92/92097.pdf.

Nye, Barbara, Spyros Konstantopoulos, and Larry V. Hedges. 2004. "How Large Are Teacher Effects?" *Educational Evaluation and Policy Analysis* 26(3): 237–57.

Orfield, Gary, and Chungmei Lee. 2006. *Racial Transformation and the Changing Nature of Segregation.* Cambridge, Mass.: The Civil Rights Project, Harvard University.

Phillips, Meredith, and Tiffani Chin. 2004. "School Inequality: What Do We Know?" In *Social Inequality,* edited by Kathryn M. Neckerman. New York: Russell Sage Foundation.

Rice, Jennifer King. 2003. *Teacher Quality: Understanding the Effectiveness of Teacher Attributes.* Washington, D.C.: Economic Policy Institute.

Rivkin, Steven G., Eric A. Hanushek, and John F. Kain. 2005. "Teachers, Schools, and Academic Achievement." *Econometrica* 73(2): 417–58.

Rockoff, Jonah E. 2004. "The Impact of Individual Teachers on Student Achievement: Evidence from Panel Data." *American Economic Review* 94(2): 247–52.

Sanders, William L., and June C. Rivers. 1996. *Cumulative and Residual Effects of Teachers on Future Student Academic Achievement.* Knoxville: Value-Added Research and Assessment Center, University of Tennessee.

Scafidi, Benjamin, David L. Sjoquist, and Todd R. Stinebrickner. 2007. "Race, Poverty, and Teacher Mobility." *Economics of Education Review* 26(2): 145–59.

Wayne, Andrew J., and Peter Youngs. 2003. "Teacher Characteristics and Student Achievement Gains." *Review of Educational Research* 73(1): 89–122.

Chapter 7

Culture and Stalled Progress in Narrowing the Black-White Test Score Gap

MEREDITH PHILLIPS

Betwen 1971 and the late 1980s, the black-white test score gap narrowed considerably in both reading and math. That progress had subsided by 1990, though it may now have resumed. Many scholars have explored why the gap narrowed—concluding that improvements in African American's socioeconomic circumstances contributed to the narrowing, and that African American students' increased access to challenging course work, smaller classes, and desegregated educational environments probably did as well (see Berends et al. 2005; Cook and Evans 2000; Ferguson 2001; Grissmer et al. 1994; Grissmer, Flanagan, and Williamson 1998). We know far less about why progress stagnated in the early 1990s, but some scholars have speculated that changes in African American culture may be at least partially responsible (see Ferguson 2001; Neal 2006). Although culture is difficult to define, let alone measure, this chapter uses available data to investigate whether changes in school-related behaviors, or changes in home environments, may have contributed to black students' stalled progress.

Racial Differences in Student Behavior and Home Environments

When scholars invoke culture as an explanation for the black-white test score gap, they often mean that African American parents or students share attitudes or behaviors that differ from those of their white counterparts, and that those differences contribute to disparities in academic success (see, for example, Ogbu 1978; see Lamont and Small 2008 for a review of new ways to incorporate culture into our understanding of inequality). We know, for example, that black and white families parent young children differently on average, and that some of those differences are associated with the black-white gap in academic skills that emerges during the first few years of life. In an excellent review of this literature, Jeanne Brooks-Gunn and Lisa Markman (2005) described seven categories of parenting practices (nurturance, discipline, teaching, language, monitoring, management, and reading materials in the home), noted that black mothers tended to rank lower than white mothers on five of these types of practices (evidence does not exist for the other two), and pointed out that ethnic differences in teaching, language, and materials helped explain a important fraction of the black-white test score gap among young children.

The evidence on whether black and white families also differ in their parenting of older children and adolescents, and whether differences in parenting styles relate to the achievement gap, is far less conclusive (see Smetana, Campione-Barr, and Metzger 2006 for a review on adolescence and parenting). But we do know that as children age, they gain more control over their environments and behavior. Differences in how older children and adolescents choose to behave and spend their time thus tend to be related to how much they learn. For example, doing more homework and spending more time reading for pleasure are related to learning more math and reading, respectively, even among students with similar academic records and family backgrounds (Jencks and Phillips 1999).

Some scholars have argued that black adolescents make poorer choices about how to spend their time than their white peers do. For example, a recent *New York Times* editorial, "A Poverty of the Mind," criticized black youth for not having their priorities straight: "Hip-hop, professional basketball and homeboy fashions are as American as cherry pie. Young white Americans are very much into these things, but selectively; they know when it is time to turn off Fifty Cent and get out the SAT prep book" (Orlando Patterson, March 26, 2006, accessed at http://www.nytimes.com/2006/03/26/opinion/26patterson.html). Similarly, Abigail and Stephan Thernstrom have attributed the achievement gap, at least in part, to the way black adolescents spend their time: "Doing well in school requires time on task and concentration, but black students spend an astonishing amount of time on their 'social homework'—namely, watching television" (2003, 147).

Culture and Stalled Progress

Because the stalled progress in narrowing the test score gap has defied easy explanation, a few scholars have suggested that cultural changes may have played some role. David Grissmer and his colleagues speculated that "changes in schools and communities that gave rise to increasing violence among black teenagers" may help explain why black teens' reading test scores fell after 1988 (1998, 219). Ronald Ferguson (2001) conjectured that the explosive popularity of hip hop music in the late 1980s and early 1990s can help explain the decline in reading test scores for black teens and suggested two related mechanisms for this effect. First, African American students may simply have become so focused on listening to this music and deciphering its lyrics that they spent less time than they otherwise would have on activities more conducive to academic success, such as reading and doing homework. Second, the values and behaviors promoted by hip hop music—especially by the antiestablishment "gangsta" rap that became so popular during this period—may have negatively influenced black students' attitudes toward academic success or their behavior at school.

Derek Neal (2006) also entertained the possibility that changes in norms were at least partially responsible for why the black-white test score gap stopped narrowing. Instead of focusing on the potential effects of hip hop, however, Neal speculated that "black-white differences in norms or culture" may have affected parenting, or what he terms "patterns of investment in children" (34). He also wondered whether normative changes associated with the crack epidemic of the late 1980s, which was generally confined to cities, may have impeded black students' academic progress.

Despite speculation about the role of culture in stalling black students' progress, empirical evidence on the topic is sparse. David Grissmer, Ann Flanagan, and Stephanie Williamson (1998) showed that the murder rate rose dramatically between 1985 and 1990 for black, but not white, teenagers. They also cited research suggesting that students learn less when they attend more violent high schools. They concluded, however, that the effects of violence are probably too small to explain the test score trends, and that black tenth graders reported feeling safer at school in 1990 than in 1980.

Ronald Ferguson (2001) examined time use data reported by seventeen-year-olds in the National Assessment of Education Long Term Trend Samples (NAEP-LTT) and found little evidence that trends in the time black students spent watching television or doing homework could explain black students' poor reading performance in the early 1990s. He did find, however, that trends in how often black students told their friends about good books and, especially, how often they read for pleasure, mirrored trends in black students' reading test scores. He concluded that "the rise of rap music may help account for the drop in leisure reading and reading scores" but also acknowledged that this conclusion "should be regarded as tentative until more evidence is found to support it" (375). Jaekyung Lee (2002) concluded the opposite—that the data on trends in youth culture do not support the cultural hypothesis for why the gap stopped narrowing. He reported that blacks had higher expectations for educational attainment, did more homework, watched less television, and attended safer schools in 1990 than in 1980. This evidence is not ideal, however, because it does not span the time period during which thirteen-year-old and seventeen-year-old black students' reading scores declined. In fact, NAEP reading scores peaked when the cohort of students Lee described (sophomores in 1990) was in eighth grade (in 1988) and only declined thereafter.

This chapter builds on this work by examining additional descriptive evidence on how black students' behavior and home environments changed during the period when the test score gap stopped narrowing. I begin by revisiting Ferguson's evidence about pleasure reading among the seventeen-year-olds in the NAEP-LTT and then ask whether a similar account can explain the stalled progress of thirteen-year-olds. I then describe changes in time spent doing homework and watching television. Next, I investigate whether changes in adolescents' school behavior might have contributed to the stalling. I then examine how adolescents' educational environments at home changed over time. I conclude by discussing which, if any, of these historical changes might have been responsible for stalled progress in narrowing the text score gap.

Test Score Trends

As discussed in the introduction to this volume, the NAEP-LTT provides the best available evidence about trends in academic progress. Those data yield several clues about likely contributors to black students' stalled gains. First, because black progress in reading stalled for black thirteen- and seventeen-year-olds at around the same time (after 1988), a period effect (rather than a cohort effect) was probably responsible for the reading decline. Second, because the black-white gap among nine-year-olds did not widen during the 1980s and early 1990s, whatever caused the decline was probably limited in its effects to early and late adolescents. A surge in the popularity of hip hop music meets both criteria as a possible cause.

The math trends tell a somewhat different story. Black students' math progress stalled out four years earlier for thirteen-year-olds (after 1986) than for seventeen-year-olds (after 1990), implying that the cause of the math decline was cohort-related and not associated exclusively with high schools or late adolescence.

Trends in Pleasure Reading

Based on evidence that trends in black students' reading test scores paralleled trends in black students' pleasure reading, Ferguson concluded that cultural changes may have played a role in the stalling of black students' reading progress (2001). Figure 7.1 displays the same data Ferguson used—data on pleasure reading from the seventeen-year-old NAEP-LTT sample—with 95 percent confidence intervals around the estimates (National Center for Education Statistics 2006b).[1] The estimates are imprecise because the NAEP-LTT surveyed very few black students about their pleasure reading after 1984.[2] Specifically, although NAEP asked more than

Figure 7.1   Trends in Daily Pleasure Reading Among Seventeen-Year-Olds

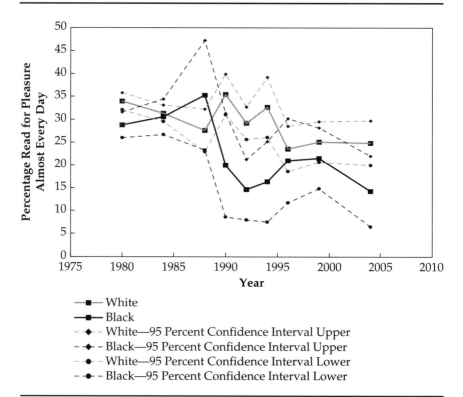

Source: Author's calculations from the NAEP-LTT (National Center for Education Statistics 2006b).
Note: Weighted estimates. Confidence intervals estimated using jackknife replication method. In 1980, the pleasure reading question offered fewer response options than in later years. However, the question contained the "almost every day" response option in all years.

1,300 black students about their pleasure reading in 1980, and more than 500 about their pleasure reading in 1984, by 1988, the numbers of black students surveyed about their literacy activities had dropped to around 100 in each survey year.[3] Another important limitation of the NAEP-LTT is that it is a school-based sample that does not survey dropouts. Consequently, black-white trends for seventeen-year-olds are potentially confounded by changing, differential dropout rates over time (Cook and Evans 2000).

Nonetheless, the data show that a statistically significant black-white gap in pleasure reading emerged during the early 1990s and persisted through 1994, and that this gap stemmed entirely, as Ferguson noted, from a drop in black students' pleasure reading. In 1988, 35 percent of black seventeen-year-olds reported that they read for pleasure every day. By 1992, this percentage had dropped to 15. The percentage of black seventeen-year-olds who reported reading for pleasure weekly, as well as the percentage who reported having told a friend about a good book at least a few times a year, also dropped statistically significantly over this time, though the percentage of white students who engaged in these activities did not change (results not shown). As Ferguson has argued, these data are consistent with the hypothesis that black adolescents focused less of their time on literacy activities after 1988, and that those changes contributed to the widening of the reading test score gap.

That conclusion rests on a single data source with few black respondents, however. To assess whether other data support this conclusion, I first turn to evidence from the Monitoring the Future (MTF) survey (Bachman, Johnston, and O'Malley 1997a, 1997b, 1998, 1999, 2003, 2004 2006; Johnston, Bachman, and O'Malley 1993, 1997, 1999, 2000). To my knowledge, MTF is the only other source of national data on the literacy activities of older adolescents that spans the historical period of interest. Since 1975, MTF has administered an annual in-school survey to high school students in the spring of their senior year.[4] Because MTF studies students so late in their high school careers it is even more susceptible than the NAEP-LTT to concerns about the confounding effects of differential changes in drop-out rates.[5] However, MTF surveyed somewhat larger samples of black students than did NAEP-LTT, and its annual samples can be pooled to obtain additional precision.[6] I pooled samples for every three years, beginning in 1980.

Figure 7.2 describes trends in twelfth graders' reading behavior. The middle set of lines shows the percentages of white and black twelfth graders who reported reading books, magazines, or newspapers "almost every day." Between 1980 and 2000, high school seniors' daily reading activities declined by about 20 percentage points. But black-white gaps in these percentages changed hardly at all. In addition, the most dramatic drop in daily reading occurred for blacks during the early 1980s—at the same time that the black-white reading test score gap was still narrowing.

Yet the MTF question about reading frequency may not accurately reflect the leisure time use changes that Ferguson suspected occurred in the wake of hip hop's growing popularity. Whereas NAEP-LTT asked students how often they read for fun on their own time, MTF asked how often they read books, magazines, or newspapers—without specifying that respondents report only pleasure reading. These question differences probably help explain the much higher percentages of students who say they read "almost every day" in the MTF compared with the NAEP-LTT. Fortunately, MTF also asked students how many books they had read in the past year, "just because you wanted to—that is without their being assigned." Figure 7.2 also displays respondents' answers to that pleasure

Figure 7.2   Trends in Time Spent Reading Among High School Seniors

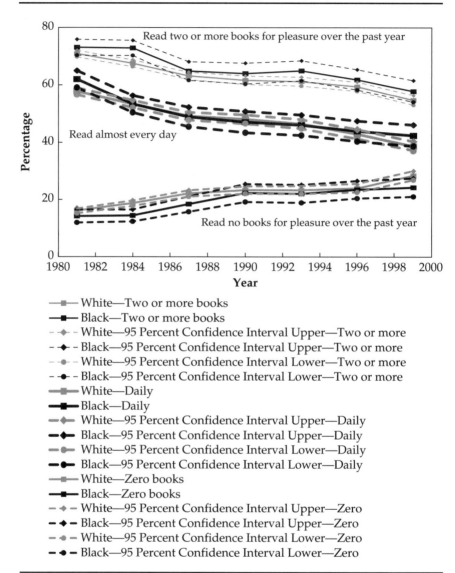

Source: Author's calculations from the public use Monitoring the Future Senior data.
Note: Weighted estimates. For additional precision, each point reflects data pooled across three adjacent years, with the point graphed at the mid-point of the three-year interval. Note that these confidence intervals are too small because they do not account for the substantial clustering of observations in schools. MTF does not provide variables on the public-use files that enable analysts to estimate correct standard errors.

reading question; the top set of lines shows the percentages who reported having read two or more books in the past year, and the bottom set shows the percentages who reported not having read any books in the past year. These data provide further confirmation that pleasure reading declined between 1980 and 2000 for both blacks and whites. These data also provide no evidence that the black-white gap in older adolescents' pleasure reading widened after 1988.

Two other data sources bear on the question of whether the stall in the narrowing of the reading gap may be attributable to changes in black students' pleasure reading. Because the black-white reading test score gap among thirteen-year-olds also reached its narrowest point in 1988 and widened thereafter, it makes sense to examine whether trends in NAEP-LTT thirteen-year-olds' pleasure reading correspond with trends in their reading test scores. As in the seventeen-year-old sample, NAEP-LTT asked few black thirteen-year-olds to answer the reading questions, but at least the trends for the thirteen-year-olds, unlike those for the seventeen-year-olds, are not affected by differential trends in dropout rates.

As figure 7.3 shows, a statistically significant black-white gap in pleasure reading among thirteen-year-olds emerged between 1992 and 1994, after the black-white test score gap in reading had already begun to widen. In addition, the gap in pleasure reading had narrowed again two years later, even though the reading test score gap did not begin to narrow again until after 1996. In general, the pleasure reading patterns for thirteen-year-olds do not appear to track test score gap patterns well. More fundamentally, such small samples of black respondents make it impossible to pin down racial differences in pleasure reading trends with any reasonable degree of certainty.

The National Education Longitudinal Study (NELS) provides an important check on patterns in the NAEP-LTT because it sampled much larger numbers of white and black adolescents, and followed them longitudinally over the period when the NAEP-LTT test score gap stopped narrowing (National Center for Education Statistics 1996). If we treat the NAEP-LTT sample of thirteen-year-olds in 1988 and seventeen-year-olds in 1992 as a cohort, we can examine whether changes in this cohort's pleasure reading between 1988 and 1992 resembled changes in NELS. The NAEP and NELS pleasure reading questions differ somewhat: NAEP asked about days of pleasure reading over the course of the year, whereas NELS asked about hours of pleasure reading per week. But when the NELS students were sophomores, in 1990, NELS asked about both yearly and weekly reading, and students' responses correlated .73. That high correlation leads me to believe that both the NAEP and the NELS pleasure reading questions measure the same construct.

The top panel of table 7.1 shows how pleasure reading in the NAEP-LTT changed for students who were thirteen years old in 1988 and seven-

Figure 7.3   Trends in Daily Pleasure Reading Among Thirteen-Year-Olds

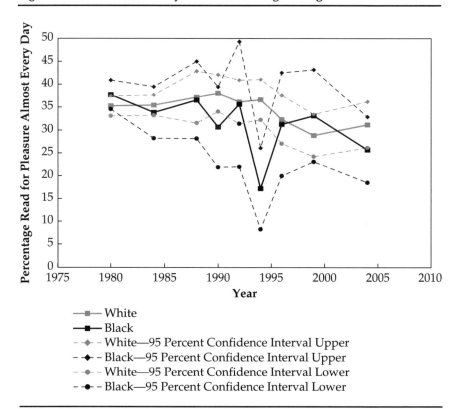

Source: Author's calculations from the NAEP-LTT (National Center for Education Statistics 2006b).
Note: Weighted estimates. Confidence intervals estimated using jackknife replication method. In 1980, the pleasure reading question offered fewer response options than in later years. However, the question contained the "almost every day" response option in all years.

teen years old in 1992; the bottom panel shows analogous changes for the same cohort in NELS. According to the NAEP-LTT, 37 percent of black thirteen-year-olds said they read for pleasure almost every day in 1988. By 1992, only 15 percent of black students in that cohort read for pleasure almost every day—a decline of nearly 22 percentage points. The percentage of white students who read for pleasure also declined over this period, but only by 8 percentage points. In contrast, NELS shows no evidence that black students did less pleasure reading in 1992 than in 1988, or that black students did relatively less pleasure reading than white students. If anything, black students who were eighth graders in 1988 increased their pleasure reading by 1992 a bit more than did their white

Table 7.1   Changes in Pleasure Reading Between 1988 and 1992

	Black					White						
	1988 (N = 98)		1992 (N = 97)		Change (1992 to 1988)	1988 (N = 500)		1992 (N = 584)		Change (1992 to 1988)	White-Black Difference in Change
	Percent	Standard Error	Percent	Standard Error	Percent	Percent	Standard Error	Percent	Standard Error	Percent	Percent
NAEP-LTT Cohort (Thirteen-year-olds in 1988 and seventeen-year-olds in 1992)											
How often read for pleasure											
Almost every day	36.6	4.1	14.7	3.3	-21.9	37.2	2.8	29.2	1.8	-8.0	13.9
Once or twice a week	30.4	4.5	36.6	4.7	6.2	30.0	2.0	32.5	1.6	2.5	-3.7
Once or twice a month	17.5	2.7	16.0	3.6	-1.5	15.2	2.1	17.2	1.6	2.0	3.5
A few times a year	8.1	2.5	20.1	3.7	12.0	7.7	1.5	10.5	1.3	2.9	-9.2
Never or hardly ever	7.5	3.2	12.6	3.6	5.2	9.9	1.2	10.7	1.5	0.7	-4.4
	Black (N = 1,214)					White (N = 10,272)					
NELS Longitudinal Cohort (Eighth graders surveyed first in 1988 and again four years later)											
How often read for pleasure											
Six hours or more	5.4	0.8	9.0	2.0	3.6	9.3	0.4	11.9	0.5	2.6	-1.0
Four to five hours	5.2	1.0	12.2	2.2	6.9	8.1	0.4	11.2	0.4	3.1	-3.8
Three hours	9.6	1.4	13.0	1.3	3.4	11.4	0.5	12.2	0.5	0.7	-2.6
Two hours	24.4	2.7	21.3	1.8	-3.1	20.8	0.7	21.9	0.7	1.1	4.2
One hour or less	34.6	2.5	27.5	2.1	-7.1	31.4	0.7	28.8	0.7	-2.6	4.5
None	20.7	2.3	17.0	2.1	-3.6	19.0	0.6	14.1	0.5	-5.0	-1.3

Source: Author's calculations from the NAEP-LTT (National Center for Education Statistics 2006b), and NELS (National Center for Education Statistics 1996).
Note: Weighted estimates. Standard errors account for the complex sampling design in each survey and are estimated using jackknife replication methods for NAEP and Taylor series methods for NELS. NELS provided additional response options at the top of the scale in 1992; I collapsed those options to "six hours or more" for comparability with the 1988 survey.

Table 7.2   Trends in Time Spent on Homework Among Thirteen-Year-Olds

	1980		1982		1988		1990	
	Percent	Standard Error	Percent	Standard Error	Percent	Standard Error	Percent	Standard Error
Black								
No homework assigned	32.1	(2.1)	28.9	(2.0)	22.0	(2.4)	20.3	(2.5)
Had homework, didn't do it	5.8	(0.4)	5.2	(0.6)	3.0	(0.9)	4.8	(1.2)
Less than one hour	31.0	(1.4)	25.2	(1.2)	34.1	(2.1)	37.6	(2.3)
Between one and two hours	22.4	(1.3)	26.0	(1.3)	29.4	(2.3)	26.4	(2.1)
More than two hours	8.7	(0.7)	14.8	(1.3)	11.6	(1.7)	10.9	(1.5)
White								
No homework assigned	30.0	(1.2)	26.6	(1.1)	16.3	(1.6)	21.9	(1.3)
Had homework, didn't do it	6.0	(0.3)	6.3	(0.4)	4.7	(0.5)	5.3	(0.5)
Less than one hour	32.7	(1.1)	27.9	(0.6)	38.4	(1.3)	37.8	(1.1)
Between one and two hours	24.4	(0.7)	28.9	(0.9)	30.4	(1.2)	28.0	(1.2)
More than two hours	6.9	(0.3)	10.3	(0.5)	10.2	(0.8)	7.1	(0.5)

Source: Author's calculations from the NAEP-LTT (National Center for Education Statistics 2006a, 2006b).
Note: Weighted estimates, with Taylor series standard errors in parentheses. Ns for black students range from a high of 3,149 in 1980 to a low of 510 in 1994. Ns for white students range from a high of 17,269 in 1980 to a low of 2,539 in 1996. These data reflect students' answers to the question: "How much time did you spend on homework yesterday?" In all years except 1982, this question was asked on the NAEP-LTT reading survey. In 1982, it was asked on the math survey.

counterparts. These results call into question the idea that a period effect reduced black students' pleasure reading in the early 1990s.

In sum, although trends for black seventeen-year-olds from the NAEP-LTT suggest that pleasure reading may have played a role in the widening of the reading gap after 1988, trends for twelfth graders from the MTF, trends for thirteen-year-olds from the NAEP-LTT, and longitudinal data on adolescents from the NELS do not confirm that story.

Trends in Homework and Television

Ferguson described trends in seventeen-year-olds' homework time and television viewing from the NAEP-LTT and found little evidence of a relationship between those time use trends and test score gap trends (2001). I present similar evidence for thirteen-year-olds from the NAEP-LTT (National Center for Education Statistics 2006a, 2006b).[7] Table 7.2 shows that both black and white thirteen-year-olds increased the amount of time

	1992		1994		1996		1999		2004
Percent	Standard Error	Percent	Standard Error	Percent	Standard Error	Percent	Standard Error	Percent	Standard Error
22.8	(2.3)	35.6	(2.6)	23.8	(3.0)	30.7	(3.1)	22.7	(2.4)
5.0	(1.0)	4.6	(0.9)	3.7	(0.9)	4.3	(0.9)	4.4	(0.9)
34.1	(2.6)	28.4	(1.9)	40.5	(2.6)	36.3	(2.7)	43.2	(2.4)
27.3	(2.9)	24.5	(1.5)	24.6	(2.8)	21.5	(1.9)	23.8	(2.1)
10.9	(1.6)	6.9	(1.3)	7.4	(1.2)	7.2	(1.0)	5.9	(1.0)
20.3	(1.3)	21.2	(1.7)	21.1	(2.0)	23.3	(1.7)	18.4	(1.2)
4.2	(0.5)	5.9	(0.6)	5.6	(0.7)	4.5	(0.5)	5.5	(0.4)
36.8	(1.1)	35.1	(1.3)	36.7	(1.4)	38.2	(1.6)	41.0	(1.5)
29.8	(1.4)	29.1	(1.3)	28.1	(1.4)	26.6	(1.3)	26.4	(1.1)
8.9	(0.8)	8.8	(0.7)	8.6	(1.2)	7.4	(0.8)	8.7	(0.7)

they spent on homework during the 1980s, largely because their teachers were more likely to assign homework.[8] By 1988, the percentages of black and white thirteen-year-olds who did at least one hour of homework a night had peaked at around 40 percent. By 2004, those percentages had declined, to about 35 percent for whites and to 30 percent for blacks. But most of the decline for black students seems to have occurred between 1992 and 1994, after the math and reading test score gaps had already stopped narrowing. In addition, if black students had suddenly rebelled against schoolwork after 1988, table 7.2 would probably show important increases in the percentages of students reporting not doing any of their assigned homework. Instead, table 7.2 shows that those percentages were largely constant over the two decades covered by the data, and that any changes tended to be temporary and statistically insignificant.

Although black and white thirteen-year-olds reported doing very similar amounts of homework during the 1980s and 1990s, the same cannot be said for how much television they watched. Between 1986 and 2004, on school

Table 7.3   Trends in Time Watching Television and Videos on School Days Among Thirteen-Year-Olds

	1986		1988		1990		1992	
	Percent	Standard Error	Percent	Standard Error	Percent	Standard Error	Percent	Standard Error
Black								
None	0.5	(0.2)	1.2	(0.5)	1.1	(0.3)	1.2	(0.3)
One hour or less	4.0	(0.6)	7.0	(1.2)	6.2	(0.8)	7.3	(0.8)
Two to three hours	22.9	(1.3)	34.0	(2.1)	30.3	(1.5)	27.7	(1.4)
Four to five hours	32.2	(1.2)	30.0	(2.6)	30.7	(1.3)	34.5	(1.8)
Six hours or more	40.4	(1.7)	27.9	(1.6)	31.7	(2.0)	29.2	(1.5)
White								
None	1.5	(0.3)	2.2	(0.3)	1.6	(0.2)	1.7	(0.2)
One hour or less	8.1	(0.9)	16.7	(0.9)	13.4	(0.5)	17.1	(0.8)
Two to three hours	40.9	(1.1)	50.2	(1.1)	48.6	(0.8)	51.2	(0.8)
Four to five hours	32.9	(1.5)	21.8	(0.9)	25.8	(0.7)	22.4	(0.8)
Six hours or more	16.5	(1.1)	9.1	(0.6)	10.7	(0.7)	7.6	(0.5)

Source: Author's calculations from the NAEP-LTT (National Center for Education Statistics 2006a, 2006
Note: Weighted estimates, with Taylor series standard errors in parentheses. Estimates are based on pooling the NAEP-LTT math and reading survey samples because both asked the same question about time spent watching television and videos on school days. I collapsed responses of two or three hours into the "two to three hours" category and responses of four or five hours into the "four to five hours" category. Ns for black students range from a high of 1,794 in 1999 to a low of 5. in 1988. Ns for white students range from a high of 8,222 in 1990 to a low of 2,946 in 1988.

days, white thirteen-year-olds were at least twice as likely as their black counterparts to watch only an hour of television or less (see table 7.3). Black thirteen-year-olds were two and a half to four and a half times as likely as their white counterparts to watch six or more hours. In 2004, for example, nearly 25 percent of black thirteen-year-olds reported watching six or more hours, compared with just 6 percent of their white counterparts. Other researchers have lamented these stark racial differences in television watching and have argued that they must be associated with differences in academic achievement (for example, Thernstrom and Thernstrom 2003). Did changes in television watching correspond with changes in the test score gap?

By 2004, both black and white thirteen-year-olds were watching far less television on school days than they had watched in 1986. This decline was greater for whites than blacks, however, and thus the gap in television watching widened. The timing of this widening is difficult to pin down because the NAEP-LTT data on television watching go back only to 1986. From 1986 to 1988, television watching declined for both blacks and whites, but declined more for whites.[9] Black students' television watching remained relatively constant from 1988 or 1990 through 1999, whereas that of white students continued to decline, and thus the gap continued to widen. Thus, although the stall in black students' academic progress cannot be blamed on increases in their television watching, it is possible that the test score gap stopped narrowing because blacks did not reduce their television viewing as much as whites did. That conjecture, however, raises two questions. First,

1994		1996		1999		2004	
Percent	Standard Error	Percent	Standard Error	Percent	Standard Error	Percent	Standard Error
1.2	(0.3)	0.4	(0.2)	1.2	(0.3)	1.4	(0.3)
7.8	(0.7)	6.7	(0.9)	7.7	(0.7)	9.6	(0.8)
28.4	(1.6)	28.2	(1.2)	27.7	(1.1)	34.5	(1.3)
29.3	(1.2)	31.9	(1.3)	33.9	(1.2)	29.7	(1.3)
33.3	(1.8)	32.8	(1.7)	29.5	(1.4)	24.8	(1.2)
2.5	(0.3)	3.5	(0.9)	3.1	(0.6)	3.4	(0.3)
18.3	(1.2)	19.0	(0.9)	20.1	(0.8)	24.3	(0.7)
50.6	(0.7)	50.9	(0.9)	51.5	(0.8)	51.4	(0.7)
20.8	(0.9)	19.5	(0.8)	18.8	(0.7)	14.5	(0.5)
7.8	(0.7)	7.1	(0.5)	6.5	(0.4)	6.4	(0.5)

to what extent did white adolescents reduce their television watching because they were spending more time using newer media, such as computers and video games? Second, do adolescents do better on math or reading tests when they watch less television? I provide an approximate answer to this second question in the conclusion of this chapter.

Figure 7.4 speaks to the first question, showing trends in the percentage of thirteen-year-olds who reported having a computer at home from 1986 to 2004 (nationally representative data on trends in video game use do not exist, as best I can tell). These data reveal a dramatic increase of more than 50 percentage points in computer ownership for both blacks and whites over the time period. The data also show that the black-white gap in computer ownership (that is, the digital divide) widened substantially during the 1990s, from about 12 percent in 1990 to nearly 30 percent by 1999, only to narrow again by 2004.[10] This pattern is consistent with the hypothesis that white students reduced their television watching more during the 1990s because they had greater and growing access to home computers during that period. In the conclusion, I discuss whether adolescents with greater computer access achieve higher math or reading scores.

Trends in Disciplinary Problems

Ferguson argued that in the late 1980s and early 1990s, black students began to "mimic the styles and behaviors of gangsta rap and other hip-hop

Figure 7.4   Trends in Home Computer Ownership Among Thirteen-Year-Olds

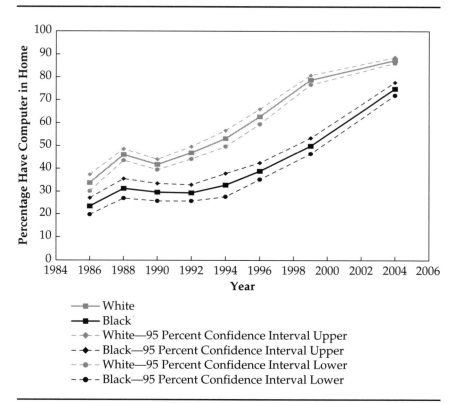

Source: Author's calculations from the NAEP-LTT (National Center for Education Statistics 2006a, 2006b).
Note: Weighted estimates. Confidence intervals estimated using Taylor series method. To obtain greater precision, I pooled data from the math and reading surveys. The question in the reading survey asked, "Is there a computer in your home?" The question in the math survey asked, "Does your family own a computer w/keyboard or screen?"

personalities" and that these newly adopted styles and behaviors probably affected the learning and school engagement of black youth (2001, 373). He also reviewed several experimental studies, some of which suggest that watching violent music videos leads adolescents to become more accepting (at least temporarily) of aggressive behaviors (see Hanson 1995; Johnson, Jackson, and Gatto 1995; see Anderson, Carnagey, and Eubanks 2003 for a more recent study about the effects of violent music lyrics—as opposed to videos—on aggressive thoughts). One of these studies also suggests a link between watching rap music videos and a reduction in students' attachment to mainstream paths to success (Johnson, Jackson, and Gatto 1995).

Figure 7.5   Trends in Disciplinary Problems at School Among Thirteen-Year-Olds

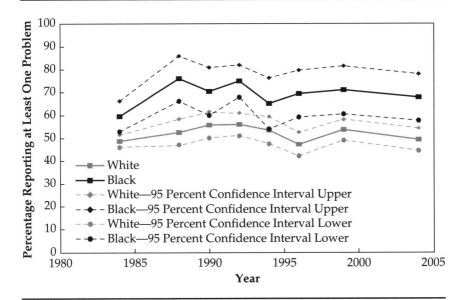

Source: Author's calculations from the NAEP-LTT (National Center for Education Statistics 2006a, 2006b).
Note: Weighted estimates. Confidence intervals estimated using jackknife replication method. The NAEP-LTT reading survey asked students a series of questions about how often during the past year they were sent to the principal's office, placed on probation, given detention, warned about attendance, or warned about behavior. Estimates show the percentage of students who reported at least one of these events over the past year.

One implication of Ferguson's argument is that black students may have behaved worse at school in the post-rap period, which could have negatively affected their academic achievement. The NAEP-LTT reading survey asked students a series of questions about how often they were sent to the principal's office, placed on probation, given detention, warned about attendance, or warned about behavior. I summed students' responses to these questions, and then graphed trends in the percentages of black and white students who reported at least one of these disciplinary problems. Figure 7.5 presents the results for the thirteen-year-old sample. In all years, larger percentages of black students (approximately 70 percent) than white (approximately 50 percent) reported having had at least one disciplinary sanction. But the percentages of black students reporting a disciplinary sanction did not increase during the period when the black-white test score gap began to widen (after 1988). If anything, the trends for thirteen-year-olds reveal a possible narrowing of the gap in disciplinary problems over the period.

**Figure 7.6   Trends in Disciplinary Problems at School Among
Seventeen-Year-Olds**

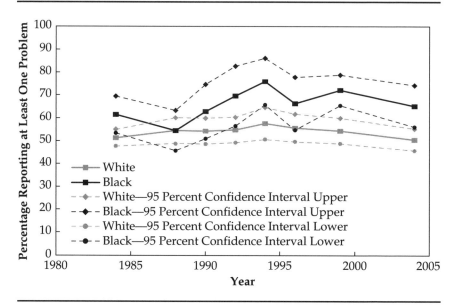

Source: Author's calculations from the NAEP-LTT (National Center for Education
Statistics 2006a, 2006b).
Note: Weighted estimates. Confidence intervals estimated using jackknife replication
method. The NAEP-LTT reading survey asked students a series of questions about how
often during the past year they were sent to the principal's office, placed on probation,
given detention, warned about attendance, or warned about behavior. Estimates show
the percentage of students who reported at least one of these events over the past year.

As with the data on pleasure reading, however, the data for seventeen-
year-olds tell a different story. Figure 7.6 shows that the percentage of black
students who experienced at least one disciplinary sanction increased
between 1988 and 1994—which is precisely the period in which the reading test score gap also widened. Unfortunately, these trends for disciplinary problems, like those for pleasure reading, are imprecise because
NAEP surveyed few black students.[11] In addition, the trends are possibly
confounded by differential trends in dropout rates. Nonetheless, the data
for seventeen-year-olds are consistent with the theory that rap music's popularity affected older black adolescents' disciplinary experiences at school.
One possibility is that rap music led older black adolescents to become
more defiant and aggressive at school. Another is that older black adolescents adopted styles of dress or expression associated with gangsta rap,
which got them into more trouble at school because school officials came
to perceive them as more oppositional.

Table 7.4   Trends in Violent Behavior Among High School Seniors

	1980 to 1982	1983 to 1985	1986 to 1988	1989 to 1991	1992 to 1994	1995 to 1997	1998 to 2000
White	11.8	13.0	12.5	14.6	14.2	13.1	12.0
	(0.4)	(0.4)	(0.5)	(0.5)	(0.6)	(0.6)	(0.6)
Black	11.2	13.2	13.6	16.1	19.7	18.9	15.6
	(1.0)	(1.0)	(1.2)	(1.4)	(1.4)	(1.5)	(1.4)
White-black difference	0.6	−0.2	−1.1	−1.5	−5.5	−5.8	−3.6

Source: Author's calculations from the public use *Monitoring the Future Senior data.*
Weighted estimates. Numbers show the percentage of students who reported committing at least two of the following violent acts in the past twelve months: hitting an instructor or supervisor; getting into a serious fight at school or at work; taking part in a gang fight; hurting someone badly enough to need bandages or a doctor; using a weapon to get something from a person. For additional precision, I pooled data from three adjacent years. Note that these standard errors are too small because they do not account for the substantial clustering of observations in schools. MTF does not provide variables on the public-use files that enable analysts to estimate correct standard errors. MTF documentation does not provide design effects documentation for these survey questions, but judging from other design effects reported for other types of questions, I suspect that these standard errors should be three to four times larger than those shown here.

A third possibility is that the popularity of rap music had little to do with these trends in behavior problems but was instead a response to trends in other conditions in black communities. As Grissmer and his colleagues (1998) noted, the black teenage murder rate soared in the late 1980s and early 1990s. Increases in black students' disciplinary problems may have been part and parcel of a more general trend of increased violence, possibly associated with the crack epidemic (Neal 2006).

The MTF survey does not ask about disciplinary problems at school, and thus we cannot use it verify the NAEP-LTT trends. It does, however, ask about violent behavior. Table 7.4 shows trends in the percentages of black and white twelfth graders who reported committing at least two of the following violent acts in the previous twelve months: hitting an instructor or supervisor; getting into a serious fight at school or at work; taking part in a gang fight; hurting someone badly enough to need bandages or a doctor; and using a weapon to get something from a person. The standard errors in this table are much too small because I have not adjusted them for the substantial clustering of students in schools in the MTF sample.[12] Nonetheless, the point estimates are consistent with the hypothesis that teenage violence began to increase in the late 1980s or early 1990s, and increased more for blacks than whites. One might expect that increased teenage violence would lead students to feel less safe at school, which in turn might affect their academic achievement. MTF asked students about their feelings of safety at school, however, and though the estimates are imprecise, they show no consistent trend in black students' perceived safety or in the black-white gap in perceived safety (results not shown).

In sum, trends in problem behaviors probably cannot help explain the drop in black thirteen-year-olds' reading scores. Trends in problem behaviors may help explain the drop in reading scores among black seventeen-year-olds, however.[13]

Trends in Literacy Environment and Parental Monitoring

Instead of speculating that black adolescent culture changed for the worse in the late 1980s, Neal speculated that black families may have reduced their investments in their children during that time (2006). Unfortunately, few data on parenting practices span the period before and after the test score gap stopped narrowing. Moreover, evidence regarding the effects of parenting practices on students' academic skills is strongest for young children, yet I know of no data that describe how the thirteen-year-olds in NAEP were parented when they were young. Nonetheless, NAEP thirteen-year-olds do report on some aspects of their home environments that may be related to their academic achievement. First, since the mid-1970s, NAEP has asked students about whether their household regularly received magazines or a newspaper, had an encyclopedia, and had more than twenty-five books. I summed these four items and pooled the data from the math and reading surveys. Figure 7.7 shows that during the nearly three decades covered by these data, black adolescents consistently had fewer reading materials in their homes than whites did. The most obvious trend is an inexplicable drop in materials in 1982, which, as best as I can tell, is not attributable to changes in how the questions were asked in that year. More important for our purposes, the data show a slight increase in black students' reading materials during the 1970s and a slight widening of the black-white gap in reading materials (of nearly a fifth of one type of reading material) between 1986 and 1996. The timing of this widening corresponds with black students' stalled test score progress.

In addition to asking students about the literacy materials in their homes, NAEP also asked a much smaller sample of students how they spent their time after school, and, if they went home, whether they were alone. To the extent that adult supervision of thirteen-year-olds makes them more likely to complete their homework or less likely to get into trouble, we might expect trends in time use after school to be related to trends in the test score gap. Unfortunately, however, the estimates are imprecise and show no consistent pattern before or after the black-white test score gap stopped narrowing (see table 7.5). Table 7.5 does suggest, however, that the percentage of thirteen-year-olds attending after school

Figure 7.7   Trends in Reading Materials in the Home Among Thirteen-Year-Olds

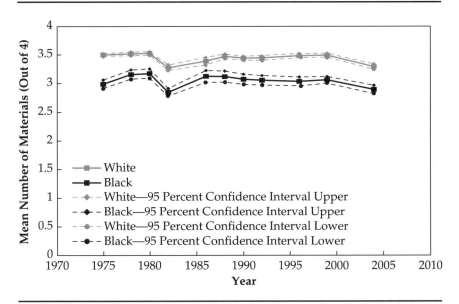

Source: Author's calculations from the NAEP-LTT (National Center for Education Statistics 2006a, 2006b).
Note: Weighted estimates. Confidence intervals estimated using the Taylor series method. To obtain greater precision, I pooled data from the math and reading surveys. The points show the mean number of reading materials in the home based on a sum of dichotomous indicators for whether the household had at least twenty-five books, an encyclopedia, regularly received magazines, and regularly received a newspaper.

programs doubled or nearly doubled for both blacks and whites between 1984 and 2004, with most of the growth in after-school program attendance occurring for blacks well after the test score gap had already stopped narrowing.

Beginning in 1986, the NAEP-LTT survey also asked students to report on their families' parenting styles. Unfortunately, NAEP-LTT asked only two questions—one about whether students' families had rules about the amount of television they were allowed to watch and one about how often someone at home asked them about their schoolwork—and respondents' answers to these questions were not correlated highly enough to justify combining them. Consequently, I show separate trends for each.

As would be expected, parents are more likely to have television rules for thirteen-year-olds than for seventeen-year-olds (see figure 7.8). And, in 1986, black parents were more likely than white parents to have television rules, despite the fact that black children watched far more television than their white counterparts on average (recall table 7.3). During the 1980s and

Table 7.5   Trends in How Thirteen-Year-Olds Usually Spend Time After School

	1984		1988		1990		1992	
	Percent	Standard Error	Percent	Standard Error	Percent	Standard Error	Percent	Standard Error
Black								
With friends	18.9	(2.2)	21.0	(3.2)	22.7	(5.2)	13.6	(3.5)
After school program	9.8	(2.2)	9.0	(2.9)	8.7	(4.0)	8.2	(3.1)
Go home	71.3	(2.4)	70.0	(4.4)	68.6	(4.6)	78.2	(4.2)
Of those who go home, percent usually home alone	17.9	(2.9)	20.1	(5.4)	23.8	(5.8)	18.2	(7.3)
White								
With friends	27.4	(0.9)	26.2	(2.0)	22.2	(1.6)	22.6	(1.7)
After school program	10.5	(0.8)	9.8	(1.6)	9.9	(1.4)	12.1	(1.4)
Go home	62.1	(0.9)	64.0	(2.6)	67.9	(1.9)	65.3	(2.1)
Of those who go home, percent usually home alone	18.4	(0.9)	22.1	(2.1)	22.6	(2.0)	26.7	(2.4)

Source: Author's calculations from NAEP-LTT (National Center for Education Statistics 2006a, 2006b).
Note: Weighted estimates, with jackknife standard errors in parentheses. I collapsed responses of "go to a friend's house" and "with friends but not at house" into one category. Data on whether students typically spent the afterschool hours home alone come from a follow up question to the afterschool question, which asks, "If you go home after school, who is usually there?"

1990s, however, black families relaxed their rules, so that the percentages of black and white families with television rules became statistically indistinguishable. Although the timing of the decline in television rules for black families corresponds with the timing of black thirteen-year-olds' stalled progress in math, the lack of data from earlier years makes it impossible to know if the downward trend observed after 1986 is merely a continuation of a trend begun when the test score gap was still narrowing. In addition, the decline was relatively modest, with 35 percent of black thirteen-year-olds having television rules in 1986 compared with 28 percent in 1999. Moreover, the decline seems to have begun in 1986 for the seventeen-year-olds as well, although the math test score gap was still narrowing for that group. Nonetheless, it is possible that the decline in the percentage of black families with television rules reflects other, unmeasured aspects of blacks' parenting styles that also became more lenient after 1986.

Table 7.6 examines whether asking one's children about their schoolwork was one of those parenting practices. As with the data on television rules, these data show that both black and white parents were more likely to ask thirteen-year-olds than seventeen-year-olds about schoolwork.

	1994		1996		1999		2004	
	Percent	Standard Error	Percent	Standard Error	Percent	Standard Error	Percent	Standard Error
	20.5	(3.3)	19.9	(5.6)	12.1	(3.6)	13.0	(2.8)
	10.6	(3.3)	18.9	(4.4)	21.1	(3.9)	20.3	(3.5)
	69.0	(4.8)	61.2	(5.3)	66.8	(4.7)	66.7	(4.1)
	28.2	(6.0)	12.9	(5.1)	24.2	(4.5)	10.6	(3.5)
	25.6	(2.5)	20.3	(2.3)	23.8	(2.7)	23.8	(2.2)
	14.6	(1.9)	16.2	(2.2)	14.1	(1.9)	17.7	(1.9)
	59.7	(2.7)	63.6	(2.6)	62.0	(2.9)	58.5	(2.1)
	25.1	(2.1)	22.2	(1.9)	21.1	(2.1)	22.9	(2.2)

And, as with the television rules data, these data suggest that in the mid-1980s, black parents were slightly more likely to ask their children about school work. However, in contrast to the data on television rules, the percentages of black parents asking about school work remained largely constant from 1986 to 2004, but the percentages of white parents asking about schoolwork increased by about 5 to 7 percentage points to match the levels of black parents.

Summary and Discussion

All these descriptive trends lead me to several conclusions about the types of changes in students' time use, behavior, and home environments that may have caused the slowdown in black students' test score gains. The data suggest that at least some of the causes differed for thirteen- and seventeen-year-olds. Among the thirteen-year-olds, gaps in television watching widened a little after 1986, largely because white students' television watching declined. About the same time, the black-white gap in computer ownership widened considerably. White families purchased

Figure 7.8   Trends in Family Rules About Amount of Television Watching Among Thirteen- and Seventeen-Year-Olds

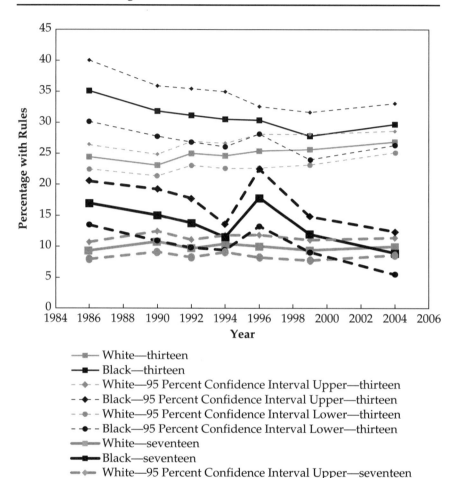

- White—thirteen
- Black—thirteen
- White—95 Percent Confidence Interval Upper—thirteen
- Black—95 Percent Confidence Interval Upper—thirteen
- White—95 Percent Confidence Interval Lower—thirteen
- Black—95 Percent Confidence Interval Lower—thirteen
- White—seventeen
- Black—seventeen
- White—95 Percent Confidence Interval Upper—seventeen
- Black—95 Percent Confidence Interval Upper—seventeen
- White—95 Percent Confidence Interval Lower—seventeen
- Black—95 Percent Confidence Interval Lower—seventeen

Source: Author's calculations from the NAEP-LTT (National Center for Education Statistics 2006a, 2006b).
Note: Weighted estimates. Confidence intervals estimated using the Taylor series method.

home computers at a faster rate than blacks, presumably because they were more able to afford them. In the late 1980s and early 1990s, the black-white gap in access to family reading materials also seems to have widened slightly, which may have been related to growing economic inequality. Finally, the gap in whether families had rules about how much television their children could watch narrowed a little during the 1990s because black families became a bit more lenient.

However, conjectures that changes in black students' leisure time use or school-related behaviors caused the gap to stop narrowing, or to widen, are not borne out by the data for thirteen-year-olds. Both before and after the test score gap stopped narrowing, black thirteen-year-olds spent similar amounts of time on pleasure reading, did similar amounts of homework, and got into similar amounts of trouble at school.[14]

In contrast, the data for seventeen-year-olds are consistent with the idea that increases in problem behaviors among blacks may have played some role in halting black progress. The NAEP-LTT data suggest that black seventeen-year-olds were more likely to get in trouble at school in 1994 than in 1988, and the MTF data suggest that they were more likely to have been involved in violent conflicts. White seventeen-year-olds' behavior changed less over this period, so the black-white gap in problem behavior widened.

The evidence on whether the black-white gap in pleasure reading widened among seventeen-year-olds is mixed. As Ferguson (2001) noted, the NAEP-LTT shows a statistically significant widening of the pleasure reading gap that corresponds with the timing of the widening of the reading test score gap. Again, the NAEP estimates are imprecise because they are based on small samples of black students. In contrast, the MTF and NELS data show no post-1988 increase in the black-white gap in pleasure reading among late adolescents.

Of course, even when trends in time use, behavior, or parenting seem to mirror test score trends, these associations may not be causal. To provide a better sense of which of these trends may be causally related to test score trends, I turn to the NELS data. NELS is the most appropriate longitudinal dataset to use for this purpose because it surveyed and tested eighth graders in 1988—the same year when the black-white reading gap in the NAEP was at its narrowest—and followed those students through the early 1990s. In addition, NELS includes far more extensive data on students' family backgrounds and academic achievement than NAEP does, making it a more useful dataset for estimating the effect of cultural variables on students' test scores. NELS and NAEP did not always ask the same questions about time use, behavior, or parenting, however, so I try to approximate the NAEP measures. I regress NELS tenth grade reading and math scores (standardized to a mean of zero and standard deviation of 1) on students' eighth grade test scores in all subjects, eighth grade grades, parent income,

Table 7.6   Trends in How Often Someone at Home Asks About Schoolwork Among Thirteen- and Seventeen-Year-Olds

	1986		1990		1992	
	Percent	Standard Error	Percent	Standard Error	Percent	Standard Error
Black						
Thirteen-year-olds						
Almost every day	81.3	(1.4)	79.0	(1.6)	83.7	(1.2)
Hardly ever or never	6.1	(0.8)	7.3	(1.2)	5.7	(0.6)
Seventeen-year-olds						
Almost every day	67.0	(2.4)	65.1	(2.5)	63.4	(2.4)
Hardly ever or never	11.7	(1.5)	10.4	(1.3)	14.5	(1.6)
White						
Thirteen-year-olds						
Almost every day	75.5	(0.9)	79.9	(0.6)	80.2	(0.8)
Hardly ever or never	7.9	(0.6)	7.0	(0.4)	5.9	(0.4)
Seventeen-year-olds						
Almost every day	59.8	(1.2)	59.3	(1.2)	59.7	(1.2)
Hardly ever or never	12.3	(0.8)	13.2	(0.8)	13.6	(0.7)

Source: Author's calculations from the NAEP-LTT (National Center for Education Statistics 200 2006b).
Weighted estimates, with Taylor series standard errors in parentheses. I omitted the two middl response options for these questions ("about once a week" and "about once a month"), which i why the percentages in each year for each group do not sum to 100.

parent education, family structure, and other eighth grade covariates.[15] I then add to these models the measures of time use, behavior, and home environment that seem to have shown widening black-white gaps (from at least one sample) during the period when the black-white test score gap stopped narrowing. Note that these equations provide relatively conservative estimates of the effects of time use, behavior, and home environment on test scores because the equations control for academic skills (test scores and grades) in the eighth grade. Because children's time use, behavior, and home environment before eighth grade probably influenced their eighth grade academic skills, my estimates probably understate the overall effects of these variables on students' tenth grade test scores. Tables 7.7 and 7.8 present the results from separate regressions for blacks and whites, respectively, showing coefficients only for the variables of interest.

Columns 1 and 2 show the association between pleasure reading and reading test scores, holding previous scores and a large set of other covariates constant. Spending more time reading for pleasure in eighth grade seems to pay off in higher reading scores for both black and white tenth graders. According to the linear point estimates, which do not differ statistically significantly for blacks and whites, each additional hour of pleasure reading per week is associated with a 0.02 to 0.04 standard deviation increase in students' tenth grade reading scores. Note that reading for pleasure is not associated with students' math score gains (see column 8),

	1994		1996		1999		2004	
	Percent	Standard Error	Percent	Standard Error	Percent	Standard Error	Percent	Standard Error
	81.5	(1.4)	84.0	(1.2)	84.7	(1.4)	83.0	(1.6)
	7.2	(1.0)	4.5	(0.6)	5.2	(0.9)	5.3	(0.7)
	67.2	(2.8)	67.7	(2.2)	67.2	(2.6)	62.9	(2.7)
	9.8	(1.4)	11.1	(1.3)	8.8	(1.4)	13.6	(2.1)
	80.8	(1.0)	80.6	(0.8)	82.7	(0.7)	82.2	(0.7)
	6.3	(0.5)	5.8	(0.3)	5.4	(0.4)	6.0	(0.6)
	64.4	(1.2)	66.4	(1.1)	67.0	(1.2)	65.2	(1.0)
	10.5	(0.7)	9.3	(0.6)	11.0	(0.7)	12.0	(0.6)

which lends credence to the notion that the coefficients in columns 1 and 2 represent a causal effect of reading for pleasure.[16] These results imply that if black students spent less time reading for pleasure after 1988 (which only one of the four datasets suggests), those changes in pleasure reading probably contributed to the stalling of black students' reading progress.

Although the gap in television watching may have widened a little among thirteen-year-olds over time, because whites' television watching declined faster than blacks', the evidence in tables 7.7 and 7.8 indicates that, if anything, those historical changes probably lowered white students' math scores. Watching television—even lots of television on weekdays (see the nonlinear estimates in columns 4 and 7)—does not seem to cause black adolescents to learn less reading or math during high school (for similar evidence, based on the effects of the introduction of television, see Gentzkow and Shapiro 2006). Moreover, television watching is positively associated with white adolescents' math gains, seemingly because students who watch at least an hour of television a day on weekdays score better in math than those who watch less or don't watch at all.

Columns 5 and 8 show the results of the other variables whose trends seemed associated with test score gap trends. For whites, and maybe for blacks as well, having a family computer in 1988 seems to have been associated with scoring higher in math in 1990, other things equal. (The coefficient for blacks is not statistically significant but its standard error is large.)

Table 7.7 Effects of Time Use, Behavior, and Home Environment on Reading and Math Gains Between Eighth and Tenth Grade, Black Students

	Reading				Math			
	1	2	3	4	5	6	7	8
Pleasure reading (hours per week)	0.023* (0.011)				0.021+ (0.011)			0.002 (0.009)
None		0.050 (0.050)						
Two hours		0.056 (0.044)						
Three hours		0.139** (0.051)						
Four to five		0.063 (0.093)						
Six or more (one hour or less omitted)		0.167* (0.066)						
Television (hrs on weekdays)			0.007 (0.011)		0.008 (0.011)	0.005 (0.009)		0.007 (0.009)
Don't watch				0.107 (0.129)			−0.116 (0.132)	
Less than one hour				0.103 (0.087)			0.040 (0.063)	
Two to three hours				0.029 (0.072)			0.041 (0.052)	

Three to four hours	0.116	−0.024
	(0.071)	(0.055)
Four to five hours	0.049	0.008
	(0.075)	(0.051)
Six or more hours (One to two hours omitted)	0.081	0.030
	(0.077)	(0.053)
Family has a computer	−0.050	0.015
	(0.037)	(0.029)
Family literacy materials	0.008	−0.016
	(0.016)	(0.014)
At least one disciplinary sanction	−0.016	−0.023
	(0.033)	(0.027)
Got into fight with other student	−0.079*	0.040
	(0.038)	(0.029)
Parents limit television rarely or never	−0.034	−0.043+
	(0.031)	(0.023)

Source: Author's calculations from NELS data (National Center for Education Statistics 1996).

Note: N = 1,500. All estimates are weighted with the f1pnlwt. Standard errors are adjusted for stratification and clustering. Estimates come from a model that regresses standardized reading or math scores in the spring of tenth grade on: reading, math, history, science scores in eighth grade, squared terms for reading and math scores in eighth grade, eighth grade grades, a squared term for grades, an indicator for whether child had ever repeated a grade, gender, a set of parent education dummies, a set of family income dummies, a set of family structure dummies, a set of students' educational expectation dummies, dummies for type of school attended in eighth grade, scales for locus of control and self concept in eighth grade, urbanism dummies, region dummies, a set of ordinal variables measuring attitudes toward math and English in the spring of eighth grade, and missing data dummies. Family literacy items include a newspaper, magazines, more than fifty books, and an encyclopedia. Disciplinary sanctions include being sent to the office for misbehaving or parents receiving warning about behavior.

Table 7.8 Effects of Time Use, Behavior, and Home Environment on Reading and Math Gains Between Eighth and Tenth Grade, White Students

	Reading				Math			
	1	2	3	4	5	6	7	8
Pleasure reading (hours per wk)	0.036*** (0.005)				0.035*** (0.005)			0.003 (0.004)
None		−0.032 (0.022)						
Two hours		0.023 (0.022)						
Three hours		0.074** (0.027)						
Four to five hours		0.151*** (0.033)						
Six or more hours (one hour or less omitted)		0.169*** (0.028)						
Television (hrs on weekdays)			0.009 (0.006)		0.012* (0.006)	0.015** (0.005)		0.015** (0.005)
Don't watch				−0.096 (0.079)			−0.104* (0.051)	
Less than one hour				−0.047 (0.032)			−0.051* (0.024)	
Two to three hours				0.001 (0.022)			0.006 (0.018)	

Three to four hours	−0.011	0.004
	(0.022)	(0.020)
Four to five hours	0.027	0.028
	(0.024)	(0.022)
Six or more (one to two hours omitted)	0.003	0.037
	(0.030)	(0.026)
Family has a computer	0.017	0.038**
	(0.016)	(0.014)
Family literacy materials	−0.002	0.002
	(0.010)	(0.008)
At least one disciplinary sanction	−0.036+	−0.043**
	(0.020)	(0.016)
Got into fight with student	−0.028	−0.026
	(0.023)	(0.020)
Parents limit television rarely or never	−0.030+	0.001
	(0.017)	(0.012)

Source: Author's calculations from NELS data (National Center for Education Statistics 1996).

Note: $N = 11,116$. All estimates are weighted with the f1pnlwt. Standard errors are adjusted for stratification and clustering. Estimates come from a model that regresses standardized reading or math scores in the spring of tenth grade on: reading, math, history, science scores in eighth grade, squared terms for reading and math scores in eighth grade, eighth grade grades, a squared term for grades, an indicator for whether child had ever repeated a grade, gender, a set of parent education dummies, a set of family income dummies, a set of family structure dummies, a set of students' educational expectation dummies, dummies for type of school attended in eighth grade, scales for locus of control and self concept in eighth grade, urbanism dummies, region dummies, a set of ordinal variables measuring attitudes toward math and English in the spring of eighth grade, and missing data dummies. Family literacy items include a newspaper, magazines, more than fifty books, and an encyclopedia. Disciplinary sanctions include being sent to the office for misbehaving or parents receiving warning about behavior.

Consequently, the faster growth in computer ownership for whites than blacks may have contributed to the widening of the black-white math gap during the 1990s. In contrast, although the black-white gap in family reading materials also widened a bit during the 1990s, adolescents do not seem to gain more in reading or math when they have more reading materials in their homes.

Other things equal, problem behaviors in eighth grade are associated with lower reading scores in tenth grade for blacks and lower reading and math scores in tenth grade for whites. Because the black-white gap in problem behaviors among seventeen-year-olds seems to have widened around the same time that the test score gap started widening, these results imply that the correspondence between the problem behavior trend and the test score trend may be causal.

Finally, the black-white gap in parents' limits on adolescent television watching narrowed a little during the 1990s because black families relaxed their rules slightly. Tables 7.7 and 7.8 suggest that this greater leniency among black parents may have contributed to the stalling of black students' math progress (and maybe also their reading progress).

Conclusion

Scholars have posited various cultural hypotheses for why the black-white test score gap stopped narrowing, and maybe even widened, during the late 1980s and early 1990s. These explanations implicitly blame either black adolescents or their families for not maintaining the very rapid academic progress they experienced during the 1980s. I hope this chapter has shown, if nothing else, that existing data are too sparse to assess cultural theories adequately. The best data for describing trends in student time use, school-related behavior, and home environments over the period when the test score gap stopped narrowing come from the NAEP-LTT for thirteen-year-olds. Unlike the data for older students, either from the NAEP-LTT or the MTF, the data for younger adolescents are not confounded by changing dropout rates. However, from the late 1980s on, NAEP posed some of the most important questions (for example, time spent on pleasure reading and disciplinary problems at school) to only around 100 African American thirteen-year-olds (and another 100 African American seventeen-year-olds). Such small samples make it impossible to describe national trends in these variables with any reasonable degree of certainty.[17]

The NAEP-LTT also has the disadvantage of asking a very limited set of questions about students' time use and family processes. Not only does this make it impossible to measure all or even most of the conceptually important dimensions of students' environments but it also forces analysts to focus on results based on single items, even though single item indicators tend to be unreliable. If twenty years from now we want to be able to move beyond speculation about how culture affects students' academic progress, we need to begin collecting time series data on a much wider array of topics from much larger samples of adolescents.

Acknowledgments

I thank the Educational Testing Service for providing the restricted use Beta Version of the NAEP Long Term Trend files. I also thank Gabriel Rossman for helpful discussions about the availability of data on rap music listening trends. I am indebted to Yougeon Lee for assembling the NAEP files and to Katherine Magnuson for supervising the file-making process. I also thank the William T. Grant foundation for supporting that work. I am also grateful to Jeanne Brooks-Gunn, Tiffani Chin, Katherine Magnuson, Jane Waldfogel, and participants at the November Russell Sage conference for providing helpful comments on this work. I am, of course, solely responsible for all errors.

Notes

1. All of my analyses of the NAEP-LTT data use observed race to classify students into ethnic groups. I use this variable not because I believe it to be more accurate than students' self-reports but because it covers more years of data than any other race variable and has been used in published LTT reports.
2. NAEP-LTT also asked fewer white students about their pleasure reading after 1984 but it still sampled approximately four times as many white respondents.
3. Between 1988 and 2004, the numbers of black seventeen-year-olds' providing data on pleasure reading for the NAEP-LTT ranged from a low of seventy-five in 1996 to a high of 119 in 1999. Although these are unusually small samples from which to estimate national trends, these respondents were reasonably well distributed across states and schools. When analyzing any of the NAEP-LTT data provided by very small samples of black respondents, I estimate standard errors using the NAEP-LTT replicate weights. These jack-knifed standard errors tend to be (though are not always) a little more precise than Taylor series standard errors.
4. MTF also began surveying eighth and tenth graders in 1991, but those surveys are less relevant because they do not span the period before and after the test score gap stopped narrowing.
5. In reading, NAEP-LTT samples students who were seventeen years old or eleventh graders in the spring (only age-eligible students are assessed in math). In contrast, MTF samples twelfth graders in the spring. Robert Hauser (2004) showed that high school dropout is much more common among twelfth than eleventh graders, implying that the MTF data are probably more biased by racial differences in dropout rate trends than the NAEP-LTT data are.
6. Between 1980 and 2000, the annual Ns of black students who responded to the MTF question about reading frequency range from a low of 274 in 1990 to a high of 522 in 1981.
7. The NAEP-LTT math and reading surveys both contain questions about homework time but the question on the reading survey (and on the math

survey only in 1982) asks about time spent on homework "yesterday," whereas the question on the math survey for other years asks about time spent "each day." Both questions also offer slightly different response options in the middle of the scale. I tried to pool data from both surveys to gain precision but because a much larger proportion of respondents chose the "no homework assigned" option for the question about homework "yesterday" than they did when asked about homework "each day," the trend results were incomparable over time. I decided to report the results for the "yesterday" question because they trend back to 1980, whereas the results on homework each day go back only to 1986.

8. This result suggests that we should think about homework effort less as a proxy for the cultural attitudes of students and more as a proxy for schools' academic expectations.

9. Note, however, that the 1986 data come from the math sample and the 1988 data come from the reading sample. Thus, apparent changes from 1986 to 1988 may not be real but may instead reflect sampling and administration differences between the math and reading samples. (Data for all the other years in the series come from both samples.)

10. The seemingly strange pattern from 1986 to 1990 can be attributed to differences in question wording over this period. The data for 1986 come solely from the math survey, which asked "Does your family own a computer w/keyboard or screen?" The data from 1988 come solely from the reading survey, which asked, "Is there a computer in your home?" Because the reading question was less restrictive, it makes sense that a greater percentage of respondents would answer it in the affirmative. From 1990 on, the estimates come from pooled samples of math and reading respondents.

11. Beginning in 1988, the reading questionnaire asked only about 100 black respondents the series of questions about disciplinary problems. Specifically, the Ns were 97 (in 1988), 100 (in 1990), 103 (in 1992), 100 (in 1994), 79 (in 1996), 100 (in 1999), and 111 (in 2004).

12. MTF does not provide outside researchers with variables that enable them to account for even the most basic elements of the complex sample design.

13. I also examined race-by-gender and race-by-parental education interactions in the NAEP-LTT and MTF samples to see if the black-white gap in problem behaviors widened more among boys or more among students from less advantaged backgrounds, but the data showed no clear trends.

14. Of course, even if gaps in these time use or behavior variables did not widen over time, these variables could still have caused the test score gap to stop narrowing or to widen if the causal association between these variables and test scores changed in a different way over time for blacks than for whites.

15. I limit the NELS sample to students who have nonmissing test score data in eighth and tenth grade and nonmissing data on race. I include missing data dummies for all other variables with missing data. I weight all estimates with the f1pnlwt and correct all standard errors for clustering and stratification using Taylor series standard errors. See table footnotes for a list of the included covariates.

16. These results replicate those found by Jencks and Phillips (1999) using the High School and Beyond dataset.

17. Note that Sheila Barron and Daniel Koretz (1994) have argued that estimates of mean test scores for black and Latino students in the NAEP-LTT are far too imprecise as well. But the Ns for the some of the variables used in this chapter are far lower than those for test scores because certain time use and behavior items appeared on only a small subset of the booklets administered to students.

References

Anderson, Craig A., Nicholas L. Carnagey, and Janie Eubanks. 2003. "Exposure to Violent Media: The Effects of Songs with Violent Lyrics on Aggressive Thoughts and Feelings." *Journal of Personality and Social Psychology* 84(5): 960–71.

Bachman, Jerald G., Lloyd D. Johnston, and Patrick M. O'Malley. 1997a. *Monitoring the Future: A Continuing Study of the Lifestyles and Values of Youth, 1990–1992* [*Computer Files*]. Conducted by the University of Michigan, Survey Research Center. ICPSR ed. Ann Arbor, Mich.: Inter-university Consortium for Political and Social Research [producer and distributor].

———. 1997b. *Monitoring the Future: A Continuing Study of American Youth, 1995* [*Computer File*]. Conducted by the University of Michigan, Survey Research Center. ICPSR ed. Ann Arbor, Mich.: Inter-university Consortium for Political and Social Research [producer and distributor].

———. 1998. *Monitoring the Future: A Continuing Study of the Lifestyles and Values of Youth, 1994* [*Computer File*]. Conducted by the University of Michigan, Survey Research Center. ICPSR ed. Ann Arbor, Mich.: Inter-university Consortium for Political and Social Research [producer and distributor].

———. 1999. *Monitoring the Future: A Continuing Study of American Youth (12th-Grade Survey), 1996* [*Computer File*]. Conducted by the University of Michigan, Survey Research Center. ICPSR ed. Ann Arbor, Mich.: Inter-university Consortium for Political and Social Research [producer and distributor].

———. 2003. *Monitoring the Future: A Continuing Study of the Lifestyles and Values of Youth, 1988 & 1989* [*Computer Files*]. Conducted by the University of Michigan, Survey Research Center. 2nd ICPSR ed. Ann Arbor, Mich.: Inter-university Consortium for Political and Social Research [producer and distributor].

———. 2004. *Monitoring the Future: A Continuing Study of the Lifestyles and Values of Youth, 1980–1987* [*Computer Files*]. Conducted by the University of Michigan, Survey Research Center. 2nd ICPSR ed. Ann Arbor, Mich.: Inter-university Consortium for Political and Social Research [producer and distributor].

———. 2006. *Monitoring the Future: A Continuing Study of American Youth (12th-Grade Survey), 1998* [*Computer File*]. Conducted by University of Michigan, Survey Research Center. ICPSR02751-v1. Ann Arbor, Mich.: Inter-university Consortium for Political and Social Research [producer and distributor].

Barron, Sheila I., and Daniel M. Koretz. 1994. "An Evaluation of the Robustness of the NAEP Trend Lines for Racial/Ethnic Subgroups." Los Angeles, Calif.: National Center for Research on Evaluation, Standards, and Student Testing.

Berends, Mark, Samuel R. Lucas, Thomas Sullivan, and R. J. Briggs. 2005. *Examining Gaps in Mathematics Achievement Among Racial-Ethnic Groups, 1972–1992*. Santa Monica, Calif.: RAND Corporation.

Brooks-Gunn, Jeanne, and Lisa B. Markman. 2005. "The Contribution of Parenting to Ethnic and Racial Gaps in School Readiness." *The Future of Children* 15(1): 139–68.

Cook, Michael D., and William N. Evans. 2000. "Families or Schools? Explaining the Convergence in White and Black Academic Performance." *Journal of Labor Economics* 18(4): 729–54.

Ferguson, Ronald R. 2001. "Test-Score Trends Along Racial Lines, 1971–1996: Popular Culture and Community Academic Standards." In *America Becoming: Racial Trends and Their Consequences*, vol. 1, edited by Neil J. Smelser, William Julius Wilson, and Faith Mitchell. Washington, D.C.: National Academy Press.

Gentzkow, Matthew, and Jesse M. Shapiro. 2006. "Does Television Rot Your Brain? New Evidence from the Coleman Study." *NBER* Working Paper 12021. Cambridge, Mass.: National Bureau of Economic Research.

Grissmer, David, Ann Flanagan, and Stephanie Williamson. 1998. "Why Did the Black-White Test Score Gap Narrow in the 1970s and 1980s?" In *The Black-White Test Score Gap*, edited by Christopher Jencks and Meredith Phillips. Washington, D.C.: Brookings Institution Press.

Grissmer, David. W, Sheila Nataraj Kirby, Mark Berends, and Stephanie Williamson. 1994. *Student Achievement and the Changing American Family*. Santa Monica, Calif.: RAND Corporation.

Hanson, Christine. 1995. "Predicting Cognitive and Behavioral Effects of Gangsta Rap." *Basic and Applied Social Psychology* 16(1-2): 43–52.

Hauser, Robert M. 2004. "Progress in Schooling." In *Social Inequality*, edited by Kathryn M. Neckerman. New York: Russell Sage Foundation.

Jencks, Christopher, and Meredith Phillips. 1999. "Aptitude or Achievement: Why Do Test Scores Predict Educational Attainment and Earnings?" In *Earning and Learning: How Schools Matter*, edited by Susan E. Mayer and Paul E. Peterson. Washington, D.C.: Brookings Institution Press.

Johnson, James D., Lee Anderson Jackson, and Leslie Gatto. 1995. "Violent Attitudes and Deferred Academic Aspirations: Deleterious Effects of Exposure to Rap Music." *Basic and Applied Social Psychology* 16(1-2): 27–41.

Johnston, Lloyd D., Jerald G. Bachman, and Patrick M. O'Malley. 1993. *Monitoring the Future: A Continuing Study of the Lifestyles and Values of Youth, 1993 [Computer File]*. Conducted by the University of Michigan, Institute for Social Research, Survey Research Center. ICPSR06367-v3. Ann Arbor, Mich.: Inter-university Consortium for Political and Social Research [producer and distributor], 2006-08-21.

———. 1997. *Monitoring the Future: A Continuing Study of American Youth (12th-Grade Survey), 1997 [Computer File]*. Conducted by University of Michigan, Survey Research Center. ICPSR02477-v3. Ann Arbor, Mich.: Inter-university Consortium for Political and Social Research [producer and distributor], 2006-05-15.

———. 1999. *Monitoring the Future: A Continuing Study of American Youth (12th-Grade Survey), 1999 [Computer File]*. Conducted by University of Michigan, Institute for Social Research, Survey Research Center. ICPSR0293nine-v2. Ann Arbor, Mich.: Inter-university Consortium for Political and Social Research [producer and distributor], 2006-05-15.

———. 2000. *Monitoring the Future: A Continuing Study of American Youth (12th-Grade Survey), 2000 [Computer File]*. Conducted by University of Michigan,

Institute for Social Research, Survey Research Center. ICPSR03184-v2. Ann Arbor, Mich.: Inter-university Consortium for Political and Social Research [producer and distributor], 2006-05-15.

Lamont, Michèle, and Mario Luis Small. 2008. "How Culture Matters: Enriching Our Understanding of Poverty." In *The Colors of Poverty*, edited by David Harris and Ann Lin. New York: Russell Sage Foundation.

Lee, Jaekyung. 2002. "Racial and Ethnic Achievement Gap Trends: Reversing the Progress Toward Equity?" *Educational Researcher* 31(1): 3–12.

National Center for Education Statistics. 1996. *National Education Longitudinal Study: 1998–94 Data Files and Electronic Codebook System.* NCES 96-130. Washington: U.S. Department of Education.

———. 2006a. *NAEP Mathematics Long-Term Trend Assessments (1978–2004), Beta One Review Draft.* Washington: U.S. Department of Education.

———. 2006b. *NAEP Reading Long-Term Trend Assessments (1971–2004), Beta One Review Draft.* Washington: U.S. Department of Education.

Neal, Derek A. 2006. "Why Has Black-White Skill Convergence Stopped?" In *Handbook of Economics of Education,* edited by Eric Hanushek and Finis Welch. Amsterdam: North-Holland.

Ogbu, John. 1978. *Minority Education and Caste: The American System in Cross-Cultural Perspective.* New York: Academic Press.

Smetana, Judith G., Nicole Campione-Barr, and Aaron Metzger. 2006. "Adolescent Development in Interpersonal and Societal Contexts." *Annual Review of Psychology* 57(2006): 255–84.

Thernstrom, Abigail, and Stephan Thernstrom. 2003. *No Excuses: Closing the Racial Gap in Learning.* New York: Simon and Schuster.

PART III

CONCLUSIONS AND
POLICY IMPLICATIONS

Chapter 8

School Policies and the Test Score Gap

HELEN F. LADD

O n average, black students in the United States achieve at lower levels than white students do. Recent evidence from the National Assessment of Educational Progress (NAEP) indicates, for example, that in 2004 the gap between thirteen-year-old black and white students was about 0.6 standard deviation in reading and about 0.8 in math. To be sure, such gaps were far larger in the 1970s, when they exceeded a full standard deviation in both subjects. The gaps fell dramatically during the 1970s and 1980s, increased during the early 1990s, and then fell again between 1999 and 2004. These ups and downs notwithstanding, the persistence of these gaps is cause for significant policy concern for reasons discussed elsewhere in this book and in Christopher Jencks and Meredith Phillips (1998).

This volume has drawn attention to school-related trends such as in the racial segregation of the schools and the widening disparities in teacher qualifications between black and white students, especially at the elementary level, that may have stalled the convergence of the black and white test scores in the 1990s (see Vigdor and Ludwig, chapter 5, and Corcoran and Evans, chapter 6, this volume). This chapter picks up from that analysis and asks what educational policies might be pursued moving forward to help reduce the black-white test score gap, or at least to offset some of the other trends that may tend to widen it, such as rising income and social inequality. Of particular interest for this review are school policies and strategies that have been proposed or justified—at least in part—on the basis of their potential for reducing black-white test score gaps. As will become apparent, not all the proposed strategies are likely to be effective in that regard and their net effect on the size of the gap is likely to be relatively small.

This discussion is divided into five sets of policy strategies. The first two focus on teachers, but from quite different perspectives. One set relates to the assignment of students to schools, with attention to how racial segregation of students affects the quality of teachers for black students relative to white students. The other focuses on more direct interventions designed to improve the quality of the teachers of black students. The third set includes the nonteacher strategies of reducing class size and implementing whole school reform. The fourth and fifth sets emerge from a more systemic view of the educational challenge and are designed to change the incentives throughout the education system. Included here are both top-down accountability strategies designed to hold schools accountable for the performance of their students and bottom up strategies such as increased parental choice and competition designed either to improve schooling options for certain groups of students or to make use of market type pressures to improve educational outcomes.

The main thrust of this chapter is that though none of the strategies discussed here is likely to be powerful enough to offset the powerful nonschool social forces that contribute to the racial achievement gap, school related strategies are a necessary component of any overall effort to reduce such gaps. Moreover, the failure of education policy makers to be vigilant about the aspects of the problem over which they do have some control could well lead to even greater gaps in the future or to lost opportunities to reduce them.

Student Assignment Policies

Vigdor and Ludwig (chapter 5, this volume) document that progress in reducing the black-white test gap stalled at about the same time that efforts to desegregate schools, as measured by the trend in the segregation of schools relative to the segregation of neighborhoods, slowed down. The authors conclude that if school desegregation had proceeded at the same rate as neighborhood desegregation, the black-white gap might have narrowed somewhat, but only slightly because of the relatively small change in the racial composition of neighborhoods during the relevant period and the small effect sizes that emerge from the literature they review. At the same time, the authors emphasize that any retreat from the goal of racially integrated schools would exacerbate black-white test score differences in the future.

Racial integration could reduce the black-white achievement gap through two main mechanisms. The first is the potential for positive spillover effects from one group of students to another. This is the one emphasized in the peer effects literature that Vigdor and Ludwig describe in chapter 5 of this volume.[1] The second mechanism works through the teacher labor market. As Corcoran and Evans discuss in chapter 6 of this volume, the evidence is increasingly compelling that certain credentials predict student achievement and that teachers with the weaker credentials are more likely to teach the more disadvantaged students. Specifically, teachers tend to sort themselves among schools in ways that work to the disadvan-

Table 8.1   **Minority Students in High and Low Percent Minority Schools, All Schools in North Carolina**

	Quartile 1 (High Minority)	Quartile 4 (Low Minority)	Difference (Percentage Points)
Elementary			
1995	67.7	4.8	−62.9
1999	74.6	6.2	−68.3
2004	81.0	8.9	−72.2
Middle			
1995	66.5	7.8	−58.7
1999	70.8	8.7	−62.1
2004	77.7	10.4	−67.2
High school			
1995	66.3	5.9	−60.4
1999	69.6	7.2	−62.4
2004	74.0	9.3	−64.8

Source: Author's compilation.
Notes: Quartile 1 and quartile 4 refer to quartiles of the distribution of schools by level and year based on the percentage of students in the school who are black, Hispanic, or Indian. The entries are the average percentages of minorities, weighted by the size of each school.

tage of students in schools disproportionately serving minority students, including black students. We now focus on this second mechanism.[2]

Racial Segregation and Teacher Disparities by Race

Assuming that access to teachers is measured at the school level, racial balancing of students across schools would ensure that students of each race would have access to similar teachers on average. To be sure, racially balanced schools need not mean that all classrooms within schools are racially integrated. Nonetheless, the more racially integrated are the schools, the more likely it is that students of different races will have teachers with similar qualifications.[3]

New evidence from North Carolina documents not only that teachers in high minority schools have weaker qualifications on average than those in schools serving white students—an observation that emerges in many states—but also that the black-white differences in teacher qualifications have been growing over time as minority students have become more concentrated in high-minority schools. Table 8.1 provides information on the racial composition of students in two groups of North Carolina schools, those in the quartile with the highest percentages of minority students (Quartile I) and those in the quartile with the lowest percentages (Quartile IV), separately by level of school and by year.[4] The table indicates that the

Table 8.2   Teachers with Less than Three Years Experience in High and Low Percent Minority Schools

	Quartile 1 (High Minority)	Quartile 4 (Low Minority)	Difference (Percentage Points)
Elementary schools			
1995	17.9	13.4	4.5
1999	21.9	14.5	7.4
2004	19.3	12.3	7.0
Middle schools			
1995	20.8	14.4	6.4
1999	25.1	17.2	7.9
2004	25.2	13.5	11.7
High schools			
1995	15.1	12.3	2.7
1999	18.1	13.4	4.7
2004	18.3	12.0	6.3

Source: Author's compilation.
Note: Quartile 1 and quartile 4 refer to quartiles of the distribution of schools by level and year based on the percentage of students in the school who are black, Hispanic, or Indian. The entries are the average percentages of minorities, weighted by the size of each school.

high minority schools at each level of schooling are becoming more racially concentrated over time, and in the process are becoming increasingly different from the low minority schools. The patterns and trends in this table provide the context for table 8.2, which, based on the same groupings of schools, reports the average percentages of teachers with fewer than three years of experience. The research literature indicates that inexperience has a clear adverse causal impact on student learning (Clotfelter, Ladd, and Vigdor 2006, 2007a, 2007b; Goldhaber 2008). Other characteristics that also predict student achievement, such as teacher test scores, exhibit similar patterns but are not shown.

For each year and each level of schooling, it is clear that the students (most of whom are black in North Carolina) in the high minority schools are more likely to have an inexperienced teacher than those in low minority schools. In addition, however, the differences in percentages between the Quartile I and IV schools have been rising over time. Thus at the same time that minority students are increasingly concentrated in the Quartile I schools, the proportions of inexperienced teachers in those schools has been rising both absolutely and relative to those in the low-minority schools.

Additional and more precise evidence of the link between changes in racial segregation and teacher credentials emerges from table 8.3, which highlights changes in the credentials of teachers faced by the typical black and typical white student in Charlotte-Mecklenburg between the

Table 8.3   Teacher Quality by Race of Student in Charlotte/Mecklenburg School District

	Three or More Years Experience		Top Quarter of Test Scores		Certified Teacher[a]	
	2000 to 2001	2005 to 2006	2000 to 2001	2005 to 2006	2000 to 2001	2005 to 2006
Black	73.7	71.2	22.4	21.4	89.7	88.4
White	76.6	75.4	30.8	30.0	91.9	92.2
Difference	2.9	4.2	8.4	8.6	2.2	3.8

Source: Author's compilation.
Note: Exposure rates of students by race to teachers in various categories are calculated as the average of teacher characteristics across schools weighted by the number of black and white students, respectively, in each school.
[a]Teachers with initial or continuing certification in LicSal licensure data.

2000 to 2001 and the 2005 to 2006 school years. This district is of interest because of the precipitous shift in its student assignment policy in 2002 as it moved away from court-induced efforts to maintain racially balanced schools to a choice-based neighborhood approach that greatly increased racial segregation. As Charles Clotfelter, Helen Ladd, and Jacob Vigdor documented (2008), the proportion of nonwhite students in that district enrolled in schools with 90 to 100 percent nonwhite students increased from 6.9 percent in the 2000 to 2001 school year to 38.5 percent in that of 2005 to 2006, which far exceeds the increase in any other large North Carolina district.[5] Table 8.3 includes information on three credentials of teachers at the school level, all of which have been shown to be predictive of student achievement: the percentage of teachers with three or more years of experience, who scored in the top quartile on standardized teacher tests and who were fully certified as teachers (Clotfelter, Ladd, and Vigdor 2007a, 2007b). The entries in the table are the weighted averages of the percentages of a school's teachers in each category where the weights are, successively, the number of white and black students in each school. Each of the credentials is defined in a positive way, so that higher proportions indicate teachers with stronger qualifications.

Consistent with the evidence for all schools in North Carolina the patterns for the 2000 to 2001 school year favored white students, though not so dramatically as in some other North Carolina urban school districts at the time.[6] Of particular interest here is how those disparities increased in the wake of the district's increase in segregation. For exposure to experienced teachers, the disparity between black and white students rose from 2.9 to 4.2 percentage points; for high-scoring teachers it rose from 8.4 to 8.6, and for certified teachers from 2.2 to 3.8. This example provides the clearest evidence to date that increases in racial segregation are likely to bring with them greater black-white disparities in teacher credentials.

Policy Strategy—Balancing Schools by SES

Although the recent rise in segregation in Charlotte-Mecklenburg exceeds that in other North Carolina districts, and possibly in most other districts as well, it might also suggest future trends because of the recent back-tracking of the federal court on the issue of school desegregation. In the early 1990s, the courts ruled that school districts declared unitary have no obligation to offset de facto segregation in schools resulting from residential segregation.[7] Subsequently, in a series of decisions meant to apply to districts not under court order, the Fourth Circuit Court of Appeals ruled that race could not be used in assigning students to schools.[8] Most recently, in *Parents Involved in the Community Schools v. Seattle School District No. 1,* the Supreme Court made a similar ruling by declaring school assignment plans based on the race of individual students unconstitutional. Hence any efforts to promote racially integrated schools at the district level from now on will have to be done indirectly. Among the policies that may pass court muster are the selective siting of schools and rezoning of school catchment areas.

One of the most commonly advanced indirect strategies is to integrate schools by the socioeconomic (SES) characteristics of their students (Kahlenberg 2001; Century Foundation Task Force 2002). The SES-based school assignment strategy pursued by Wake County, North Carolina, exemplifies this approach.[9] Designed to ensure that all schools are middle-class schools, the district limits the percentage of low-income students in each school to 40 percent and the percentage of students scoring below grade level to 25 percent. Some supporters of SES balancing would prefer such a strategy to a race-based strategy in any case. Because black students within a district are likely to be overrepresented among students from low-income families, however, the SES strategy has also been justified in part on its potential to reduce racial segregation and in some areas has succeeded (Kahlenberg 2001; Chaplin 2002). In the 2005 to 2006 school year, for example, Wake County had only 2.3 percent of its nonwhite students enrolled in 90 to 100 percent nonwhite schools, far below the 38.5 percent already noted for Charlotte and also well below that for other large districts in North Carolina.[10]

A 2002 study based on national data on the distributions of black and white students provides additional support for this race-based rationale for SES balancing (Chaplin 2002). More recent research, however, highlights the limitations of an income-based balancing strategy for reducing racial disparities across schools (Reardon, Tun, and Kurlaender 2006). At one extreme, if all black students were poor but no white students were, distributing poor students equally among schools would be tantamount to distributing black students evenly among schools. The authors show, however, that within large urban areas in the United States, the income distributions of blacks and whites are not different enough in practice to guarantee much racial integration even with a strictly defined income integration scheme. In practice, the effects on racial integration depend on the disparity between the incomes of whites and blacks in the area and the details of the income-based integration plan. Further, given the observed patterns of residential segregation by race and income within urban districts in the United States, for income balancing to lead to racial balancing of schools most districts would have to make transportation readily available to all students so that they can attend schools outside their residentially segregated neighborhoods and to invest resources in particular schools to counter the preferences of some parents to enroll their children in schools near their homes (Reardon, Yin, and Kurlaender 2006, 68).

Although the authors correctly emphasize that balancing schools by income might be desirable for reasons other than their effects on racial integration, their main conclusion is that integrating schools by income is at best a poor substitute for integrating schools by race. From the perspective of the black-white achievement gap, that is disappointing because, as Corcoran and Evans document in chapter 6 of this volume, sorting decisions of teachers appear to be influenced more by the race of a school's students than by their SES. Nonetheless, given the limits imposed by the courts on the power of districts to use the race of individual students in making school assignments, some districts may find that a carefully designed strategy for balancing schools by SES is the best tool available to them for promoting racial balance and thereby indirectly leveling the distribution of teachers across students of different races.[11]

At the same time, given that schools are likely to remain racially segregated and may well become even more so in the future, other more direct strategies will also be needed to counter the disadvantage black students face relative to white students in the quality of their teachers. I now turn to some of those strategies.

Teacher Quality—Direct Policy Interventions

Among the direct policy interventions for reducing the black-white disparities in teacher quality are financial incentives intended to make schools serving minority students more attractive to teachers and new pathways into teaching designed to provide more teachers for hard-to-staff schools. In addition, attention to professional development is potentially important for the black-white gap because of the weak credentials of many of the teachers in high-minority schools.

Financial Incentives to Alter the Distribution of Teachers

That the teachers of black students have on average weaker credentials than those of white students reflects the way teachers are distributed both across and within school districts. At both levels, policy interventions related to teacher salaries could potentially be part of a productive policy strategy.

Across Districts   The distribution of teachers across districts largely reflects considerations of supply and demand, including the preferences of teachers. Various authors have investigated the effects of a number of factors on the ability of districts to attract and retain teachers and have found that teacher retention tends to be higher in districts with better salaries, higher pupil test scores, smaller classes, and lower proportions of low-income and minority students (Murnane and Olsen 1989; Mont and Rees 1996; Hanushek, Kain, and Rivkin 1999; Scafidi, Sjoquist, and Stinebrickner 2002).

If money were no object, the offer of high teacher salaries would be a logical component of any policy strategy for attracting and retaining more highly qualified teachers to districts serving large proportions of minority students. Such salaries would have to be high enough, however, to compensate teachers who would otherwise prefer to teach in districts with more congenial working conditions. Some studies suggest that such salary differentials would need to be quite high. Eric Hanushek, John Kain, and Steven Rivkin (2004) estimate that reducing the rate of attrition in a large urban district to that in suburban schools would require a 43 percent salary difference for female nonminority teachers with three-to-five years of experience. Emerging from similar research for New York State is that salary differentials of $10,000 to $16,000 would be required to attract equally qualified teachers to low-performing public schools away from suburban schools (Boyd et al. 2006).[12] The rub is that districts with large proportions of minority students are often unable to raise adequate local tax revenue or they receive inadequate aid from their states to offer the higher salaries needed to attract high quality teachers.

Within Districts   The distribution of teachers within districts introduces some additional considerations in part because district and school officials play a major role not only in assigning teachers to schools and to classrooms but also, as discussed earlier, in assigning students. Another key difference is that though salary schedules differ across districts they are uniform within districts. Under the current system, a teacher at any step in the salary schedule would receive the same salary regardless of the school at which she teaches within the district. As a result, the easiest way a district administrator can improve the real income, or job satisfaction, of an experienced teacher who remains within a district is to permit that individual to move to a school offering a more satisfying teaching experience. Such transfers generally work to the disadvantage of black students, particularly those from low-income families, when they are concentrated in specific schools.

Once again, financial incentives may be required to change the incentives for teachers to move among schools in this way. An example of this approach is North Carolina's $1,800 annual bonus program for certified teachers in the shortage areas of math, science, and special education teaching in eligible middle and high schools. School eligibility was determined based on the percentages of low-income students and of students performing poorly in math and biology. Importantly the program was designed so that eligible teachers would continue to receive the bonus even if the school became ineligible as a result of its improved performance. Despite flaws in the way the program was implemented, the evaluators found that the program reduced turnover in the eligible schools by 17 percent (Clotfelter, Ladd, and Vigdor 2008). The program was not in place long enough for it to have any measurable impact on teacher recruitment.

Policy Implications   Financial incentives are only one of several policy options to attract quality teachers to high-minority schools. Another is for urban districts to hire teachers earlier in the year to avoid much of the late hiring that historically has put them at a disadvantage relative to suburban districts in competing for quality teachers (Jacob 2007). Yet another is to improve the working conditions for teachers in high-minority schools, possibly by improving the leadership of those schools. At this point, the research is not adequate to determine which strategy or combination of strategies is likely to be most effective. Ideally, states and districts would experiment with various forms of financial and other incentives, and researchers would be actively engaged in their evaluation.

Alternative Pathways into the Profession

Consistent with the theme already discussed, schools serving low-performing minority students are likely to have the greatest difficulties attracting teachers of any quality to teach their students. As a result, their teachers are more likely to be uncertified, to be on some form of temporary license, or to be a novice teacher than those of other schools. Some cities, including most notably New York City, have set up programs, including the NYC Teaching Fellows Program, to address this challenge by providing new pathways for potential teachers to enter the profession. Although these new pathways require far less initial training than the traditional pathway of standard teacher training and certification, the goal is to attract teachers able to offset their initial lack of training. The best-known national program of this form, Teach for America (TFA), recruits corps members from top universities, provides intensive training during the summer, and gives additional support as they pursue their teaching assignments in hard-to-teach schools in communities throughout the country. A potential difference between the TFA program and the new New York City–specific pathways is that there is no expectation in the TFA program that teachers will remain after their second year of required teaching.

A major policy question is how the teachers entering through these alternative pathways fare in the classroom. Studies of TFA teachers in Houston generated somewhat mixed results, with the conclusions differing in part on whether TFA teachers were compared only to certified teachers or to all teachers, regardless of their certification status (see summary in Goldhaber 2008, 151). A recent randomized national field experiment of the TFA program presents a clearer picture. Regardless of the comparison group, the students with TFA teachers outperformed the students of other teachers in the relevant schools in math by as much as 0.15 standard deviations, but performed no better or worse in reading (Glazerman, Mayer, and Decker 2006). Positive findings for the TFA teachers also emerge from a careful study of the alternative entry paths in New York City. At the same time, the students of teachers who entered through one of the New York City specific programs exhibited slightly smaller gains than those of other teachers (Boyd et al. 2006). Consistent with that finding, a more general study of the effects of teacher credentials in North Carolina also shows lower achievement gains for students of teachers who obtained their licenses under that state's alternative entry program (Clotfelter, Ladd, and Vigdor 2007a, 2007b).

The positive findings for TFA teachers notwithstanding, the jury is still out on the power of alternative entry programs to raise the quality of teaching in low-performing schools serving large minority populations. One characteristic of the TFA program that stands out, and is worthy of further attention, is the greater support it provides for its teachers once they are in the classroom than most other alternative entry programs do.

Professional Development

Despite the particular importance of professional development for many of the teachers in low-performing schools, the evidence on how best to proceed is scanty.[13] At the same time, the evidence is increasingly clear about what districts should avoid. In that category are financial incentives for teachers to complete Master's degrees not tightly linked to their teaching responsibilities and investments in short-term, generic professional development activities. Instead, professional development should be longer and deeper, and should be linked to the relevant standards, curriculum, and assessment system of the district or state. Even professional development programs that meet those general criteria, however, may not be effective. The challenge for educational policy makers is therefore to find programs that are demonstrably effective and are tightly aligned with the needs of the teachers and the goals of the district.

Policies Directed Toward Classrooms and Schools

The strategies I discuss here shift attention away from the quality of teachers to the size of classrooms and to school-based comprehensive reform efforts. As will become clear, though, concerns about teacher quality cannot be avoided, especially with respect to the class size discussion.

Smaller Class Sizes

Reducing the size of classes has long been on the policy agenda of state policy makers. As Corcoran and Evans noted earlier (chapter 6, this volume, figure 6.1), average class sizes, as approximated by pupil-teacher ratios, declined from just over nineteen (19.3) in the mid-1980s to seventeen in 2004. For smaller class size to serve as a strategy to reduce the black-white test score gap, smaller class sizes would have to generate higher achievement for minority students than for white students.

Evidence on how class size affects student achievement emerges from two main sources: empirical studies of observational data and a well-known randomized field trial, called the Tennessee STAR (Student/Teacher Achievement Ratio) project. Though his periodic reviews of the various observational studies have led the economist Eric Hanushek (1999) to conclude that smaller class sizes have no systematic positive effect on student achievement, his methodology and conclusions are subject to significant criticism.[14] The STAR study, in contrast, provides compelling evidence not only that smaller class sizes generate higher achievement in the early grades but also that the effects are larger for minority students.

The STAR project, which was financed by the Tennessee legislature and ran for four years in the mid-1980s, is highly touted because it was based on an experiment in which students were randomly assigned to classrooms of different sizes. Kindergarten, first, second, and third classrooms of thirteen to seventeen students were compared to classrooms of twenty-one to twenty-five students. The curriculum and the tests were standardized to compare about 6,500 pupils in about 330 classrooms, at approximately eighty schools in math, reading, and basic study skills. The initial study concluded that smaller classes generated gains in achievement scores, especially in kindergarten and grade one and for minority children (Finn and Achilles 1990; Mosteller 1995). Moreover, the effect size for minority students was about double that for majority students. These findings emerged not only from the original study, but also from careful follow-up studies by Alan Krueger (1999) and Nye, Hedges, and Konstantopoulos (2000), in which the authors explicitly addressed some of the flaws in the implementation of the STAR experiment. The largest increase in test scores emerges for students the first year they attend a small class. After that year, additional time spent in a small class has a positive, but weaker association with test scores.[15]

Subsequent studies using follow-up data indicate that the positive achievement effects of small class sizes in the early grades appear to persist through eighth grade (Nye, Hedges, and Konstantopoulos 2004). Moreover, consistent with the initial studies of short-term benefits, the benefits as of eighth grade were larger for minority students than for white, though the difference between minority and white students was statistically significant only for reading. Across the five years of the follow-up, minorities benefited from the early class size reductions on average in reading by an amount that was about 67 percent larger than the benefit to white students.

Most researchers now agree that small classes can be beneficial in the early grades, and particularly for minority students.[16] For policy purposes, however, three caveats are worth noting. The first is that smaller class sizes do not guarantee higher student achievement. This point clearly emerges from Murnane and Levy's study of fifteen schools in Austin, Texas (1996). As a result of a desegregation court order, all fifteen schools were given additional funding to reduce class sizes. Although all the schools hired more teachers and reduced class sizes, achievement rose only in the two schools that made other changes as well, such as adopting new curriculum, bringing in health services, and involving parents. The second caveat is that reducing class size is expensive because it requires additional teachers and classrooms. Positive effects on student achievement alone thus do not make it a cost-effective strategy.

The third caveat is that policy makers must be careful in extrapolating the results from an experiment such as Project STAR to a district or statewide policy to reduce class size. The reason is that large-scale changes set in motion a variety of other adjustments that are not incorporated into the small-scale experiment. Most obvious in the case of a class-size reduction is that it creates a need for many additional teachers and classrooms and is likely to induce some teachers to move from one school or district to another. As a result, when California enacted legislation in 1996 to reduce K–3 classes by about ten students per class, the hoped-for benefits for minority students did not materialize. The problem was that the larger teaching force required to staff the smaller classrooms led to a deterioration in the average quality of teachers in schools serving a predominantly black student body. This outcome occurred because such schools found it increasingly difficult to attract and retain quality teachers (Jepsen and Rivkin 2002; Bohrnstedt and Stecher 2002).

Whole School Reform

In contrast to piecemeal reforms that address specific inputs to the educational process, such as the quality of teachers or the size of their classes, whole school reforms are designed to improve achievement by changing multiple factors within a school simultaneously and methodically. A variation of this reform effort is the promotion of small high schools, an effort supported in recent years by significant funding from the Bill and Melinda Gates Foundation. Whole school reform models are typically designed for schools serving low-performing students. Because many of these schools disproportionately serve minority students, a successful reform effort of this type could potentially reduce the black-white achievement gap by raising the performance of low-scoring black students.

Because no one has a monopoly on ideas of how to reform schools, numerous whole school reform models exist, the best known of which is Success for All, developed by Robert Slavin at Johns Hopkins. Many other whole school reform models are connected with the New American Schools initiative that began in 1991. That nonprofit set up a competition for the best whole school reform model and ultimately chose to support eleven models from 600 proposed designs. In 2002, Rand reported the results of its comprehensive study of the models, representing seven of the design teams, that were in 550 schools.

The results of the New American Schools (NAS) project have been disappointing largely because many of the schools were unable to implement the model fully (Kirby, Berends, and Bodilly 2002). In practice, they needed considerable assistance and often faced barriers in the form of district bureaucracies, state and district polices, and resistance from unions. Emerging from this experience are two lessons. One is that individual schools are part of a larger system, which makes it hard to change them without changing the system of which they are a part. Another is that, within schools, the quality of leadership is key.

In contrast, most of the more than forty-five studies of the Success for All model generate positive achievement effects. Success for All is an early intervention model designed to ensure that every student reaches third grade ready to read. Critics of the program argue that the positive findings may be biased upward either because most studies include the model designer, Robert Slavin, as a member of the evaluation team or because of the way students or schools select into the program. The selection problem is at least partially addressed in a recent study, in which schools interested in participating in the program were randomly selected to receive the Success for All program in grades K through two or grades three through five (Borman et al. 2007). As was true of most of the earlier related studies, this national randomized field trial in high poverty schools across eleven states generates statistically significant positive achievement effects in reading for the Success for All program.[17]

One thorny issue that arises in the context of any school-level reform is the extent to which a model that works well at the initial site under the close supervision of the team that designed the model can be replicated elsewhere. Another is whether the results can be generalized to schools beyond those that choose to participate in the program. Even in the randomized study of Success for All just mentioned, the results are at best generalizable to schools interested in implementing the program.

These issues are further illustrated by the First Things First (FTF) program, a small-school reform model designed to improve the achievement of economically disadvantaged middle and high school students. Although FTF generated impressive achievement gains in math and reading and improvements in other outcomes for students in its home site of Kansas City, Kansas, the effects were far less positive and far less consistent in the expansion sites. The evaluators speculate that among the reasons for the less impressive results were the weaker support from the districts in the new sites, the relatively long time needed for program development, and the inability of the designer to provide adequate technical support for the project over an extended period (Quint et al. 2005). The evaluators conclude that implementing such a program is hard work and requires significant commitment of educators not only at the school level but also at the district level.

The bottom line is that some school-based reform models appear to have the potential to raise student achievement of some low-performing students, including minority students. Taking such programs to scale, however, is a difficult undertaking with no guarantee of widespread success. Further, the success of any school-based strategy will inevitably require the involvement and commitment of district-, as well as school-, level officials.

School-Based Accountability Programs

By school-based accountability programs, I am referring to systems that use measures of student outcomes—primarily student achievement as measured by test scores—to hold schools accountable for improving the performance of their students. The federal No Child Left Behind Act (NCLB) of 2001 is the most prominent example. That legislation requires every state to test all students in reading and math annually in grades three through eight and once in high school. It uses those test scores, reported separately by racial and income subgroups within schools, to hold individual schools accountable for making adequate yearly progress toward the ultimate goal of 100 percent proficiency. Many states, particularly southern states such as Texas and North Carolina, had their own quite well-developed accountability systems well before the federal law spread school based accountability to all states.

This type of top-down administrative system differs from other forms of accountability, such as political accountability that would hold policy makers accountable through the political process or to accountability through market processes. In the next section on choice and competition, I return to market-based accountability. In this section, I restrict the discussion to test-based administrative accountability.

There are at least three rationales for this type of accountability, not all of which have direct links to the racial achievement gap. For the proponents of standards-based reform, for example, test-based accountability is simply one part of a more coherent reform strategy designed to promote the ambitious educational outcomes required in this increasingly global society. The goal is to align all components of the education system, including teacher training and capacity building, toward the overall goal of high student performance, progress toward which is measured by student test scores. Though such proponents emphasize the importance of high standards for all students, the standards-based reform strategy is not directly targeted on achievement gaps. Instead, the goal is to increase overall achievement.

A second rationale for test-based accountability it that it serves as a stand-alone policy designed to address the perceived problem that educators are shirking their responsibilities and simply are not working hard enough or smart enough to generate the desired outcomes. Economists often use the language of the principal agent model to describe this situation. In the context of such a model, the challenge is to set up an appropriate incentive system to induce the agents—in this case, the educators—to operate in ways compatible with the interests of the principal—in this case state policy makers and the public. By measuring, reporting, and attaching positive consequences to strong performance and negative consequences to weak school performance, policy makers provide incentives for schools and school districts to focus attention on what is being measured and ultimately to alter the way they operate. Concerns about the capacity of schools to respond or inadequate resources clearly take a back seat to confidence in the power of incentives and sanctions to change behavior.

To the extent that teacher shirking is the policy problem, rather than, for example, lack of resources, knowledge or professional skills, a test-based accountability system could help narrow the black-white test score gap. For accountability to narrow the gap, however, two things would have to be true. The first is that, in the absence of an accountability system, the parents of black students would have to be less vigilant than their white counterparts in monitoring the quality of the children's schools and classrooms so that the introduction of accountability would have a differentially positive effect on black students. Although information on this point is lacking, the lower levels of education or income of black parents relative to white parents could well render them less able or willing to exert an influence in the schools. In addition, any differential monitoring would have to occur in schools that were not racially balanced. Otherwise, monitoring by white parents would benefit black students along with white and hence the introduction of an accountability system would have little or no effect on the black-white achievement gap. If shirking is indeed the problem, accountability could well be a useful tool for closing gaps. To the extent that the low achievement of minorities reflects either larger social forces or their exposure to teachers with weak credentials, however, simply putting pressure on teachers to work harder or smarter will do little to reduce the gap.

Finally, as groups such as the Citizens' Commission on Civil Rights and the Education Trust have emphasized, school accountability—especially as implemented under NCLB with its attention to subgroups—can be viewed as a tool for directly addressing the problem of educational inequities and, in particular, racial achievement gaps. By setting high standards for all students and by focusing attention on the students whom the education system has been leaving behind, namely minorities, students from low-income families and those who are disabled, school accountability programs could raise the achievement of those historically low-performing groups.

Design Matters

Regardless of the rationale, the potential for test-based accountability systems to contribute to reducing the black-white test score gap will depend on how the system is designed. Among the many important design issues, perhaps the most important is whether to use a status model or a model based on individual student growth to judge the effectiveness of individual schools. A status model essentially looks at levels of achievement—typically defined as the percentage of students who reach a designated level of proficiency—whereas a growth model—often called a value-added model—focuses on the average gains in learning of individual students from one year to the next. NCLB is currently based on the status approach.

The status model is appealing to some observers because it sends a clear signal that the goal is high achievement for all students. The problem, though, is that simply sending a signal does not ensure that the outcome will be achieved, and may well lead to unintended and undesired side effects such as narrow teaching to the test or possibly even cheating. As has been documented in many studies, including Clotfelter and Ladd (1996), status models are not well designed to promote an equity agenda because they inevitably favor the schools with the most advantaged students. This pattern emerges because of the high positive correlation across schools between the socioeconomic status of the students and their achievement. As a result, the more advantaged schools have greater incentives to improve than schools serving low-performing students who perceive little chance of positive recognition.

If the important values are providing realistic incentives for school improvement, especially for schools at the low end of the performance distribution, the growth approach, though itself somewhat flawed, is clearly preferred to the status model.

Achievement Effects of Accountability

At this point, less is known about how accountability programs affect student achievement than one might expect, given its centrality to the current education policy debate.[18] Although a recent study found that student achievement in reading and math has risen in most states with three or more years of comparable test score data since NCLB was enacted, the authors emphasized the difficulty of determining whether NCLB caused the increase (Center for Education Policy 2007). In addition, national trends of test scores based on the National Assessment of Educational Progress (NAEP) provide no support for a large and demonstrable effect of NCLB on student achievement. Although the reading scores of eighth graders were rising before NCLB was enacted, they have remained generally constant since then. At the same time, the upward trend in eighth grade math scores both before and after NCLB is consistent with the view that the state-level accountability programs that preceded the federal legislation have raised student achievement in math.

In general, the state-level experiences provide a better source of information on the achievement effects of accountability, both because many states have been using test-based accountability systems longer than the federal government has and because of the possibility of comparing trends in a particular state to those in other states or to the nation. Even, here, however, the effects are not clear.

Of particular interest for the black-white achievement gap is the Texas experience, because that state provided the model for the federal approach of focusing attention on subgroups within schools. Other evidence about the achievement effects of accountability emerge from cross-state studies that make use of the variation across states in the strength of their state accountability systems or in the timing of their introduction to tease out their causal impacts on student achievement. A central issue in all the studies is how best to measure achievement. The main choices are the high-stakes state test on which a particular accountability system is based, or the NAEP to which no specific stakes are attached but which has the advantage of being comparable across states. As illustrated for Texas, positive results on the high-stakes test may not translate into positive results on the low-stakes test. In general, the low-stakes NAEP test is probably the better indicator of student learning. The exception is in those cases in which the state or district's curriculum differs significantly from the material tested on NAEP.

Texas   Perhaps of most interest are the results for Texas, because that state's accountability system served as the model for NCLB. After a series of education reforms starting in the early 1980s, Texas introduced in 1990 a criterion-referenced testing program called the Texas Assessment of Academic Skills (TAAS) that was designed to shift the focus from minimum skills to higher-order thinking skills (see Haney 2000.) Schools were held accountable not only for the overall pass rates on TAAS in the school but also for the pass rates of four student subgroups: African Americans, Hispanics, whites, and economically disadvantaged students

Between 1994 and 1998, TAAS test scores in both math and reading increased dramatically, suggesting that the state's accountability program had a large and positive impact on student achievement. Analysis by Stephen Klein and his colleagues, however, showed that the large gains on TAAS did not translate into comparable large gains in the lower-stakes Texas NAEP scores (2000).[19] Moreover, only for the white fourth graders did the reading gains of Texas students on NAEP exceed the gains of their counterparts nationwide. A somewhat more positive story emerges for Texas fourth graders in math. Once again, the TAAS gains exceeded the Texas NAEP gains but in this case, the latter gains exceeded the national gains for all three racial groups.

Most relevant for this discussion is that the TAAS and NAEP results generate conflicting stories about how accountability affected racial achievement gaps in Texas. In particular, the gaps between blacks and whites in fourth grade reading and math and in eighth grade math based on the TAAS scores decreased significantly between 1994 and 1998, but the comparable gaps based on the NAEP increased slightly (Klein et al. 2000, 10–11). Similar patterns also emerge for Hispanics. Klein and his colleagues speculated that the reasons for the differing patterns for TAAS and NAEP results is that Texas teachers may be teaching very narrowly to the TAAS and that the schools serving minority students may be doing so even more than other schools. Thus, even in Texas, the evidence is at best mixed about the power of an accountability system to reduce racial gaps.

Cross State Studies   Other studies generate similarly mixed results with respect to effects by racial group. At least one careful study (Carnoy and Loeb 2002) for the late 1990s found larger effect sizes on passing rates at the basic level on NAEP for black and Hispanic students than for white students. Other studies with different outcome measures found different patterns. In particular, Eric Hanushek and Margaret Raymond (2005) found essentially no effects of accountability on the gains in achievement between fourth and eighth grade of black students, but positive effects for Hispanic students, effects that are consistent with early findings by racial-ethnic group for seventh graders in Dallas (Ladd 1999). Effects of accountability on racial-ethnic achievement gaps are similarly mixed. The Hanushek and Raymond study determined that state accountability systems may have reduced the gap for Hispanics but expanded it for blacks.

Conclusions About Accountability

Although accountability programs that focus on specific groups may have some potential for reducing black-white achievement gaps, the overall evidence suggests their effects are likely to be small and most likely to emerge in the lower grades. There is little evidence to date of their ability to reduce the gap at higher grades and in terms of higher-order skills. Though somewhat discouraging, this conclusion should not be too surprising. These findings are consistent with the view that the underperformance of black children relative to white children in many cases has far less to do with the teacher shirking that motivates stand-alone accountability programs and far more to do with a host of other factors both inside and outside the schools. The challenge for education policy makers at this point is to develop accountability systems that take greater account of the different skills and capacities that children bring to school, that shift the focus away from test score results to the strengthening of instructional practices within schools, and that cast the bright light of accountability on participants other than just teachers in the education process, including district and state policy makers who determine the terms under which individual schools operate.

School Choice Programs

As is the case for test-based accountability programs, expanded parental choice of schools has been promoted for many reasons, not all of which are related to the challenge of reducing the black-white test score gap. The following discussion briefly evaluates three mechanisms through which expanded parental choice of schools might conceivably reduce the black-white test score gap. That the evidence for success in each case is at best mixed raises doubts about the potential for parental choice programs to reduce the gap. Indeed, the more general concern is that expansion of choice could well widen achievement gaps. Because additional choice serves multiple goals, this conclusion need not mean that additional choice is undesirable. It does mean, however, that as policy makers respond to rising demands for more parental choice, they need to take care in designing those programs in ways that are least likely to widen racial achievement gaps.

Effects on Achievement Through Competition

Some proponents favor more parental choice because they believe that when schools are faced with the possibility of losing students and the funding that accompanies them, the schools will be forced to become less complacent and more productive. The evidence in the United States to date, however, suggests that competitive pressures of this type are not likely to have much impact on the black-white test score gap. One reason is that even at best competitive pressure appears to have very small positive impacts on student achievement (Gill and Booker 2008). That conclusion is based on existing studies of various types of choice programs, many of which are still quite small. Although larger positive results could conceivably emerge as the United States introduces more choice and competition, the evidence from other countries with more extensive choice, such as Chile, tends to confirm this conclusion.

Another is that parental choice and competition may exacerbate the challenges that low-performing schools serving many black students face. To the extent that the students who exercise their power to leave are more motivated or are from families who are more actively involved in the school, the outcome could well be greater concentration of low-performing students, and hence more challenging-to-educate students, in those schools (Fiske and Ladd 2000). The result is that the performance of students in those schools, including many black students, may well fall in the face of competitive pressures.

Achievement Effects on the Choosers

Potentially more important from the perspective of the black-white test score gap is that giving parents more choice may improve the schooling options—and outcomes—for black students more than for white. Two considerations appear to support this possibility. One is that black students, especially those from low-income families, typically have fewer schooling options than their white counterparts. That occurs because the combination of their lower family incomes and various features of the housing market, including zoning restrictions and discrimination, tend to limit the neighborhoods—hence schools—available to them under a geographic school assignment system and because the lower average incomes of their families restricts their ability to enroll in private schools. The other consideration is the perception, and to some extent the evidence, that private schools, particularly Catholic schools, generate higher achievement than public schools. In fact, the positive achievement effects of Catholic schools are far smaller than once believed. At the same time, the evidence is consistent with positive differential effects for African Americans in urban areas.

These considerations, along with others, open the possibility for charter schools or voucher programs to reduce gaps to the extent they give black students access to better schools. Charter schools, which are now enabled by state legislation in forty states plus the District of Columbia, are public schools that are publicly funded but operated by nongovernmental organizations under charter from a public agency and are schools of choice in that no students are assigned to such schools. Although the state enabling laws differ from state to state, one of the goals of such laws is typically to provide additional options for disadvantaged students. Voucher programs, in contrast, expand the options for students not explicitly by the introduction of new schools but rather by providing public funding for students to attend private schools. Such demand-side funding may simply increase the demand for slots in existing private schools or, depending on the scale of the program, expand the supply of private schools. Charter school programs are currently far more common than voucher programs in the United States. The most well-known publicly funded voucher programs are in Milwaukee, Cleveland, and Washington, D.C. A number of privately funded voucher programs, typically called scholarship programs, have operated in other cities, including New York City, Washington, D.C., and Dayton, Ohio.

The key policy question of interest here is whether black students who exercise their option to choose a different school under either of these programs achieve at higher levels than they would have had they remained in the traditional public schools. Answering that question with confidence is challenging because the students who take advantage of the new schooling options are likely to differ in systematic ways from those who remain in the traditional public schools. Hence, researchers have had to develop empirical methods that keep to a minimum the biases that arise from self-selection.

Charter Schools   One method used quite extensively in the literature on charter school effects involves the estimation of longitudinal models based on the test scores of individual students who are observed in both traditional public schools and in charter schools, with indicator variables to control for the characteristics of students, such as their motivation, that do not change over time. Such models solve the selection problem by measuring the gains in achievement of students when they are in charter schools relative to those of the same students when they are in traditional public schools. The disadvantage of this approach is that the sample is restricted to the students who are switching from one type of school to the other and may not be representative of all charter school students. A second method is to make use of the multiple natural experiments that arise when charter schools are oversubscribed and have to select students through a random lottery process. With this approach, the students who lose the lottery can serve as a control for the students who are selected into the school. The random assignment component of this approach solves the selection program but has a downside in that the results are generalizable only to the types of charter schools that are oversubscribed.

Careful studies of charter schools based on longitudinal data typically show little or no positive overall achievement effects. In fact, research of this type finds large negative achievement effects in North Carolina, negative overall effects in Texas for newly established charter schools and no differential effects for more mature charter schools, and similar patterns in Florida (Bifulco and Ladd 2006; Sass 2006; Hanushek, Rivkin, and Branch 2005). The more negative effects in North Carolina may well reflect the failure of that state to remove the charters of underperforming schools.

The results from studies based on oversubscribed charter schools are generally more positive (Hoxby and Rockoff 2005). These studies are important as an existence proof. That is, they document the potential for certain types of charter schools—the oversubscribed ones included in the studies—to raise achievement for the types of students likely to apply to them. To the extent that such models can be successfully expanded to other sites, and that such models serve black students, their success indicates the potential for some black students to benefit from charter schools. At the same time, however, other black students could well be harmed by the availability of charter schools. That conclusion emerges clearly from the North Carolina experience, where the black students who end up in racially segregated charter schools fare far less well than other charter school students. As Robert Bifulco and Helen Ladd documented, the net effect of charter schools in that state has been to expand the black-white test score gap (2007). Although that outcome may not emerge in other states, it highlights the need for policy makers to be alert to the effects of their policy decisions on the black-white test score gap.

Voucher Programs   With respect to voucher programs, evaluation of the heavily studied initial Milwaukee program shows that means-tested voucher programs can be designed to successfully expand the schooling opportunities for black families. Whether such programs increase the learning of the participants, however, is more controversial. The best of the three studies of the initial Milwaukee program finds small positive achievement gains in math but none in reading (Rouse 1998). All the studies of that program, however, are bedeviled by the challenge of finding an appropriate control group, given that students were not randomly assigned to receive a voucher.

A better approach for measuring achievement effects is to do field experiments in which applicants to the voucher program are randomly selected into the program or into a control group. Such experiments have been used to evaluate privately funded voucher programs in New York City, Dayton, Ohio, and Washington, D.C. Based on three years of the voucher programs in New York and Washington, D.C., and two years in Dayton, researchers William Howell and Paul Peterson (2002) find no evidence of a general achievement difference between the public and the private schools. In no year and in no individual city (other than the second year in Washington) was there evidence that students who shifted to private schools achieved at higher average levels than those who remained in the public school system. Further, when the analysis was disaggregated by the race of the students, no differences emerged for either white or Hispanic students.

Positive differences in achievement did emerge, however, for black students. Based on their preferred estimates, which disproportionately weight the results from New York City on the ground they were the most stable over time, the authors conclude that blacks who switched to private schools scored about 3.9, 6.3, and 6.5 percentile points higher than comparable students in the control group in the first three years of the program (Howell and Peterson 2002). These effects are about two-thirds the size of the differences that emerged for minority students exposed to smaller classes in the Tennessee experiment. The differences were consistent, however, across neither cities nor grades. In New York City, for example, the positive differential emerged clearly and consistently only for students in the fifth grade (Howell and Peterson 2002, tables 6.2 and D.1). Further, a reanalysis of the New York data (Krueger and Zhu 2002) has generated questions about the robustness of the positive findings for blacks in that city. Finally, it is not at all clear that any positive effects of private schools can be extrapolated to an expanded voucher program, even one targeted at black students. There is no guarantee that any new private schools established in response to an expanded voucher program would be of the same quality as the more established schools involved in this small scale initiative.

Thus the power of voucher programs to reduce the black-white achievement gap by raising the achievement of black students who use vouchers to attend private schools remains to be documented. The evidence to date is not promising.

Promoting Racial Integration Through Parental Choice   One final mechanism, albeit an unlikely route, through which greater choice could potentially reduce the black-white gap is worth exploring. To the extent that parental choice were to reduce racial segregation it could, for the reasons discussed earlier, potentially lead to a more even distribution of teacher quality across racial groups.

To be sure, the expansion of options for parents to choose the schools their children attend has historically generated greater, not less, racial segregation in the United States. That outcome has resulted in part from white flight, which may have been motivated in part by "outgroup avoidance" (Saporito 2003), that is, the desire of the dominant group to minimize contact with the other group. Greater choice would also increase segregation if members of each racial group prefer to associate with others like themselves. Nonetheless, two other mechanisms could operate in the other direction. Given the high levels of residential segregation in metropolitan areas in the United States, greater choice could possibly reduce school segregation by providing families access to schools that are more integrated than the neighborhoods available to them. This mechanism is most applicable to the black families whose housing decisions are constrained by zoning restrictions or racial discrimination in the housing market. In addition, explicit policy decisions about resources and the location of schools could promote greater integration. If parents prefer schools with more resources, the generous funding of schools in minority neighborhoods in the form of magnet schools, for example, might attract students from other neighborhoods with different family backgrounds. Also, the creation of specialized schools with specific themes, such as district-wide magnet schools in science or theater, may draw students from across the district or even from other districts. In this way, school specialization can widen a school's catchment area beyond racially isolated neighborhoods, thereby reducing racial segregation. Whether choice programs are likely to increase or decrease racial segregation is thus an empirical question.

Robert Bifulco, Helen Ladd, and Stephen Ross (2008) used data from Durham, North Carolina, to examine that issue in the context of choice programs consistent with the 2007 Supreme Court ruling. This urban school district is a useful case study for several reasons. One, it has avoided using racial criteria in its school assignment programs since the 1999 Fourth Circuit Supreme Court case that put a damper on race based policies in that circuit. Second, it has long had a liberal school transfer program. Third, it offers a variety of schools of choice, including magnet schools, charter schools and year round schools. The availability of data on individual students makes it possible for the authors to track students to the schools they attend. The main question is whether the choice programs in that urban district increased or decreased the racial segregation of the schools.

Consistent with various predictions from the literature, the authors find evidence that substantial numbers of white families used the school choice options to avoid schools with concentrations of racial minorities, and that some black families used the options to select more racially isolated environments. The segregating effects of such choices, however, were largely offset, especially at the middle school level, where the district has had some success in establishing magnet schools attractive to white families, by the students who made racially integrating choices. As a result, Durham's school choice programs increased racial segregation but only by a small amount. Although the small size of the increase may be welcomed by some observers, the finding that racial segregation increased at all is not good news for those hoping that choice programs might serve as a mechanism for reducing racial segregation. Moreover, such programs resulted in far greater segregation by class and student achievement, an outcome that might also work to the disadvantage of black students who tend to be overrepresented among low SES and low-performing students. At the same time, studies such as this one are unable to explore the broader, general equilibrium effects of school choice policies. The availability of such policies might, for example, affect the residential choices that parents make and thereby indirectly influence a range of other policy outcomes.

Conclusion

Emerging from this discussion is that none of the various school-related policies discussed here is likely to play a major role in reducing the black-white achievement gap. Some policies, however, undoubtedly have more potential than others. Most promising appear to be strategies to promote small class sizes in the early grades and to even out the quality of teachers across schools serving different racial groups. Instead, major reductions in the achievement gap will require policy attention to the larger social forces that lead to differences by race in what children bring to the classroom.

Despite this pessimistic conclusion about the power of school policies by themselves, well-designed policies are still a critical component of any gap-reduction strategy. The reason is that even vast improvements in various social policies relevant for education, such as improved health care or nutrition for infants and young children and expanded access to high quality preschool opportunities for children from disadvantaged families, will fail to reduce the gap if the education system itself distributes resources unequally across students of different races (for evidence on Head Start, see Currie and Thomas 1995; Garces, Thomas, and Currie 2002). As highlighted earlier, the more unevenly that students of different races are distributed across schools, the more potential there is for resources, such as quality teachers, to be unevenly distributed by race. Hence, a major challenge for policy makers is to maintain whatever pressure they can to limit the resegregation of schools. Unfortunately, the Supreme Court has limited the direct powers of districts to promote racial integration through explicitly race-based student assignment programs. Districts must therefore rely on less direct strategies, such as balancing schools by socioeconomic status, the judicious use of funding for magnet schools, the location of new charter schools, or special programs to promote the goal of racial balance. As illustrated by the recent experience in Charlotte-Mecklenburg, North Carolina, failure to pay attention to racial balance can have serious consequences for the black-white distribution of teachers. Even in the absence of future changes of this type in the distributions of students and teachers, however, policy makers will need to be vigilant in pursuing strategies designed to counter the black-white differences in educational inputs that currently exist. That will require policies specifically designed to improve the skills of the teachers serving black children and to improve the schools they attend.

Acknowledgments

The author thanks Charles Clotfelter, Jens Ludwig, Jacob Vigdor, and the editors of this volume for their helpful suggestions.

Notes

1. Having more advantaged peers need not always lead to more positive outcomes. As Christopher Jencks and Susan Mayer emphasized, another possibility is that children in schools with more advantaged peers may become discouraged by their relative deprivation (1990). In that case, having more advantaged peers could reduce student achievement.
2. As Jacob Vigdor and Jens Ludwig noted, the methodology used in the peer effects literature typically does not incorporate the effects of this second mechanism. In particular, the inclusion of school fixed effects in the regression models holds constant the time-invariant characteristics of schools, including the mix of their teachers.
3. Charles Clotfelter, Helen Ladd, and Jacob Vigdor (2003, 2008) documented for North Carolina that at the elementary level, most of the racial segregation is between, not within, schools. At the high school level, within-school segregation plays a far larger role.
4. The quartiles are redefined for each year.
5. A more nuanced measure of segregation indicates a similar increase. That measure increased from 0.20 to 0.33 over the same period, again a huge increase relative to that of other districts.
6. Data not shown. The one exception to the statement in the text is Wake County, which explicitly promoted racial balance across schools before 1999 and since then has promoted economic balance.
7. *Board of Education of Oklahoma v. Dowell*, U.S. 237 (1991) and *Freeman v. Pitts* (1972).
8. *Capacchione v. Charlotte-Mecklenberg Schools*, 57 F. Supp. 2d 228 (W.D.N.C. 1999); *Eisenberg v. Montgomery County Public Schools*, 197 F.3d 123 (4th Cir. 1999); *Tuttle v. Arlington County School Board*, 195 F.3d 698 (4th Cir. 1999) (for an analysis of these decisions, see Boger 2000).

9. Other districts that have implemented socioeconomic integration plans include LaCrosse, Wisconsin, Cambridge, Massachusetts, and San Francisco (for descriptions of the plans in these three districts, see Reardon, Yin, and Kurlaender 2006).

10. The percentages for other large districts are 30.9 for Guilford, 9.4 for Cumberland, and 23.9 for Winston/Salem/Forsyth (Clotfelter, Ladd, and Vigdor 2008, table 2).

11. For a discussion of the argument that parental choice might conceivably serve the same goal, see the section on parental choice.

12. Such estimates would overstate the required salary increases if the estimated wage elasticities of supply are too low. A study based on an $1800 bonus program for eligible teachers in low-performing middle and high schools in North Carolina finds retention elasticities that are significantly larger than other estimates in the literature (Clotfelter et al. 2008). These larger estimates may emerge from the bonus program because the researchers are better able to separate the effects of the salary differential from the working conditions in the school given that the bonus applies to only a subset of the teachers within each school.

13. This section draws heavily on Heather Hill (2007).

14. Hanushek's approach and conclusions have been criticized on methodological ground by Larry Hedges, Richard Laine, and Rob Greenwald (1994) and Alan Krueger (2002) Particularly compelling is Alan Krueger's criticism that Hanushek's method of aggregating results across studies gives far too much weight to multiple estimates from studies that find no effects. With a more appropriate weighting based on the same set of studies that Hanushek reviewed, Krueger (2002) concluded that student achievement is higher in the smaller classes, after other factors that affect student achievement are appropriately controlled for.

15. Joshua Angrist and Victor Lavy (1999) also found that smaller class sizes increased achievement in Israel using the natural, but quite random, variation in class sizes associated with that country's explicit policy of capping class sizes.

16. One possible exception is Eric Hanushek (1999), who emphasized that the benefits of smaller classes are limited to kindergarten and first grade and that the huge variation in student achievement suggests that teacher quality is much more important that class size.

17. At the same time, no such effects emerged from a completely independent observational study of three whole school reform models, including Success for All, in New York City (Bifulco, Duncombe, and Yinger 2005). Although carefully done, however, that study is subject to all the caveats of studies based on quasi-experimental data.

18. Much of the following discussion is based on Figlio and Ladd (2008).

19. Using effect sizes, which are measured in standard deviations and thus can be compared across tests, Klein and his colleagues reported the following effect sizes for achievement gains in reading for Texas fourth graders between 1994 and 1998: TAAS scores increased by 0.39 for white fourth graders, 0.49 for black fourth graders, and 0.39 for Hispanic fourth graders. In contrast, the gains on the Texas NAEP were far smaller at 0.13, 0.14, and 0.14, respectively (2000).

References

Angrist, Joshua D., and Victor Lavy. 1999. "Using Maimonides' Rule to Estimate the Effect of Class Size on Scholastic Achievement." *Quarterly Journal of Economics* 114(2): 533–74.

Bifulco, Robert, William Duncombe, and John Yinger. 2005. "Does Whole-School Reform Boost Student Performance? The Case of New York City." *Journal of Policy Analysis and Management* 24(1): 47–72.

Bifulco, Robert, and Helen F. Ladd. 2006. "The Impact of Charter Schools on Student Achievement: Evidence from North Carolina." *Education Finance and Policy* 1(1): 50–90.

———. 2007. "School Choice, Racial Segregation and Test Score Gaps: Evidence from North Carolina's Charter School Program." *Journal of Policy Analysis and Management* 26(1): 31–56.

Bifulco, Robert, Helen F. Ladd, and Stephen Ross. 2008. "Public School Choice and Integration: Evidence from Durham, North Carolina." CALDER Working Paper No. 14. Washington, D.C.: The Urban Institute.

Boger, John Charles. 2000. "Willful Colorblindness: The New Racial Piety and the Resegregation of Public Schools," *North Carolina Law Review* 78(September): 1719–96.

Bohrnstedt, George W., and Brian M. Stecher, editors. 2002. *Class Size Reduction in California*. Sacramento, Calif.: CSR Research Consortium, California Department of Education.

Borman, Geoffrey, Robert E. Slavin, Alan C. K. Cheung, Anne M. Chamberlain, Nancy A. Madden, and Bette Chambers. 2007. "Final Reading Outcomes of the National Randomized Field Trial of Success for All." *American Educational Research Journal* 44(3): 703–31.

Boyd, Donald, Hamilton Lankford, Susanna Loeb, and James Wyckoff. 2006. "How Changes in Entry Requirements Alter the Teacher Workforce and Affect Student Achievement." *Education Finance and Policy* 1(2): 176–216.

Carnoy, Martin, and Susanna Loeb. 2002. "Does External Accountability Affect Student Outcomes? A Cross-State Analysis." *Educational Evaluation and Policy Analysis* 24(4): 305–31.

Center on Education Policy. 2007. *Answering the Question That Matters Most: Has Student Achievement Increased Since No Child Left Behind*. Washington, D.C.: Center on Education Policy.

Century Foundation Task Force on the Common School. 2002. *Divided We Fail: Coming Together Throughout Public School Choice*. New York: The Century Foundation Press.

Chaplin, Duncan. 2002. "Estimating the Impact of Economic Integration of Schools on racial Integration." In *Divided We Fail: Coming Together Throughout Public School Choice*. New York: The Century Foundation Press.

Clotfelter, Charles, Elizabeth Glennie, Helen F, Ladd, and Jacob L. Vigdor. 2008. "Would Higher Salaries Keep Teachers in High Poverty Schools? Evidence from a Policy Intervention in North Carolina." *Journal of Public Economics* 92(5–6): 1352–70.

Clotfelter, Charles T., and Helen F. Ladd. 1996. "Recognizing and Rewarding Success in Public Schools." In *Holding Schools Accountable: Performance-Based*

Reform in Education, edited by Helen F. Ladd. Washington, D.C.: Brookings Institution Press.

Clotfelter, Charles T., Helen F. Ladd, and Jacob L. Vigdor. 2003. "Segregation and Resegregation in North Carolina's Public School Classrooms." *North Carolina Law Review* 81(4): 1463–512.

———. 2006. "Teacher-Student Matching and the Assessment of Teacher Effectiveness." *Journal of Human Resources* 41(4): 778–820.

———. 2007a. "Teacher Credentials and Student Achievement: Longitudinal Analysis with Student Fixed Effects." *Economics of Education Review* 26(6): 673–82.

———. 2007b. "Teacher Credentials and Student Achievement in High School: A Cross-Subject Analysis with Student Fixed Effects." CALDER Working Paper 11. Washington, D.C.: The Urban Institute. Accessed at http://www.urban.org/url.cfm?ID=1001104.

———. 2008. "School Segregation under Color-Blind Jurisprudence: The Case of North Carolina." CALDER Working Paper 16. Washington, D.C.: The Urban Institute. Accessed at http://www.urban.org/url.cfm?ID=1001152. Forthcoming in *Virginia Journal of Social Policy and the Law.*

Currie, Janet, and Duncan Thomas. 1995. "Does Head Start Make a Difference?" *American Economic Review* 85(3): 341–64.

Figlio, David, and Helen F. Ladd. 2008. "School Accountability and Student Achievement." In *Handbook of Research in Education Finance and Policy,* edited by Helen F. Ladd and Edward B. Fiske. New York: Routledge.

Finn, Jeremy D., and Charles M. Achilles. 1990. "Answers and Questions about Class Size: A Statewide Experiment." *American Educational Research Journal* 27(3): 557–77.

Fiske, Edward B., and Helen F. Ladd. 2000. *When Schools Compete: A Cautionary Tale.* Washington, D.C.: Brookings Institution Press.

Garces, Eliana, Duncan Thomas, and Janet Currie. 2002. "Longer-Term Effects of Head Start." *American Economic Review* 92(4): 999–1012.

Gill, Brian P., and Kevin Booker. 2008. "School Competition and Student Outcomes." In *Handbook of Research in Education Finance and Policy,* edited by Helen F. Ladd and Edward B. Fiske. New York: Routledge.

Glazerman, Steven, Daniel P. Mayer, and Paul T. Decker. 2006 . "Alternative Routes to Teaching: The Impacts of Teach for America on Student Achievement and Other Outcomes." *Journal of Policy Analysis and Management* 25(1): 75–96.

Goldhaber, Dan D. 2008. "Teachers Matter, but Effective Teacher Quality Policies Are Elusive." In *Handbook of Research in Education Finance and Policy,* edited by Helen F. Ladd and Edward B. Fiske. New York: Routledge

Haney, Walter M. 2000. "The Myth of the Texas Miracle in Education." *Educational Policy Analysis Archives* 8(41). Accessed at http://epaa.asu.edu/epaa/v8n41.

Hanushek, Eric A. 1999. "Some Findings from an Independent Investigation of the Tennessee STAR Experiment and From Other Investigations of Class Size Effects." *Educational Evaluation and Policy Analysis* 21(2): 143–63.

Hanushek, Eric A., John F. Kain, and Steven G. Rivkin. 1999. "Do Higher Salaries Buy Better Teachers?" NBER Working Paper #W7082 (April).

———. 2004. "Why Public Schools Lose Teachers." *Journal of Human Resources* 39(20): 326–54.

Hanushek, Eric A., and Margaret E. Raymond. 2005. "Does School Accountability Lead to Improved School Performance?" *Journal of Policy Analysis and Management* 24(2): 297–329.

Hanushek, Eric A., Steven G. Rivkin, and Gregory F. Branch. 2005. "Charter School Quality and Parental Decision Making with School Choice." NBER Working Paper 11252. Cambridge, Mass.: National Bureau of Economic Research.

Hedges, Larry V., Richard D. Laine, and Rob Greenwald. 1994. "An Exchange Part I: Does Money Matter? A Meta-Analysis of Studies of the Effects of Differential School Inputs on Student Outcomes." *Educational Researcher* 23(3): 5–14.

Hill, Heather C. 2007. "Learning in the Teaching Workforce." *Future of Children* 17(1): 111–27.

Howell, William G., and Paul E. Peterson. 2002 *The Education Gap: Vouchers and Urban Schools*. Washington, D.C.: Brookings Institution Press.

Hoxby, Caroline M., and Jonah E. Rockoff. 2005. "The Impact of Charter Schools on Student Achievement." Unpublished paper. Harvard University.

Jacob, Brian A. 2007. "The Challenges of Staffing Urban Schools with Effective Teachers." *Future of Children* 17(1): 129–53.

Jencks, Christopher, and Susan E. Mayer. 1990. "The Social Consequences of Growing Up in a Poor Neighborhood." In *Inner City Poverty in the United States*, edited by Laurence E. Lynn, Jr., and Michael G. H. McGeary. Washington, D.C.: National Academy Press.

Jencks, Christopher, and Meredith Phillips, editors. 1998. *The Black-White Test-Score Gap* Washington, D.C.: Brookings Institution Press.

Jepsen, Christopher, and Steven G. Rivkin. 2002. "What Is the Trade-Off Between Smaller Classes and Teacher Quality?" NBER Working Paper 9205. Cambridge, Mass.: National Bureau of Economic Research.

Kahlenberg, Richard D. 2001. *All Together Now: Creating Middle-Class Schools Through Public School Choice*. Washington, D.C.: Brookings Institution Press.

Kirby, Sheila N., Mark Berends, and Susan J. Bodilly. 2002. "A Decade of Whole School Reform: The New American Schools Experience." RAND Research Brief 8019. Santa Monica, Calif.: RAND Corporation.

Klein, Stephen P., Laura S. Hamilton, Daniel F. McCaffrey, and Brian M. Stecher. 2000. "What Do Test Scores in Texas Tell Us?" *Education Policy Analysis Archives* 8(49). Accessed at http://epaa.asu.edu/epaa/v8n49.

Krueger, Alan B. 1999. "Experimental Estimates of Education Production Functions." *Quarterly Journal of Economics* 114(2): 197–532.

———. 2002. "Understanding the Magnitude and Effect of Class Size on Student Achievement." In *The Class Size Debate*, edited by Lawrence Mischel and Richard Rothstein. Washington, D.C.: Economic Policy Institute.

Krueger, Alan B., and Pei Zhu. 2002. "Another Look at the New York City School Voucher Experiment." NBER Working Paper 9418. Cambridge Mass.: National Bureau of Economic Research.

Ladd, Helen F. 1999. "The Dallas School Accountability and Incentive Program: An Evaluation of Its Impacts on Student Outcomes." *Economics of Education Review* 18(1): 1–16.

Mont, Daniel, and Daniel I. Rees. 1996. "The Influence of Classroom Characteristics on High School Teacher Turnover." *Economic Inquiry* 34(January): 152–67.

Mosteller, Frederick. 1995. "The Tennessee Study of Class Size in the Early School Grades." *Future of Children* 5(2): 113–27.

Murnane, Richard J., and Frank Levy. 1996. "Evidence from Fifteen Schools in Austin, Texas." In *Does Money Matter?* edited by Gary Burtless. Washington, D.C.: The Brookings Institution Press.

Murnane, Richard J., and Randall J. Olson. 1989. "Will There be Enough Teachers?" *American Economic Review* 79(2): 242–46.

Nye, Barbara, Larry V. Hedges, and Spyros Konstantopoulos. 2000. "Do Minorities and the Disadvantaged Benefit More from Small Classes? Evidence from the Tennessee Class Size Experiment." *American Journal of Education* 109(1): 1–26.

———. 2004. "Do Minorities Experience Longer Lasting Benefits from Small Classes?" *Journal of Educational Research* 98(2): 94–100.

Quint, Janet, Howard S. Bloom, Alison Rebeck Black, LaFleur Stephens, and Theresa M. Akey. 2005. *The Challenge of Scaling up Educational Reform.* New York: MDRC.

Reardon, Sean F., John T. Yin, and Michael Kurlaender. 2006. "Implications of Income-Based School Assignment Policies for Racial School Segregation." *Educational Evaluation and Policy Analysis* 28(1): 49–76.

Rouse, Cecilia E. 1998. "Private School Vouchers and Student Achievement: An Evaluation of the Milwaukee Parental Choice Program." *Quarterly Journal of Economics* 113(2): 553–602.

Saporito, Salvatore. 2003. "Private Choices, Public Consequences: Magnet School Choice and Segregation by Race and Poverty." *Social Problems* 50(2): 181–203.

Sass, Tim. 2006. "Charter Schools and Student Achievement in Florida." *Education Finance and Policy* 1(1): 91–122.

Scafidi, Benjamin, David L. Sjoquist, and Todd R. Stinebrickner. 2002. "The Impact of Wages and School Characteristics on Teacher Mobility and Retention." Unpublished paper. Georgia State University.

Chapter 9

What We've Learned About Stalled Progress in Closing the Black-White Achievement Gap

RONALD F. FERGUSON

Overcoming academic, social, and economic disparities between blacks and whites in the United States is an aspiration that dates back to when teaching a black person to read was against the law—an act of civil disobedience. Even then, before the emancipation, some people dared challenge the idea that race should determine a person's destiny. There have been many successes in living out this aspiration. American blacks have performed outstandingly at all levels of society and in all walks of life. At the same time, blacks as a group remain overrepresented among the poor and the incarcerated. As a group, they remain underrepresented at high school graduations, on college campuses, and in jobs that require and reward academic achievement.

Less than half a century from now, blacks and other nonwhites will make up the majority of the U.S. population and it is important that being black not remain so strong a predictor of negative life outcomes. Success will depend at least in part on the types of learning that academic test scores measure. As Katherine Magnuson and Jane Waldfogel explain in the introduction, test scores are key predictors of success across a broad range of social and economic domains, including labor market earnings. They will therefore be key precursors of how well the United States fares in its long-term national pursuit to vanquish racial disparities.

Before 1970, it was easy for many to believe that racial differences in ability were immutable facts of nature and the quest for racial equality a naive dream. Some defend this position even today. Fortunately, evidence has accumulated since 1970 to justify cautious optimism that the black-white achievement gap can someday be closed. Much of the evidence comes from the National Assessment of Educational Progress Long Term Trend Assessment (NAEP-LTT), mandated by the U.S. Congress in the 1960s and launched as a national testing series in 1971. As other chapters in this volume have explained, it is the only nationally representative source of trend data on academic performance, including breakdowns by racial and gender groups.

Between 1971 and 1988, the black-white reading score gap in NAEP-LTT for nine-, thirteen-, and seventeen-year-olds narrowed by 34, 54, and 62 percent, respectively. Between 1973 and 1990, the black-white gap in NAEP-LTT math scores for the same three age groups narrowed by 23, 41, and 48 percent. Further, William Dickens and James Flynn have produced evidence of a 25 percent narrowing of the black-white IQ gap between 1972 and 2002 (2005). These findings confirm that even IQ tests are skills tests, not gauges of innate, immutable ability. Finally, using the Early Childhood Longitudinal Survey Birth Cohort, Roland Fryer and Steven Levitt (2007) present evidence that racial differences in mental ability are essentially absent just prior to infants' first birthdays.

Despite all of these reasons to be hopeful, the problem that this volume confronts is that progress in narrowing black-white test score differences has been uneven over time. For teenagers in particular, researchers, parents, activists, and policy makers still seek to understand why progress stalled around 1990. In this, the final chapter in the volume, I review what we have learned from the varying contributions to this collection and offer a few additional ideas.

As we proceed, it is useful to keep in mind three things that need to be true about a phenomenon for it to contribute to the narrowing or expansion of the black-white test score gap over time. First, the phenomenon needs to be something that actually affects achievement, as measured by test scores. Second, it needs to be something that can differ for blacks and whites, with regard to either level or impact—even when groups have or experience the same levels, it may have a greater impact. Third, the phenomenon needs to be something that has changed over time for at least one of the groups, either in magnitude or in how much any given magnitude matters in determining test scores.

This volume examines a number of phenomena that might plausibly fit the cited criteria. The story that emerges is nuanced and hopeful, adding to our understanding even as it highlights remaining puzzles.

Income Inequality and Family Background Effects

Three chapters in this book offer new evidence on ways that income inequality and family background characteristics may have influenced test scores and black-white achievement gaps over the past few decades. In chapter 1, Katherine Magnuson, Dan Rosenbaum, and Jane Waldfogel focus on nine-year-olds' reading and math scores in the NAEP-LTT. In chapter 2, Mark Berends and Roberto Peñaloza track predictors of math scores across four cohorts of high school seniors from 1972 to 2004. In chapter 3, Mary Campbell, Robert Haveman, Tina Wildhagen, and Barbara Wolfe study vocabulary scores among youth from the National Longitudinal Study of Adolescent Health (Add Health). Each considers aspects of family and community resources other than simply income, but each also reaches conclusions about the importance of income or income inequality as an explanation for changes in black-white test score disparities.[1] I first consider their findings on the effects of income inequality and associated disparities, and then on parental income and education and other aspects of family background.

Income Inequality

Growing income inequality in the American economy, including race-based income inequality, has been a theme in public discourse over the past two decades, but its possible role in affecting achievement disparities has gone largely unexamined. Income disparities have grown between the middle and the bottom of the distribution and also from the middle to the top. Gaps have grown most between the middle and the top, as the highest incomes have risen most rapidly (see figures I.1 through I.9).

In chapter 1 of this volume, Magnuson, Rosenbaum, and Waldfogel are interested in whether growing inequality in the economy may have contributed to the black-white test score gap between nine-year-olds. The authors justify focusing on nine-year-olds by citing the growing evidence, which David Grissmer and Elizabeth Eiseman also emphasize in their chapter, that most of the test score gap develops before children enter school and during the first few years of schooling. Preschool and the first few years of elementary school are years that one would expect the family and its experience with inequality to have the greatest impact on achievement, as compared with the influence of school and peers. If inequality affects achievement in this context, it probably operates mainly through its impact on parenting. However, it could also affect achievement-related social norms and public policies, if the collective commitment to children through finances for schools, health care, or out-of-school programs were somehow affected.

Magnuson, Rosenbaum, and Waldfogel summarize a number of reasons to believe that income inequality might matter, ranging from the affordability of resources for learning at home, to possible feelings of relative deprivation that might affect judgments about effort and educational investments. Citing Richard Freeman and Alexander Gelber (2006) and Susan Mayer (2001), they make the important point that effects on effort might be either positive or negative. For example, Mayer compared states from 1970 to 1990 and found evidence that greater state-level income inequality appeared to decrease rates at which lower income students enrolled in and graduated from college. Conversely, greater inequality appeared to increase enrollment and graduation rates among youths from higher income families. Again, there are a number of mechanisms through which such effects might operate.

In chapter 1, the authors use a cross-sectional time-series panel of test scores and family characteristics from the NAEP-LTT. They augment it with racially specific state-level data on average family characteristics from the March Current Population Survey (CPS). Generally, they assign black nine-year-olds the state-level averages of selected family characteristics for blacks and do the same for whites. Their measures of income inequality, however, use data from the overall (not race-specific) family income distribution in the state. The measures form one measure that is the ratio of the 50th percentile to the 10th percentile income (the 50:10 ratio) and another that is the ratio of the 90th to the 10th percentile (the 90:10 ratio).

The greater is state-level income inequality among families, the more depressed are nine-year-olds' reading and math test scores for both blacks and whites. The similarity of impacts across racial groups indicates that there was little if any effect on black-white test score gaps. When the authors segmented the sample by the level of parental education that the student reported, they found roughly the same predicted effect of inequality on math outcomes for each parental education level. For reading, they found the most negative effects of inequality for children of the least educated parents, and little if any effect for parents with more than high school degrees.[2]

Although statistically significant, the effects on test scores that Magnuson, Rosenbaum, and Waldfogel find for income inequality are generally quite small. By 2004, scores would have been 1 point higher in reading (the reading standard deviation is 41 points) and 2 points higher in math (the math standard deviation is 36 points) if income inequality, measured by the 50:10 ratio, had remained at its 1978 level. The fact that they find any effect at all is interesting. Nonetheless, there is little support in their findings for the idea that inequality, per se, affected the black-white achievement gap.

In chapter 3, Campbell, Haveman, Wildhagen, and Wolfe predict vocabulary test scores of nineteen- to twenty-four-year-olds, interviewed in wave 3 of the Add Health survey during 2001 and 2002. The family and school measures that the authors use as predictors come from seven years earlier in 1994 and 1995, when the youths were surveyed as middle and high school students as part of wave 1. The authors include in their analysis a measure of family income inequality at the school level, based on data collected in parent interviews. The variable the authors use is the ratio of family incomes at the 90th and 10th percentiles in the school—the 90:10 ratio.

They find that the effect of school-level income inequality is to significantly lower scores for blacks and to slightly raise scores for whites: "If the average black student experienced the same level of inequality in their school as the average white student (a 90:10 ratio of 9.0 instead of 11.4), the full model would predict a statistically significant increase in their test score rank." The difference would equal a 7 percent reduction in the black-white gap.

It is important to point out that there may not be much correlation between school-level inequality and inequality in the state or nation. Still, this finding that greater school level inequality has different effects on blacks and whites is reminiscent of the findings in Mayer (2001). In Mayer, as indicated, rates of college enrollment and completion among students in the bottom half of the income distribution (where blacks are overrepresented) declined with increased state-level income inequality, and rates in the top half of the distribution rose. The effect was not mostly attributable to students' family income conditions, for which Mayer had good statistical controls. Similarly, recall the finding in Magnuson, Rosenbaum, and Waldfogel where, at least for reading, state-level inequality is associated with more negative outcomes for the children of the least educated parents. Although the effects are often small, each is a case in which the group on the lower side of the hierarchy fares worse under conditions of greater inequality, and those on the top side are unaffected or seem to be affected positively. The reasons remain unclear.

Ways that people respond to income inequality may be mediated and moderated by racial, social class, and gender identities and by such things as criminal justice system policies, the severity of drug problems in local neighborhoods, and images that news and entertainment outlets disseminate. Thus, income inequality is only one among a cluster of conditions that affect whether life seems fair and feasible for individuals, and whether the society seems just in its treatment of both individuals and groups. People may cope in a variety of ways with the feelings that this messy mix of phenomena engenders. As isolated individuals, they may feel more stressed and self-protective as conditions seem to deteriorate. However, as members of groups, they may reach out through various forms of social commentary and political action. Later in the chapter, I ask whether conditions associated with income disparities, escalating incarceration rates for black youth, the crack cocaine epidemic, and other forms of social inequality may have helped trigger shifts in youth behavior at the end of the 1980s and affected trends in achievement gains for both black and white teens through the 1990s.

Family Income

Beyond income disparity in the school, state, or national economy, family income (or poverty status, and so on) is an obvious candidate to consider with regard to all three of the criteria outlined for phenomena that could help explain trends in the gap. First, it is plausible that income affects school achievement through several channels. Second, its level and impact can differ by race. Third, it changes over time, sometimes at different rates for different groups.

In chapter 1, Magnuson, Rosenbaum, and Waldfogel include a race-specific state-level poverty rate in some of their equations predicting nine-year-olds' reading and math scores. In contrast to the state-level inequality measures discussed, the estimated effect of the race-specific poverty rate on reading scores is small and statistically insignificant. In the most basic form of the equation, the same measure has a large and statistically significant predicted effect on math scores. However, when other state-average family background variables are added to the equation for math scores, the estimated effect of the poverty measure drops by a almost half, its standard error rises, and it becomes statistically insignificant.

In chapter 3, Campbell, Haveman, Wildhagen, and Wolfe have a more direct measure of family income in their analysis, collected directly from parents. They find that the specification best suited for predicting vocabulary scores is one that allows the impact of income on scores to differ for families in three income ranges: below the poverty line, from the poverty line up to twice the poverty level, and above twice the poverty level. When the authors do not control for any other family or school background variables, income is a statistically significant predictor of vocabulary scores, but only if family income at the wave 1 interview was below twice the poverty level. When other school and family background measures are added, the estimated impact of income becomes smaller and statistically insignificant for both blacks and whites in all three income ranges.

In chapter 2, Berends and Peñaloza define income quintiles for measures in each of the four data sets they use to study high school seniors from 1972 to 2004. They find statistically significant effects of income in predicting math scores, even after controlling for other family background measures. The estimated effects of income grew stronger in later years, especially in the top two quintiles.[3] Still, the simulated effect of family income on changes in the black-white test score gap is small.

Concerning the conditions set out above for affecting test score gaps, it is clear that the first obtains: black-white gaps in family income exist. However, concerning the second condition, the evidence that income per se affects achievement levels is at best mixed when a parental education measure is included in the analysis. Two of the studies here produce weak results for income effects on achievement, but Berends and Peñaloza find stronger effects. Of course, if our goal is to understand changes in achievement gaps, whether family income predicts achievement does not matter if there is minimal change over time in the family income gap.

Have black-white disparities in family income grown? According to the U.S. Census data for 1970 and 2000, mean family income for blacks grew from $31,857 in 1970 to $40,628 in the year 2000 (adjusted to 2000 dollars). This is a 27.5 percent increase in real income. Mean family income for whites grew from $50,780 in 1970 to $64,150 in 2000, for a 26.3 percent increase. Although blacks gained slightly more in percentage terms, whites gained $4,599 more in absolute purchasing power, thereby increasing income inequality in absolute terms. However, the ratio of black-to-white mean income rounds off to 63 percent in both 1970 and 2000. The similarity of income growth rates for blacks and whites in their data is probably why Berends and Peñaloza find small effects of income as a predictor of changes in the math achievement gap.

Campbell, Haveman, Wildhagen, and Wolfe emphasize that growing inequality in the economy has been driven most strongly by growth at the top of the distribution. At that end of the distribution, additional income growth may affect how many years of schooling parents buy for their children, but it does not have much effect on the children's test scores. "It appears," they write, "that there is a threshold effect; you cannot use huge incomes to buy test scores, even if you can use them to buy other important educational outcomes, such as educational attainment [that is, years of schooling]." Income growth for blacks and whites is more similar in parts of the distribution where higher income stands a better chance of raising scores.

Distinguishing Family Effects

Can we reliably distinguish the effects of family income from those of parental education, and the effects of both from the impacts of other family characteristics or resources? Not completely. Parental education, family income, household structure, numbers of children, social network supports, and other resources are typically correlated. Each tends to be measured with error in any particular study. Their relative importance can differ from one study to another in ways difficult to explain. In most cases, researchers tend to be less concerned with distinguishing the impact of any particular family background characteristic than with making sure to include as well-measured and complete a collection of family measures as possible. The central question is typically not how much parental education or income contributes as a separate variable, but instead how much family resources collectively matter to the outcome under study.

Nonetheless, for predicting test scores, parental education is often the strongest predictor among the available family background measures. As an indicator of the type of skills available for translation into earnings over time (which determine family income), parental education can be an even better income measure than actual monetary measures—it can be a proxy for what economists call permanent income.[4]

Parental Education and Other Family Characteristics

In chapter 1, Magnuson, Rosenbaum, and Waldfogel use racially specific, state-average measures from the CPS for parental education and other family background measures as well as two measures reported by student test takers. The student-reported measures are parental education and whether the family receives a newspaper. The authors test whether their student-reported measure of parental education predicts test scores as strongly for blacks as for whites. Like Ronald Ferguson (2007), Roland Fryer and Steven Levitt (2004), and Selcuk Sirin (2005), they find a smaller achievement payoff to parental education for blacks than for whites. The effect they estimate is almost one-third smaller for blacks than for whites. Because black parents, on average, have less education than white parents, the gap in parental education predicts less of the black-white test score gap than it would if the estimated impact of parents' education on children's achievement were as great for blacks as for whites. Even so, Magnuson, Rosenbaum, and Waldfogel estimate that the black-white parental education gap predicts about one-sixth of the base year black-white test score difference for both reading and math.[5] In addition, for math (but not reading) scores, parental education predicts between 10 and 20 percent of the gains that white students achieved from the 1980s to the 1990s and about a quarter of the gap-narrowing that blacks achieved in comparison to whites over the same period.

Beyond the student-reported measure of parental education, the within-race state-average measures of mothers' education that Magnuson, Rosenbaum, and Waldfogel take from the CPS are important predictors of scores for both reading and math—more than a third of the base-year math gap between blacks and whites and a sixth of the base-year reading gap. They also predict some of the gains that both groups achieved over time and some of the narrowing of the black-white score gap in math. However, because the CPS measures are state averages, it is difficult to know with any confidence what the mechanisms might be through which these predicted effects are generated. They could include a variety of factors outside the family.

Parental education measures in chapters 2 and 3 are easier to interpret. As introduced, the Berends and Peñaloza study in chapter 2 uses data for twelfth graders in 1972, 1982, 1992 and 2004, from four nationally representative longitudinal samples. Their data do not include 1990, the year that black math scores for seventeen-year-olds peaked in the NAEP-LTT. Otherwise, however, the narrowing of the black-white math-score gap that Berends and Peñaloza track over the twenty-two years of their study closely approximates that found in the NAEP-LTT. Berends and Peñaloza find that the narrowing of parental education gaps predicts about a fifth of the decrease in the black-white math score gap that transpired for twelfth graders between 1972 and 2004. Relatively greater improvement for blacks in parental occupational status also predicts narrowing of the gap in math achievement.

Campbell, Haveman, Wildhagen, and Wolfe find in chapter 3 that not only do one's parents' education levels matter, friends' parents matter as well, and to about the same degree. Recall that the dependent variable in chapter 3 is vocabulary scores for older teens and young adults. A one-year increase in parental education in these authors' results predicts a 1.6 percent increase in the young person's vocabulary score. The size of this effect doubles if his or her friends' parents also have an additional year of education.

Confirmation of Earlier Studies

Findings in this volume build on the work of several previous research teams that studied the importance of parental income and education and other socioeconomic measures as possible predictors of black-white test score convergence in the 1970s and 1980s (see Cook and Evans 1998; Grissmer, Flanagan, and Williamson 1998; Hedges and Nowell 1998). These studies concluded that one reason for test score convergence was that black-white gaps in parents' education and family size had narrowed for children who attended elementary and secondary schools in the United States between 1970 and 1990. Conversely, during the same two decades, blacks suffered more decline than whites in the percentages of children living in two-parent households and with older, more mature mothers. The latter trends partially offset the beneficial impacts of rising parental education and falling family size. Income growth was similar for blacks and whites and therefore did not seem to contribute to changing test score disparities.

Each of the earlier studies concluded that parental education, in particular, was responsible for at least some of the narrowing that occurred in the black-white achievement gap from the early 1970s to the late 1980s. They agreed as well that their estimates left most of the narrowing that occurred during the 1980s unexplained.

The chapters in this volume track scores through 2004, but the basic conclusions of the earlier studies remain intact. Family background variables, especially parental education, help predict achievement. Narrowing of gaps in parental education, in particular, has contributed to the narrowing of black-white test score gaps. Certain turning points in the test score series, however, are not predicted by parental education or other socioeconomic variables. We must therefore look elsewhere for more nuanced explanations.

Segregation

Did desegregation help narrow the black-white achievement gap? Is reseg-regation an explanation for stalled progress? There is agreement that segregation declined between 1970 and 1990, during the period of most rapid progress. The average white student attended a school that was 86 percent white in 1968 and 83 percent white in 1990. Meanwhile, the average black student's school was 19 percent white in 1968 and 34 percent white in 1990 (Logan 2004). In chapter 5, Jacob Vigdor and Jens Ludwig report that "the best available evidence suggests that a 10 percent increase in the black share of a school's student body would reduce the achievement test scores for black students by between 0.025 and 0.08 standard deviation, and reduce test scores for whites by perhaps one-quarter to two-fifths as much."

The numbers in the last paragraph are the basis for a simple (and very rough) estimate of how much difference desegregation made from 1968 to 1990. If we use the 15 percent that John Logan (2004) reports for increased integration (that is, 34 percent white classmates in 1990 in −19 percent in 1968) and assume for simplicity that desegregation did not reduce whites' scores, then the expected change in the black-white score gap due to deseg-regation between 1968 and 1990 is roughly 0.04 to 0.12 standard deviation. How do these numbers compare to the actual gap reductions in the 1970s and 1980s? We will use the 0.12 standard deviation impact estimate to get an upper bound and we will assume that it applies equally to reading and math. Then, for nine-, thirteen- and seventeen-year-olds respectively, desegregation may have accounted for up to 50 percent of the reduction in the black-white math score gap for nine-year-olds and up to 20 percent of that for thirteen- and seventeen-year-olds.[6] For reading, desegregation may have accounted for up to 30 percent of the reduction for nine-year-olds, 25 percent of the reduction for thirteen-year-olds, and 15 percent of the reduction for seventeen-year-olds.

Has there been resegregation since 1990? Reports of resegregation center on facts such as the following: the percentage white students in schools that blacks attend declined from 34 percent in 1990 to 29 percent by 2000. Whether the decline represents resegregation of blacks is a topic of active debate. If the percentage white in schools that whites attend did not increase, then some would prefer not to label the decline in black exposure to whites as resegregation. Instead, they would say simply that blacks have less exposure to whites. Logan (2004) reports that the average white student attended a school that was 86 percent white in 1968, dropping to 83 percent in 1990 and to 79 percent in 2000. In chapter 5, Jacob Vigdor and Jens Ludwig argue that studies such as Clotfelter (2004) and Orfield and Eaton (1996), which emphasize the increasing average percentage of nonwhite children in the schools that black children attend, "confound the increasing diversity of the student body in the American public schools with increases in the separation of blacks from students of other races."

Vigdor and Ludwig report that for the average black student in public schools, the percentage black among schoolmates dropped from 51.5 percent in 1987 to 48.3 percent by 2003. Blacks also became less exposed to whites, because of the increased percentages of Hispanics and Asians in the schools they attended.

If, as Vigdor and Ludwig argue, increased concentration of blacks in schools that other blacks attend should be the emphasis of discussions about black resegregation, then the conclusions should be that there was little if any resegregation during the 1990s, except in particular school districts. However, if isolation from whites is the issue, then Vigdor and Ludwig agree that isolation of this nature did increase from the late 1980s to the present. Whether increases in this type of isolation tend to depress test scores and increase black-white achievement gaps is an empirical question.

The Berends and Peñaloza chapter offers at least one piece of evidence on the question for twelfth graders. Their racial composition measure is the proportion minority in the schools that their survey respondents attended. For 1972, 1982, 1992, and 2004, respectively, the proportions minority in schools that white twelfth graders attended were 0.17, 0.21, 0.18, and 0.14. Hence, at least in these samples, it appears that whites after 1982 became more segregated not just from blacks but from minorities more generally. For blacks in the same four years, the proportions minority were 0.38, 0.37, 0.42, and 0.60.[7]

The Berends-Peñaloza estimates indicate that the increased proportion minority for black twelfth graders over the twelve years from 1992 to 2004 fully offsets the estimated effects that more parental education and better occupational status had over the thirty-two years from 1972 to 2004 on reducing the black-white math score gap. Their estimates indicate that the math score gap in 2004 would have been 0.14 standard deviation smaller if the proportions minority in 2004 were the same as in 1972. To put this in perspective, 0.14 standard deviation equates to about 15 percent of the black-white math score gap among twelfth graders in 2004.

The focus of the Vigdor and Ludwig study is on black segregation from nonblacks, not black segregation from whites. They point out that school segregation of blacks from nonblacks remained mostly unchanged during the 1990s, but that residential segregation of blacks from nonblacks was reduced. They report that if school segregation of blacks from nonblacks had been reduced as much as neighborhood segregation, then their "best estimate is that the black-white test score gap would be roughly 0.01 to 0.02 standard deviation narrower." This is a very small amount.

Thus it seems that Vigdor and Ludwig come to different conclusions than Berends and Peñaloza do on whether increased segregation contributed to stalled progress on closing black-white achievement gaps after the late 1980s. Perhaps the differences are because the Berends and Peñaloza estimates concern the effects for blacks of being segregated with nonwhites, away from whites, and Vigdor and Ludwig's focus is on the effects of being segregated with other blacks, away from nonblacks.

Teacher Quality

One mechanism through which segregation might have an effect on achievement gaps is that schools where blacks and other nonwhites are more represented may attract and hire teachers with lower qualifications (Ferguson 1998a). Or, the average effort that teachers expend may differ depending upon whom they are teaching, perhaps because of lower expectations for students from particular backgrounds (Ferguson 1998b). For example, Sean Corcoran and William Evans find in chapter 6 that teachers of the average white student are at school the same number of hours per week as teachers of the average black student. However, there is a difference outside of school hours: teachers of the average white student devote 0.80 hours more per week outside of school.

Concerning teacher quality, Corcoran and Evans conclude that "the teachers of the average black student are consistently more likely to be inexperienced, uncertified, and unhappy with their career choice than teachers of the average white student." The authors acknowledge that such differences tend to have only small estimated effects on black-white score gaps in standard cross-section analyses at single points in time. However, they remind readers that over a child's twelve years in elementary and secondary school, small annual effects of poor teaching may accumulate.

Concerning changes in the quality of instruction, Corcoran and Evans report "no evidence to suggest that changes in exposure to high-quality teachers adversely affected the black-white achievement gap during the 1990s." This is because quality patterns were mostly unchanged.[8]

Youth Cultures, School Cultures, and Stalled Progress

The topics covered so far can help explain achievement levels at points in time and basic trends over time in achievement disparities, but probably not sudden fluctuations around longer term trajectories. Some aspects of the stalled progress at the end of the 1980s, for example, ups and downs in reading scores for black seventeen-year-olds, seemed sudden and jerky.[9] Also, the time paths differed for reading and math. How might teen cultures enter the story? Teenage cultures express themselves to a substantial degree around phenomena that have the character of fashions.

New teen fashions can spread quickly across the entire nation, as can fashions in school rules, grading, instruction, and curriculum.

In chapter 7 of this volume, Meredith Phillips takes up the question of whether shifts in youth behaviors might help explain stalled progress in closing the black-white achievement gap. It is worth emphasizing that this is not the same as asking whether black youth or their families are to blame. Youth cultures and school cultures are subcultures of larger societies. Like the larger macro culture, youth and school cultures have subcultures that have subcultures that have subcultures. Any culture or subculture is a way of being—a collection of beliefs, behaviors, and preoccupations that are shared among members and to which they tend to conform. No single entity has the power to set the norms to which participants are held informally accountable. All of this is to say that consideration of culture as a source of achievement differences is not about blaming groups or individuals.

What Might School and Youth Cultures Help Explain?

Meredith Phillips did not find any noteworthy evidence of black-white differences in behavior trends for thirteen-year-olds.[10] Perhaps blacks and whites in this age range were engaged to similar degrees in learning. With the exception of the middle to late 1980s and 2004, the ups and downs in gains follow similar patterns for blacks and whites. Some small differences are that, for most cohorts, blacks' reading scores tend to rise a bit more than whites' and whites' math scores tend to rise a bit more than blacks' during the nine-to-thirteen age bracket.

It seems likely that shifting emphases in school improvement efforts might help account for why reading and math gains tend to move in opposite directions for both blacks and whites. Reading gains were falling from the 1970s through the middle 1980s, at the same time that math gains were rising (see the synthetic cohort charts in the introduction). Then reading gains were flat for both racial groups through the 1990s while math gains were falling. It seems very likely that this pattern is grounded to a large degree in what was happening across the nation with instruction. It is possible that a cycle in the culture of instruction periodically shifts the relative emphasis on reading versus math improvement in the upper elementary and middle school grades.

If we seek culture-related explanations for stalled progress toward closing black-white achievement gaps among teenagers, the point should be mainly to learn why, and in what ways, youth, family, or school cultures motivated or enabled blacks during the middle to late 1980s and again in 2004, to gain more than whites as they matured from ages nine to thirteen.

Similarly, with regard to high school math gains, the big story is that blacks substantially outgained whites during the 1970s and 1980s. Then, blacks and whites had roughly equal gains for the cohort that reached seventeen years of age in 1994. Both groups trended downward after 1994. The stalled progress was that blacks had failed to sustain gains that were greater than those for whites, and then both blacks and whites seemed to drift downward in the gains they achieved as teenagers. This downward drift needs to be understood for both groups.

The most interesting patterns are for reading. Total reading score trends for black and white seventeen-year-olds during the 1970s were essentially flat, with scores by 1980 only slightly better than those in 1971 or 1975. In addition to a stagnant trend, blacks' gains of fewer than 20 points from ages thirteen to seventeen seemed meager compared to whites' gains of just over 30. Blacks at age seventeen in 1980 were 50 points (1.25 standard deviations) behind whites. Progress then turned sharply upward for blacks. Reading scores for the cohort that reached seventeen years of age in 1984 rose by 31 points from the time the cohort was thirteen years old in 1980. This equaled what white peers gained over the same period. Scores for blacks who were seventeen-year-olds in 1988 rose by even more—38 points—from the time that the cohort was thirteen-year-olds in 1984. This latter gain was more than whites achieved from ages thirteen to seventeen at any time and it caused the achievement gap to narrow.

After the 1988 cohort of black seventeen-year-olds achieved such outstanding gains, the 1992 cohort performed quite poorly. Consider blacks who turned seventeen in 1988, versus 1992. As nine-year-olds, the two cohorts were only 3 points apart at 189 and 186, respectively. As thirteen-year-olds, those who were seventeen-year-olds in 1992 had scored 10 points higher than the 1988 cohort of seventeen-year-olds had scored as thirteen-year-olds. Despite this lead at age thirteen, the 1992 cohort of black seventeen-year-olds made meager gains during their teen years. Their 18-point gain from ages thirteen to seventeen was less than half the 38-point gain by the older cohort.

Consecutive cohorts of black teens after 1992 gradually recovered from the low performance of 1992, but never returned to the level of performance achieved in the middle to late 1980s. Also, white gains declined after 1992 in reading and after 1994 in math.

Evidence for Some Plausible Explanations

Why was there was such a sudden collapse of reading scores for black teens at the end of the 1980s? And why was the recovery after 1992 so anemic? Why did whites' gains also seem to be drifting downward after the early 1990s, after having risen modestly by the early 1990s?

In chapter 7, Meredith Phillips explores whether there may have been parenting or behavior shifts to help account for stalled progress. As I indicated above, she finds no evidence of such shifts for thirteen-year-olds. However, she does find some evidence of behavior changes for seventeen-year-olds:

> In contrast, the data for seventeen-year-olds are consistent with the idea that increases in problem behaviors among blacks may have played some role in halting black progress. The NAEP-LTT data suggest that black seventeen-year-olds were more likely to get into trouble at school in 1994 than in 1988 and the MTF data that they were more likely to have been involved in violent conflicts. White seventeen-year-olds' behavior changed less over this period, so the black-white gap in problem behavior widened.

Phillips found only mixed evidence on whether leisure reading changed in ways that seem likely to have contributed to stalled progress.

Here I introduce two additional pieces of evidence on changes in behavior, both from the Monitoring the Future Survey (MTF). This, as Phillips explains in chapter 7, is an annual national survey of high school seniors, focused mostly on substance use, but also covering a variety of lifestyle and time-use topics.

The MTF survey asks students whether they have cut any classes during the month before the survey (see figure 9.1). Spread across the years since 1976, a total of more than 60,000 blacks and 360,000 whites have answered the class-cutting question. From the late 1970s through the first few years of the twenty-first century, the percentage of black respondents reporting that they never cut class was highest from 1984 through 1988, the same years that black thirteen- to seventeen-year-olds experienced their peak reading-score gains and when math gains for this age group were high as well. During this period, about 5 percent more blacks than whites reported that they never cut class. Class attendance then dropped for blacks, but not whites, from 1988 to 1992—the four years when black teens made only meager reading-score gains and whites reached their peak. By 1992, the gap in class attendance was about the same as from 1984 to 1988, but the group on top had flipped; whites were more likely than blacks to report that they never cut class.

Further, there was a correlation with grades. The number of black students reporting that they never cut class fell the most for students with lowest grade point averages, though it fell somewhat even for students with GPAs of A or A-minus. For whites, class attendance was steady from 1984 through 1992, then drifted downward a bit during the early 1990s. For black and white high school seniors, in 1996 they had almost identical score gains from ages thirteen to seventeen and similarly close rates of class attendance. After 1997, class attendance rose for whites and fell for blacks for several years.

Figure 9.1   Black and White Twelfth Graders Who Did Not Cut Class in Month Before Survey

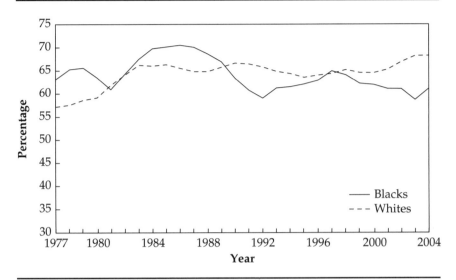

Source: Author's compilation from the Monitoring the Future Survey.
Note: Smoothed using a three-year moving average.

Next, there is an interesting pattern of grade inflation in the MTF data. Figure 9.2 shows percentages of students reporting GPAs in each of three grade ranges: the A range, the B range, and the C range or lower. From 1984 through about 1988, about 40 percent of black students reported C-range or lower grade point averages. This was of course the period of high score gains. Then, during the 1988 to 1992 interval, the percentage with C-range or lower GPAs fell and the percentage with A- and B-range GPAs rose. Statistical regression analysis indicates a distinctly steeper decline in C-range or lower GPAs for black high school seniors during these four years compared to the time just before or just afterward.

Thus, for black youth who were high school students between 1988 and 1992, the NAEP-LTT tells us there were meager achievement gains in reading (though math gains were not bad), class attendance was drifting downward more rapidly than before, and grades were drifting upward.

When grades are drifting upward but gains in achievement are drifting in the other direction, there may be some grade inflation. This seems to have happened not only for blacks, but also for whites. The charts in the introduction show that test score gains for whites in the thirteen- to seventeen-year-old age range drifted downward in reading after 1992 and then for both reading and math after 1994. Figure 9.2 suggests that 1992 is the year grade inflation began in earnest for whites. The percent-

Figure 9.2   Blacks and White Twelfth Grade Reporting GPAs in Each Range

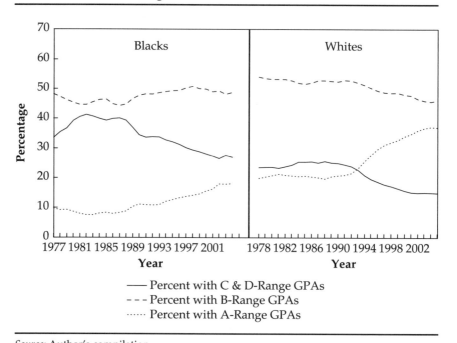

Source: Author's compilation.
Note: Three-year moving averages.

age of white seniors with A-range GPAs rose from about 23 percent in 1992 to 37 percent by 2004. At the same time, their gains in reading and math were drifting downward.

It seems clear that factors contributing to achievement for black and white teenagers during the 1980s and 1990s went beyond the rise in their parents' education levels or changes in the racial compositions of the schools they attended, though the latter were probably important. Exactly what those additional factors were and how they affected achievement are things for which current knowledge only scratches the surface (Neal 2006). In another volume, I speculate in more detail about the importance of rap music's rise to prominence during 1988 to 1992 (2001). Glenn Loury (2007) has countered that the flooding of black neighborhoods with men returning from prisons may be part of the story as well. The crack-cocaine epidemic that began in 1984 is implicated in both hip-hop music messages of the time and the historically high rates of black men circulating through the prisons system. All these things and more, including the rise in economic inequality discussed earlier in this chapter, may have affected black youths' behaviors and preoccupations in ways that influenced their achievement gains and helped retard progress toward closing achievement gaps.

Finally, part of the reason black youth who reached age seventeen in the late 1980s scored so well on the NAEP-LTT reading and math exams is that, compared to previous cohorts, they were ahead by age nine. Further, part of the reason people have mostly failed to notice a downward drift in four-year gains by both black and white adolescents in the NAEP-LTT math test is that the upward drift in the foundations established by age nine has been propping up the scores observed at ages thirteen and seventeen. It seems that high schools have maintained constant performance targets even though elementary schools have sent up better prepared students. We need secondary school cultures that work to build more effectively on the improvements that our elementary schools are achieving.

Gains Before Age Nine (or Five or Two)

I have saved for last a topic that in the long run may be the most important for closing the black-white achievement gap. The brief treatment that I give it here is not an indication of its relative importance. It is what David Grissmer and Elizabeth Eiseman cover in chapter 4—early learning.

Grissmer and Eiseman do not address the question of why progress stalled during the school years. Instead, they are concerned with the importance of social, emotional, and motor skills that develop interactively with the cognitive skills that test scores later measure. The authors review the existing literature and add several additional estimates to suggest that "fine motor skills and approaches to learning, then, but not social skills, would seem to be much more strongly linked to cognitive measures of reading readiness at kindergarten entrance than any single family characteristic." They continue: "Black children have large gaps in these noncognitive skills compared to white children, and the differences would predict up to 40 percent of the math and reading gap at kindergarten entrance."

Grissmer and Eiseman use data from three sets of children—identical twins, nonidentical twins, and unrelated pairs—to test for genetic bases of the various skills they use for predicting kindergarten readiness scores. Based on their analysis, they conclude that the fine motor skills and learning characteristics so important for kindergarten readiness "have little or no genetic influence" and are shaped almost entirely by differences in the environments that children experience between their first day in the world and their first day at school. Therefore, making early learning environments as effectively nurturing as possible should be a priority.

The agenda for research, policy, and practice that Grissmer and Eiseman propose is in very early stages of development. Theirs is among a collection of new interdisciplinary efforts to understand deeply how social, psychological, and physiological processes work together in learning environments to affect early childhood development across multiple skill domains. This is exciting work. It will be important to develop effective mechanisms for disseminating emerging insights to parents and early childhood caregivers. At the same time, through research such as that which Grissmer and Eiseman report in their chapter, we need to stay serious about expanding what we know.

Black-white achievement gaps are clearly present on average by the age of three, but Grissmer and Eiseman remind us that recent evidence indicates equal measured abilities across racial groups in infancy, just before children's first birthdays (Fryer and Levitt 2007). By focusing on the learning that begins in infancy, before racial skill gaps have developed, the Grissmer-Eiseman chapter contributes evidence and recommendations aimed at preventing the black-white achievement gap from ever opening. The authors suggest that with a focused research agenda around the issues they highlight, we can develop the knowledge to give many more children successful launches in life and that this in turn may well inspire the political will to build the required vehicles. They also warn that without attending to differences in early childhood learning environments, we may never close the gap.

School Policies

Among all the learning environments that children inhabit, school classrooms are the ones for which we agree to take the greatest collective responsibility as a society. It is therefore appropriate to inquire whether the achievement trends and gaps that this book considers have been and can be significantly affected by schooling policies. Certainly, school policies can affect achievement, their impacts on schooling experiences can differ for children on opposite sides of the achievement gap, and they can change over time.

Based on a variety of research and practical wisdom, there are reasons to expect that students will learn more when their teachers are more skilled and hard working, when their class sizes permit ample individualized attention, and when the teaching staff and student body are stable enough that teaching, learning, and school improvement in the building can be cumulative. Policies have thus been established over the past few decades that aim to improve teachers' skills, give them incentives to work hard, reduce class sizes, and help reduce turnover of both students and teachers.

Helen Ladd's chapter does a good job of reviewing a number of such policies and the research evidence for the impacts they have had. In particular, she considers "policies and strategies that have been proposed or justified—at least in part—on the basis of their potential for reducing black-white test score gaps." She concludes that "not all the proposed strategies are likely to be effective . . . and their net effect on the size of the gap is likely to be relatively small." At the same time, she asserts that along with efforts to deal with broader social forces, "school-related strategies are a necessary component of any overall effort to reduce such gaps." There are some reasons to be hopeful, but not much to be excited about.

We can do better. Although class size, funding, accountability, school choice, and other relatively easy-to-mandate policies will continue to receive attention in public discourse, I expect that the focus of attention concerning schools over the next decade will shift. Like high-performance organizations in the private sector, the driving goal will need to be quality improvement at the point of production. Technologic and competitive pressures in the private sector forced many firms in the American business sector through this type of transformation from the late 1970s through the 1990s. Policy matters, but not in the absence of a broader change in social consciousness and priorities.

To produce more high-performance schools, I expect a closer focus on issues of teacher selection and retention and on the identification, refinement and implementation of effective instructional practices. These will require stronger school cultures and leadership, supported by public policies that allocate resources with these purposes in mind. We know for a fact that some schools are much more effective than others at helping children from a diverse range of backgrounds to achieve at high levels. I see growing agreement (though not a consensus) among people who spend lots of time in schooling environments about the norms and practices that seem to account for school-to-school differences in how much children learn. I expect policies that support the distillation, dissemination, implementation, and evaluation of lessons from high-performance schools to play an increasingly prominent role over the next few decades.

Conclusion

There is not a single story of stalled progress. Still, the chapters of this volume support the plausibility of the proposition that more progress is possible—that what appeared to be stalled progress at the end of the 1980s was a set of fluctuations around a cluster of long-term trends toward closing the black-white achievement gap. But long-term progress is not inevitable. It is the product of ongoing, collective striving and our willingness to grope along together, motivated at least in part by the aspiration I discussed earlier in this chapter. The authors of this volume have tried to play their roles by searching for insights that others will find useful. One finishes the book with a sense that many forces affect the outcomes that concern us and we should strive to understand the issues broadly, not fixating too narrowly on one or another idea for how to avoid stalled progress in the future. We should be cautiously optimistic.

There is not a single story of stalled progress for reading and math. Reading skills improved faster for black than for white nine-year-olds during the 1970s, and this caused the achievement gap to narrow not only for nine-year-olds but also for the thirteen- and seventeen-year-olds that the nine-year-olds later became. Reading scores for nine-year-olds stopped improving around 1980 and sat still for the next twenty years before resuming their rise at the end of the 1990s, peaking in 2004. Meanwhile, math scores for nine-year-olds rose steadily. Progress toward closing the math achievement gap stalled for nine-year-olds after 1986 only because white children progressed as swiftly as blacks did. The engine that raised skill levels in math for nine-year-olds did not stall, however. Comparing reading and math for nine-year-olds, we know that there is not a single story of stalled progress. In the same way, at times over the past three decades, compared to the cohorts behind them, teenagers learned more math after age nine or thirteen but fewer reading skills, or expanded their reading skills but made less progress in math.

There is also not a single story of stalled progress across age groups. Efforts in the United States have raised the NAEP-LTT scores of nine-year-olds since the late 1990s in both reading and math, for both blacks and whites, and narrowed the black-white gap in both subjects. Indeed, among nine-year-olds, black-white achievement gaps in the NAEP-LTT were smaller for both reading and math in 2004 than ever before. At the same time, scores for black and white seventeen-year-olds have been stagnant for more than a decade. Additionally, black seventeen-year-olds were further behind white peers in both reading and math as of 2004 than they were at age nine in 1996. Effective high school reform and other measures to help teens to reach their potential are pressing needs.

As people struggle to make progress on the issues this book addresses, there is not a single story of striving. Instead, there are people in schools and homes and communities with scarce resources and competing priorities, working with varying degrees of effectiveness to give children experiences that will equip them along multiple dimensions to thrive in a future world that none of us has visited. The composite of their efforts produces the aggregate numbers we observe in the NAEP-LTT and other sources of achievement information. In the many stories hidden within the aggregate numbers, a common theme is that every community wants its children to excel, no matter their racial or ethnic identities. Narrowing gaps between groups will be sustainable over time as a national aspiration only if the goal of raising achievement among children from every racial and ethnic background is also stressed alongside closing the achievement gap. The nation's progress among nine-year-olds over the past several years is evidence that the two goals need not conflict.

The chapters in this volume do not explicitly articulate any particular menu of activities for raising achievement and closing gaps. It was never the intention that they would. Nonetheless, they implicate all of the following as ways of raising achievement levels and of reducing the likelihood that future progress will stall as often as it otherwise might:

- augment family resources, including but not limited to income, in ways that strengthen capacities for successful parenting
- avoid isolating children of any racial group in schools that serve only others like themselves
- avoid or offset huge income inequities
- provide children with competent and caring teachers who are willing to work hard
- help young people cope with social forces that might distort their judgment and support young people's efforts to cooperate and behave in ways that enable themselves and others to learn
- strengthen early learning environments to equip children with social, emotional, cognitive, and noncognitive skills that support kindergarten readiness
- connect children with adults and other youth who will care for them as part of an extended, nurturing community

Findings and discussions in this volume support each of these as points of emphasis.

All in all, most of what I already believed has survived my engagement with these authors. But I learned a few things as well.

Notes

1. Each is also careful to acknowledge uncertainty about the mechanisms through which income might affect achievement and about the ways that estimated effects of income may be due to omitted variable bias related to income-correlated factors not included in their analyses.
2. Perhaps this is related to the affordability of books. It resonates with the fact that while inequality grew most in the top half of the income distribution, the effect of income on achievement is probably greatest for the poorest families.
3. Specifically, in 1972 and 1982, a family income in the top two quintiles did not predict that math scores would be any different than if family income ranked in the middle quintile. By 1992, family income in the fifth (but not the fourth) quintile was a statistically significant predictor, as compared with the middle quintile. By 2004, both the fourth and fifth quintiles predicted scores that were higher by statistically significant margins, compared to the middle quintile of the family income distribution.
4. For example, looking backward, parents' education levels are correlated with the accumulated skill-building resources that family members have invested

over a child's lifetime, not just in the current year. Test scores measure some of the skills that the accumulated experiences enabled by family resources have produced. Looking forward, youngsters whose parents have more education have more reasons to be optimistic that, if they work hard, material, and informational supports will be available for making plans come true. We might therefore expect that children from more highly educated families will have higher scores because they have worked harder. Of course, there will be exceptions, since parental resources can also substitute for a child's own efforts.

5. The base years for the analysis are 1975 for reading and 1978 for math.

6. In standard deviation units, the reductions in the black-white math score gap from 1973 to 1990 were about 0.5 for nine-year-olds and 0.6 for thirteen- and seventeen-year-olds.

7. The jump in proportion minority for black twelfth graders from 0.42 in 1990 to 0.60 in 2004 is huge by any reasonable standard. It is also curious in these data that, for blacks, there was no meaningful reduction in exposure to minorities after 1972. The reasons are unclear.

8. In "Can Schools Narrow the Black-White Test Score Gap?" (1998a), I discussed reasons to believe that teacher quality rose more for blacks than for whites during the 1980s, before the period that Corcoran and Evans examine.

9. For nine-year-olds, the period when reading scores were improving and the black-white gap was narrowing had stopped ten years earlier, around 1980. Conversely, in math, nine-year-olds never experienced stalled growth for any sustained period. The math gap narrowed among nine-year-olds in those periods when blacks experienced faster score-growth than whites, and stabilized during those when black and white scores grew at similar rates. Explanations for why math and reading followed different patterns of progress for nine-year-olds are probably to be found in shifting cultures of basic skills instruction, but that is beyond the scope of this chapter.

10. Neither did she find any shifting behavioral trends: "Both before and after the test score gap stopped narrowing, black thirteen-year-olds spent similar amounts of time on pleasure reading, did similar amounts of homework, and got into similar amounts of trouble at school."

References

Clotfelter, Charles T. 2004. *After Brown: The Rise and Retreat of School Desegregation.* Princeton, N.J.: Princeton University Press.

Cook, Michael D., and William N. Evans. 2000. "Families or Schools? Explaining the Convergence in White and Black Academic Performance." *Journal of Labor Economics* 18(4): 729–54.

Dickens, William T., and James R. Flynn. 2005. "Black Americans Reduce the Racial IQ Gap: Evidence From Standardization Samples." Washington, D.C.: The Brookings Institution.

Ferguson, Ronald F. 1998a. "Can Schools Narrow the Black-White Test Score Gap?" In *The Black-White Test Score Gap*, edited by Christopher Jencks and Meredith Phillips. Washington, D.C.: Brookings Institution Press.

————. 1998b. "Teacher Perceptions and Expectations and the Black-White Test Score Gap." In *The Black-White Test Score Gap*, edited by Christopher Jencks and Meredith Phillips. Washington, D.C.: Brookings Institution Press.

————. 2001. "Racial Test-Score Trends 1971–1996, Popular Culture and Community Academic Standards." In *America Becoming: Racial Trends and Their Consequences*, edited by Neil Smelser, William Julius Wilson and Faith Mitchell. Washington, D.C.: National Academy Press.

————. 2007. *Toward Excellence with Equity: An Emerging Vision for Closing the Achievement Gap.* Cambridge, Mass.: Harvard Education Press.

Freeman, Richard B., and Alexander M. Gelber. 2006. "Optimal Inequality/ Optimal Incentives: Evidence from a Tournament." NBER Working Paper 12588. Cambridge, Mass.: National Bureau of Economic Research.

Fryer, Roland G., and Steven D. Levitt. 2004. "Understanding the Black-White Test Score Gap in the First Two Years of School" *Review of Economics and Statistics* 86(2): 447–64.

————. 2007. "Testing for Racial Differences in the Mental Ability of Young Children." Accessed at http://post.economics.harvard.edu/faculty/fryer/papers/fryer_levittbabiesrevision.pdf.

Grissmer, David, Ann Flanagan, and Stephanie Williamson. 1998. "Why Did the Black-White Test Score Gap Narrow in the 1970s and 1980s?" In *The Black-White Test Score Gap*, edited by Christopher Jencks and Meredith Phillips. Washington, D.C.: Brookings Institution Press.

Hedges, Larry V., and Amy Nowell. 1998. "Black-White Test Score Convergence since 1965." In *The Black-White Test Score Gap*, edited by Christopher Jencks and Meredith Phillips. Washington, D.C.: Brookings Institution Press.

Logan, John. 2004. "Resegregation in American Public Schools? Not in the 1990s." Albany, N.Y.: Mumford Center for Comparative Urban and Regional Research. Accessed at http://mumford.albany.edu/census/noresegregation/noresegregation01.htm.

Loury, Glenn C. 2007. "Racial Stigma, Mass Incarceration and American Values." Paper presented at the Tanner Lectures in Human Values. Stanford, Calif., April 4–5, 2007. Accessed at http://www.econ.brown.edu/fac/Glenn_Loury/louryhomepage.

Mayer, Susan E. 2001. "How Did the Increase in Economic Inequality Between 1970 and 1990 Affect Children's Educational Attainment?" *The American Journal of Sociology* 107(1): 1–32.

Neal, Derek A. 2006. "Why Has Black-White Skill Convergence Stopped?" In *Handbook of Economics of Education*, edited by Eric Hanushek and Finis Welch. Amsterdam: North-Holland.

Orfield, Gary, and Susan Eaton. 1996. *Dismantling Desegregation: The Quiet Reversal of Brown v. Board of Education.* New York: The New Press.

Sirin, Selcuk. 2005. "Socioeconomic Status and Academic Achievement: A Meta-Analytic Review of Research." *Review of Educational Research* 75(3): 417–53.

Index

Boldface numbers refer to figures and tables.

Aaronson, D., 199, 216, 217
accountability, school, 58, 302–7. *See also* No Child Left Behind Act (NCLB) (2001)
achievement: and desegregation, 113, 290–91; and executive function, 145; explanations for gaps in, 1–2; and family environment, 66; and family income, 35–37; measurement of, 42–43; and residential segregation, 114, 141–42; and school environment, 66; and socioeconomic characteristics, 34, 111, 182, 201. *See also* early childhood education and achievement, math skills and scores, and reading skills and scores
Add Health (National Longitudinal Study of Adolescent Health), 115–16
adolescent behavior and home environments: after-school supervision, 268–69, **270**; computers, 263, 275; data sources, 253, 280–81; disciplinary problems, 263–68, 280; homework, 251, 252, 260–61, 270–71; parenting practices, 269–71; racial differences, 250–53; reading for pleasure, 251, 252, 253–60, 273, 274–75; television, 251, 252, 261–63, 269–73, 275; test score gap, 271–80; videogames, 263

advanced degrees, in teaching, 215–16, 224
African Americans. *See specific entries*
after-school supervision, 268–69, **270**
age: of kindergarten entrance and achievement gap, 148–49, 151, 174; and skills development, 154
Allison, P., 117
Angrist, J., 315n15
approaches to learning, 152, 154–58, 339
aptitude, of teachers, 217, 218
Arlington County School Board; Tuttle v., 314n8
assessments, 146–47, 154. *See also specific assessments*
attendance, student, 334–35
Aughinbaugh, A., 112
Austin, Tex., class size study, 300

Bacolod, M., 236, 244n13
Baltimore, Md., Moving to Opportunity (MTO), 193–99
Barron, S., 283n17
Barrow, L., 216, 217
behavior, 140. *See also* adolescent behavior and home environments
Bifulco, R., 310, 312
Bigelow, J., 160
Bill and Melinda Gates Foundation, 301

birth weight, 159
Blair, C., 155
Blau, D., 112, 121, 131n1
books, in home, 149, 151. *See also* reading
Boyd, D., 216, 219, 243n6
boys, 6–9, 156
Bradley; Milliken v., 205–6
Brewer, D., 216, 217, 244n11
Brooks-Gunn, J., 194, 251
Burkam, D., 173n4
busing, 205. *See also* desegregation, of
    schools

California, class size reduction initia-
    tive, 239, 300–301
Campbell, M., 60n3, 61n5, 114
Capacchione v. Charlotte-
    Mecklenburg Schools, 314n8
Card, D., 201
Catholic schools, 308–9
CCD (Common Core of Data), 74,
    188–89, 226, **228**, 229
census data, 36, 96–97, **114**, 199
certification and licensure, of teachers,
    217, 220, 225, 292–94, 297–98
Charlotte-Mecklenburg School
    District, 292–94, 314
Charlotte-Mecklenburg Schools;
    Capacchione v., 314n8
charter schools, 309–10
Chicago, Ill., Moving to Opportunity
    (MTO), 193–99
child poverty. *See* poverty
Chile, school choice programs in, 308
Chin, T., 219, 244–45n17
Citizens' Commission on Civil Rights,
    304
CLARIFY, 132n12
class attendance, 334–35
class-cutting behavior, 334–35
class size, 214, 239–41, 299–301, 313
Clotfelter, C., 213, 217, 232, 244n11,
    244n14, 293, 304, 314n3, 329
cognitive development, 139–41,
    144–45, 146, 154–55, 159–60
cohort data, 9–11, 92
Coleman, J., 142, 201
college education, and family income,
    128

college financial aid programs, 24
college preparatory classes, 114
Common Core of Data (CCD), 74,
    188–89, 226, **228**, 229
compensation, teachers, 226, 296–97
computers, 263, **264**, 275
Cook, M., 34, 70–71, 72, 77
Cooley, J., 203
Corcoran, S., 244n13
CPS (Current Population Survey), 16,
    33, 34, 39, 41
crack cocaine, 252, 336
Crain, R., 113
credentialing, of teachers, 217, 220,
    225, 292–94, 297–98
crime, 197, 198, 199
cultural attitudes and practices, 143,
    250–53, 331–37. *See also* adolescent
    behavior and home environments
Current Population Survey (CPS), 16,
    33, 34, 39, 41
Cutler, D., 199

Dallas, Tex., school accountability
    study, 307
Dee, T., 216, 218, 244n10
desegregation, of schools: and
    achievement gap reduction, 113,
    290–91; and math scores, 92; mea-
    surement of, 290; research consider-
    ations and conclusions, 329–31; and
    school choice programs, 312–13;
    and school dropout rates, 199; by
    socioeconomic characteristics,
    294–95; Supreme Court rulings, 294,
    313; and teacher quality, 291–94;
    trends, 184–85; and violent crime
    victimizations, 199
Diamond, A., 161
Dickens, W., 24, 321
disciplinary problems, 263–68, 280
discrimination, 141–42, 142
dissimilarity index, 185, 187, 188–91
dropout rate, 60n3, 93–94, 199
Duncan, G., 148, 194, 208n5
Duncan, O., 80, 83
Durham, N.C., school choice pro-
    grams, 312–13

early achievement: age at kindergarten entry, 148–49, 151, 174; birth weight and health status, 149, 151; data sources, 140, 145–47; family variables, 149, 151–52, 153; gap at kindergarten entrance, 152–56; home environment, 149, 151–52; importance of, 337–38; and maternal education, 153–54; methodology, 147–50; noncognitive skills, 140, 144–45, 149–50, 152, 154–56; parent-child activities, 149, 152; policy issues, 153, 158–61, 174; preschool attendance, 149, 152; research considerations, 139–45; twin data, 156–58. *See also* achievement

Early Childhood Longitudinal Survey of Kindergartners (ECLS-K), 140, 145–50, 200

earnings. *See* wages and earnings

Eaton, S., 329

economic inequality, 12–16. *See also* income inequality

educational attainment, of children, 36, 110, 127–28

educational attainment, of parents: and black-white test score gap, 34–35, 57; and early childhood test score gap, 149, 153–54; and family income, 326; measurement, 34–35, 96, 327; NAEP analysis, 39, 56; research considerations and conclusions, 327–28; trends, 80; and vocabulary test scores, 122. *See also* maternal education

educational attainment, of teachers, 215–16

educational reform, 66, 95, 301–2

Education Department, U.S., 93, **189**

Education Longitudinal Study (ELS), 74, 232–35

Education Trust, 304

EEO (Equality of Educational Opportunity) data, 70, 104*n*1

Ehrenberg, R., 216, 217, 244*n*11, 12

Eisenberg v. Montgomery County Public Schools, 314*n*8

Elementary and Secondary Education Act (ESEA), 66–67, 243*n*1

elementary schools, 214, 216, 239–41

ELS (Education Longitudinal Study), 74, 232–35

endogenous variables, 148–49, 155

English teachers, 225, 232–35

Equality of Educational Opportunity (Coleman), 142

Equality of Educational Opportunity (EEO) data, 70, 104*n*1

ESEA (Elementary and Secondary Education Act), 66–67, 243*n*1

Evans, W., 12–13, 34, 70–71, 72, 77, 244*n*13

executive function, 145, 161

fair housing laws, 186

family characteristics: and cognitive development gap, 141; data sources, 33, 68, 72–75; and early childhood achievement, 149, 151–52, 153; and math skills and scores, 46–47, 68–69, 85, **86**, **88**, 91–92; measurement of, 39, 41, 70, 71, 75–79; and reading scores, 52; research considerations, 66–67; and test score gap, 42–43, 44–46, 58, 67–72, 84–86, 91–92; trends, 80–81. *See also* adolescent behavior and home environments

family income: and children's achievement, 35–37; and educational attainment, 110, 127–28; measurement of, 41, 96–97, 325; research considerations and conclusions, 324–26; school balancing by, 294–95; and test scores, 111–13, 120–22, 325; trends, 14, **114**, 325–26. *See also* income inequality

family structure: measurement of, 41; and NAEP math scores, 47; single-parent families, 12, 16; two-parent families, **17**

federal courts, 294

federal free lunch program, 191, **206**, **207**, 236

Ferguson, R., 10, 244*n*12, 252, 253–55, 263–65, 273, 327

field experiments, voucher programs, 311

Figlio, D., 315*n*18
financial aid programs, 24
fine motor skills, 146–47, 152, 154–58
First Things First (FTF) program, 302
Flanagan, A., 34, 69, 252
Flynn, J., 24, 321
free lunch program, 191, **206**, **207**, 236
Freeman, R., 322
Freeman v. Pitts, 314*n*7
Fryer, R., 153, 173*n*4, 174*n*11, 200, 321, 327
FTF (First Things First) program, 302

Gamoran, A., 76
Gates Foundation, 301
Gautreaux residential mobility program, 193, 197
Gelber, A., 322
gender: math score differences, 8–9; NAEP data, 39; noncognitive skill differences, 156; reading score differences, 6–7; of teachers, 218, 235, 244*n*12
General Educational Development (GED) certificate, 34–35
genetic influence, 1–2, 141, 150, 156–58
Georgia, school racial composition and teacher attrition, 236
girls, 6–9, 156, 216, 244*n*12
Gittleman, M., 112
Glaeser, E., 199
Goldhaber, D., 216
grade inflation, 335–36
grade point average (GPA), 335–36
Greenwald, R., 315*n*14
Grissmer, D., 34, 68, 69–70, 71, 72, 251–52, 267
Grodsky, E., 42
gross motor skills, 146–47
Guryan, J., 199

Hamre, B., 173*n*4
Hanushek, E., 200, 201–2, 203, 216, 236, 296, 299, 307, 315*n*14, 16
Harding, D., 199
Hauser, R., 281*n*5
Head Start, 149, 160
Heckman, J., 60*n*2

Hedges, L., 69–70, 71, 72, 215, 216, 300, 315*n*14
High School and Beyond (HSB), 73, 104, 282*n*16
high school dropout rate, 60*n*3, 93–94, 199
high school graduation, 128
high schools, 214, 239–40, **242**. *See also* adolescent behavior and home environments; tracking
hip hop music, 252, 255, 263–68, 336–37
Hispanics, 110, 111, 306–7. *See also* income inequality, and vocabulary test score gap
home environment, and early childhood achievement, 149, 151–52. *See also* adolescent behavior and home environments
homework, 251, 252, 260–61, 270–71
Housing and Urban Development (HUD) Department, Moving to Opportunity (MTO), 193–99
Hout, M., 12–13
Howell, W., 311
Hoxby, C., 202, 203
HSB (High School and Beyond), 73, 104, 282*n*16

imprisonment, 336
income inequality: and educational attainment, 36–37, 322–23, 324; and math scores, 51, 57–58, 323; measurement of, 37, 41–42; and public program funding support, 61*n*4; and reading scores, 52, 56, 57–58, 323; research considerations and conclusions, 33, 322–24; and school quality, 36; social consequences of, 12–13; and student motivation, 35–36; trends, 13–16, 45–46, **47**, 110, 113
income inequality, and vocabulary test score gap: conclusion, 128, 130; data sources, 115; findings, 117–26, 323–24; methodology, 115–17; reasons for, 114; research considerations, 113–14
integration, of schools. *See* desegregation, of schools

intelligence quotient (IQ), 2, 321

Jefferson Co. Board of Ed; Meredith
    v., 208n6
Jencks, C., 2, 5, 243n4, 282n16, 289,
    314n1
Jepsen, C., 239
job satisfaction, among teachers,
    225–26, 229

Kain, J., 201–2, 203, 216, 236, 296
Kalogrides, D., 42
Kansas City, Kans., First Things First
    (FTF) program, 302
Karoly, L., 160
Katz, L., 198
kindergarten and kindergartners: age
    of entrance and achievement gap,
    148–49, 151, 174; Early Childhood
    Longitudinal Survey of
    Kindergartners, 140, 145–50, 200;
    reading skills upon entrance, 152–53
King, J., 216
Klebanov, P. K., 194
Klein, S., 306, 315n19
Kling, J., 198
Konstantopoulos, S., 215, 216, 300
Koretz, D., 283n17
Krueger, A., 300, 315n14

labor markets, 13–14, 213, 242
Ladd, H., 217, 232, 244n11, 244n14,
    293, 304, 310, 312, 314n3, 315n18
LaFontaine, P., 60n2
Laine, R., 315n14
Lankford, H., 219
Latinos, 110, 111, 306–7. See also
    income inequality, and vocabulary
    test score gap
Lavy, V., 315n15
learning approaches, 152, 154–58, 339
learning disabilities, 152
Lee, C., 213
Lee, J., 252–53
Lee, V., 173n4
Levitt, S., 153, 173n4, 174n11, 200, 321,
    327
Levy, F., 300

licensure and certification, of teachers,
    217, 220, 225, 292–94, 297–98
Liebman, J., 198
Loeb, S., 219
Logan, J., 329
Los Angeles, Calif., Moving to
    Opportunity (MTO), 193–99
Loury, G., 336
Ludwig, J., 148, 314n2
Lutz, B., 199

magnet schools, 312, 313, 314
Magnuson, K., 148, 173n4
Mahard, R., 113
male teachers, 244n12
March Current Population Survey, 16,
    33, 34, 39, 41
Markman, L., 251
marriage, 12, 16
masters' degrees, 215–16, 224
maternal education: and black-white
    test score gap, 57; and early child-
    hood achievement gap, 153–54; and
    math scores, 47; NAEP data, 41; and
    newspaper receipt, 44, **45**; and read-
    ing scores, 52, 57; trends, 45, **46**, 80,
    81. See also educational attainment,
    of parents
mathematics teachers, 225, 232–35
math skills and scores: cohort data, **11**;
    and computer ownership, 275; and
    disciplinary problems, 280; Early
    Childhood Longitudinal Survey of
    Kindergartners, 146; and family
    characteristics, 46–51, 68–69, 85, **86**,
    88; and income inequality, 51, 58;
    methodology, 75; Moving to
    Opportunity program impact, 197;
    NAEP data, 38–39, **62–63**; and
    NCLB, 305; and school desegrega-
    tion, 329; and school environment,
    85–87, **88**; and teacher quality, 216;
    and television viewing habits, 275,
    280; test score gap, 56–59, 89, 91;
    trends, 7–9, **11**, 43–46, 56, 67–68, 213,
    253, 332, 333, 340
Mayer, S., 12–13, 36–37, 42, 314n1, 322,
    324

measurement. *See* methodology
Menaghan, E., 131n1
Meredith v. Jefferson Co. Board of Ed, 208n6
methodology: achievement, 42–43; charter schools, 309–10; desegregation of schools, 290; early childhood environment, 147–50; educational attainment of parents, 34–35, 96, 327; family characteristics, 39, 41, 70, 71, 75–79; family income, 41, 96–97, 325; family structure, 41; income inequality, 37, 41–42, 115–17; math skills and scores, 75; NAEP-LTT analysis, 42–43; occupational status of parents, 96; poverty, 42, 51; residential segregation, 182–84, 185; school environment, 71, 75–79, 97; school segregation, 182–84, 186–91, 199–203; teacher quality, 215; test score gap, 25n4; tracking, 97; voucher programs, 310–11
Mexican Americans, 111
middle schools, 214, 218
Milliken v. Bradley, 205–6
Milwaukee, Wis., voucher program, 310
mobility, of family, 150–51, 159, 193–99
Monitoring the Future (MTF) survey, 255–57, 260, 267–68, 281n5, 334–35
Monk, D., 216
Montgomery County Public Schools; Eisenberg v., 314n8
motor skills, 140, 146–47
Moving to Opportunity (MTO), 193–99, 203
MTF (Monitoring the Future) survey, 255–57, 260, 267–68, 281n5, 334–35
MTO (Moving to Opportunity), 193–99, 203
Murnane, R., 300
music, 252, 255, 263–68, 336–37

NAS (New American Schools) initiative, 301
National Assessment of Educational Progress (NAEP), 305–6
National Assessment of Educational Progress Long-Term Trend (NAEP-LTT): after-school supervision, 268–69; as benchmark for test score trends, 74–75; cohort data, 9–11; computer ownership, 263, **264**; conclusions, 56–59; data description, 5, 37–42, 320–21; disciplinary problems, 265–66; early childhood achievement gap analysis, 152–53; and educational attainment of parents, 34–35; family background measures, 71; home environment, 268–71; homework, 260–61; and income inequality, 35–37; limitations of, 33, 58–59, 254, 280–81; math scores, 7–9, 46–51, 253, 321; methodology, 42–43; reading for pleasure, 253–60; reading scores, 5–7, 51–56, 252–54; television, 261–63; trends, 5–11, 43–46, 67–68, 79–80, 253, 289, 321
National Board for Professional Teaching Standards (NBPTS) certification, 217
National Education Longitudinal Study (NELS), 73–74, 79–80, 257–60, 273–74
National Education Longitudinal Study of 1988 (NELS-88), 68, 104n1, 232–35
National Longitudinal Study of Adolescent Health (Add Health), 115–16
National Longitudinal Study of the High School Class of 1972 (NLS-72), 72–73, 104n1
National Longitudinal Survey of Youth (NLSY), 199–200
National Longitudinal Survey of Youth (NLSY-80), 68, 68106n1
National School Lunch Program, 191, **206**, **207**, 236
nature vs. nurture debate, 1–2
NBPTS (National Board for Professional Teaching Standards) certification, 217
NCLB (No Child Left Behind) Act (2001). *See* No Child Left Behind Act (NCLB) (2001)

Neal, D., 5, 143, 252, 268
Nechyba, T., 202–21
neighborhoods, 113, 114, 191–99. *See also* segregation, residential
NELS (National Education Longitudinal Study), 73–74, 79–80, 257–60, 273–74
NELS-88 (National Education Longitudinal Study of 1988), 68, 104n1, 232–35
Nevada, class size reduction initiative, 239
New American Schools (NAS) initiative, 301
newspapers, receipt of, 39, 44, 52
New York, N.Y.: Moving to Opportunity, 193–99; teacher aptitude, 244n15; Teaching Fellows Program, 297; voucher program, 311
New York State: teacher distribution study, 219; teacher salary incentives, 296
New York Times, 251
NLS-72 (National Longitudinal Study of the High School Class of 1972), 72–73, 104n1
NLSY (National Longitudinal Survey of Youth), 199–200
NLSY-80 (National Longitudinal Survey of Youth), 68, 68106n1
No Child Left Behind Act (NCLB) (2001): accountability approach, 304; effectiveness, 305; purpose of, 212; requirements, 3–4, 66–67, 302
noncognitive skills, 140, 144–45, 149–50, 152, 154–56
NORM, 117
North Carolina: charter school studies, 310; class size reduction initiative, 239; school accountability programs, 303; school choice programs, 312–13; school desegregation, 294; school segregation and test score gap study, 202–3; teacher bonus program, 297; teacher experience, 244n14, 291–94
Nowell, A., 69–70, 71, 72
Nye, B., 215, 216, 300

occupational status, of parents, 80–81, 81, 96
Orfield, G., 213, 329
Orr, L., 208n4

Page, M., 208n5
Panel Study of Income Dynamics (PSID), 36, 199, 208n5
Parcell, T., 131n1
parenting practices, 143, 149, 152, 251, 269–71
Parents Involved in the Community Schools v. Seattle School District No. 1, 208n6, 294
paternal education, 80, 81
Peabody Individual Achievement Test (PIAT), 112
Peabody Picture Vocabulary Test (PPVT), 115, 121–22
Peer: contagion, 192; environment, 122, 126–27, 201–3; percentage non-white measure, 187–88
Peterson, P., 311
Phillips, M., 2, 5, 219, 243n4, 244–45n17, 282n16, 289
physical assessments, in early childhood, 146–47
Pianta, R., 173n4
PIAT (Peabody Individual Achievement Test), 112
Picture Vocabulary Test (PVT), 115
Pitts; Freeman v., 314n7
pleasure reading, 251, 252, 253–60, 273, 274–75
policy: class size, 214, 239–41, 299–301, 313; early childhood education, 153, 158–61, 174; educational reform, 66, 95, 301–2; future issues, 338–39; recommendations, 24, 341; research considerations, 289–90; school accountability, 58, 302–7; school choice programs, 307–13; teacher quality, 242–43, 295–99, 313. *See also* desegregation, of schools
poverty: average years spent in, 1; measurement of, 42, 51; by race, **16**; and teacher sorting patterns, 235–39; and test scores, 56, 57, 121–22

PPVT (Peabody Picture Vocabulary Test), 115, 121–22
preschool, 141, 159, 160–61, 173n4, 313. *See also* early childhood education and achievement
private schools, 82, 83, 308–9, 310–11
Private School Survey (PSS), 74
professional development, 298–99
proximal processes, 143–44, 153, 159
PSID (Panel Study of Income Dynamics), 36, 199, 208n5
PSS (Private School Survey), 74
psychomotor assessment, 146–47
public housing, 193–99
PVT (Picture Vocabulary Test), 115

quality, of schools, 70–71
quality, of teachers. *See* teacher quality

racial background: of students, 39, 235–39; of teachers, 218, 220, 235
racial balancing, 294–95, 314
racial composition of schools, **228**. *See also* segregation, school
racial-ethnic identity, 96
RAND research, 68, 69, 301
rap music, 252, 263–68, 336–37
Raymond, M., 307
readiness, for reading, 160, **170–72**
readiness, for school, 337–38
reading: material availability in home, 149, 151, 268, **269**, 273, 280; for pleasure, 251, 252, 253–60, 273, 274–75; readiness for, 160, **170–72**
reading skills and scores: cohort data, **10**; and disciplinary problems, 280; Early Childhood Longitudinal Survey of Kindergartners, 146; and family characteristics, 52, 68–69; and hip hop music, 252; and home reading material availability, 280; and income inequality, 52, 56, 58; at kindergarten entrance, 152–53; Moving to Opportunity program impact, 197; NAEP data, 38–39, **60–61**, 152; and reading for pleasure, 251, 252, 253–60, 274–75; and school desegregation, 329; test score gap,

56–59, 213; trends, 5–7, **10**, 43–46, 56, 67–68, 213, 252–54, 332, 333, 340
reform, school, 66, 95, 301–2
regression analysis: family background, 77–79; math scores, 46–51; reading scores, 52–56; school environment, 77–79
research considerations and conclusions: desegregation of schools, 329–31; early childhood environment, 139–45; educational attainment of parents, 327–28; family characteristics, 66–67; family environment, 66–67; family income, 324–26; income inequality, 33, 113–14, 322–24; residential segregation, 181–82; school environment, 66–67; school segregation, 181–82, 186, 199–206, 329–31; teacher quality, 212–14, 331; test score gap, 4–5, 16–24
residential mobility interventions, 193–99
residential segregation. *See* segregation, residential
retention, of teachers, 236, 296
Rivkin, S., 200, 201–2, 203, 216, 236, 239, 296
Rockoff, J., 216
role models, 192
Ross, S., 312
Rothstein, J., 201
Ruhm, C., 173n4

safety, school, 252, 267–68
Sanbonmatsu, L., 197
Sander, W., 216, 217
SASS (Schools and Staffing Survey) data. *See* Schools and Staffing Survey (SASS) data
SAT scores, 111, 201
Scafidi, B., 236
school accountability, 58, 302–7. *See also* No Child Left Behind Act (NCLB) (2001)
school choice programs, 307–13
school districts: dissimilarity indices, **189**; teacher salaries, 296–97

school environment: and black-white test score gap, 67–72, 84–91, 92; data sources, 72–75; and math skills, 85–87, **88**, 92–93; measurement of, 71, 75–79, 97; research considerations, 66–67; trends, 81–84; and vocabulary test scores, 122, 126–27. *See also* segregation, school

school expenditures, 66

school quality, 70–71

school racial balancing, 294–95, 314

school readiness, 337–38

school reform, 66, 95, 301–2

Schools and Staffing Survey (SASS) data: description of, 219; gap in exposure to qualified teachers, 220, 223–29; school racial composition, 236; teacher quality components, 219–20, **221–22**, 236

school segregation. *See* segregation, school

school tracking. *See* tracking

school work, 251, 252, 260–61, 270–71

Schwab, R., 244*n*13

science, 216

science teachers, 225

Seattle School District No. 1; Parents Involved in the Community Schools v., 208*n*6, 294

secondary schools, 214, 239–40, **242**. *See also* adolescent behavior and home environments; tracking

Section 8 housing, 193–94

segregation, economic, 36, 186

segregation, residential: and achievement gaps, 114, 141–42; and economic inequality, 13; measurement of, 182–84, 185; research considerations, 181–82; trends, 184–87, 204

segregation, school: and math score gap, 92; measurement of, 182–84, 186–91, 199–203; research considerations and conclusions, 181–82, 186, 199–206, 329–31; and school choice, 311–13; and teacher quality, 291–94; and test score gap, 191, 199–206; trends, 82, 83, 183–91, 204, 226, **228**, 229, 329

SES (socioeconomic status). *See* socioeconomic status (SES)

shirking problem, 303–4

Siebens, J., 42

single-parent families, 12, 16

Sirin, S., 327

Sjoquist, D., 236

skill-biased technological change, 13–14

Slavin, R., 301

social skills, 140, 152

socioeconomic composition of schools, 83, 89, 91, 201

socioeconomic status (SES): and school achievement, 34, 111, 182, 201; school racial balancing by, 294–95, 314

socioemotional development, 147

Solon, G., 208*n*5

South: earnings gap, 199–200; school desegregation, 184

spatial mismatch, 192

special education, 152

STAR experiment, 215, 216, 239, 244*n*10, 299–300

STATA, 43

states: dissimilarity indices, **190**; free lunch eligible-ineligible dissimilarity, **207**; income inequality, 36–37; school segregation and test score gap, **192**

status model, of school accountability, 304–5

Stinebrickner, T., 236

student assignment policies, 290–95

student-teacher ratio, 214, 239–41, **242**, 299

subject matter preparation, of teachers, 225

suburbs, 186

Success for All, 301–2

summer breaks, from school, 173*n*2

Supreme Court, U.S., 205, 294, 313

TAAS (Texas Assessment of Academic Skills), 306

teacher bonus programs, 297

teacher quality: advanced degrees,
215–16, 224; certification and licensure, 217, 220, 225, 292–94, 297–98;
and class size, 239–41; components
of, 214–20, **221–22**, 236; conclusion,
241–43; data sources, 213, 219, 232;
distribution across schools, 212, 213,
219; experience level of, 216, 220,
229, 291–94; gap in students' exposure to, 220, 223–29; matched
teacher-student data, 232–35; and
math scores, 216; measurement of,
215; No Child Left Behind requirements, 212; policy interventions,
242–43, 295–99, 313; research considerations and conclusions, 212–14,
331; and school segregation, 291–94;
and student poverty or race, 235–39;
work experience, 216, 220, 229,
291–94
teachers: approaches to learning
assessments, 154; compensation,
226, 296–97; gender of, 218, 235,
244n12; job satisfaction, 225–26, 229;
labor markets, 213, 242
teacher-student ratio, 214, 239–41, **242**,
299
Teach for America, 217
teenage culture, 331–37. *See also* adolescent behavior and home environments
television, 251, 252, 261–63, 269–73,
275
Tennessee, STAR experiment, 215,
216, 239, 244n10, 299–300
tenure, of teachers, 245n19
test-based accountability, 302–7
test score gap: future of, 24; importance of, 3; measurement of, 25n4;
research considerations, 4–5,
16–21; trends, 3, 5–11, 43–46,
67–68, 79–80, 111. *See also specific
entries*
Texas: charter school studies, 310;
school accountability programs,
303, 306–7; school segregation and
test score gap study, 201–2

Texas Assessment of Academic Skills
(TAAS), 306
Thernstrom, A., 251
Thernstrom, S., 251
Title I, of Elementary and Secondary
Education Act, 66–67
Tools of the Mind, 161
Toronto public housing study, 199
tracking: and math score gap, 87, **88**,
89, 92–93, 95; measurement of,
76–77, 97; self-reports of, 83–84, **85**
Tuttle v. Arlington County School
Board, 314n8
twin studies, 150, 156–58
two-parent families, **17**

universal preschool programs, 160–61
urban schools, 82, 83, 97
U.S. Census Bureau, 36, 96–97, **114**,
199
U.S. Department of Education, 93,
189
U.S. Department of Housing and
Urban Development (HUD),
Moving to Opportunity (MTO),
193–99
U.S. Supreme Court, 205, 294, 313
Utah, class size reduction initiative,
239

videogames, 263
Vigdor, J., 199–200, 202–3, 217, 232,
244n11, 14, 293, 314n2, 3
violence, 197, 198, 251, 252, 267
vocabulary tests, 112, 115–16. *See also*
income inequality, and vocabulary
test score gap
Votruba-Drzal, E., 112
voucher programs, 309

wages and earnings: earnings gap,
199–200; inequality trends, 13–16; of
teachers, 226, 296–97. *See also*
income inequality
Wake County, N. C., school desegregation, 294
Waldfogel, J., 173n4

Washington, D.C., voucher program, 311

wealth inequality, 16

white flight, 312

Williamson, S., 34, 69, 252

Wilson, W. Julius, 95

Woodcock-Johnson-Revised (WJ-R) tests, 197

work experience, of teachers, 216, 220, 229, 291–94

work hours, of teachers, 226, 331

working conditions, 225, 229, 297

Wyckoff, J., 219

youth culture, 331–37. *See also* adolescent behavior and home environments